DISCARD

A Stranger and a Sojourner

DATE DUE

A Stranger
AND A Sojourner

*Peter Caulder,
Free Black
Frontiersman
in Antebellum
Arkansas*

BILLY D. HIGGINS

THE UNIVERSITY
OF ARKANSAS PRESS
Fayetteville
2004

08   07   06   05   04   5   4   3   2   1

First paperback edition printed in 2005

Designed by Liz Lester

⊗ The paper used in this publication meets the minimum requirements of the
American National Standard for Permanence of Paper for Printed Library Materials
Z39.48–1984.

LIBRARY OF CONGRESS CATALOGING-IN-PUBLICATION DATA

Higgins, Billy D., 1938–
    A stranger and a sojourner : Peter Caulder, free Black frontiersman in
antebellum Arkansas / Billy D. Higgins.
        p.   cm.
    Includes bibliographical references and index.
    ISBN 1-55728-777-5 (case-bound : alk. paper)
    1. Caulder, Peter, 1795–ca. 1859. 2. Free African Americans—White
River Region (Ark. and Mo.)—Biography. 3. African American pioneers—
White River Region (Ark. and Mo.)—Biography. 4. Frontier and pioneer
life—White River Region (Ark. and Mo.) 5. White River Region (Ark. and
Mo.)—Social life and customs—19th century. 6. White River Region (Ark.
and Mo.)—Biography. 7. Arkansas—Biography. 8. Arkansas—Race
relations. 9. African American soldiers—Biography. 10. United States—
History—War of 1812—Participation, African American. I. Title.

F417.W5H54 2004
976.7'2'00496073—dc22
                                                    2004008879

*This project is supported in part by a grant from the Arkansas
Humanities Council and the Department of Arkansas Heritage.*

TO OPE AND HIG

CONTENTS

Acknowledgments

My students energized me as I wrote this book. On the occasions when the prospects for locating more factual information on Peter Caulder had dimmed, a sincere inquiry or a clever suggestion from one of them would rekindle the questing spirit.

Early interest in Peter Caulder's military career came from Juliet Galonska, then the park historian for the Fort Smith National Historic Site. She supplied the initial evidence that Caulder was categorized differently than his white counterparts in the Rifle Regiment. Research assistance by Carolyn Filippelli proved vital. Her advice and corrections strengthened the work. Margie Hicks was my indispensable arranger of interlibrary loans. Jeannie Whayne recognized that the early drafts held some promise and published a segment in the *Arkansas Historical Quarterly*. Patrick Williams, associate editor of the *Quarterly*, added his support. Willard B. Gatewood Jr. assisted the research, writing, and rewriting of the manuscript. It is accurate to say that without his superb and gracious mentoring, the book would never have seen the light of day.

In tracing documents related to the Caulder story, Andrea Cantrell of the University of Arkansas Special Collections, Linda Pine of the University of Arkansas at Little Rock Archives, Russell Baker of the Arkansas History Commission, Sarah Erwin of the Gilcrease Museum Archives, Kathy Huber of the Tulsa City-County Public Library, and staff members of the National Archives in Washington, D.C., gave me every consideration and many ideas. Tom Wing showed me details concerning life, dress, and drink experienced by riflemen at the early fort. The Arkansas Humanities Council provided a grant that sped research for the book, for which I am grateful.

Dolores Abernathy Jackson, Max George, Marty Grant, Bill Holmes, Jerry Caulder, Leo Mills, and Marilyn Bacon provided information on genealogy and supplied me with photographs and leads on possible descendants of Peter Caulder and David Hall. Roy and Ginni Linton of Yellville assisted me with landownership records of Marion

County. Douglas Watkins of Sharp County, Arkansas, and Jimmy Calder of Marion, South Carolina, each allowed me to sit on the fender of their tractors while covering their farmlands once walked over by Peter Caulder.

Dan Maher suggested improvements. He, Edward Levy, and Lonnie Watts explored the Caulder project with me at every stage of its development. I am grateful for their customary good humor, and without my conversations with these three scholars, I would have missed much about Caulder's persona. The completed book owes much to Anna Moore and Debbie Self, who made many valuable suggestions and corrections. Ernest Cialone provided artwork that allowed me to *see* historical scenes that I had only imagined. I thank Sarah White for her meticulous proofreading.

Steadying me during seven years of travel to libraries, court-houses, cemeteries, archives, farms, old forts, and the houses of strangers (who usually became friends) was my wife, dear friend, and connoisseur of country roads, Peggy Higgins. She may have secretly preferred to visit our children, Tim and Lea, on her weekends, but instead she summoned her best smile and stayed with me on the trail, driving while I deduced. I humbly thank you, Peggy. I would also like to express my deepest appreciation for my "friends of youth" and "friends from the valley" who encouraged me in writing this book.

INTRODUCTION:
A STRANGER AND A SOJOURNER

Nineteen-year-old Peter Caulder departed his rural South Carolina home at the height of the War of 1812, a stranger to his country beyond Marion County. Three years later, he clambered out of a skiff at a flat rock called Belle Point on the Arkansas River, one of the first eight American soldiers to set foot in what is now Fort Smith, Arkansas. Young, strong, and raw, like the country that he served, Caulder refined his soldiering and navigation skills on the country's frontier. By 1827, well before Arkansas Territory had quite matured, Caulder was ready for a personal transition from bachelor rifleman who spent much of his time in the saddle to a homesteader, husband, and father. A sojourner, Caulder's relationships with his white and black neighbors in the territory, his integrated service in the United States Army, and his liberty about where to live and how to earn a living reveal a remarkable degree of independence for a free black man in the antebellum South. The historical documents that allow the tracing of his life—army returns, county tax records, trader account books, censuses, a folklorist, and travelers' journals—constitute pieces of a puzzle that when put together present a rather detailed view of the stranger/sojourner and the developing frontier community into which he was cast. To draw an accurate historical sketch of him, the background of officers, friends, fellow soldiers, relatives, and neighbors, those who worked shoulder to shoulder with him, had to be brought into focus. Caulder's knack of being in places and with people of historical significance resulted in an event-filled life. But he could and did keep to himself at times. He fathered seven children while residing peacefully and self-sufficiently on Cawlder Mountain, a flat-bench farm above the White River six miles from the Missouri border. Eventually growing antagonisms over slavery shattered his personal paradise. After a lifetime of acceptance by scores of white friends and neighbors in Arkansas and in South Carolina, Peter Caulder finally felt the bitter sting of racism. His and other free black people's designation by the Arkansas legislature as enemies of the state lacked the drama of jack boots on the pavement and a thumping on the door. Nevertheless, a chilling message had been sent, and to protect his family, just before the Civil War Caulder pulled up stakes and left Arkansas.

Although he worked hard, Caulder never accumulated the education, the estate, the wealth, or the slaves that distinguished a few unusual free black people of the antebellum period. He seemed happy enough to be an ordinary American who pursued common goals, high among them to be a loyal comrade, a provider for his family, and a member of the community. Caulder's assured attitude, his skilled hands, his willingness to serve, and his effectiveness in carrying out duties led to his acceptance as a trusted guide and a capable peer by a variety of men over a long period of time. After noting his color on a few early muster rolls, Caulder's commanding officers in the U.S. Army began to disregard it. So did many civilian whites on the frontier who knew him and dealt with him. How did an individual in that racially sensitive time succeed, to a surprising degree, in transcending his "race?"

Retained in the army following the War of 1812, twenty-year-old Pvt. Peter Caulder paddled his way up the Arkansas River as part of a rifle company sent into the heart of a newly expanded United States. This adventure resulted in his settling far from the Carolina sandhills where he was born and spent his boyhood. As a soldier at Fort Smith and Fort Gibson, he compiled a commendable record. Combined, he served more than fourteen years in the South Carolina militia, the U.S. Rifles, and the Seventh Infantry. After the military years, Caulder located his land of promise and a wife near the White River in present-day Marion County, Arkansas, on a branch called the Little North Fork. Caulder's ability to provide food, shelter, and security for his young wife and many children, the accomplishments of his extended family, his financial independence, and his material accumulations that included a homestead, farm animals, a horse, and hounds together add up to a yeoman's satisfaction in the South. For thirty-five years he lived what could be reasonably called the "good life" of that day.

Caulder signed his land bounty applications and army records with an "x" mark. Like many on the frontier, he was not a man of letters. Documentation of his actions exists, but not his actual words that explain or interpret those actions. Nevertheless, a record of Caulder can be traced through antebellum Arkansas. Despite obstacles to his pursuit of happiness, such as lack of opportunity for education, lifelong illiteracy, and denial of army promotions that he had earned, Caulder established a law-abiding, bill-paying, tax-paying citizen's role for himself. He avoided adverse legal actions and physical conflict with whites. Caulder held the respect of diverse people, both military and civilian, with whom he came into contact. His patience and avoidance of scrapes may have been a blessing to potential foes or antagonists. Peter Caulder would have made a formidable opponent, since he was a crack shot, rode well, was an expert tracker, and had a strong physical build, standing a little above average height. No photograph or sketch exists, but Caulder had a dark skin color and was African featured enough for whites who had to categorize him. Army records of 1815 referred to him, and his father, as "colored" men. His childhood neighbors and army comrades, James and Martin Turner, were categorized by the U.S. Army as colored. Census marshals in two Arkansas counties over a thirty-year period designated him, and later his wife and children, as mulatto. Maj. William Bradford, a skilled army officer, veteran of the War of 1812, and the commander of the first Fort Smith, described Caulder's complexion, eyes, and hair all as "dark." Caulder forged his closest and most enduring bonds with black people.

Caulder married Eliza Hall, a daughter of David Hall, a free black pioneer who settled on the White River in 1819. Hall's sons and sons-in-law, the three South Carolinian army veterans among them, married and raised large families. The Hall-Caulder-Turner families cleared trees, planted crops, raised livestock, and patented their lands, which lay adjacent to the White River.

Although ostensibly barred from the state by law, mulattoes from Tennessee and Illinois migrated to Marion County and by 1850, at least one hundred twenty-nine people resided in nineteen households in the county. It was the largest congregation of free blacks in Arkansas. The Marion County free black population was rural, self-sufficient, agricultural, and viral. Fully half the population was between the ages fifteen and sixty-five, and included a number of young adult males. Kinship and close friendships unified the free black people who embarked on land purchases, improvements to farms, material advancement, and even education. The Marion County community was defined to include this important segment of the county's population.

Growth and prosperity abruptly halted in 1852. A murder trial involving one of their own and a white man, a ferry operator, riddled the mulatto communities in north Arkansas, putting them on the wan. Finally, the expulsion law of 1859 drove the Hall-Caulder-Turner settlement in Marion County and the smaller Madewell mulatto cluster at Turkey Crossroads, west of Yellville, from the state. The free black families, including that of Peter Caulder, not knowing whether authorities intended to enforce the law or not, became refugees. As they pulled away from lands on which they held United States government patents and had lived for thirty years, three generations of free black family members said good-bye to all that they had known. David Hall, the old pioneer and patriarch of the community, was spared this final grief. He already lay in his grave near the waters of the White River.

Descendants of David Hall, including his daughter, Eliza Caulder, did not let their discouragement endure, however. Eliza, without Peter, who became a casualty of the times, settled with her remaining family in Bollinger County, a region in southeast Missouri with good trees, roaring creeks, and elbow room for pioneer-spirited people like the Caulders and the Halls. In an area traveled through by her husband in 1818 on a return trip to St. Louis while with Maj. Stephen Long, Eliza, her oldest son, David, and the core of the Caulder family began to put down their roots again. This time their sojourn would at last be transformed into full citizenship.

An early Arkansas statute specified a person with one-eighth black blood as being legally black and therefore eligible to be enslaved. The 1859 expulsion of free black people law required them to revert to slavery. Of course with seven-eighths white blood, a person could be so light skinned and European featured that they could "pass," and actually had to admit that he or she was black. Yet, passing was not easy nor often accomplished, although it did present a path for survival taken by some black people of fair complexion in a slave society. Antebellum Southerners were used to making racial determinations based on appearance. A relative of David Hall, Thomas Hall, tried to prove with an affidavit that he was a "white" person of Portuguese descent.[1] Peter Caulder's African ancestry seemed never to be in doubt during his career, but that did not prevent Maj. William Bradford and other commanders from placing trust and responsibility in Caulder, just as his fellow soldiers placed their respect and confidence in him.

Trust, bearing, accomplishments, and forty-two years of Arkansas residency aside, Peter Caulder could in the end echo Abraham's statement that he was a stranger and a sojourner.

PROLOGUE

Peter Caulder stood on his cabin porch gazing toward the path that emerged from the line of stout oaks at the edge of his clearing. At the end of a sloping path that Caulder had carved into the hillside, a landing bordered the White River. Caulder thought about the stream two hundred feet below this flat-topped bench where he had settled thirty years ago. Heavy downpours could turn the trusted waterway with its fishing holes into a rampaging giant. During high water, the roar of fast moving and powerful currents warned of danger. Muddy waters carrying whole uprooted trees jumped banks at times threatening the farmsteads of Caulder's kinsmen whose riverbank farms adjoined the swirling waters. Once, fearful for his neighbors and kinfolk, Caulder had plunged down the path to the edge of a flooding river. He clung to vines and branches as he made his way toward his sister-in-law Rachel Hall's endangered cabin. Caulder had found Rachel and her children huddled together on a rock ledge a few feet above the dark, sucking water and had rescued them, carrying them on his back one at a time to safety. Such trials from nature made up much of life in the remote hills where the Little North Fork joined the White River. Peter and Eliza Caulder and their seven children bonded in meeting tests, making them a confident family, proud, loving, and supportive of each other.

Today, Caulder cast a farewell glance around the flat-top mountain that bore his name. He heard familiar, soul-satisfying sounds: the mellow call of a catbird, an excited bark from a gray squirrel, and the snort of his saddled horse. In spite of these little pleasures, Caulder was saddened more than he had ever been in his sixty-four years. His sorrow welled up from the great trial that his family now faced. This present test came not from nature, but from a law passed by a group of white men who had no idea about the quality or the history of the people that their legal maneuverings were most directly, and most adversely, affecting. Negro slavery, John Brown, and fear of insurrection had clouded minds in Little Rock, and finally even in Marion County.

Children just out of bed rustled around in the cabin. Caulder heard his wife's voice prompting the children to go about their chores for the day. Caulder made a slight turn to view the white oaks that defined Cawlder Mountain. Turning back to the path, Caulder saw his oldest son, David, of strong build, buoyant spirit, dark skin, dark eyes, and dark hair, leading a pair of Grandfather David Hall's mules. Snorting about the move that lay ahead, Caulder stepped off the porch. A tan hound arose from behind the flat rock that served as a step and stretched a cold nose to meet the hand of Caulder, who spoke gently to his beloved hunting partner. "No 'bar' scent today, ol' Buck. Us'ens got plenty of work to do." Peter Caulder, War of 1812 veteran, elite rifleman, pioneer of Arkansas Territory, his wife, Eliza Hall Caulder, and their seven children were about to become refugees from the state of Arkansas.

CHAPTER ONE

Catfish Creek

PETER CAULDER, BORN IN 1795, WAS THE SON OF MOSES CAULDER and his wife, who lived on a fifty-acre tract in the South Carolina sand hills bordered by the placid and murky Catfish Creek. Moses Caulder's farmstead abutted property owned by an older Peter Calder, listed in the 1800 census as a white man and perhaps a relative as well as a namesake. The white Peter Calder and his wife, Nancy, had a grown son, Peter Calder Jr., who was also a head of household as listed in the 1790 census, the nation's first. No free persons of color or slaves resided in either Calder household, but the elder Peter Calder may have helped support Moses, perhaps his son by a slave wife.[1] Moses Caulder maintained a household for fifteen years on Catfish Creek and had heard the enlightened rhetoric of the American Revolution. Moses's mother was most likely a slave manumitted by the elder Peter in the flush of the spirit of liberty generated by the Declaration of Independence. Moses and his son Peter may have registered their appreciation for that era and the freedom it inspired by volunteering for military service in the War of 1812.

Free and with support from the white Peter Calders as he grew up on Catfish Creek, young Peter lived comfortably in a mixed community that helped prepare him for integrated duties in the United States Army. It was his confidence—a lack of fear of white men—that enabled a young black man to operate in a country divided by the idea of "race," a crevice between classes of men that grew deeper and wider with each passing year. How did South Carolina, a state so committed to race-based slavery that it later sought to dissolve the union, spawn such a native son?[2]

The Southern states were not only different from Northern states in 1795 at the time of Caulder's birth, they were basically different from one another as well. In Michael Kammen's analysis, the colonies between 1660 and 1760 represented an "invertebrate America . . .

a series of water-tight compartments none of which felt very much curiosity toward events in the domain of the others."[3] Charles II, the restored king of England, granted chartered estates on the North American mainland to eight Barbados petitioners who named their territories in honor of their king, and its port Charles Town. The grantees, known legally as the Lords Proprietors, set out to wring profits from their Carolina possessions by installing an agricultural plantation system. One historian noted that "everyone involved in the founding of South Carolina planned on making money out of the venture."[4] The Proprietors had in mind a cash crop tended by African slaves, a scheme modeled after their lucrative Barbados sugar plantations. Before enough Africans could be imported, Carolina planters relied on Native Americans for the labor needed in indigo patches and rice fields. The offspring of Indian and African unions, a byproduct of working side by side as Carolina plantation slaves, became commonplace, so whites invented a term, *mustee,* to describe such mixed-blooded people. *Mulatto,* another term coined by white colonists, referred to people with one European and one African parent—"new people," as the historian Joel Williamson described them. Peter Caulder and his father, Moses, would be among America's "new people," men and women who had black ancestors but who were linked also to their white neighbors by "bonds of kinship and culture."[5]

Thousands of Angolans initially entered the North American realm by stepping onto the wharves at Charles Town. By 1708, blacks equaled the number of whites in South Carolina. Black hands provided production energy in the fields, forests, and trades, becoming the principal factor in the South Carolina economy. "The Negro Slaves . . . do all the Labour or hard Work in the Country, and are a considerable Part of the Riches of the Province."[6] By the time of the 1775 revolt from Britain, blacks outnumbered whites in a colony where slavery was less peculiar than in any of its mainland cousins.[7]

Untitled whites, including former indentured servants from Virginia (the "bounty Irish"), settled by the hundreds in the interior sand hills of South Carolina. Settlers clad in homespun set about hacking out a living with axe, saw, hoe, and a sense of humor. Mostly Protestant and fully competitive, these Scotch-Irish pioneers brought with them a hardy individualistic and democratic spirit. Before 1800, beasts roamed and most in the sand hills hunted deer to put on the family's table, making gun "ownership . . . common in the Carolina backcountry."[8] It would be the rare individual from the sand hills who could rise from subsistence level to join the wealthy as plantation owners, though enough did so to continue the dream if not the guarantee of upward mobility.

A courthouse was built near Catfish Creek between the Big and Little Pee Dee rivers and named in 1798 after Francis Marion. As the two Pee Dees come together, they form a V-shaped peninsula of trackless, cane-choked wetlands that sheltered Marion, hero of the southern phase of the American Revolution. A painting shows the Swamp Fox in a clearing amidst giant sweetgums and black oaks sharing his evening dinner of roasted sweet potatoes with a wayward British officer. In the background of the painting, lean, buckskin-clad veterans who made up Marion's superb strike force stand, arms crossed and rested on the muzzles of their long tom muskets, and watch the formalities. A black man, obviously the cook, pulls the yams from the coals of an open fire. Chinua Achebe writes that in East Africa, the "Yam is King." The tuber gained a place of importance in South Carolina's inner coastal plain, too.[9]

In the flush of liberty following the Revolution, a spate of manumissions attested to the power of an idea even in South Carolina, which owed its existence to slavery. Of course, there were many in South Carolina who detested slavery—slaves and free black people. But their opinion counted for little. The power was in the hands of well-educated planters who did not ponder moral justifications for the peculiar institution in South Carolina anymore than did planters in Barbados.

In contrast, a few hundred miles north the concept of slavery, if not its practice presented a moral dilemma to enlightened Virginia tidewater planters, who after all were Anglican gentlemen steeped in the republican writings of Montesquieu, Locke, and Paine. In much of the Virginia colonial era, blacks formed only a part of the labor force, indentured whites another part. Eventually, indentured labor in the tobacco fields ended and slave labor remained. As the institution of slavery grew in Virginia, so did vexing questions about its nature. Many Virginians thought slavery a doomed institution. The Northern colonies had shown that with industrial maturity, slavery became less useful. The dynamic free-enterprise economy of the North caused many of its citizens to condemn the stagnant "peculiar institution."

In the wake of the Nat Turner Rebellion, racial issues dominated Southern public consciousness and decision-making processes more than ever. People with an African ancestor had "Negro blood" and were sucked in a vortex that led to degradation of their character *by definition*. In systematically withholding education, opportunity, and prosperity from blacks, Southern whites had created a system that could verify their charges of black inferiority.

———————

Because legal slavery was based on "Negro blood," some accepted mechanism had to evolve in order to decide judicial cases involving people with mixed heritage. What made a person black or white before the law? How did the new people, the mulattoes, fit in? South Carolina courts came to rely on the decision of the jury in determining racial classification for litigants. Nothing else made as much sense or sufficed. Peer opinion, not laws handed down by the legislature, mattered most. Medical science simply could not demonstrate conclusive proof of "race," though some doctors of medicine postulated so on witness stands.[10]

During the Reconstruction that followed the Civil War, embittered Southern whites targeted the handiest, most-visible scapegoat around, black people. Unfettered by Yankees in 1876, Bourbon Democrats in the ex-Confederate states returned to power to systematically disenfranchise black voters and segregate blacks from whites. Southern state after state passed antimiscegenation laws to protect "white womanhood," a false premise that led not only to the age of the lynch rope, but also to the paranoia of an entire region.[11] One "drop of black blood," regardless if that gene showed up on the exterior of a person or not, segregated that person as a Negro. (Homer Plessy, the litigant in that famous *Plessy v. Ferguson* Supreme Court decision of 1896 that ruled segregation of public facilities constitutional, was seven-eighths white with fair hair and blue eyes.)

In mandating racial categories, post–Reconstruction-era Southerners kindled fierce hatreds within themselves and within their culture. People of African ancestry were vilified and humiliated, regardless of their accomplishment, contribution, citizenship, or hue. Blacks responded (not with discriminatory laws or by lynching whites, because they were powerless to do so) by returning white hatred evinced in veiled looks and the denial of white values where possible.[12]

Before Reconstruction, the South was a land of contradictions and ambivalence where racial categorization was concerned.[13] Certainly, historians have documented wretched conditions under which a great many free blacks lived in slave societies. But in parallel existence, there were well-treated and prosperous free black people. Frequently, men and women of mixed ancestry, were, on an individual basis, shown respect and valued by their white contemporaries. One historian observed that "until the 1850's South Carolinians maintained a striking tolerance of free mulattoes and an amazing resistance to the outright outlawing of interracial marriage."[14]

Tolerance may have bred an assurance in Peter Caulder that he had some control over his life. When he, his father, Moses Caulder, his friends Martin Turner, James Turner, Joseph Clark, and his brother-in-law Caleb Cook volunteered for the United States Army and marched out of South Carolina, they believed that they were of use to their society and that their society would reward their usefulness. While they may not have imagined complete equality for themselves, they must have had some idea of independence at least. In the case of Peter Caulder, that idea of independence was fulfilled.[15] He trusted his country, the army, and his countrymen with his future. That future, as it turned out, would be in Arkansas far from the safety and security of his childhood home.

Unlike yeomen farmers and army recruiters, the planter class of South Carolina was not so sure that a free black man like Peter Caulder could be trusted at any time. Tidewater men had serious misgivings about the intentions of people of color. These planters, after all, had created a slave society based on the idea of "race," coercion, physical punishment, and total control. Free black people were suspected as dangerous mavericks in such an unstable world. Planters recognized the intelligence of free blacks and their opposition to slavery and sought to reduce their numbers in South Carolina. This they could do because few white men were altruistic enough to defend free black interests from the planters. A landowner in Marion County might trust his neighboring black family and send their son to Charleston and back with valuable products and cash receipts, but how could this same white man take on the slave owners and argue in public forums for toleration and equality? Thus, slave owners, forming an elite class of society that gossiped continually about black inferiority with great energy and no fear of social stigma and that controlled the state government, could easily win public approval to curtail the free blacks. In 1800, the network of state laws aimed at restraining liberties and opportunities of free people of African ancestry in South Carolina began. William Faux, an English traveler, observed that at "Charleston, no black man, though free and rich and having horses and carriages . . . is permitted . . . to be seen out of his house after ten at night."[16] What the non-slave owning white hill farmer could do and did do, however, was to ignore such laws on the books that adversely and unfairly affected his black neighbors. As another approach to the problem, local citizens often just redescribed their free black neighbors as white. External appearance mattered to Southerners in placing people in social strata, but those mixed people who looked and acted white enough could be and often were so termed. The legal stature of "whiteness" provided, of course, an important advantage for an individual's future in a racially based slave society.

In Marion County, white neighbors seemed comfortable with the black families who lived in their midst. Eighty-one free people of color, including the household of Moses Caulder, resided in a continuous row of eleven rural households to make up a significant free black community. Extended families with numerous children and elder relatives lived together under one roof, such as in the household of Harmon Shoemake, patriarch of a large clan. Some residents, such as John Turner Jr. and Reuben Turner, nonwhites of 1800, were reclassified as white by the 1810 marshal.[17] Not only were free black people tolerated, apparently they were viewed by whites with so little of the suspicion held by the planter class that the local census marshals could perpetrate reclassification of the "race" of certain people in the households of their districts without so much as the raise of an eyebrow. Moses Caulder and Reuben Turner were such men of variable classification.[18]

Universal racial identification standards hardly existed. Census marshals categorized individuals relying as much on the reputation one enjoyed in the community as on visible skin tones. Faux, an 1819 visitor to South Carolina, wrote that any man with a "robust habit and swarthy dark complexion" might be confused with a Negro, mulatto, or yellow man because "it is sometimes difficult to distinguish from a white or brown person."[19] Free blacks in rural areas could and did quietly integrate themselves into their village and community society. Far removed from coastal plantations or urban areas, pioneering settlers pursued small-scale operations based on family and neighborhood labor. Common concerns and travails bonded these hardworking yeomen, a shared ethic that sometimes transcended racial grouping. Under such familiar circumstances, free blacks occasionally had close ties to whites. Miscegenation, a pejorative term in post–Civil War vocabularies, raised much less reaction among Southern whites in early accounts. Nor were interracial unions only between white men and black females. A contemporary observer, Josiah Quincy, noted with some surprise that South Carolinians had "no reluctance, delicacy, or shame . . . about speaking of interracial affairs." Gideon Gibson, a free black carpenter from Virginia, moved to South Carolina and settled on the Santee River. He owned seven slaves and had a white wife. Gibson, a contemporary pointed out, was "whiter than any Huguenot descendent."[20]

In at least one case, a mixed marriage proceeded over the years in Marion County without evidence of the kind of white indignation and commentary that such an arrangement was sure to bring on fifty years later. The "natural aversion" of Southern whites to mixing may have been an inculcated behavior, learned by each generation of children after decades of vitriolic, callused, and systematic "arguments" against black people and their culture.

John Turner, "a free person of color" and his wife, Patience, a white woman, owned a diamond-shaped tract of land along Catfish Creek adjoining that of Moses Caulder. John Turner, whose mother was a slave on his white father's plantation, came to freedom through purchase and manumission by his Irish-born wife, Patience.[21] In colonial Carolina on sandy lands at the edge of a pine forest, the couple set up their homestead and acquired not only land, but livestock and a bank account as well. The Turner family grew to include several children, including John Turner Jr., and grandchildren, two of whom were Martin and James Turner. These brothers, six years apart in age, came to be the childhood friends and military comrades of Peter Caulder of the neighboring farm, who stood between the Turner brothers in age.

In 1797, John Turner Sr. gained another mouth to feed as he took a ten-year-old white youth named John G. Powers into the Turner household. Young Powers's white parents bound the boy to John Turner as an apprentice. For the eight years before his death in 1805, John Turner seemed to have been a stable influence on Powers, teaching his young apprentice a trade on which he could build a livelihood. What Turner's particular professional skill may have been is not known to history. Rope making, indigo processing, chimney building, horse training, and leather tanning brought cash income to white and black tradesmen in the backcountry. Shoemaking was an important part-time trade that supplemented incomes of subsistence farmers. Turner's free black neighbor, Solomon Shoemake, supported his large household by plying the trade after which he was named. Martin Turner seemed to have had opportunities to handle mule and horse teams. From his neighbor Solomon Shoemake, Martin Turner may have learned how to tan cowhides and make leather harnesses. If so, that would have given Martin Turner a toolkit for his army and pioneering careers.[22]

John Turner Sr. owned 213 acres of good land drained by Catfish Creek in an area known as Pigeon Bay. Around Turner, his white neighbors, such as the Betheas, Tarts, and Basses, prospered in diverse agricultural businesses. Black slaves were present here on the fringes of the one-crop plantation country, but in small numbers. Pioneers, husbands, wives, and children did the manual labor in this part of the backcountry. Cattle fed on lush cane stands and hogs rooted through the hardwood forests, feasting and fattening on the mast. Along with livestock husbandry, farmers of the low-lying areas cultivated indigo, a crop that preceded cotton as the sand hill country's principal staple. In Marion County, indigo stalks reached four or five feet in height and limbed out vigorously.[23]

Members of the Caulder and Turner families most likely did seasonal work for whites along Catfish Creek. Exporting indigo through the port of Charleston and driving cattle to Virginia markets required travel outside Marion County, jobs that young Peter Caulder and his friends Martin and James Turner may have relished.[24] Lumbering posed a much less enticing field for teenage laborers. Cutting huge swamp oaks and sycamores, pulling the logs out of the woods and into a yard, squaring them, and splitting out boards were back-breaking pioneering tasks. Peter Caulder and the Turners learned to handle an axe and a splitting hammer. During their military careers at Belle Point and as they homesteaded along the White River in territorial Arkansas, they would have ample opportunity to practice these skills.

The Betheas and Tarts used their influence at times to advance the interest of their neighbors, the Turner and Caulder families, helping them, for instance, in becoming militia substitutes or in changing their color classification by the local census taker. In 1800, John Turner Sr., John Turner Jr., and Reuben Turner are counted in the census as free blacks (nonwhite). But in the 1810 census, after the death of John Turner Sr., his sons, Reuben Turner and William Turner, were listed as white. As historian Joel Williamson writes, "the door to whiteness for free people of some color was kept firmly and judiciously open in South Carolina. Known and visible mulattoes could by behavior and reputation be 'white.'"[25]

Apprentice John G. Powers stayed on with the Turner family until well into his teen-age years. The white youngster acquired land, perhaps inheriting some of John Turner Sr.'s property as did Turner's biological sons, Reuben and William. Powers's long-term relationship with the Turners sparked a romance in the household and eventually a marriage proposal. On January 4, 1813, sixteen-year-old John Powers, a future Confederate soldier, and Sarah, daughter of John and Patience Turner, wedded. The union lasted seven years and produced one son and three daughters. Sarah Turner Powers, a "free woman of

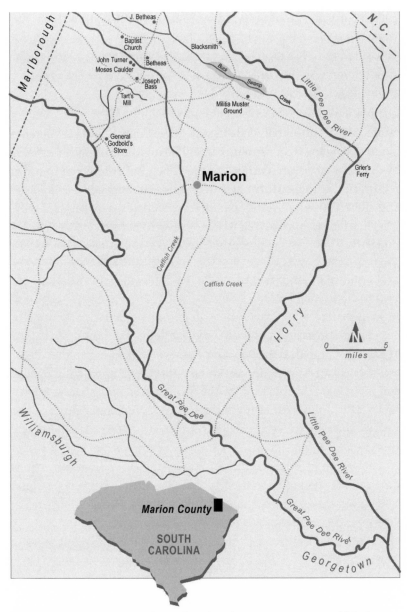

Map of Marion County, South Carolina, based on an *1818* survey published in Mills Atlas (*1825*). Farms of John Turner and Moses Caulder bordered Catfish Creek near Bethea's Road adjoining the Joseph Bass farm. Peter Caulder drilled on the muster ground by Buck Swamp Creek, two miles northeast of Marion.

MAP BY TOM PARADISE.

color," left her white husband and took her children to Alabama in 1820. Later, she settled in Georgia where she lived until her death on May 8, 1859. In the backlash of his abandonment, Powers wed Sarah Ann Conner, a white woman with whom he lived for the next forty-seven years. John Powers died in 1867 and the heirs of his two families, one black and one white, entered into prolonged litigation over his estate, a legal battle that made its way to the South Carolina Supreme Court during the Reconstruction era. The high court decided in favor of the heirs of Sarah Turner Powers. The civil trial turned on the recognition of the legality of the 1813 marriage between a white man and a black woman. In the year of Powers's first marriage, the South Carolina legislature enacted its famous Negro Laws that severely curtailed the legal rights in property of black people. In 1873, Martin W. Turner of Marion, South Carolina, a namesake of the Martin Turner who enlisted in 1814, was summoned to appear before the court as a credible witness favorable to the Sarah Turner Powers heirs in this hearing.[26]

As the Turner name existed in early land, court, and clerk records of Marion County, so did that of the early Caulder family. Moses and his wife seemed destined for a stable and relatively prosperous life. Boundary references to Caulder's property in deeds recorded in Marion County indicate that Moses Caulder had name recognition among whites in the community.[27] In 1796, near the end of George Washington's administration, Moses and his wife were blessed with a second child, a girl whom the young couple named Mourning. Indeed, upon the birth of their daughter, the world may have looked as bright as a morning star to the young couple. By 1810, however, Moses Caulder had had some reversals and had fallen on hard times. His mother, who had lived with the family and who perhaps was the source of Moses's and Peter's freedom, died. In the midst of this grief, Moses lost his wife, perhaps in the birthing of the new child.

These deaths placed a pall on the Moses Caulder household. On March 10, 1812, a bittersweet day for most fathers, forty-year-old Moses gave his daughter Mourning's hand in marriage to Caleb Cook, a free black man born in Connecticut who had wended his way to Marion County, South Carolina. Free blacks from northeastern states often shipped out, making the sea their highway to the world and launching themselves on careers before the mast. But life aboard ship was not for everyone. Maybe after a merchant sloop docked at Charleston's waterfront, a teen-age Caleb, seasick or just thrashed by the ship's first mate or both, decided to jump ship, an action that occurred frequently enough in Charleston, though illegal.[28] A furtive Cook could have met Peter Caulder and Martin Turner at a shop operated by free blacks and hitched a wagon ride out of town and back to Marion with them. The older Turner lad was most likely a teamster and may on occasion have brought a wagonload of Bethea's cattle hides or deerskins to an export buyer in the big port city. Once in Marion, Caleb Cook, the Connecticut Yankee, began to court Mourning Caulder.

The romance blossomed and on lands belonging to Henry Berry, a white farmer, the newly wed nineteen-year-olds built a cabin in which they lived. In the spring of their marriage, Caleb and Mourning bent to the plow helping their landlord put in a cash crop, and earning a new set of calluses for the ex-sailor. For themselves, one imagines, they laid out a vegetable garden complete with yams and butter peas. This state of married bliss for Mourning lasted a little more than two years, ending when Caleb Cook enlisted in the army. He marched away to defend his country in the autumn of 1814 leaving his young wife on Catfish Creek. She would stay in Marion for the rest of her life. He apparently never returned and never again saw his spouse.[29]

So it seems that neither Moses nor Peter Caulder returned to Marion. Yet, the name remains entrenched in Marion County where the current telephone directory lists thirty Caulders or Calders, some of whom reside on Calder Road. The Caulder/Calder cemetery borders the Marion city limits. In this small graveyard, several veterans of World War I and World War II are buried, demonstrating that the tradition of family members enlisting as regular soldiers in time of national peril continued from the earlier days. All of the present-day Caulders/Calders of Marion County are white people, descendants most likely of the elder Peter Calder or of Dr. William Calder, a physician who died on August 19, 1797, after a ten-year medical residency on Edisto Island.

William Calder owned forty-five slaves. Archibald Calder, a

white man no doubt related to William, owned twenty-five slaves in a separate estate. Edisto Island is in the tidewater region of South Carolina and was an entry point for new slaves coming from Africa.[30]

In the summer of 1819, an English traveler by the name of William Faux stayed on Sullivan's Island in the tidewater, renting a room in a stilt house from a Mrs. Calder, a "Caledonian." Evenings were spent around a billiard table. One night with cool sea breezes and roaring tides, Mr. Calder, the landlady's husband, related a story to Faux about the time he took a Negro to his homeland on a visit and then was prevented on pain of arrest from forcing the black man to return to America with him. A bemused Faux entered into his journal this summary, "the poor negro's [sic] chains fell off when he reached old Scotland, where he now lives, a free man." How Calder felt about the loss went unrecorded, but Faux's stay must have delighted the Calders, because at the Englishman's departure by boat for Philadelphia, he was presented a gift by Mrs. Calder ("a mark of special favor") of an eighty-year-old black female servant, Cassandra. Cassandra protested her impending transfer, however, and in the end, Faux, to his credit, declined to accept the human gift and traveled on without the servant.[31]

Family tradition has it that Caulder is a Scottish name, and that emigrant brothers, apparently on the heels of a narrow escape, went their separate ways once in the New World and may have deliberately spelled their last name differently to confuse any would-be trackers.[32] The actual reason for the spelling variation might be more prosaic. Early nineteenth-century census marshals, tax collectors, and military clerks resorted to phonetic spelling in many cases when recording names. Thus Caulder becomes Calder, Colder, or even Cawlder on separate documents that refer to the same person. Army records go so far as to include the varieties of spelling of a soldier's surname. The Caulders themselves being frontiersmen who could not write their own names were unable or unwilling to correct misspellings of their surname.

On June 18, 1812, President James Madison signed into law the war bill that the Twelfth Congress had narrowly passed the day before.[33]

The sixty-one-year-old president was known more for his compromising spirit than for aggression. But Madison, indeed the nation, had been provoked by continual illegal British actions at sea against American shipping and seamen. The president probably was also swayed by the vocal nationalism of new congressmen from the South and West. To almost all Americans, Britain's detestable habit of impressing sailors was matched in repugnance by their habit of making Indian alliances to thwart western expansion of the young United States. Felix Grundy of Tennessee reflected the attitude of the frontier as he remarked in Congress that Britain should be driven from Canada to end the "intriguing with our Indian neighbors . . . to tomahawk our women and children."[34]

President Madison and the United States Army counted on a tide of militia volunteers from the states. Thousands of new men indeed flocked to recruiting booths to join their country's military, if for only three months at a time.[35] An enthusiastic response to the war call occurred in South Carolina, where local battles had been particularly bloody during the Revolutionary War. Indeed, a twenty-nine-year-old congressman and a rising star in the Palmetto state, John C. Calhoun, named after an uncle who had been singled out and murdered by Tories in 1781, had advocated war.[36] John Randolph, an anti-Jeffersonian Virginian, labeled Calhoun and his South Carolina congressional colleague Langdon Cheeves "War Hawks" because they supported Madison's call. That was a smear in Randolph's Federalist eyes, but most South Carolinians as well as future authors of textbooks loved the appellation.[37]

South Carolina militia law "called to duty all able bodied white men, free blacks, and slaves between the ages of eighteen and forty-five."[38] With a few exceptions, the act made serving in the militia compulsory, but substitutes were permitted. Eleven days after the Declaration of War with Britain, Marion County resident Alexander Lane sent in his place eighteen-year-old Peter Caulder. Thus, the military record of Caulder, whose years in the army would take him to (and leave him in) pre-territorial Arkansas, began with his being substituted for his white neighbor in the county militia. Lane had to provide young Caulder with musket and accouterments to begin his military service.

Peter Caulder became part of his neighbor Capt. Elisha Bethea's company of the Fifth Regiment. His two life-long friends, twenty-two-year-old Martin Turner and eighteen-year-old James Turner, enlisted along with Caulder, on the same Monday, June 29, 1812, and also as substitutes for white citizens of Marion County.[39] Substituting was a practice that dated back to the Revolutionary era. In colonial and early America, volunteers who were well off either served as officers or hired men to take their place in the enlisted ranks.[40]

In the first two weeks of their enlistment, the company's sixty-four men and officers (at the most) bivouacked in a field near a crossroads store and a mill northeast of Marion. During the first weeks of enlistment, Captain Bethea marched his green recruits and practiced them in close-order drill according to Baron von Steuben's *Blue Book*, the American army standard adopted by George Washington in 1779.[41] The captain probably on occasion marched his men to the battalion mustering grounds six miles down Buck Swamp River. The company stayed in Marion County for three months readying itself for a battle that never came. Caulder and mates never assembled with the full regiment, which was under the command of John Keith, a politician who owned 143 slaves and a plantation on the Black River.[42]

Free black men and slaves, as auxiliaries, supplied the labor for colonial militia units and served as musicians.[43] Privates Peter Caulder, Martin Turner, and James Turner, however, may have differed from this norm and drilled side by side with their white comrades since they drew the same six-dollar-a-month pay as the white militiamen.[44] Black men did serve as combat soldiers in integrated units, such as the New Jersey Brigade, during the Revolutionary War. They suffered hardships and casualties alongside white troops and presumably shared in the glories and comradeship that battle offers. Between 1797 and 1808, however, black volunteers discovered that the welcome they had received during times of crisis when manpower was needed substantially cooled in peacetime.

In Marion County, after a month of training, the men returned to live and eat at home. With a need to take care of their farm chores, the militia troops mustered for readiness drills perhaps no more than once or twice a month. No great peril loomed on the horizon for the South Carolina militia, despite the constant fear in Charleston that the British Navy might attack. But, unlike their strategy in 1780, the Redcoats stayed away from South Carolina. On September 29, 1812, the ninety-day terms of service for Peter Caulder, Martin Turner, and James Turner expired. Returning to civilian ways, Caulder went to work in the harvests. Hay and indigo had to be gathered. Hog and cow pens needed to be rebuilt for the fall roundup. The boom of war cannon was too distant to be heard on Catfish Creek. Caulder's discharge removed him from the disorders that spread through the South Carolina militia in 1813, when enlisted men rebelled against their officers. Commanders had tried to impose Articles of War that disciplined troops and required that they retire to their sleeping quarters at evening curfew, arise at dawn, perform soldier duties during the day, and share in mess duties.[45]

Except, perhaps, for these disorders in South Carolina militia units, Lt. Col. Thomas Adams Smith would have summoned some of their units to reinforce his regiment of regular army riflemen who were engaged in the "Patriot War" on the St. John's River near Savannah, Georgia. Smith in 1817 sent Pvt. Peter Caulder as part of a rifle company under Capt. William Bradford to Belle Point on the Arkansas River in 1817 to establish a fort that came to bear Smith's name.[46]

CHAPTER TWO

Rifleman

AT THE TIME OF THE WAR OF 1812, THE MARION COUNTY SHERIFF WAS
Enos Tart, who owned land adjoining the farms of John Turner and
Moses Caulder on Catfish Creek, six miles above the courthouse. Tart,
"a most remarkable man, a giant in strength and size, weighing about
three hundred pounds and not over corpulent," kept the peace by being
strong enough to pick up and hold two men by their collars until they
promised to stop fighting. Marion citizens liked Tart's good nature and
his restraint in dealing with drunks and other recalcitrant persons who
stood to be physically injured in case the sheriff lost his composure.[1]

Perhaps protected by the goodwill of neighbors like the generous
and tolerant giant sheriff, Moses Caulder lived peacefully with his
young wife along Catfish Creek. The couple had toddlers, two boys
and a girl, and an elderly mother-in-law who lived with the family.
The world looked bright. During the next decade, however, Caulder's
fortunes turned. The couple lost a young son, not uncommon for
families of the period, but no less hard for that fact. Caulder's wife may
have had complications in her next pregnancy, and her early death
made Caulder a widower. The death of his mother-in-law, who had
been a part of the household, left him alone to raise his teen-aged son
Peter, his daughter Mourning, and an infant daughter.

With the war raging, Americans were beginning to realize that
the state militias were not the answer for the long haul. In 1814,
Congress acted to strengthen the regular army by voting to increase
cash incentives and offer a one-hundred-sixty-acre land bounty to
recruits. Military leaders eased the unwritten restriction that recruits
were to be drawn only from the white citizenry in order to widen the
manpower pool.[2] The ninety-day South Carolina militia service of
Peter Caulder, Moses's son, had convinced this young landless man
that adventure and advancement awaited him in the army, and his
father, too, was swayed by these feelings.

Patriotism played a role, too. On August 23, 1814, British troops under the command of Gen. Robert Ross had swept aside American defenders, seized the federal city, occupied it for two days, and burned notable public properties including the White House, the Capitol, the National Archives, the Treasury building, and the Library of Congress. The news of the national disaster spread along the "cumbersome mail stages that linked the country together." *Niles' Weekly Register* reported that "the spirit of the nation is roused."[3] This unity of purpose and renewed willingness to put it on the line by men and women alike made the defense of Baltimore and New Orleans successful. Moses Caulder, Peter Caulder, and other men of Marion County shared this surge of patriotism.

Moses and Peter took a fateful trip to the Marion County Courthouse. With Spanish moss hanging limply from the water oaks in the sultry air of a hot Friday afternoon on the second of September 1814, the two men gazed at each other and listened as the uniformed recruiter explained the terms of service to them. At the end of the day, with witnesses attesting to their marks, Moses and Peter had enlisted in the Third Rifle Regiment for five years. The Third Rifles had posted Lieutenant Gadi Crawford in South Carolina to raise part of the regiment's authorized twelve hundred men. Martin Turner and James Turner had enlisted two weeks earlier than did the Caulders. In September, Joseph Clark and Caleb Cook, Peter Caulder's brother-in-law, joined the Third Rifles, too. These six Marion County men, whom the army classified as "colored men," joined the Third Rifle Regiment as pioneers.

Throughout the colonies before Independence, militia officers had employed free black men and slaves as laborers or fatigue men for their companies and regiments. Gen. James Oglethorpe's Florida expedition in 1740 used the nickname, "pioneers" for ox team drivers, most of whom were slaves sent by their masters to earn task money.[4] The practice of employing black men to fortify and provision local units continued during the Revolutionary War and afterward as state militias warred with Indians. As military organizations developed regulations, commanders placed "fatigue men" or "pioneers" on their rosters. These were soldiers who could effectively cut trees, saw lumber, and build. Pioneer units were not restricted to blacks nor did ordinary troops escape construction of campsites, trails, bridges, and wagon roads altogether. But tasks associated with moving and encamping an army fell to the pioneers, allowing officers to devote more time for practice of their military arts by the infantry and artillery soldiers. Winfield Scott insisted on organizing pioneer units within each of his regiments. The pioneers were paid at the same monthly rate as other soldiers. Usually, the burly soldiers picked for these construction squads were issued axes and shovels instead of muskets and swords and were readily identified by their white canvas "aprons." For pioneers, company officers wanted hardy men able to work full days until the job was completed. Since these men were often placed "on command," which meant they performed construction tasks without direct supervision, they had to be reliable and inventive. Though sometimes not issued rifles, pioneers were fully integrated into fighting units and were instructed to use their axes and brush hooks as combat weapons when face to face with the enemy. During later wars, pioneer units were assigned battlefield duties that included laying and clearing minefields. In fact, by the War of 1812, these roles were overlapping, some soldiers being designated as "miners" or "sappers."[5]

Lieutenant Crawford combed Marion County for recruits and signed up at least twelve men for the Third Rifles, including the six black privates. White enlistee Knightly Barfield had served in the militia along with Caulder and the Turners. Other white recruits were three Parker brothers, James Crosby, and John Franks. Franks gained the stripes of a corporal, the highest enlisted rank any of these Marion County men ever achieved.[6] The enlistment of a sizable group from a small village marked the corporate spirit that motivated young men to join military units in nineteenth-century wars.[7] Infused with patriotic spirit, women of Marion knitted socks and patched shirts for their young men. Perhaps Marion ladies fashioned a battle flag under which their heroes would fight on behalf of their homes. In such ways, the community let their young soldiers know that they were valued as fighters for liberty and for the homeland.

On an October day in 1814, well-wishers and family gathered at the Marion courthouse for goodbyes to their volunteers. The men in uniform received farewell hugs and kisses from family and friends, along with a bit of adulation from village lads and girls. Mourning Caulder bid farewell to her husband, her brother, and her father. She who was losing so much to the patriotic chore at hand may have shed more than a few tears as the Third Rifle Regiment, accompanied by fife and drum music, marched north along the Charlotte road toward North Carolina. Did Moses, Peter, Martin, Caleb Cook, and their friends have a premonition that they were embarking on an adventure that would take them out of Marion County, South Carolina, for good? They could not have known that even though all would survive the war, they would never set foot in Marion County again. One of the young white enlistees, James Crosby, must have had second thoughts about these very prospects. On October 17, the day of the march from Marion, the twenty-one-year-old Crosby slipped away from the company. The army advertised extensively for Crosby, and despite offers of a fifty-dollar reward for anyone furnishing information about the deserter, he never returned.[8]

As the regiment consolidated from recruiting stations, the South Carolinians commingled with men from other Southern states. At cantonment Greene, located in Mecklenburg County, North Carolina, Capt. Thomas. J. Robison swore in a number of Fayetteville men. Enlistees came from Columbia, York, and Union courthouses in South Carolina. Some men enlisted at Chambersburg and Marietta, Georgia. They came from North Carolina recruiting stations set up at Charlotte and Wardsborough. A group of volunteers came from Knoxville, Tennessee. One recruit came from Abington, Virginia, near the Cumberland Gap in the southern Appalachians. The men of the Third Rifles were young, rural Southerners, familiar with sand hill and mountain farms, but for the most part not landowners themselves.[9]

After three weeks of drill and adjusting to army life, the riflemen departed North Carolina bound for the nation's capital. As they traveled the rutted National Road into Virginia, the soldiers passed a steady stream of southbound wagons loaded with tobacco for the Charleston export markets. Despite adding to their numbers with recruits in Pendleton, North Carolina, and in southeast Virginia, the regiment never got up to its authorized strength. Heading north bivouacking in fields, and warming themselves on nippy Virginia nights by fires built by the pioneers, the Third Rifles numbered about six hundred men.

Caulder and his pioneer squad set up camp at Bottoms Bridge, Virginia, for an extended stay. In this low country with its late season swarms of mosquitoes and perhaps tainted drinking water, a number of troops fell to malaria and dysentery, diseases actually more deadly foes of nineteenth-century warriors than the steel of opposing armies. The Marion County mulattoes stayed healthy. Threats by Adm. Alexander Cochrane, nicknamed "the Goth" by terrorized seaboard residents, to burn "every assailable city" on the east coast may have forced the riflemen to remain longer in southeast Virginia in order to defend Norfolk. In mid-November the regiment now beefed up with two hundred additional infantrymen moved north to Fredericksburg where Peter Caulder spent his first Christmas away from Marion, South Carolina, in company with his fellow soldiers. The regiment stayed along the Rappahannock for the month of January because of the general ill health of a number of riflemen and because of British threats to the Potomac estuary. The riflemen moved into positions around Washington in early February 1815, arriving just as citizens of the capital received twin strokes of good news.[10] A copy of the Ghent treaty had reached the president's desk and three days before that news of Andrew Jackson's splendid victory at New Orleans had flashed through the capital. Peter Caulder and his fellow soldiers had to have participated in a Saturday night celebration that marked the end of the war. At 7 P.M. on February 18, the roar of cannons signaled the city's happy citizens to illuminate their homes. As celebrants touched off blunderbusses and rockets, the mayor of Washington, James H. Blake, saluted the "star-spangled banner" hoisted at city hall. Peter and Moses Caulder, Martin and James Turner, Caleb Cook, Joseph Clark, and the rest of the regiment witnessed this patriotic excitement along with leaders of the American government. The young riflemen from rural South Carolina, "hale, hard, generous men" who had enlisted to save their country, wound up in the nation's capital with propitious timing.[11]

Maybe the color and goodwill of the occasion, the stirring band music, and claps on the backs for men in uniform by grateful civilians formed a lasting imprint on Caulder. He decided on a career as an enlisted man in the United States Army.

At Greenleaf Point, the young nation's third-oldest army establishment after West Point and Carlisle Barracks, Peter and Moses Caulder and the riflemen set up white canvas tents. On level grassy lands shaded by giant oak trees, Caulder could see the broad waters of the Potomac at the tip of the small peninsula. Fort McNair sits today on the site, which is southeast of the city center. Maj. Pierre L'Enfant laid out Greenleaf Point as a military defense post for the federal city, but it was later converted to an arsenal. American soldiers who manned the site when the British invaded the capital on August 24, 1814, had destroyed what munitions they could, but retreated before the powder magazine had been emptied. On the second day of occupation, a British column of four officers and two hundred troops marched from Capitol Hill to the arsenal intent on destroying any usable ordinance to prevent its recovery by the Americans. The Redcoats dumped 150 kegs of gunpowder into a well before an enormous explosion rocked the premises, killing from twelve to thirty Redcoats and badly injuring forty-four others. The losses suffered by the British with the gunpowder accident at Greenleaf Point represented the worst single moment in Gen. Robert Ross's week-long inland campaign to take the nation's capital.[12]

Upon their arrival, Caulder and the Third Rifles found that buildings had been blown into "a huge, jumbled, mangled mass." He and his comrades were assigned rebuilding tasks such as hewing timbers and manufacturing replacement supplies of gunpowder from local raw materials. Soldiers in the War of 1812 at times had to make gunpowder, a chemistry skill important to Peter Caulder in Arkansas Territory. Free black craftsmen of the city were hired, at decent wages, to help rebuild the arsenal. In striking up friendships with these professionals, Caulder could well have extended his masonry abilities, another skill he employed later in his career.

Aside from repairing facilities, more training in the arts of war occupied the Third Rifles. Six hours a day spent in drill had become the guiding strategy for Winfield Scott and other emerging United

States military leaders. The stern routines and discipline resulted in fewer desertions apparently than those that occurred in infantry regiments. The list of deserters from the three rifle companies at Greenleaf Point numbered thirty-one men, about 5 percent of the total on the muster rolls. The higher retention rates in the Third Rifles perhaps can be explained by the commitment of the troops from the South.

As part of the tradition of that era, riflemen received a daily rum ration to ease the pains that beset men at war or on peacetime duty. Soldiers in good standing like Peter and Moses Caulder and Martin and James Turner could receive a pass to venture off post. A Washington city grog house or two catered to black men. Washington's population of about twenty-eight thousand was one-third black, of which more than three thousand were free men and women.[13] Like Caulder and the Turners, the majority of these were of mixed heritage. During their ninety-day stay in the capital, Caulder and Turner had opportunities to visit such black-owned businesses as a shoe shop or a barbershop where stories were exchanged and black Washingtonians made one another laugh— and think. In browsing a fruit stand or sampling oysters at one of the walk-in bars operated by free black people in Washington, the riflemen extended their horizons well beyond rural South Carolina and beyond army tents, mess lines, and close-order drill sessions.[14] The sons of Marion were taking in new sights, meeting diverse people, listening to new conversations, and gaining an expanding view of the United States. However, as out of the country as Peter Caulder was while in Washington, the country remained in him. If the urban way of life appealed at all to him, there is no evidence of it. In fact, he was destined for a life on the frontier quite different from that enjoyed by free blacks in the capital city.

For the men of the Third Rifles at Greenleaf Point, the end of the war spelled a turning point in their personal lives. Congress ratified the peace agreement on February 17, 1815. The next day, army commanders were ordered to discharge all militiamen and volunteers.

United States Army troops were held in their positions for a while longer. Private Caulder learned that he was to remain in uniform until the government fixed the peacetime army. Only the "duration" soldiers were released. In starting for home, the discharged men took with them the satisfaction of good service in the name of national honor, a pay bounty that averaged seventy-five dollars, and a promise of one hundred and sixty acres of land for their enlistment.

For some, including the black pioneers from South Carolina, the mustering out process became a little more complicated because of their five-year term of enlistment. Nevertheless, the Marion men had reason to be optimistic. Army rumors had it that any rifleman who wanted out could soon get his discharge. Furthermore, newspaper reports from Baltimore and New Orleans had mentioned the valiant and loyal efforts of black volunteers in the stirring defense for each city. The white community noted the patriotism of blacks to their country, and race relations in the United States, a country that felt as though it had won a victory over Britain, reached a high point of harmony. Perhaps in this spirit, Col. James C. Hamilton directed his company officer, Capt. Walter Coles, to continue the service of Peter Caulder, Moses Caulder, Joseph Clark, Martin Turner, James Turner, and Caleb Cook in the Rifle Regiment, and the "colored men" were placed on the company muster roll in alphabetical order with the other soldiers.[15]

The Military Peace Establishment Act passed by Congress reduced the army to a total of ten thousand men. Nothing was mentioned in the act about excluding blacks from the U.S. military. During the war, with the exception of all-black militia units in Louisiana, black soldiers and sailors had been integrated into regular army units, albeit most often as pioneers or musicians.[16] Nevertheless, as Marquis de Lafayette said of the Revolutionary War, "black and white soldiers messed together without hesitation." Black sailors made up almost 20 percent of the navy after 1813, and a navy surgeon wrote that "the white and colored seamen mess together. . . . There seems to be an entire absence of prejudice against the blacks as messmates among the crew."[17]

As an example of the cutback in the military, the four Rifle Regiments that had been authorized during 1814 were consolidated into one. Selection of officers and men to remain in the army were based on their competency "to engage an enemy in the field of battle." Men disabled by wounds or infirmities were released from active duty. Troops of the Third Rifle Regiment who had just begun five-year hitches could now apply for a discharge, or they could seek to stay in the army by passing a series of stringent qualification tests.[18]

On a spring day early in April 1815, Pvt. Peter Caulder mustered for the last time at Greenleaf Point. At the morning inspection, the Potomac River at their backs, the riflemen heard orders read for their company assigning it to Carlisle Barracks where their new regiment, to be known as the United States Rifles, would be housed and where qualification tests would be conducted. Soon, with drum and fife music keeping the cadence, the riflemen marched north from Washington toward Carlisle Barracks in south-central Pennsylvania. Caulder and the pioneers may have preceded the main body of troops, marking the trail and, at the end of each day's march, setting up camps amidst apple orchards and tall hardwood forests.

Situated along the north bank of the Susquehanna River fifteen and a half miles west of Harrisburg on the wagon road to Pittsburgh, the post of Carlisle faced a heavily wooded, flat-topped ridge that bordered a lengthy plain on its north edge. The south edge of the plain touched the river. Since the Washington administration, Carlisle had maintained its role as a training post for the U.S. Army. The small garrison, whose unit was officially called "rifles," tended to the receiving and training of small numbers of regular army recruits. Five well-built brick buildings and an ordinance magazine completed installations on the twenty-seven-acre site, which today houses the United States Army War College. The routines of the post went on quietly except when "fights between soldiers and the citizenry, of which there seem to have been many," occurred.[19] A local purveyor supplied beef, pork, bread, whiskey, soap, candles, vinegar, and salt rations for the troops. Soldiers manufactured their own gunpowder, there being ample blocks of sulfur in a nearby swamp. Quartermaster soldiers at Carlisle seined fish from the Susquehanna, salting and preserving the catch for the army, part of the self-sufficient principle under which frontier units would operate over the next two decades.[20]

Route of the Third Rifles from Marion County to Carlisle, Pennsylvania. In February 1815, Peter Caulder arrived at Greenleaf Point, in Washington City. After the war ended, Caulder and his fellow riflemen were transferred to Carlisle Barracks, Pennsylvania, the army's second-oldest military installation. The freshly trained companies of the newly organized Rifle Regiment were assigned to the western frontiers of the United States. Bradford's company of riflemen including Peter Caulder boated down the Ohio and Mississippi rivers to their new station in Louisiana.

MAP BY TOM PARADISE.

When Coles's company arrived at Carlisle in April 1815, they were the first unit to gather at what proved to be a way station for the new Rifle Regiment. The regimental quartermaster issued each enlisted man a rifle, except for the pioneers and the musicians. Clothing and pay issued to the Caulders and the Turners equaled that of the rest of the men.

The lack of regular pay added to chronic shortages of rations and led to some foraging on the part of soldiers. On weekends, southern-born riflemen might venture four miles into the village of Carlisle. Most of the young troops were unmarried, and they could have been looking for female companionship or maybe just enjoying an outing. Instead of sticking to the thoroughfare, soldiers occasionally crossed through orchards and fields. Apparently plucking a few green apples caused farmers to complain to the post commander, who issued orders that "in the future, soldiers of this garrison going to and from town keep to the publick [sic] road." Officers were "strictly enjoined to prevent . . . trespass on private ground" and soldiers so deviating would be confined and subject to court martial. The punishments sounded sufficiently fierce to Caulder, Martin Turner, and James Turner, so they avoided the temptations, as did their compatriots. The black soldiers seemed to do little to attract adverse attention to themselves while at Carlisle.[21]

In late May 1815, the riflemen received back pay and bonuses, an occasion that restored morale and lightened the mood of Caulder and his mates. Arising from their cots at reveille, the soldiers hit the surrounding countryside for daily training, perfecting their skill at tracking, survival, and evasion. At the post rifle range, the riflemen gained full command and knowledge of their Model 1812 rifled muskets. At times, Caulder squeezed off a few rounds. By the next year at Fort Claiborne, Louisiana, the black soldiers would be issued rifles. The quartermaster provided enough gunpowder and ball to ensure the marksmanship and the smoothness that comes with practice. Riflemen had long been recognized as elite soldiers. In a letter dated June 17, 1775, John Adams, Massachusetts's representative to the Continental Congress at the outset of the Revolutionary War, had written his wife, Abigail, and made this statement:

> The Continent is really in earnest in defending the Country. They have voted Ten Companies of Rifle Men to be sent from Pennsylvania, Maryland, and Virginia, to join the Army before Boston. These are an excellent Species of Light Infantry. They use a peculiar Kind of [ ] call'd a Rifle — it has circular or [ ] grooves within the Barrell, and carries a Ball, with great Exactness to great Distances. They are the most accurate Marksmen in the World.[22]

By the end of the summer of 1815, it was clear that this "excellent Species of Light Infantry" was destined for duty on the western frontier of the United States. To Natchitoches, Detroit, and St. Louis in proximity to possible foes, the Spaniards, the British, and dissatisfied Indians of the Mississippi Valley region, the riflemen would go to form the first line of defense for the new nation on its far frontiers.

So who were these defenders of sparsely populated American territories? Who were the riflemen who went beyond the Mississippi to embark on some of the most remarkable, if little publicized, military episodes in the early years of continental expansion? How did they appear to contemporaries and what backgrounds shaped them? Evidently, Moses and Peter Caulder and their four comrades from Marion County were the only black soldiers enlisted in the Rifle Regiment, the only band of brothers. No other men listed on the existing muster rolls were so identified. Their white comrades were veterans of the War of 1812, most of whom enlisted in 1814. Daguerreotypes were twenty-five years in the future and individual sketches of Bradford's enlisted men are nonexistent. Physical descriptions in army records of that period are standardized, with officers listing color of eyes, hair, and complexion on each soldier along with height, place of birth, and civilian occupation. Ironically, officers went to greater lengths in describing physical appearances of deserters.

The riflemen came mostly from farming stock as was the case with the Caulders, the Turners, and Joseph Clark. Two men in Coles's company had been carpenters, two more, shoemakers. Several were laborers from cities and two were surveyor's chainmen. Four, including Caleb Cook, had been sailors. Only a few had enlisted for the duration of the war, the great majority having signed on for a five-year hitch, most of them in the summer or fall of 1814. Their average height was five feet, six inches. Peter at five feet, nine inches, Moses Caulder at six feet, and the Turner brothers at five-ten were above average in height. Hair, eye, and complexion colors ranged from sandy to dark to black to fair, blue, or hazel. Ruddy and fair were common complexion entries. Only seven men in Coles's company at Carlisle were listed as having dark hair, dark eyes, and dark complexion, and six of these men were mulattoes from Marion County. The rest of the men in the company were described with other combinations, normally including a fair or light or blue entry. A small sample, but since commanders of this era did not specifically report race in post returns, perhaps an unwritten code existed whereas this particular combination could be read by other officers as designating men of color. Later, however, when the army recruited from central European immigrants, this combination appeared more often.[23]

Peter Caulder's rifle comrades bore scars of prior civilian work (a gunsmith had gunpowder marks in his face) and scars of knives indicating active lives in an age when daily risks were of a different nature. A fellow South Carolinian had a "sallow" complexion, another "yellow eyes." Many soldiers had blue eyes, a few were described with gray eyes. Some, but apparently not Caulder, had missing teeth. Riflemen gambled, wore whiskers, tried to bilk or bet one another out of wages, taught one another their skills, talked and acted optimistically (sprightly) or related tales of gloom (downcast). One was described as "quick in speech," another "slow of speech." Caulder had to watch out for one private known for being "addicted to taking things not his own, particularly watches." Another soldier, "can't look a man in his face." Some were careless in appearance, while others were "fond of dress." The soldiers ranged in age from eighteen to forty, most of them in their twenties. At Carlisle, Peter Caulder was twenty-one years old. They were to a man born in the United States and in the years 1815 through 1819, the majority of men on frontier duty came from seaboard states. Replenishing the Rifle Regiment after five-year terms began to expire became difficult for the army. Young white men coming into the age of adventure in a growing nation had other choices, but only Peter Caulder and Joseph Clark among the black soldiers reenlisted after their first hitch despite being offered chances to do so. Public dislike of the regular standing army curtailed enlistments. The army came to depend on foreign-born recruits. Soldiers born in Poland, Austria, or England became common on the western frontier.[24]

The War of 1812 provided command officers with name recognition throughout the United States. Peter Caulder could recognize Andrew Jackson, William Henry Harrison, and Zachary Taylor, men with whom he had shared bonds of military service. Their fame vaulted them into the White House. Perhaps Caulder and the southern-born riflemen had heard about the exploits of such men from Major Bradford, who had witnessed two of these famous leaders in battle and could have recounted war stories to the men. Photographs do exist for War of 1812 officers who extended their careers or lives beyond 1840, men like John E. Wool, Winfield Scott, and Zachary Taylor. But for most men of the era, word pictures must suffice, as is the case with Maj. William Bradford. Despite his prominence in army circles, his army responsibilities, his political race in Arkansas, and his valor in the War of 1812, not even a sketch of Bradford has been located.

Along benches, ridges, and streams in the vicinity of Carlisle, the riflemen steadily trained under the watchful eye of company officers through an "uncommonly clear" June. In July, Caulder and the men who had been in Capt. Walter Coles's company for six months fell out to receive their new commander, Bvt. Maj. William Bradford. During the summer of 1815, Caulder, Cook, and Clark surveyed, cleared land, laid out roads, built bridges, and honed their pioneering skills in the Pennsylvania countryside. No existing record verifies that Martin and James Turner acted as teamsters or horse traders for the regiment, but this duty seemed to be their specialty, a carryover from their South Carolina trade and work experiences.

Whether Caulder or Cook sent mail to Marion County or received any is unknown. Illiterate soldiers sometimes persuaded officers to write letters on their behalf. Caleb Cook had left his young wife, Mourning, in Marion. The couple must have dreamed about seeing each other again. The army granted neither Caulder nor Cook furloughs while they were at Carlisle, and even if time had been available, the lack of pay might have prevented these young soldiers from undertaking a trip to South Carolina. Moreover, the men were competing for slots in the Rifle Regiment. If they were successful in staying in the army, the odds were long that Caulder, Cook, and the Turners would ever again see relatives in South Carolina. Their destiny lay to the west.

The western frontier was in a state of flux. British troops had at last withdrawn from their continental strongholds including Prairie du Chein along the Wisconsin River, and the vacuum had to be filled soon by American arms in the name of security and stability for venturesome American settlers.[25] To enforce American claims, the six hundred riflemen training at Carlisle making up twelve companies prepared to take up new assignments in the upper and lower Mississippi regions as outlined by an act of Congress. These troops would be the vacuum fillers and the peacekeepers. Maj. Gen. Andrew Jackson transferred the Rifle Regiment from Carlisle west via flatboats down the Ohio and on to St. Louis.[26]

Discipline, regular pay, reliable rations, and the retrenchment had worked wonders for the now-confident regiment. The riflemen wore a green tunic with gold trim worn over green canvas trousers, distinctive sharpshooter colors that harked back to European tradition. On August 30, 1815, as Colonel Hamilton marched his proud regiment toward Pittsburgh, an observer noted that "we have seldom witnessed better looking (men) as to health and dress, and in every respect (they appeared) martial."[27]

As Peter Caulder and his fellow riflemen set out from Carlisle, one old friend did not accompany them. Moses Caulder had been discharged from the army because of his age. With the general order of the redeployment, company officers were instructed that "all riflemen within their respective commands who may be *actually unfit* for any corps, to be *at once* discharged." What pangs of regret Moses must have had as he realized that he would not be joining Peter and his younger comrades on this great western adventure! Rather than return to South Carolina, Moses Caulder apparently stayed north of the Mason-Dixon line, most likely migrating west into Illinois Territory. A few years later, he applied for and received a veteran's land bounty in Hancock County, Illinois. The government deeded him one hundred sixty acres near where Joseph Smith and his Latter Day Saints would locate Nauvoo.[28]

In September 1815, Caulder and several hundred riflemen loaded onto ten flatboats at Pittsburgh for the voyage down the Ohio as seasonally early north winds brought chilly air. When not poling,

Caulder and his fellow soldiers cooked, scrubbed, relaxed, or slept on deck, wrapping themselves in their blankets at night. To keep the eye of their marksmen, officers organized periods of target practice, firing from the sides of the flatboats as they drifted down the river. Discipline prevailed, however, and a soldier had to seek permission before discharging his weapon, even if a likely turtle presented itself.[29] Stopping only for food, to make repairs, or to stretch legs in between ports of call, the forty-two men of Bradford's company who had been transformed from green recruits into tough soldiers during the long weeks at Carlisle, reached the Mississippi River by early October. As the waters of the Ohio mixed with the muddy Mississippi, Caulder helped head two of the flatboats downstream toward Louisiana in the far southwest reaches of the United States as it existed in 1815. A week or so later reaching the mouth of the Red River, the two boats were turned northwesterly to go upstream on the tributary river. Caulder and the riflemen poled and cordelled the boats toward their destination, a hundred miles upriver in the new western lands. By the time days were short and nights cold in December, Peter Caulder, Joseph Clark, Martin Turner, and James Turner were pitching their bedrolls at a tiny fort named Claiborne near the settlement of Natchitoches in the state of Louisiana. In their fourteen months of army service, the men from Marion, South Carolina, had traveled a great arc from Catfish Creek to Washington to Pennsylvania, down the Ohio and Mississippi Rivers to Louisiana and up the Red to the very limits of their country. Peter Caulder and his Marion County comrades were being paid in the service of their country and were being treated with respect by their white peers. Not only were they seeing exotic lands for the first time, they were part of a group charged with defending U.S. territory. None of the five black men had yet reached the age of twenty-five.[30]

Natchitoches, a few miles from Texas, had been an administrative center for Spanish Louisiana since 1763. Native Americans, French colonials, and Spanish soldiers had traveled the Red River for decades despite a clogging raft of driftwood, a tangled jumble of floating trees that stretched one hundred miles long, above present-day Shreveport. The indistinct border between Spanish Texas and

Louisiana invited filibusters. Some four hundred whites lived above Natchitoches. A few clamored to occupy lands weakly held by the Spanish government, the power center of which seemed so far away. The quieting of continental issues by treaty between Spain and the United States still lay a few months in the future when Caulder and his mates took up their positions on the frontier. The riflemen spent part of their first weeks in setting up patrols and mapping the region for its defense. Caddo Indians of the region did not yet consider themselves as under jurisdiction of the United States and had their own ideas about freedom of movement, hunting land, and trading rights. Caulder and the Turner brothers probably did trade with the Caddos as well as with white settlers, giving Indians and settlers issue items such as shot, gunpowder, candles, cloth, and needles in return for food, particularly cornmeal and dried venison.

Caulder and his mates had to make do for a part of their diet and most of their protein. They hunted deer and small game. Hunting and gardening became essential duties for frontier soldiers. In his study of fort building by the army in the old northwest, the historian Francis Paul Prucha was so impressed by the logging and construction demands placed on frontier soldiers that he entitled his work, *Broadax and Bayonet.* In certain Mississippi Valley cantonments, especially those manned by companies and detachments of the Rifle Regiment, the riflemen "pioneered" as well as soldiered.[31]

During his Louisiana and Arkansas Territory commands, Bradford makes no mention in his correspondence or on his monthly returns of the race of the five men from South Carolina who accompanied him throughout the trans-Mississippi. No longer are Caulder, the Turners, Clark, and Caleb Cook designated as pioneers and set apart as colored as they were in company books of Walter Coles at Greenleaf Point and Carlisle. These men are issued rifles at Fort Claiborne, maybe even before they left Carlisle. Caulder, like his South Carolina friends, wanted to stay in the army, was good enough to stay, and won the respect and friendship of white men in the regiment. Hard as it is for those who know what unfolds in the next decades to comprehend, Caulder's integration into an army unit occurred without documented objections. Col. James Hamilton, who stayed on active duty in the Rifle Regiment as commander of Fort Crawford until 1819, knew definitely that Caulder was colored (a designation that he specified for the official record and a designation that all five mulatto soldiers accepted). Bradford was aware of the designation, just as the previous commander of the company Captain Coles had been.

There is, however, a possibility that "race" did surface as a distinction if not as an issue in company duty assignments during 1816 at Fort Claiborne, Louisiana. In the April, October, and December 1816 returns, the only ones that survive, Major Bradford was marked absent from the post on other assignments. The five black soldiers along with several other enlisted men are placed on "extra duty" or "daily duty" by order of Bvt. Maj. Joseph Selden. This signified that soldiers had road-building or other construction assignments apart from their military duties. Selden commanded a detachment of riflemen at Baton Rouge and may have transferred Caulder and the others into it, a considerable distance from Natchitoches, to carry out construction assignments at Baton Rouge. Selden was a Virginian and old hand in the army, having served in the Revolutionary War as well in as the recent contest with Britain. His preemption of Bradford's troops might have caused a dispute over command that arose between him and Major Bradford. In March 1816, Gen. Thomas Smith wrote a letter to Andrew Jackson in which he discussed the Bradford-Selden "quarrel" over seniority. Bradford argued in a letter to Jackson that his battlefield and command experiences underlay his seniority over Selden's claims. Secretary of War William H. Crawford resolved the dispute in Bradford's favor, perhaps with the help of Jackson.[32] The two officers would soon be separated from each other and from their Louisiana commands. Early in 1817, Smith summoned Bradford to Belle Fontaine.

CHAPTER THREE

Stranger at Belle Point

LOUISIANA QUALIFIED FOR ADMISSION AS THE EIGHTEENTH STATE IN 1812. Only three years later, Peter Caulder, Martin Turner, James Turner, and Joseph Clark poled their way up the Red River feeling the excitement that the frontier brings to young men. The riflemen passed plantations and a few communities of settlers, but mostly they witnessed the wildness of the land. In 1815, Louisiana had a large city, New Orleans, and a few forward towns such as Natchitoches, but rustic settings and nature dominated the new state. The riflemen would join these primitive surroundings in a life governed by the hunt, firearms, horses, wary strangers, and beasts of the forest.

Huge Missouri Territory to the north was more sparsely settled, but poised to grow quickly. Indeed by 1816, St. Louis had two thousand residents with another fifty-four hundred people living in the hinterland of the zestful city. Riflemen passing through this gateway, as Caulder did at least once, must have marveled at the sights. St. Louis's muddy waterfront streets thronged with fur-clad trappers, beaver-hatted merchants, tall, silent Osage Indians in moccasins, women in long dresses, booted land speculators, burly boatmen in homespun, and barefooted black men. Caulder may have noticed the women of St. Louis and perhaps dreamed of finding the right one and settling down in this wild, but promising territory. The city at the juncture of America's two longest navigable rivers attracted hundreds of adventurers eager to make their fortunes in new lands accessible by the wide Missouri that bordered its north edge. An eastern minister once noted that observance of the Sabbath did not extend across the Mississippi. Despite that hindrance, people forded or ferried their way across the broad, muddy waters in droves.

Brig. Gen. Thomas Adams Smith had arrived at St. Louis earlier to superintend the vast Ninth Military District. To carry out his duties, he deployed infantry, artillery, and riflemen, sometimes referred to in more gallant nomenclature as the United States Rifles. Smith set up his headquarters at Belle Fontaine, two miles north of St. Louis on the Missouri River, a site chosen in 1804 by James Wilkinson while he was governor of Louisiana Territory and occupied by military units since.

When the Rifle Regiment arrived from Carlisle in late 1815, it was split up and companies were further deployed along the northwestern and southwestern frontiers to forward stations. Confident that the southwestern sector was in good hands under Bradford, General Smith himself led two rifle companies composed mostly of riflemen from northern states up the mighty river toward lands of the still-hostile Fox, Sauk, and Kickapoo Indians.[1] Smith placed garrisons of riflemen in extreme and isolated spots of the territories, to show might and keep the Indians in check. The fort that Bradford would build at Belle Point on the Arkansas frontier, of course, came to bear Smith's name and its establishment would involve Caulder, Clark, the Turners, and two score of riflemen initially assigned to Louisiana.

Thomas Adams Smith was a decorated veteran of the War of 1812. Born in Virginia and raised in Georgia, he was commissioned a lieutenant of artillery on December 15, 1803, at the age of twenty-two. Assigned to Gen. James Wilkinson's staff in New Orleans, the nefarious general selected Smith to carry news for President Jefferson that Aaron Burr was in a conspiracy to pry part of the west away from U.S. control. Smith apparently was not instructed to reveal that Wilkerson had been involved in the conspiracy with Burr.

Emerging from this chapter of political intrigue, Brig. Gen. Thomas A. Smith now found himself swept up in another sort of intrigue, that of romance. Smith began a courtship with Cynthia Berry, then proposed marriage, and the couple wedded in 1807. The Smiths had eight children, by any index a successful marriage even though the army allowed the officer little time at home with his wife and family over the next eight years.

Smith transferred from an artillery unit into the U.S. Rifles in 1808 and with the outbreak of the war in 1812, became a colonel in that regiment. Following his undertaking of the Patriot's War, he was moved to the northern theater and his brave actions at Sacket's Harbor and at Plattsburgh in New York earned him a reputation for being a fighter. Breveted to brigadier general in 1814, Smith accompanied Gen. George Izard on a four-hundred-mile diversionary march to Lake Erie. In 1825, Izard, "a prominent South Carolina Federalist," was appointed by President James Monroe as the second governor of territorial Arkansas and came to Little Rock to administer the territory.[2]

Smith's trip up the Mississippi with his riflemen gave him a first-hand look at the geography and at Indian adversaries. Back at his desk at Belle Fontaine in August 1816, Smith opened a letter from Albany, New York, and read an introduction for a former engineering instructor at West Point, Stephen Harriman Long. General Smith invited the young, adventuresome officer to his quarters for dinner and introduced him to Mrs. Smith.[3] The professional association of the two officers blossomed into a friendship. Long closed one report sent to Smith with a personal note, taking care to inquire about the health and well-being of the general's wife.[4]

General Smith maintained the peace and security of the northwest and the southwest frontiers with his elite force of riflemen who wore green tunics trimmed with yellow fringe, green trousers, and shaklo hats. Some men carried the army's latest in individual weaponry, the 1812 breechloaders, while others were issued rifled muskets. The six-pound cannon, a formidable artillery piece for the era, lent punch and prestige to Rifle Regiment maneuvers. Occasionally, the rifle companies on the frontier faced Indian disturbances. For Peter Caulder and his fellow soldiers in Louisiana, the trouble brewed out of migrations and arguments over territory. Cherokee streamed into Arkansas district of Missouri Territory after the Treaty of Fort Clark in 1808 in which the Osages had ceded their ancient claims to hunting lands north of the Arkansas River. The Jefferson administration encouraged Cherokees to move from their homelands in Tennessee, North Carolina, and Georgia into Arkansas district.[5]

The Cherokee reserve, shaped like a diamond, stretched from the Missouri line to the Arkansas River. Hunting whitetail deer, Waipiti elk, and buffalo and fishing the river for the table added to the nutrition as well as the scope of life for these native Americans. The Cherokees picked up Christian names and were determined to create for themselves in these new lands the Valhalla that Jefferson had envisioned.[6] Despite a promising start, two embedded dangers imperiled the Cherokee future in Arkansas: the fury of the Osages and the land lust of the whites. Both of these forces would soon involve Peter Caulder. The Cherokee migrations and the resulting conflicts with the Osage tribes hurled new challenges for Peter Caulder and the other riflemen at Fort Claiborne.

Oral traditions of the Osage make mention of their warriors from Missouri who traveled afar, in the fall of 1754, to join the French in the ambush of Gen. William Braddock's Redcoats in Pennsylvania. The Osages had long been trading partners with the heavy eyebrows, part of that natural division of North American Indians into either French or British spheres. French was a second language among the Osages. In a single year, the Osages exported forty thousand pounds of deer hides, twelve thousand raccoon pelts, almost three thousand beaver pelts, and five hundred bear skins through French traders. In the eighteenth century, the Ozarks were indeed rich hunting grounds providing the Osages with a hefty balance of trade in the best years. French and Spanish officials were willing to overlook a few of the worst habits of the Osages, like their occasional roasting over a fire of captured vagabond woodsmen.[7] The Cherokees, though, had been prone to trade with the British and fought alongside the English during the wars of the eighteenth century. No friendship or trading relationships ever developed between the Osages and the Cherokees, whom the former contemptuously referred to as *Sah-La-Keh*, That-Thing-on-Its-Head, because they wore calico headbands that held a tail plume of the snowy egret.[8] The Osages, in fact, had few allies among other Indians, and for that reason attempted to keep up a bluff by circulating tales of their ferocity.[9]

As Peter Caulder and the men of Bradford's company patrolled the Red River for bandits and tried to quell other border disturbances, about two thousand Cherokees came into Arkansas. Sauk, Fox, Shawnee, Iowa, and Kansas Indians who had accepted federal exchanges began to arrive in Arkansas, as well, to walk over lands set aside for them out of the Osage cession. A few dozen Delaware Indians settled above Batesville.[10]

Over the next two years, some forty-six thousand Indians of these tribes, thirteen thousand of them warriors, migrated from the north, many of them passing through Arkansas to relocate further to the southwest along the Red River.[11] The number of clashes with Osages had increased to the point that a state of ongoing warfare existed. With the loss of hunting lands and the threatened game supply, the Osages turned to cattle and horse stealing from the Cherokees and other eastern Indians to compensate for their losses. The Cherokees retaliated with vengeance. Rising levels of violence endangered voluntary Indian removal plans of the federal government.

Probably thinking that other tribes were faring better with Americans, the Osages had asked for the government to furnish them with an agent to be located at their tribal core site where the Verdigris flows into the Arkansas River. One branch of Osages revered this location known to them as the Place-of-the-Many-Swans. The Osages tried to hold onto old ways, such as hunting buffalo, stealing horses, and warring with rivals. They had little use for the white man, other than getting needed articles like firearms through trade. The Osages sought to stem the tide of a changing frontier rather than accommodate it. They were not cultivators or lettered men like the Cherokees. Nomads and meat eaters who depended on the deer, the beaver, the elk, and the buffalo as their source of livelihood, the Osages had not thought they had ceded those vital game and fur animals along with the Ozark land. To make matters worse, bloody conflict tended to mark their first contacts with Americans—outlaws on the lam, "men more savage than those whom they called Injuns." These barbarians would have been hanged for rape and murder had they not fled their own white law. Yet when such men met their deserved fate at the hands of the Osages, who proudly displayed scalps in their lodges as proof of their capable defense of home, hearth, and hunting ground, whites, incredibly to the Osages, suddenly would cast the slaughtered rogues as victims.[12] Only gradually did the Osages drop their hatred of Americans and seek to work out their differences with governors, agents, and military commanders.

William Clark, governor of Missouri Territory from 1812 to 1815, forwarded requests for a military presence in Arkansas to the secretary of war John C. Calhoun and late in 1816 the secretary took action. He sent a directive to General Jackson at Nashville to set up a cantonment and a garrison at the point where the southeastern Osage boundary met the Arkansas River. Jackson forwarded the order to Gen. Thomas Smith at Belle Fontaine.[13]

To carry out the order, Smith turned to his topographical engineer Stephen H. Long and to his capable commander in the southwest, William Bradford, whom Brigadier General Smith summoned from Louisiana.[14] Upon his arrival in St. Louis in April 1817, Bradford set about organizing the expedition to Arkansas. He secured a keelboat, a pilot, and boatsmen, and stockpiled the necessary ordnance, which included two six-pound cannons, powder, and shot. A civilian contractor, Hugh Glenn, assembled the supplies Bradford would need for a three-month-long river journey.[15] Steadily, stores arrived at the Belle Fontaine wharf and were loaded onto the keelboat: blankets, issue tunics made of gray wool, white canvas pants, wool socks, and boots for the men; bags of rice and dried beans, cured meat, barrels of flour, tins of salt, coffee, and sugar; kegs of brandy and whiskey; live chickens; leather tracings; harness for oxen; pots of grease for axles; and lard for cooking.

Bradford compiled his roster of riflemen who would accompany him, twenty-eight of whom he had commanded since his days at Carlisle, Peter Caulder, Joseph Clark, Martin Turner, and James Turner among them. The War Department transferred another thirty riflemen from Joseph Selden's company to Bradford's command. Bradford was to proceed down the Mississippi to meet his core of veterans coming up from Louisiana under the wing of Selden, the fifty-nine-year-old veteran of the Revolutionary War and the War of 1812.[16] General Smith noted the southern riflemen's adjustment to hot weather and mosquitoes. He wrote to Jackson's adjutant in Nashville that "the detachment from Natchitoches being inured to a Southern climate will be liable to experience less mortality on the Arkansaw than recruits from so high a latitude as Albany, New York."[17]

At summer's end, the complicated plan swung into action. On September 15, 1817, Bradford began his descent of the river. A newspaper reported that Bradford and Long had "left St. Louis for the purpose of establishing a military post on the Arkansas, near the Osage boundary."[18]

At Cape Girardeau, Bradford met Bvt. Maj. Joseph Selden and his men who had ascended the Mississippi to that point. Selden was in the grip of an illness and many of the riflemen apparently suffered from the same epidemic. Leaving Selden to tend to his own recovery, Bradford loaded his keelboat and two flatboats with the increasingly incapacitated riflemen and pushed into the Mississippi current to continue the downstream float to Arkansas. Shortly, Long and Bradford arrived at the confluence of the Ohio and Mississippi near the present-day city of Cairo, Illinois, where they beached the boats and camped, perhaps to allow some of the men a chance to recover. Long, who was a ceaseless observer of terrain and climate conditions, took the opportunity to make notes. He was not impressed with the location and described the area as "covered with a heavy growth of timber which at present not only renders it gloomy, but subjects the people living upon it to much sickness." Major Long, ever the engineer, thought that clearing three or four hundred acres of forest would be a great improvement. Thomas Nuttall, observing the same area but with a naturalist's viewpoint, opposed Long's evaluation. Nuttall visited the same spot two years later and came away impressed with the abundance of "various kinds of game, but particularly deer and bears, turkeys, geese and swans with hosts of other aquatic fowls."[19]

Setting out on the river again, riflemen continued to fall out and the deck of the keelboat became littered with soldiers wrapped in blankets. Bradford had to order an emergency halt at New Madrid so that he could attend to some dangerously ill soldiers. Bradford had medicines and hospital stores with him, but no doctor.[20] Accordingly, Long and Bradford went to work treating the men, offering them such medical assistance as they could. In time, twenty-four of the riflemen regained strength enough for duty on the next leg of the journey to Arkansas Post. But Long wrote Smith that three men "who were judged incurable before we met them" died, meaning that the officers had to consign some members of the expedition to the hard ground of Missouri Territory before the company ever arrived at the mouth of the Arkansas.[21] Neither officer identified the causes of the epidemic or offered an opinion on it. In late summer, tributaries of the Mississippi, the source of drinking water for the riflemen, may have carried harmful bacteria.[22] Early Americans fell in staggering numbers to cholera and dysentery, diseases caused by impure water. Long had to abandon his anticipated side trip to the "country of the St. Francis," lands that he wanted to explore and survey while en route to Arkansas.[23]

While Bradford was en route from St. Louis and trying to bring his reinforcements back to health, Peter Caulder and thirty Natchitoches riflemen, left at the mouth of the Arkansas by Selden, poled their flatboat thirty-six miles up the Arkansas River to reach a settlement known as the Village or Post of Arkansas. As the men reached the mouth of the White River they may have found that stream as John James Audubon described it three years later: "full and run violently, the Watter a Dull Red Clay Color."[24] Audubon noted the presence of buntings, meadowlarks, and cardinals that cheered the break of each sunny morning. Peter Caulder when not poling might have relaxed on the deck for a bit of similar bird watching and gazed at a string of farms that stretched along the north side of the river beginning some seven miles down from the village. The stubble of harvested fields of wheat, hemp, and cotton provided grazing for sheep that might have bleated out their awareness of the passing soldiers. The grunting of root hogs told of mast-carpeted thickets, and cattle bawled from the thick canebrakes that adjoined crop fields bounded by split-rail fences. Caulder and his old friends from Marion County may have felt a touch of nostalgia as they glided by, the landscape here so much like home on Catfish Creek.[25]

Along the Arkansas, crops were best produced on lands long ago cleared and tamed by Quapaws.[26] New ground gave difficulties because its sod was so thick that wooden plows had difficulty in breaking it. Family holdings ran back away from the water's edge in accordance with the French method for laying out farms, called long lots. Perhaps seven hundred whites and sixty slaves lived in the vicinity of the river. The occasional free man of color from New Orleans visited Arkansas Post and at times could have become a short-term resident in the area, though free blacks do not appear on existing census records. Beyond the pale of cultivation, wildflowers blanketed a vast prairie that extended back ninety miles, uninhabited and waiting. The hub of this modest plantation community was the Post where a mixed heritage revealed itself in the daily life. Several village residents spoke French. Dark-complexioned people with diverse ethnic origins lived and worked in the community both as residents and transients. A villager at the wharf when the army flatboat pulled alongside it and tied up would hardly have been surprised when Peter Caulder and other mulatto soldiers jumped ashore.[27]

A cluster of farmers lived near the fort. The isolated clearing in the forest that had a few residents and a few log buildings, accessible only by boat or path, signified what little civilization there was in Arkansas, but it was, ironically, a rather cosmopolitan place when Peter Caulder and his fellow riflemen set foot in the village.

Caulder and the soldiers who had come north had been exposed to tropical diseases during their year in Louisiana. Peter Caulder spent two months of 1816 either in the tiny hospital at Fort Claiborne or recovering in his quarters from the sicknesses that struck down riflemen. Joseph Clark, too, had a severe bout with disease. Martin Turner and James Turner seemed to be more resistant or perhaps more careful. For five years these brothers stayed fit for duty. No record of their going on sick call during any month at any station appears on returns. Caulder remained essentially healthy and ready for duty while in the army. Only one other time in his twelve-year career was he reported as "sick in quarters." Thus the men from Louisiana appeared in contrast to the regiment's recruits from Albany. In rejoining his Carlisle veterans upon his arrival at Arkansas Post, Major Bradford must have been gladdened to see these reliable (and healthy) men with whom he already had served for two years.[28]

In the grassy commons of the old military site near the village, surrounded by massive bare limb walnuts, water oak, and cottonwood trees, the riflemen pitched camp. Bradford tended to the men who were slow in recovering from dysentery and drilled those who were fit for duty. He sent foragers in search of fresh provisions to supply the men. White and Indian hunters trafficked through the village, the only sizable settlement in Arkansas district. At the wharf, Caulder had an opportunity to witness bargaining for the dried venison and bear meat offered for barter by these "woods runners." He saw the honeyed results of the fine art of bee tree robbing, a skill that he came to practice while in the army and while homesteading in the White River hills.[29]

Migratory ducks along the Mississippi flyway surely provided sport and food for the inhabitants. The village probably boasted dogs trained or bred to retrieve the downed waterfowl. Peter Caulder liked working dogs, and he could have picked up tips on the care and handling of retrievers. Protein in the soldiers' diets came from sources like bird and turtle eggs, buffalo tongues, alligator snouts, and crayfish. Major Bradford had government vouchers to offer sellers of such delicacies and may have authorized Privates Joseph Clark or James Turner, as camp cooks, to acquire local food for the mess offerings. While the last of the sick soldiers recuperated, Bradford, as a distinguished and news-bearing guest, may have dined with prominent villagers. Around the table would have been typical fare for such semi-formal social occasions, including a bottle of wine, slices of ham or mutton, and bread. If loosened by this bit of civilization at the Post, a more relaxed Bradford could have issued passes for his riflemen to walk the mile or so from the camp to the village where one of the log buildings along Front Street housed a billiard table. Did Caulder and his Marion friends join other soldiers in a pool game at Arkansas Post? It is true that a new deck of cards could be had in one store, stocked for the village inhabitants who were remarked on by some travelers for their love of card games such as whist.[30] It is equally true that Bradford looked after military details such as posting sentries and setting up a duty schedule. The soldiers operated under the Articles of War discipline and expected strict order and military bearing from Bradford. No incidents between local people and soldiers marred the bivouac at Arkansas Post. One of those small pleasures that enlisted men eagerly anticipated came at the bottom of the day, the daily whiskey ration. From a local vintner, Caulder may have procured jugs of elderberry wine or hard cider made from wild plums to buttress the gill of alcoholic beverage a day he received. Gardeners around the village grew tobacco as a companion to garlic in their herb plots. Peter Caulder chewed or smoked a pipe and may have traded rations or candles for twists of dried tobacco. As did the Arkansas Indians they had come to keep peace among, the riflemen pursued a barter economy. Caulder had no money with which to buy anything since he had not been paid for almost a year, but trading offered an opportunity for not only picking up goods, but of competing with another male.

The riflemen certainly made up a male culture. Danger and outside work, elements of their existence, called for aggressive and tough men. No doubt, pranks, tests of strength, rough satires, and games of chance spiced the soldiers' lives. The average age of the enlisted men, twenty-five, and the fact that they were veterans of a war, if not of actual battle, intensified what one historian has characterized as "the pleasures of male culture." Southern white male culture of the eighteenth century commonly relegated black men, when they were included at all, as attendants or liegemen. Whether Caulder and the men from Marion interacted as full-scale partners with white soldiers in those "pleasures of male culture" is speculative.[31] During duty hours, no apparent difference was made in the tasks, assignments, or treatment between whites and the five black men from Marion County in Bradford's company. It is difficult to see how working relationships among enlisted men could be maintained if the company was stratified by race as in civilian society. Definitely, ideas and gossip of race and slavery were well known to the young riflemen. How it affected the treatment of Private Caulder seems less clear. In today's society, we often see, especially among young people, a voluntary social segregation. Caulder chose to stay close to his friends from Marion County, South Carolina. They obviously enjoyed one another's company and depended on one another.

Even though the company of riflemen that founded Fort Smith was essentially masculine, it was not totally so. Four women accompanied the expeditionary force and were authorized by Bradford to draw rations. In return, the women washed uniforms and blankets for the soldiers and may have also barbered, trimming the men's hair and beards to military standards. These women went unnamed on official reports, but Susan Loving appears in an 1820 sutler's account book at Fort Smith and may have been the wife of William R. Loving, a rifleman from South Carolina, a Carlisle veteran, and occasional duty mate of Caulder. Probably, Susan Loving stepped ashore at Belle Point on Christmas Day, 1817.

Another married soldier in the company, Sgt. Balthazar Kramer, had left his wife in Kentucky. The German-born Kramer had heard the crash of muskets and the whine of bullets on a War of 1812 battlefield in New York. Bradford, who had known him since Carlisle, no doubt depended on his first sergeant's army experiences and organizational skills in bringing the detachment up from Natchitoches. He was a proven sergeant who could maintain the discipline and military bearing of the company.[32]

While at Arkansas Post, Caulder may have preferred to sleep under the stars in cool, dry October weather that normally was slightly beyond the insect season. In sweltering summers, swarms of mosquitoes discomforted people at the village, some of whom tried to escape the sharp proboscis by sleeping under netting. Outbreaks of yellow fever, a virus, and malaria, a debilitating disease rendered by parasites in the blood, took lives and slowed the coming of civilization to eastern Arkansas. Despite the insects, throwing a log on the fire and stretching out beside it while comrades played the harmonica, sang, or dealt a few hands of poker may have seemed idyllic to Caulder and his fellow riflemen. Especially since poling and cordelling boats four hundred and fifty miles into Indian country lay in store.

During their extended stay at Arkansas Post, conversations between Bradford and Long occurred, some of them overheard no doubt by Peter Caulder, who became a traveling companion to both officers. Having recently been introduced to each other at Belle Fontaine, the two officers who Smith jointly assigned to carry out an important mission in a remote and volatile part of the United States came from different backgrounds. Long was an articulate New Englander, a former schoolmaster, and a West Point instructor. He had been promoted from lieutenant directly to major. Officers rarely skipped two grades in the peacetime army and that reflected the army's estimation of Long's value. Bradford, a one-time Kentucky politician turned militia officer, had risen in the ranks by his battlefield valor, a true mustang. Bradford, a courteous officer, but a stern disciplinarian, engendered loyalty among his troops with his consistency and his toughness.

Often, Long burrowed into his books. He carried with him such printed fare as the account of the 1805 Hunter-Dunbar exploration of the Ouachita River valley. Other times found him sitting alone writing his copious notes on which he based his expedition journals and official letters describing his observations and explorations. Bradford was literate but probably not literary and had a small correspondence. He generally confined his writing to reports. Long became a noted explorer and evidently was happiest while on the move. He usually avoided staying in any one place for too long a time. Bradford, a tenacious sort, held his ground, worked through multiple problems at early Fort Smith, and delved into local and territorial politics. In the late fall of 1817, the two sat together on the banks of the Arkansas River, one small, dark eyed, and intense, the other tall, angular, with sharp nose, a fair complexion, and long side whiskers. Both were eager to be on their way. Perhaps in a candle-lit tent, the two compared notes on how to best accomplish the difficult task that lay ahead.

Three months earlier, Long had visited Fort Crawford on the Wisconsin River, spending a day measuring the buildings.[33] At Arkansas Post, placing his preliminary sketches on his lap desk, he may have gone over his fort-building ideas with Major Bradford. The army officers concurred on a two-stage advance up the river. Long intended to ascend the river one hundred miles beyond Belle Point to "the forks" in his skiff and return in time to meet the arrival of Bradford's company. Long had taken this very skiff to Saint Anthony falls at the headwaters of the Mississippi the previous year. William Clark, the former governor of Louisiana Territory and a famed explorer himself, had presented it to Stephen Long prior to the voyage up the

Mississippi. The skiff had the appearance and dimensions of a long boat, being outfitted with six oar locks and a mast holder, and could carry ten men with provisions for three weeks.[34] Peter Caulder, Martin Turner, and five other men from Carlisle and Natchitoches, Bradford's senior troops, were chosen to make up Long's advance detachment. In late October, the seven men and their officer pushed off from the wharf at the Post and paddled the skiff into eddies of the river, probably flying a fifteen-stripe American flag. To reach Belle Point where the Poteau River joins the Arkansas by mid-November, Long kept the men at the oars ten to twelve hours a day. On the upper Mississippi expedition the previous year, Long had his crew up and in the water each day by 4:30 A.M. and spent at least twelve hours on the river normally covering about twenty-six miles and once making thirty-two miles in a single day. His biographers noted that Long had "a compulsion for rapid travel."[35]

On his present mission, the determined explorer wanted with him tested men who could, without complaint, hustle up river, clear land, and lay out the fortification in anticipation of Bradford's arrival. Caulder and Martin Turner, former army pioneers, certainly knew how to swing an axe. While awaiting the main body of troops, the men could fell trees, stack firewood, and start to build huts. Bradford and Long chose Sgt. Balthazar Kramer and Cpl. Daniel Norman as the non-commissioned officers. Privates Thomas Cole, Perry Watkins, and Robert Sloan, veterans of the Carlisle training and of duty on the southwestern frontier, joined Long, Kramer, Norman, Caulder, and Turner in the advance party.[36]

Along the way, Peter Caulder occasionally fished the river and sloughs. Long agreed that adding catfish and drum to the diet would help keep the men healthy. Long had learned the natural vegetation of the Mississippi River valley and knew on sight the various hardwood trees of the area, such as sycamores, red, white, and water oaks, sugar maples, black cherries, and basswoods. Caulder growing up in Marion County, South Carolina, had the woodsman's knowledge and may have helped Long identify many of the wildflowers—red and white roses and morning glory. The men scrutinized the shrubbery along the river looking for healing plants like rue, parsley, and spikenard and for small trees with edible fruit like the plum, persimmon, and paw paw.[37] When Sergeant Kramer fell out with what was believed to be a rheumatism attack, Long probably treated it with a natural remedy that he had used earlier in the year to cure a sick man on the voyage up the Mississippi. He recorded that

> The mode of treatment I adopted towards them (men attacked with fever and ague) was to administer a cathartic of clomel and jalap soon after the shake or chill was off, and the next day, sometime before the return of the fever was expected, require the patient to take freely of wine and bark, which invariably had the desired effect.[38]

Kramer, however, did not respond and may have been incapacitated, curled up in the bottom of the boat for much of the run, a misfortune that acted to slow the progress of the advance party. Nevertheless, twenty days after departing Arkansas Post, Caulder helped pull the skiff onto a smooth rock shore at a location near the Osage boundary point where the Poteau River flowed into the Arkansas. Fur trappers had referred to this spot as Belle Point and used it as a rendezvous location. Marking it as a promising spot to build the fortification, Long and his men pushed on up the Arkansas to the conjuncture of the Verdigris River. Here, at "the forks" in a stop of twenty-four hours, Long uncased his sextant. The major noted the November constellations visible in the night sky. Perhaps while the major stargazed, Caulder and Martin Turner or other riflemen had a chance to practice their marksmanship in the surrounding oak woods. A squirrel and gravy breakfast might have tasted especially good to the soldiers if poached from this heartland of the mighty Osages. Done with the brief inspection and leaving their imprint on a strategic and sensitive point of land, the crew turned around and steered the skiff for the mouth of the Poteau that they had passed ten days previously. With six oars hitting the water in unison and with the current pushing, the skiff must have cut the water smartly on the one-hundred-thirty-mile trip back to Belle Point. One can almost imagine a young, enthusiastic Long perched in the bow, calling cadence so much like the coxswain, Caulder and his strong companions bending their backs in unison.[39]

In the next two weeks, Long explored the country around Belle

Point on foot, probably in the company of Peter Caulder. The topographical engineer liked what he saw and decided the site to be ideal for building a cantonment and establishing a permanent garrison. An uninhabited plain stretched for several miles to the north and east. The fort could be built well above the river out of danger by flooding, yet the landing was only a short distance down the slope. The gently undulating ground could be cultivated and a surrounding climax hardwood forest could be logged for palisades and huts. An abundance of black walnut and ash trees made it apparent that a good water table underlay the site. Limestone outcroppings guaranteed that water from the ground would be potable and accessible from consolidated aquifers. Hand-dug wells could supply a permanent camp with its most essential requirement, water. The availability of a reliable, sweet, and safe water supply proved to be a first consideration in locating western forts. With this asset, Fort Smith would be a key to the army's march toward the south plains. Fort Smith, now a city that attracts industries, long has advertised and prided itself on its good-tasting water supply.[40]

With Sergeant Kramer disabled and Caulder exploring with Long, Corporal Norman took charge and put Privates Martin Turner, Cole, Sloan, and Watkins at work blazing trees to mark the perimeter for the cantonment. The unfortunate Kramer had to be tended to by the other men. He had lost the use of his hands and legs and retrospective diagnosis suggested poliomyelitis.[41]

In the meantime, Bradford, and his fifty-seven-man company, most of whom were now fit for duty, and the four women boarded the keelboat and the two flatboats and pushed off into the Arkansas River pointing their bows into the current. In early November, low water levels in the river would seem to be less formidable to upstream navigation, yet the miles seemed to stretch on and on. Progress was slow. Major Bradford probably developed a daily routine much like that of Long, but with a considerably slower rate of speed. The riflemen arose at 4:30 A.M. The drummer beat out a breakfast call at 5:00 A.M. Joseph Clark may have acted as a cook on the trip upriver. After eating their hard biscuits and bacon, the men were on the river in position to pole or cordel the boats by daybreak. Poling the boats

Skiff at Belle Point. Major Long and the riflemen pulled their boat ashore in November 1817. On a bench just above the landing, Long laid out the fort.

ILLUSTRATION BY ERNEST CIALONE.

was an exhausting exercise and the men probably took two-hour shifts. From the front of the boat, a soldier thrust a long pole down into the bed of the river. A man walking to the back of the boat while pushing on the pole provided the power to go up current. Two or three men poling on each side of the boat kept a steady if slow rate of speed. Hidden shoals could result in an overturn as could collision with a submerged snag, throwing men into the water. Five years later, Colonel Arbuckle in bringing the Seventh Infantry to Fort Smith, lost one of his soldiers in this manner. The young soldier drowned in the quirky, muddy waters of the river, sucked under by the cross currents before his mates could find and rescue him. To the credit of Bradford and his keelboat pilots, his 1817 voyage up the Arkansas lost no one despite the occasional grounding in shallow water on a sandbar.

The riflemen ate and slept aboard the flatboats. Like all travelers of the era, they were beset with lice and fleas. The boats were partially covered to protect supplies and the men from cold rains of late autumn. Bradford stopped occasionally on the sandbars that frequented the middle of the low river. The men could catch and roast catfish over a fire for dinner on some days. Paths developed by generations of Indians and trappers ran along both banks of the river. Riflemen assigned as hunters to bring in fresh meat walked with their kill over such riverside paths to rejoin the company at prearranged stops. Bradford did not report any close calls with hostile Indians or bandits on the voyage to Belle Point, but no doubt hidden eyes watched in silence the migration of soldiers. Though having horses and mules was a possibility and mounted riflemen would have been valuable in guarding the flank and bringing in game, Bradford does not refer to mounts or pack animals and so probably did not have any with him on his voyage to Belle Point. He had available, though, a saddler and straps of leather. By the time that Thomas Nuttall arrived at Fort Smith in 1819, the command had acquired a number of horses, apparently from Indian traders. The Osages were great keepers of horses, and in one case a traveler counted two hundred horses in one small Osage village. For the trip up the Arkansas, Major Bradford, the lone officer, depended on two sergeants and three corporals to make duty rosters and see to it that assignments were carried out. The noncommissioned officers kept a firm hold on the troops, who apparently worked well together.

Zacheus Waldo, the drummer, and Joseph Cross, the fifer, played spirited tunes for morale and to signal divisions of the days' routines. The bouts with illnesses and the death of at least three riflemen on the Mississippi had in a way bonded the troops and created cama-raderie on this wilderness adventure. The riflemen left no record about their thoughts, but they must have been well aware of their mission and its perils.

No sample or description exists of the caliber of Bradford's speak-ing voice. He could read and write, though his spelling lacked. He was described as a small man, but wiry and strong. He was brave, assertive when he had to be, and never ostentatious.[42] Leading sixty men into unknown territories and toward an uncertain fate required a steady hand. Bradford's riflemen, half of whom had been with him for almost two years, backed him whether in the face of hostile forces or on hard work details, equally serious enemies of frontier soldiery.[43]

Osage Indians had a fierce reputation and looked for opportun-ities to attack the Cherokees and their Caddo and Delaware allies. Indians on the warpath, especially the Osages, might not be particu-lar about whom they scalped.[44] The riflemen were in harms' way and they knew it. Their six-pound cannons, though lashed in for the transit, must have conveyed the sense of confidence that superior firepower can do for a mobile army. Perhaps on the journey the wary troops talked little during the day, the sighs, groans, and expletives of typical hard-working soldiers carried well enough across the broad expanse of river water over which they were laboring. None of the black soldiers nor most of the white privates knew how to read or write. Oral tradition sufficed for entertainment. Where bands of sol-diers face hardships, jokesters and tellers of tales arise. On dark November and December nights, with sentries posted, the riflemen might have dozed in tents, spooning with one another against the cold, as a comrade spun stories or as one of the washerwomen sang her lullaby. But these scenes could have happened only in the dark of the moon. When full, Bradford would have had the men laying in a supply of wood, kindling a fire in the boat's cabouse, and poling their heavily laden boats through the night into the next day.[45] Not as obsessed with speedy travel as Long, Bradford nevertheless wanted to arrive at his new station as soon as he could.

People along the banks of the river at the few settlements marveled at the sight of a military expedition, stars and stripes fluttering to the cadence of a drumbeat, and even hailed the soldiers as they passed. There must have been excitement and hoorays from the banks at Cadron and at the Big Mulberry to see this many men in the uniform of the United States Army coming so far up the river. Settlers would have fired shots into the air, and Bradford would have had a squad of his men to fire their muskets to salute the whites in return. One can imagine the sound of the gunfire and the uproar of startled birds shattering the stillness of an afternoon on the river. Even the dullest observer could recognize that the distinct crackling of the army muskets meant that a new day was dawning for Arkansas.

Thus with teamwork and with encouraging nods and shouts from whites and Indians, the band of elite riflemen came up the Arkansas. These experiences infused Bradford's company with an *esprit de corps*. The signs were that the company had created good morale for itself, and that was the overriding atmosphere in the early days of the fort on the Arkansas.

At Belle Point, Caulder and Martin Turner helped the major finish the survey. Eager to move on to his next exploring objective, Long fretted about Bradford, who was overdue. He had estimated that the keelboat, though laden with twenty tons of cargo, could progress fifteen miles a day and therefore cover the distance in forty-two days. His party had averaged considerably more distance than that even with time lost tending to Sergeant Kramer. After laying out the ground plan for the fort, Long found a seller of horses, either the whites on the Big Mulberry, the nearest settlement, or passing Indians. Long intended for himself, Caulder, and two enlisted men to leave Belle Point by horse and travel overland to the Red River for further observations of the country as ordered by Jackson. The other men were to continue their work at clearing and surveying until Bradford arrived. Cpl. Daniel Norman was left in charge of this detail and was entrusted with the building sketches of the fortification that Long had drawn up.[46]

CHAPTER FOUR

Army Guide

LEAVING BELLE POINT, STEPHEN LONG, PETER CAULDER AS HIS GUIDE, and two soldiers, Robert Sloan and Perry Watkins, set out to the southwest on a route along the Poteau. Branching off from the sluggish river south by southwest of Fort Smith, the party followed a buffalo trail through the Ouachita Mountains. After three or four days of up and down travel through the rugged terrain, they struck level land once again and the Kiamichi River. This they followed to the Red River, passing over the site of the future Fort Towson. Taking the downstream path on the north bank of the Red River, they intersected a well-worn trace that led northeast. Long and Caulder forded a number of southeast-flowing streams, icy waters that no doubt refreshed the plunging horses and their riders. After days of such travel through quartz-strewn benches and hill valleys, they reached what is today's city of Hot Springs on the last day of 1817. Long had with him a copy of William Dunbar's alluring description of the springs from his exploration of the Ouachita River region. Despite the chill in the air, the warm water basins carved into limestone outcroppings no doubt beckoned to Long and Caulder, affording the hardy explorers a moment of ultimate relaxation. Perhaps the major and the private found their bath at the steamy springs as therapeutic and marvelous as had Dunbar and George Hunter in December of 1805.[1] Though their enjoyment went unrecorded, the magical waters must have well relieved the dirt encrusted and parasitic hair of these wintertime travelers.

After sampling the unusual "thermal springs there," Long, Caulder, Sloan, and Watkins continued on to the Arkansas River, fording it at about where Little Rock is now located. Leaving Sloan and Watkins at the river to await Privates Martin Turner and Thomas Cole, who were bringing the skiff downstream from Belle Point, Long accompanied by Caulder took the horses and set out

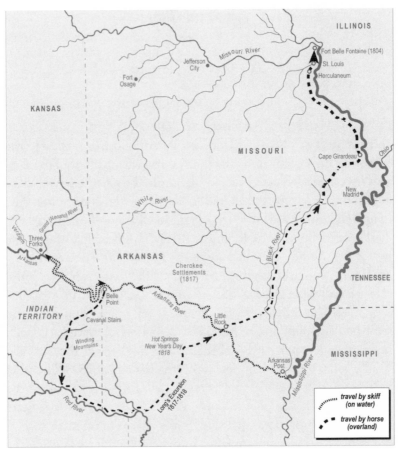

Stephen H. Long's excursion from Belle Point to Hot Springs via the Red River. Peter Caulder accompanied Major Long by skiff to Belle Point and then to Three Forks. After returning to Belle Point and leaving a vanguard there to await Bradford's arrival, Long, accompanied by Peter Caulder, proceeded by horse to the Red River. Long and Caulder returned to Gen. Thomas A. Smith's headquarters near St. Louis via Hot Springs of Arkansas.

MAP BY TOM PARADISE.

overland "on the west of the Mississippi to St. Louis."[2] In a few days Turner and Cole regrouped with Sloan and Watkins at the "Little Rock" landmark and continued their journey down the Arkansas to the Mississippi. Once there, the riflemen turned the skiff into the December-cold waters of the Father of Waters and bent the oars for an upstream pull back to St. Louis.[3]

Long and Caulder followed the trail that led to St. Louis through northeastern Arkansas and southeast Missouri. Caulder may have noted the landscapes of the area west of Cape Girardeau in what would one day become Bollinger County, Missouri. Arriving safely but weary after a trip of some two thousand miles, Peter Caulder recuperated from his exertions on the expedition. His fellow soldiers had succeeded in paddling the skiff up the Mississippi and, along with Caulder, stayed a month at Belle Fontaine to recoup before setting out in midwinter to return to Belle Point.[4] When the weather looked promising, or at least not threatening for river travel, Caulder, Martin Turner, Thomas Cole, Robert Sloan, and Perry Watkins loaded themselves in the skiff for the trip back to Camp Smith. After two voyages of discovery, the six-oared skiff had ended its usefulness to Long, and he bid it farewell in its new guise as an "express" boat carrying dispatches between St. Louis and Camp Smith. January brought ice, snow, sleet, and freezing rain to Missouri, and these raw winter elements hindered the five privates in their return. Not until the end of February did the men pull the boat on to the flat landing rock at Belle Point and report to Major Bradford. Caulder, Perry Watkins, and Martin Turner were in good health. The winter trip, however, had exhausted Sloan, who wound up abed for a month, ill perhaps with flu or pneumonia. Although Sloan recovered, a month later Thomas Cole succumbed to an illness. So serious was Cole's condition that he remained bedfast in his quarters for the next nine months, and after that, because of or despite his prolonged acquaintance with therapies and treatments, became the hospital orderly.

On Thursday, December 25, 1817, a cold Christmas Day while Long and Caulder approached the hot springs, Bradford stepped ashore at Belle Point and was greeted by Corporal Norman, who had campfires crackling on the plain above the river. The late December sun cast its slanting rays onto the gathering as the men heaved boats onto a rock ledge and secured them. Biting winds and freeze-hardened ground may have confronted the new arrivals, but they were cheered by the small comforts of fire and huts afforded them by the advance detachment. Presently, Major Bradford set up building and clearing routines for the company. One of the corporals, perhaps Andrew

Calhoun, directed the unloading of the keelboat, an assignment that included placing the six-pound cannons on their firing platforms. Marksmen took to the woods to hunt meat. Buffalo, elk, bear, and deer came under their sights, and the fruits of their hunt at chow time, sautéed tongue or back strap for example, did much to sustain morale and keep the troops dedicated to completing the work at hand. In the first week, satisfactory progress had been made in setting up a facility soon christened Camp Smith. Washington's Continental Army had learned the fine art of hut building during the Revolution. The riflemen at Belle Point continued the tradition. Day by day, the men worked steadily, arising at 5 A.M. to further secure their stronghold and make the improvements that would mark Fort Smith as a permanent establishment, a settlement in the wilderness that arose from the hammers and axes in their hands. A sense of community transcended grievances among the men and allowed Bradford, as the lone officer, to concentrate on progress in building. He knew that he commanded good men, and they felt well led by the little major. Recognizing Daniel Norman's effort in the advance guard, Bradford promoted the reliable corporal to sergeant. The little major, his own hut under construction, sat in the cabin of the keelboat on New Year's Day to write a long letter to Gen. Andrew Jackson, bringing his commander and acquaintance up to date on the building of America's newest frontier fort.[5] In this epistle, Bradford does not refer to his enlisted men by name, nor in any fashion mentions his mulatto soldiers.

Obviously in this, their great endeavor on the frontier, both Bradford and Long trusted the Marion men to perform up to and perhaps exceed standards they set for all the soldiers. In all respects except for promotion, Long and Bradford treated Peter Caulder as a reliable, trusted, and likable soldier. Caulder evidently had the right stuff that made him a welcomed companion on long, uncharted missions. If either of the officers thought anything detrimental about the race or color of Caulder, the Turners, or Clark, they did not mention it in written reports or journals that survived. From the vantage of today, it seems incredible that not even the slightest mention was made in official records or letters that black soldiers served alongside whites in Arkansas. But that incredulity is based on what we know happened in the next decades of American history. We know, but Bradford and Long could not, how important the establishment of a man's race became to almost all Americans. In the period from 1817 to 1824, Bradford, Long, Arbuckle, and other officers at frontier posts insulated by distance from recruiting centers had a desperate need for capable, loyal enlisted men. Regiments and companies on the frontier normally mustered an ethnic assortment of soldiers from heaven only knew where (many had to be taken at their word as to their country or place of origin). Some foreign-born recruits were in the United States for only a short period before joining the army. Desertions, illnesses, fights, loafing, and theft by the enlisted men plagued good military order. The last thing a commanding officer would want to do, therefore, was to discredit, and discard, a soldier like Peter Caulder through an uncalled for racial categorization. In making out annual description rolls, officers reported color of hair, eyes, and complexion. No column for race appeared on the preprinted army return forms. Perhaps, too, officers in command at Fort Smith felt the tolerance and respect evinced by a fellow officer, Capt. John R. Bell. Bell wrote in his journal praise for a black farmer whom he encountered on a trip down the Ohio:

> Robert Wilson, a coloured man, who has resided here eleven years, opened his farm and erected buildings which are of brick, and cost him five thousand dollars, his dwelling house, which is new, and out house, are planned & finished in a degree of taste and style not often to be met with among farmers. This mulatto fellow is an example of industry and economy rarely to be met with and is worthy the imitation of thousands of whites emigrating to this country.[6]

The duties of Peter Caulder, Martin Turner, James Turner, and Joseph Clark certainly included "pioneer" work for Bradford's company. But on the frontier, all of the troops performed pioneering duties of road construction, camp clearing, fort building, gardening, and livestock tending. The Marion men's duties assignments, except for Caulder's detached services, were fully consistent with those of the white troops. The integration of Caulder and the other mulattoes into the routine went unrecorded; therefore, we might think of these "colored men" as being ordinary soldiers. Does this full integration into a front-line military unit then cause Caulder to think that he is "passing" as white? As tempting as that assumption might be, it seems not to be the case. Actions of Caulder and his peers from Marion speak to the issue. Officers picked Caulder many times for detached duties of significance. By 1827, Caulder was senior to all enlisted men at Fort Gibson. The fact that he did not rise in rank indicated that something held back his army career. Maybe his illiteracy worked that much against him. But more likely, it was because he had been designated in early army records as a "colored" man, and his assignments further separated him as they often took him away from the barracks for extended periods. At Fort Smith in the 1820s, Caulder, the Turner brothers, and Joseph Clark frequented the sutler's store. They bought whiskey, knives, lead for shot, and extra gunpowder on credit as did the other men. The storekeeper's confidence in them proved justified as they settled up their accounts as soon as they got paid. But the sutler's account book demonstrated the closeness between the old friends from Marion, South Carolina: they made credit purchases in one another's names and paid off debts for one another. White enlisted men had no record of this kind of reliance upon one another in settling their store accounts.

Even though the close friendships among the men from Marion endured, only Peter Caulder decided to make the army his career or, apparently, Arkansas his permanent home. Caulder reenlisted for the second tour after coming to Fort Smith. Joseph Clark reenlisted for one other hitch, but only after a few months of civilian life between enlistments. Martin Turner, James Turner, and Caleb Cook rejected the army's offers after their first five-year terms were up. They favored civilian pursuits, indicating that they had found little to fear because of their color in frontier Arkansas so did not mind leaving whatever sanctity the army might have afforded them.

The Osage-Cherokee friction that had drawn Bradford's company up the river to Belle Point continued to heat up. The riflemen arrived shortly after a murderous attack by Cherokees and their allies on the village of Osage chief Clermont. The presence of the U.S. Rifles in

Arkansas reflected the federal government's desire to impose firm control over its westernmost territories and if not to suppress war between the Osages and the Cherokees, at least to keep the fallout from jeopardizing the entire territory. In fact, Bradford did not seem to consider his mission one of "peace-keeping" between the tribes at all. His battles during the War of 1812 at Fort Meigs and at Horseshoe Bend had cast him no less an "Indian fighter" than his friend and commanding general, Andrew Jackson. Bradford superseded orders from Washington to remove all whites from Indian lands on at least two occasions, finding reason to delay those removals. One of his fellow officers was not so lenient to white settlers, resorting to burning buildings and crops to force out the interlopers.[7] Bradford evidently could not bring himself to such radical actions against whites. While Governor Miller diligently worked to negotiate a permanent peace between the Cherokees and the Osages upon his arrival in the territory, Bradford preferred to let Indians settle their differences even when that meant bloody reprisals and continued violence between the tribes. In the end, the building of Fort Smith and garrisoning it with riflemen encouraged white settlement of Arkansas, an expansion that had been heretofore restrained by the wildness of the district. The steady increase of population brought development, more wealth, and definite political maneuvering to the Arkansas River valley. Bradford knew that increased activity of his men stymied boredom and prevented time for feuds among the men. He may have accepted as his primary mission and rallied his men to their efforts not as passive peacekeepers on temporary frontier duty, but the chosen, active, and capable builders of a new settlement on the edge of civilization. Bradford continually interacted well with his white neighbors, both depending on them and supporting them when necessary. Peter Caulder and the riflemen at Belle Point no doubt took their cue from Bradford's outlook. Bradford and Caulder were to stay in Arkansas until the end of their lives, both finishing their sojourns as civilians. As a corollary to development and white population gains, white spokesmen lobbied Congress to abrogate Native American claims in Arkansas. The founding of Fort Smith under Bradford's command, far from smoothing troubled waters for Indian inhabitants of the vast land west of the Mississippi, actually fueled the tempest besetting Osages, Cherokees, and whites in Arkansas. The Cherokees felt emboldened by the army's presence, as though the United States government had not only sanctioned their move west of the Mississippi, but were now willing to protect their settlements. The Osages had held a trade monopoly during the French and Spanish colonial period in Arkansas. Like the Iroquois and the Chickasaws, the Osages were a particular tribe of Indians who had prospered with European intervention. The Osages realized what had created their largess. Their chiefs defended their status and monopoly with a studied ferocity that in turn built onto their reputation as being so bad as to be avoided. Now, the Osages, who for a century had let no encroachment go unchallenged, felt they were being forced out by eastern Indians. They resisted with all their wile and might. The Osages again would show the ferocity that had cowed the French and other tribes and had left them masters in their land for so long.

――――――――

Peter Caulder's generation of Americans completed the hold of their young country on lands north of the Ohio River and south of the Great Lakes. Pulled as though by gravity toward the Mississippi River, frontiersmen and militiamen extinguished, tier by tier, through wars and subsequent treaties of cession, all Indian claims to the rich soils of what would become the Corn Belt, even today America's most-productive farmland. Whites followed streambeds and game trails north of the Ohio toward these ceded lands. Muscle, youthful energy, and a shared development ethic pushed settlers to drastically alter countrysides and engineer landscapes a far cry from those known only a few years before by the previous inhabitants. A trickle of free black people such as Caulder's future father-in-law, David Hall, joined this human flow to the west. Given the social attitudes that existed in the United States in the decade after the War of 1812, Peter Caulder or David Hall could imagine themselves yeoman farmers, cultivating a corn crop, husbanding livestock, hunting in the surrounding woods, and raising a family. That dream must have seemed to these men of color idyllic and, if not easy, at least possible.[8] As a member of a rifle company hacking out a cantonment four hundred miles up the Arkansas River early in 1818, Peter Caulder directly participated in American expansion. He may never have heard the phrase "Manifest Destiny," but he and his comrades worked in the vanguard of the American spread across the continent. He may have been less certain about the racial conflicts being brewed up by the westward movement, although he would feel those effects even at Belle Point from which he could literally view vistas of open prairies in Indian territory. As congressmen discussed statehood conditions for Missouri and questioned the permanency of slavery there and in Arkansas Territory, Thomas Jefferson, from his plantation home in Virginia, referred to such debates over the future of slavery as ringing a "firebell in the night."[9] In the ranks of frontier rifle companies, where few had owned real estate before their enlistment, the men probably did not bother to imagine themselves as slave owners or slaves. Arguing over abstract political issues, it would seem, took up little of their energy. Perhaps, though, Peter Caulder, Martin Turner, or Daniel Norman had heard of or discussed something called the American Colonization Society. Yet that organization would instigate a preposterous "solution" to the problem of race mixing in the United States, a mixing that already had occurred in the life of Peter Caulder and would, of course, have seemed normal to him.

One of the fifty-four sovereign, recognized countries on the African continent has a capital named after an American president. That president, James Monroe, along with Henry Clay, Andrew Jackson, Francis Scott Key, and Daniel Webster met on December 21, 1816, with other whites to organize a plan for black migration out of the United States. In the Davis Hotel, a trendy Washington gathering spot, the American Colonization Society (ACS) was born at the hands of that era's "best and brightest." Henry Clay said that he was motivated to participate in a resettlement effort because free blacks in the United States faced "unconquerable prejudice resulting from their color, [and] they never could amalgamate with the free whites of this country."[10]

In 1816, when Clay uttered this rhetoric, men of color were already amalgamated with whites in Bradford's company of the Rifle Regiment posted at Fort Claiborne, Louisiana. In addition, a considerable number of free black pioneers were busily amalgamating themselves with fellow white homesteaders in frontier settings. Early in the nineteenth century, mulattoes, free blacks, and a mixed-blooded people known as "melungeons" migrated west into Kentucky and Tennessee to set up pioneer homesteads. Caulder's future father-in-law, David Hall, born in North Carolina in 1782, moved to Tennessee as a single man. In Tennessee, Hall married Sarah and began his family. Black men could vote in Tennessee elections before 1832, yet Hall's desire for more independence provided him with ample reason to move further west and pioneer in the White River hills.[11]

Just as the ACS offered a radical and impracticable solution for anticipated problems created by emancipated blacks, supply and demand and free enterprise in the American system were offering, by the "invisible hand," other dynamics that worked much better. In the decades before the Civil War, black people operated businesses, plied trades necessary to village life, held savings accounts in banks, and owned land and farms. Most of these routine economic and social activities went on without opposition from whites and certainly without fanfare. It is a mystery why more white politicians could not see the de facto and mutually beneficial "amalgamation" of whites and blacks going on in the South under their very noses.[12]

Of all post–War of 1812 telltales that revealed the white elite's deep prejudices toward free black people, the organization of the American Colonization Society seems clearest in retrospect. The good feelings between the races generated by fighting wars of national survival against a common enemy sank below sight with the meeting at the Davis Hotel. Yet slavery remained under attack, even in slave states. Herekiah Niles, editor of the influential *Niles' Weekly Register*, a Baltimore newspaper that concentrated on its self-proclaimed destiny as a historical source for future researchers, encouraged the emancipation of blacks. Niles called for dispersion of freed blacks around the country as the practical solution to amalgamation. Niles wrote that in "a few generations, a black person would be a rarity . . . the sable color (would) retire by degrees."[13] A group of delegates at a meeting of the Manumition (*sic*) Society of Tennessee in November 1816 addressed the nation in a reprinted appeal for "the gradual abolition of the slavery of the people of color" and charged that the government should "do away with this evil."[14] More voices called for its end. Clay's 1820 compromise bridged these rising waters of slavery condemnation by drawing up for Congress a method for admitting new states with regard to their slave or free status. States, one free and one slave admitted together as pairs, would preserve the sectional numbers in the Senate—Clay and his wonderful symmetry. Clay's compromise directly involved Arkansas Territory. With slavery in Arkansas a foregone conclusion, in increasing numbers, neophyte planters ferried their coffles across the Mississippi to promising lands in Arkansas Territory. Never would the "boy planters" of Arkansas have to fear legislated emancipation.[15] Free black pioneers in Arkansas like Hall and Caulder were ultimately doomed. Both the American Colonization Society and the 1820 compromise, each designed by Henry Clay, arguably the most influential politician of his era and a three-time losing candidate for the presidency, represented a major failure of democracy to protect the interest of all of the people in the United States. Ironically, John C. Calhoun used the argument that American democracy in its present form could not protect minority rights in his 1847 treatise, *South Carolina Exposition and Protest*. In Calhoun's view, the minority left unprotected was the Southern slaveowners.[16] Peter Caulder, with unsettling issues of race and slavery swirling in the background, nevertheless may well have felt that the first two years at Fort Smith offered ample adventures and satisfactions for his personal life. Back at Belle Point with Major Bradford after his four-month detached duty at the side of Stephen Long, Caulder found himself busy with army duties.

The sun arose on early spring mornings in 1818 at Belle Point whether Peter Caulder could see it or not through heavy cloud cover. By this time in his army career, the twenty-three-year-old Caulder had slept outside on the ground as much as he had in a bed with a roof over his head. When the sun did break through, some hardier riflemen might have bathed in the Arkansas, but most probably went unwashed for long periods. Other facets of the primitive life on the frontier could be equally daunting. Food was probably available on a limited basis, three meals a day being a civilized habit rather than common in primitive surroundings as Fort Smith offered. The heavy work must have seemed endless. Constructing a fort meant that the soldiers saw to chopping down large trees, trimming branches, hand sawing and splitting out boards, quarrying rock, digging a foundation, and hauling the building materials to the site. All troops were pioneers now. To compound difficulties, the paymaster had not visited in over a year. In spite of these hardships, morale seemed intact. Bradford kept his men busy and despondency did not sweep through the ranks, at least not for having idle hands.

Preparing a garden in time for spring planting absorbed the energies of the band of soldiers in 1818 and on a larger scale in 1819. Far-flung cantonments faced limited transportation and spotty supply lines. Deciding that the army had to produce its own food supply, the War Department directed frontier forts to cultivate crops for their use. Troops were to be like the yeoman whom they protected, self-sufficient sons of soil and toil. The majority of riflemen in Bradford's company, Caulder and the men from Marion included, had listed farming as their preenlistment occupation. By 1820, the Fort Smith garrison boasted a large truck patch that grew an array of grains and vegetables. Troops, traders, and women of the post depended on this food production. It seems doubtful that Peter Caulder was placed on garden duty since he was often away guiding and hunting instead. Martin Turner may have seen to the care of a growing herd of horses. Livestock, horses, milch (milk) cows, and pigs acquired by the rifle company were fed on corn grown by the soldiers. So good did soldiers become at agriculture that the dean of inspector generals who made visits annually to selected frontier posts protested the practice as being a constant distraction to good soldiering.[17]

Peter Caulder and the riflemen interacted constantly with their wild surroundings, as explorers, hunters, trappers, boatmen, and trail builders. Along Arkansas streams, a plethora of native fauna and flora species could be observed. The naturalist Edwin James in 1820 ranked mammals of the Arkansas River watershed into a hierarchy of importance: bison, bear, deer, elk, wolves, and beavers in that order.[18] Some of these mammalian neighbors of Belle Point, including the prowling cougar, could endanger unsuspecting humans at any given moment. Though venomous snakes rarely posed a lethal problem for inhabitants, almost any encounters with these fascinating creatures excited men to tell tales. Around a campfire, Major Long may have regaled his soldiers with a first-hand account about a trio of Indians on the upper Mississippi the year before, one of whom had just been struck by a rattler. Long watched while the Indians "cut out a piece of the flesh containing the wounded part" and applied a compress above the bite. Long attempted to help by washing the gashes with salt and water, but the Indians refused him, "being prejudiced against admitting water to a wound in any case." Since Long had no "sweet oil" he could only watch as the pair carted off their pain-racked companion to their hunting encampment for what was hoped to be a recovery. Once during the dog days of July, a friend of Major Long, Captain Duffhey, was bitten by a rattlesnake. Long described the episode:

> He received the wound in the instep where the tooth of the snake penetrated to the bone. He applied a bandage upon his leg in the first instance, and resorted to medical aid as soon as it was practicable. When he was bitten he was in the woods four miles from home, consequently the poison must have had a considerable time to diffuse itself, before he could apply a remedy. His foot and leg swelled very much and became black, but the remedies applied proved efficacious, and he is now past danger, and is so far recovered that he is able to walk about with ease.[19]

White headed eagles, passenger pigeons, ivory-billed woodpeckers, and even stray pelicans brought feathered beauty, and in the case of the pigeons, a tasty target for a Caulder's rifle. The bison that ranged along the Arkansas River were not as numerous as their cousins on the plains, nor as tasty. The normal buffalo kill made by Belle Point soldiers, lone thin bulls that habituated thick canebrakes along the river, yielded tough, stringy meat, reason enough for riflemen, as did Indians, to use mainly the tender hump and tongue of the animal. Turkeys, raccoons, rabbits, squirrels, bears, and white-tailed deer provided food for the table not only for soldiers, but also for Indian inhabitants and white settlers. Probably 1818–21 represented the high point in protein supplied by game animals for the soldiers. The lack of supplies coming upriver in the first years forced a dependence on game as well as garden produce for the sixty-man company at Belle Point. After a few years of intense hunting, populations of large game mammals in the vicinity of the fort plunged. As at posts on the northwest frontier, hunters and woodcutters had to increase their range, foraging several miles away, after the first years because of the army's heavy consumption of local natural resources.[20]

For Bradford to accomplish the primary mission of making the fort a formidable position representing United States power, a staggering number of other goals had to be set and completed. First the men had to be suitably housed for the remainder of the winter. The fort had to be supplied with a clean, handy, and reliable source of drinking and cooking water, meaning that a well soon had to be dug. To erect the fort's walls, squads of men used pick and shovel to level the site and dig the trench for the foundation stones. Quarrying rock and cutting and hewing timbers were major labor undertakings. Caulder, a man of thick chest and broad shoulders who had been issued a pick, probably dug out and shaped limestone blocks. Bradford had to buy horses and mules from Osages, Cherokees, and local white settlers for the work of sledding rock, timber, sand, and gravel. Martin Turner, an experienced teamster, could have been detailed to buy and train draft and saddle stock. Having these animals meant in turn building corrals and stalls, more carpentry chores. The soldiers set up a blacksmith shop to make shoes and metal parts. The washerwomen may have helped manufacture leather harnesses, hames, and reins for the teams. Major Bradford set into operation a postal express boat that shuttled dispatches and correspondence between Belle Point and Arkansas Post. Caleb Cook, Caulder's brother-in-law and former seaman, rejoined the company for a year in 1818 at Belle Point, apparently assigned to the express boat that carried dispatch pouches to and from headquarters at Belle Fontaine.[21] Soldiers acting as hunters, skinners, butchers, processors, and cooks carried out their daily routines for the mess. The army provided recipes and details for cooking in the *General Regulations for the Army*. Rotating squads of privates each took a tour in baking bread and making soup.

The army way with meat was to boil it; "sometimes roasted or baked, but never fried."[22]

Ordnance, especially the two six-pound cannons, had to be inspected and periodically fired. Exploring and mapping of the region had to be carried out. Nor did Bradford neglect military regimen at early Fort Smith. He filled out the returns to keep regimental officers happy with his paperwork, and had the drill manual imposed by his sergeants on the troops, who no doubt were scheduled for firing on the range as well. Fifer Joseph Cross sounded reveille at daybreak Monday through Saturday. Able-bodied riflemen fell out on the parade ground for a routine roll call to start the day. Corporals would cry out, "All present or accounted for, sir!" to Bradford or his subaltern. The 1818 flag of twenty stars in the blue field and fifteen red and white stripes waved atop the tall flag pole made from peeled logs spliced together to obtain a forty-foot height. Kitchen duty, woodcutting, kindling, splitting, skinning animals and tanning of hides, breaking and shoeing horses, milking cows or goats, plowing new ground for the coming garden, patching uniforms, digging latrines, and building boats to ferry the river filled the days of the men and women at Fort Smith. The riflemen dined together at evening mess as an integrated company. Upon completing duties for the day, Caulder, the Turners, Clark, and Cook, having worked the equal of the other men, stood in line among them for their daily whiskey ration. At dusk, each man could relax at least briefly. In front of their white canvas tents neatly pitched on the point above the river before retiring to slumber under an Arkansas moon, young soldiers spoke in low voices to one another. They talked about duty lists, quality of food, the women, Indians, and deer hunting before drifting away to thoughts of their boyhood homes that lay hundreds of miles to the east.

Peter Caulder may have acquired building skills as a youth in South Carolina. A farmer was, by the very nature of being self-sufficient, knowledgeable and a man who could work with his hands. It seems plausible, though, that Caulder learned the trade of chimney building, which would have presumed stonework and carpentry experiences for him. Caulder would have had abundant opportunities to design and build chimneys for the fort and for the huts of the men. Although wooden chimneys were used because of easier and faster construction, they were prone to fires and rot. Stone chimneys were preferred. Caulder knew how to handle pick, mattock, and rock hammer. Expertly fitted stones held chimneys together where mortar was of low quality and sometimes not available at all. In August 1820, William R. Loving, a twenty-three-year-old married soldier paid Hugh Glenn, sutler for the cantonment, $4.00 for "building a chimbley" and another $1.75 for "laying a hearth [in front of] and covering [the] chimbley." Glenn may have acted as the contractor and employed Caulder, who had a line of credit at Glenn's store beyond that of other privates, to do the work of building the chimney. Bradford allowed Private Loving and his wife, Susan, to build a cabin across the river from Belle Point.[23] Mrs. Loving took in washing to earn additional money for the couple. Probably in the cabin that Caulder had helped build—just in time it seems—Fort Smith's first child was born. Capt. John R. Bell recorded that on Sunday, September 17, 1820, a "soldier's wife of the garrison was delivered of a fine boy weighing 12 pounds." It seems likely that the child belonged to William and Susan Loving.[24]

After the Loving cabin was finished, Caulder asked for and got a furlough from company commander Capt. James H. Ballard to accompany Glenn to Three Forks up the Arkansas River for more supplementary work for pay. Glenn wanted Caulder and another worker to help him build an addition, most likely a chimney, to his new trading post on the Verdigris.[25]

Chimneys that drafted well could burn less than prime firewood, a considerable convenience of the era when people depended solely on wood heat. Weather reports from 1815 to 1820 indicated a wide variance in yearly temperatures. Nuttall's temperature record for 1819 in Arkansas Territory shows very warm spring and summer seasons. Wheat harvests in the United States reached record-setting levels in 1817. Yet some winters were colder than normal. *Niles' Weekly Register* referred to ice floes large enough to halt shipping on the Mississippi below Cape Girardeau and heavy July snows in New

England.[26] Riflemen on woodcutting details about Fort Smith, just trying to stay warm or cook their food, represented an activity multiplied over and over in the nineteenth century. The soldiers at Belle Point played their part in what has been analyzed as a major impact on the environment.[27]

A major influence on the environment had an insidious entry in 1807, as Robert Fulton, a New York City school chum of Benjamin L. E. Bonneville, launched a steamboat, the *North River*. Mark Twain commented on the one hundredth anniversary of Fulton's launching of the *North River* that, "the rivers were at last made useful." Steamboats overcame the obstacles to Manifest Destiny presented by backward- (eastward-) flowing rivers like the Arkansas and the Missouri. Remarkably, this huge stride for transportation coincided with Bradford's establishment of Fort Smith on the Arkansas River. As Peter Caulder departed Belle Fontaine in 1818 by skiff with oars to return to cantonment Smith and his frontier duties, Stephen H. Long started a journey in another direction, to Washington, D.C. While in the east with the encouragement of Secretary of War Calhoun, Long designed and had built at Pittsburgh a steam-engine-powered boat for an expedition up the Missouri River. The boat, named the *Western Engineer,* was first steam vessel to be financed out of the army budget. Aboard the *Western Engineer,* Long returned to Belle Fontaine in 1819 to set out on the first leg of the expedition that would not be completed until the fall of 1820 and which would, at its end, involve both Peter Caulder and Fort Smith.

Native Americans had perfected the birch-bark *canoe*, an ingenious invention recognized as a superior means for traversing country north of the Ohio, a land sliced by streamlets. But canoes were labor intensive in construction, and therefore expensive. French traders who could not afford canoes settled for the one-piece boat, carved, hacked, or burned out of a large tree. The resulting craft, termed a *pirogue*, could be used by one or two trappers on a given river, but was not easily portaged between waterways because of its weight. The pirogue stood up to bumps and smashes in rapids and could be large enough to carry several ninety-pound bales of furs. It served its purpose and made its way across the Mississippi into Arkansas during the years of Spanish administration, the word *pirogue* itself being of Spanish derivation. William Woodruff, his second-hand printing press, and a wooden box of type arrived at Arkansas Post on October 30, 1819, in two pirogues lashed together.[28]

Peter Caulder's life would be touched by other newcomers to Arkansas who arrived in 1819 by boat, including David Hall, a free black man, and his wife, Sarah, parents of the woman whom Caulder would marry two decades later. But perhaps as significant as the Halls would be to Caulder, the editor of the soon to appear *Arkansas Gazette* might have had an equally profound, if tragic effect on his life. Woodruff, though a New Yorker, was a staunch foe of free black people in Arkansas and through his newspaper helped influence public opinion among Arkansas whites against those particular residents. Two other men, prominent in the history of the territory, came to Arkansas Post in 1819 by boat from the east and would travel up the Arkansas to visit Fort Smith, Thomas Nuttall, the English naturalist, and New Englander James E. Miller, the first territorial governor of Arkansas. Peter Caulder no doubt saw and perhaps spoke to both Nuttall and Miller, and they he, as their paths crossed on the frontier.[29]

Nuttall wrote sparingly about the post surgeon, Thomas Russell, M.D., and about Major Bradford. But, separated by customs of the day from the enlisted men, Nuttall did not mention Caulder or any other soldiers by name in his journal. Although while at Arkansas Post, he had referred to a "negro" whom he had hired as a poler on his flatboat, Nuttall says nothing about blacks being among the riflemen at Belle Point. Perhaps he was unaware of or unconcerned about the ethnicity of soldiers, but Nuttall may have had considerable contact with Peter Caulder and probably saw Martin and James Turner, too. Nuttall did describe much of what he saw at the fort, if not who. He wrote that "two block houses, and lines of cabins or barracks for the accommodation of 70 men whom it contains . . . (was) agreeably situated . . . on ground rising 50 feet above the 'washing of the current.'"[30] Bradford liked the young British visitor, with his enthusiasm for nature, and provided mounts for Nuttall and Russell, who on several occasions together explored the prairies around the fort for the purpose of cataloging plants and animals. On one excursion, the naturalist, the doctor, and an unnamed soldier who accompanied them pitched a tent and slept on blankets alongside a stream in the middle of the prairie serenaded by "music of the frogs" and the "vociferations of two species of whip-poor-wills." The "cheerless howling of a distant wolf" and swarms of mosquitoes only slightly disturbed Nuttall's tranquillity at the overnight camp just a few miles from the fort. At Belle Point fifty feet above the churning waters of the river, Caulder and his comrades at Fort Smith often had the same nighttime sensations. The outdoor life had its rewards as well as its pests.

Late April rains swelled the Arkansas and Poteau Rivers submerging sandbars and presenting Nuttall a view of wildness as the Arkansas's booming, milky-colored waters flowed past Belle Point. When the waters receded on May 16, 1819, Major Bradford departed the fort on a mission to remove white settlers from territory set apart for Cherokees. Bradford did not look forward to this duty and probably was in a sour mood. Nevertheless, Bradford invited Nuttall to ride along with the mounted detachment that included six riflemen. James and Lewis Rogers, sons of Cherokee chief John Rogers, came too in order to verify the army's fulfillment of their obligation to remove white settlers from Cherokee claims. Their route would take this motley group up the Poteau River via "Cavanoil" (sic) Mountain and from there across the Winding Stairs uplands to the "Kiamesha" (sic) River and finally to the valley of the Red River. One soldier, most likely Peter Caulder, acted as a guide since he had traveled a similar route from Belle Point to the Red River in the winter of 1817 with Stephen Long. In his journal, Nuttall did not name the guide, nor did he make any reference to or give any description of the soldiers along on this excursion that lasted one month. That, of course, meant a lot of time "roughing it."[31]

Ironically, at the very time that this duty was being carried out by Bradford, Stephen Long departed Pittsburgh for Belle Fontaine aboard the steamboat *Western Engineer*. Long's hand-picked party was on the first leg of a well-publicized exploring expedition to the Rocky Mountains. John C. Calhoun had approved funds for Long's exploration in order to gain information about the West and tangentially to impress plains Indian tribes about U.S. might and intentions. What occurred instead was somewhat of a boondoggle. The *Western Engineer* spent most of the time under repair, information gathered about western geography left more questions than gave answers, and Indians encountered were not impressed about U.S. might. The ragged expedition and its pitiful trade items induced baleful reactions among Comanche Indians. The enterprise, however, resulted in two detailed accounts about it. Journals by Edwin James and Capt. John R. Bell cataloged a variety of natural landscapes in the Platte, Arkansas, and Canadian watersheds and the people, plants, and animals that inhabited this vast, virgin country. Surprisingly, one of these journals provided important clues to the character and activities of Peter Caulder.

The vicissitudes of camp life or "roughing it" agreed with Peter Caulder's constitution. Repeatedly Bradford or his officers sent Caulder into the wilds of Arkansas and Oklahoma. As in the spring 1819 excursion to the Red River to remove whites who had illegally settled on Indian lands, each day in the saddle for Caulder and other mounted riflemen broke down into routines — scouting, foraging, hunting, strapping on their horses' grain bag, and finding clear springs to refill canteens. When away from the post, Caulder rode long days, pitched camp at dusk, and spread his blanket roll or buffalo robe on the ground for a few hours' sleep between watches.

To take the troop to the Red River in May 1819, the guide led it along narrow traces, originally beaten into the mountain benches by buffalo and elk and later marked with piles of stone left as monuments by the Osages war parties. Descending into a valley of Birney Creek in the Winding Stairs, the party surprised a buffalo herd, "wallowing in the dust." The alarmed buffaloes galloped away and the riflemen in the lead of the column spurred their horses forward to give chase. A marksman dropped a young bull out of the panicked herd and Bradford called an early halt to preserve the meat. Perhaps the task of skinning and butchering the carcass went to the Cherokees accompanying the small expedition, although by this time at Belle Point some riflemen had specialized in this chore, which required keenly sharpened knives and an understanding of the anatomy of the great beast. As the skinning progressed, some soldiers kindled a fire and set up a rack over it to smoke choice portions. Sampling roasted tongue around the fire soon had the party in good spirits. Thomas Nuttall used the short break in the march to search for plants to catalog.[32] The thirty-two-year-old Englishman already had been published, and though short of obsessive about his calling, he certainly qualified as highly conscientious in finding and describing unrecorded species on this and his other excursions.

On the long ride to the Red River, Caulder scouted out gaps through the hills, and the detachment covered eighteen to twenty miles a day over the forbidding terrain. On midday stops, the men fed their horses from the bags of corn they carried and pulled buffalo jerky and hard biscuits from their saddlebags for themselves. When fortunate, the group enjoyed their noon meal in a shady glen by cool, flowing water. Once, Caulder regaled the group with wild honey taken from a bee tree that he had discovered. The delights of foraging for natural foods did not evade the riflemen when on detached duty away from the fort's mess kitchen and the normal army fare that tended to be grease laden.[33]

Caulder unfurled his buffalo robe and smoked his tobacco in a pipe in the evenings before he fell asleep. Chilly mornings greeted the early risers of the expedition and on one day, a cold rain drenched the men who had no wet weather gear issued to them beyond the green linen frocks and knitted caps that constituted their standard attire when on duty. The men usually rode single file in silence, but in camp or on occasion when the party partook of overnight lodging with a settler, the soldiers and the Rogers brothers exchanged lively gossip. Caulder, a handler of hounds, told the group a hair-raising anecdote about missing his best hound one night and following its trail the next day. Coming to a stream bank, Caulder discovered his badly mauled dog lying beneath a tree alongside a dead wolf. He deduced, probably with only a bit of the hyperbole common to many of these campfire stories, that a panther had leaped from an overhead tree branch to attack his canine rivals that had sniffed out the deer kill on which the big cat was feasting. The cougar is called catamount, puma, or mountain lion in various parts of the country. South Carolinians and Arkansans nor-

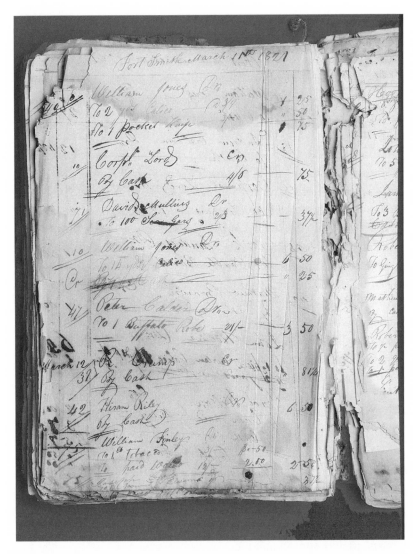

A March 10, 1821, entry from Fort Smith Trader's Ledger recorded Caulder's purchase of a buffalo robe. Caulder's store purchases as recorded in these account books included gunpowder, buttons, calico, and "looking glasses." Adam Lawyer, one of Caulder's closest white comrades, bought silk and buttons. Apparently the soldiers had lady friends whom they supplied with material for dress and clothes making.

mally used the term *panther* to denote the largest feline predator in their woods. Riflemen on the frontier lived close to nature, and their observances of habits and habitats of wildlife delighted Thomas Nuttall, who was well liked by both officers and enlisted men and who probably did not attempt to correct the exaggerations that he heard. The riflemen, a few years younger than the scientist, had already gathered a store of thrilling tales for campfires.[34]

Cherokees typically carried vermilion and in the evenings around the fire after chow, the Rogers brothers may have casually rubbed the ceremonial dye into the stock of their muskets. Intrigued with the stylish firearms of the Cherokees, Caulder and other riflemen may have followed their lead and polished their rifles with vermilion. The men of Bradford's company when absorbed into the Seventh Infantry at Fort Smith passed on this art of wood staining to their new comrades. In a summer 1827 visit to Fort Towson, the inspector general Col. George Croghan found "arms in the hands of the men in the highest possible degree of polish . . . they have here, as at Cantonment Jesup, a fashion of staining the stock of the musket with vermilion."[35] Towson and Jesup were Red River outposts of the Seventh Infantry. Peter Caulder's friend, Pvt. Joseph Clark, pulled an 1827 tour of duty at Fort Jesup, part of a detachment sent from Fort Gibson. Clark may have carried the vermilion technique with him and taught it to the men at Jesup.

Caulder and his fellow soldiers had chances to fire their rifles on the ride to the Red. White-tailed deer and wild pigs offered sport and targets that when plunked could wind up on the evening spit. Varmints like coral snakes and water moccasins, "both of them . . . furnished with mortal fangs," slithered through "swampy alluvions and ponds" that bordered the Kiamichi and gave occasional opportunity for impromptu shooting matches. Riflemen, so well drilled in marksmanship as part of their reason for being, sought such chances to showcase their ability. Capt. John R. Bell once observed soldiers at Fort Missouri attempting to recover a runaway mule by "creasing" him with a bullet across the back of the neck. The aim was slightly off, sending the bullet low, mortally wounding rather than just stunning the poor mule.[36] Once while his men made camp on the Red River, Major Bradford rode out a few miles to visit settlers. At dusk, instead of Bradford returning, two suspicious characters appeared out of the shadows. The sentry cocked his rifle. The soldiers had been warned that desperados, who had stolen horses and murdered a Cherokee, were at large. But the riders, upon being ordered to halt by the guard, instead bolted their horses into the canebrake and "effected [sic] their escape into neighboring Texas."[37] Along the sparsely populated frontier line in the early nineteenth century, gossip, much of it about misdeeds or crimes such as stealing horses, formed the essence of conversations and stood as the reality. No one knew the truth of events for sure where stories passed around without much in the way of verification or critique. Much of the official correspondence in the territorial papers was devoted to clearing up misrepresentations involving Indians, factors, agents, military officers, and territorial officials. Events of local interest and gossip continue today to dominate conversations in the Arkansas-Oklahoma borderlands. Opinions are shaped by news that is carried from person to person, and from those opinions a general perception emerges. These locally shaped perceptions then influence values and dictate social decisions in a community.

Near the Red River, Caulder picked up on a lightly marked trail that led the party to the house of William Styles. Styles may have heard of Bradford's presence in the area, but what must the pioneer have thought as he watched a large group of mounted and armed men approach through open ground toward his tiny cabin, scattering his animals and rousting his hounds to the howl? Furthermore, the message that they brought to him was, in the literal sense of the word, unsettling. John C. Calhoun in his letter of instruction for this mission specified to Bradford that any white settler who resisted peaceful evacuation was to be "removed by force."[38] The case of William Styles demonstrated how well Bradford carried out difficult military duties. The major did not provoke Styles or threaten him, but instead displayed a calm and reasonable manner that eased the settler. Styles showed hospitality to the troops, giving them a breakfast topped with a rare treat of milk and butter. Later on, Styles sheltered and provided meals to the penniless Nuttall for a week after the naturalist tarried too long in his gathering and became separated from the rest of the expedition. On the morning of May 24, 1819, a Red River settler named Martin Varner prepared a breakfast for Bradford's detachment. Varner further ingratiated himself with his visitors by bringing out for show the dried skin of a collared peccary that he had bagged along the Red. An amazed Nuttall had not realized that the range of the peccary was as far north. On such relaxing and memorable occasions, Caulder must have taken in the sights, pleasures, and methods of pioneer life and pictured himself living as the people on the Red were. Caulder knew that he was in line for a grant of one hundred sixty acres because of his War of 1812 service, although surveying Arkansas bounty lands was progressing slowly. In fact, Caulder would not be able to initiate his claim until 1822. Nevertheless, the private kept his dream of a farm that one day would be his, free and clear. He may have imagined that a cow like Styles had would be necessary for his homestead so that he, too, could furnish sweet-tasting milk and butter for family, friends, and visitors.

In the valley of the Red, Bradford visited the homes of Daniel Davis, John Davis, William Gates, and Charles Gates. The major read the order to these whites that they must pull up stakes and leave the Cherokee lands. Davis and Gates, like other white "intruders," took the news grimly, pointing out that they had wrested improvements and should not be forced to abandon them. Nuttall observed the plight of people "who had cleared considerable farms (and) were thus unexpectedly thrust out into the inhospitable wilderness." Bradford sympathized as well, because as he did in 1818 when he issued similar orders to the Billingsley settlement north of the Arkansas River, but extended their time for evacuation, in 1819 he turned for home without actually supervising the evacuation of the land. Consequently, Styles, Varner, and others stayed on and in the next years became petitioners to the territorial government against the Indian claims. Many of the settlers remained in Indian territories; others crossed the Red to settle in Texas.[39]

Bradford reached the limit of his jurisdiction at the banks of the Red, and having served notice on some two hundred whites that they must vacate Cherokee-claimed lands, the major considered his mission completed. On May 26, the party spent most of the day at Styles's house. As their string of horses grazed greedily on the orchard grasses (*Tripsacum dactyloides*) in the prairies that adjoined the homestead, Caulder and the riflemen cooked rations and made preparations to return by the route over which they had come. On a Monday, May 31, after hard days in the saddle, the riflemen again saw Fort Smith.[40]

Bradford, Caulder, and the riflemen had reluctantly left Thomas Nuttall behind in the Red River valley. As a show of his resourcefulness and dedication to biological science, Nuttall not only found accompaniment to Belle Point later in June, but while awaiting a chance to return, described dozens of plant species during his prolonged stay in southeastern Oklahoma. Upon his arrival, on June 21 at Belle Point, Nuttall found a warm greeting from Bradford, Dr. Russell, and perhaps, Caulder as well. Some aspects of frontier life go unrecorded by Nuttall in his journal—sex, religion, and politics, for instance. Like other journalists, except for one, who passed through the "Little Gibraltar on the Arkansas," Nuttall does not refer to Private Caulder, the guide, *or any other enlisted rifleman* by name in his journal. Nuttall, a discreet scientist, skirts commentary on race in his 1819 journal and only briefly comments on two free Negro rivermen he encountered.[41]

Major Bradford must have been pleased with Peter Caulder's performance of duty on the Red River expedition. A few days after returning to Fort Smith, Bradford summoned the scout to his hut. Bradford, in what must have been a frank and no-frills conversation between these terse, active men, convinced Peter Caulder, his trusted and valued private, to reenlist for a second hitch of five years. Bradford sealed this bargain right away in an unusual clerical move. He wrote out an honorable discharge two full months before Caulder's original five-year tour of duty expired in mid-September 1819. No other rifleman was given this kind of early release for the purpose of reenlistment. Obviously Bradford liked and valued Caulder, and the two agreed to continue their military relationship for at least another five years. On a Friday, June 4, 1819, the major filled in the enlistment papers, and the private scratched his mark so beginning his second tour of duty with the U.S. Army. Bradford could see that much work—construction, diplomacy, scouting, and perhaps even fighting—remained for the frontier company. The commander would have to depend on veterans like Caulder to get these jobs done. The newly appointed governor of Arkansas, James E. Miller, was not yet in the territory, and Indian troubles rumbled. What Bradford or Caulder could not foresee was how soon the U.S. Rifles would be disbanded. Growing white settlement and wilting peace negotiations between the Cherokees and the Osages pressured the War Department to increase military presence on the border. Before the five years had lapsed, Caulder would be transferred into the Seventh Infantry and Bradford would be reassigned.

CHAPTER FIVE

Fort Smith

MOST IN BRADFORD'S COMPANY, LIKE CAULDER, HAD ENLISTED FOR A five-year hitch in the war year of 1814, and their terms would be expiring in August and September of 1819. Always hard up to keep a full roster of enlisted men at Fort Smith, Bradford may have sought to start reenlistment momentum with Caulder. That ploy did not work completely, but a few riflemen did follow Caulder's example. William Loving, Bennett Webb, and Jacob Rose, friends and comrades of Caulder since the 1816 Natchitoches days, reenlisted. But, the majority of riflemen, including Caulder's Marion County friends, declined Major Bradford's offer to continue their army careers as enlisted men.[1]

One private, George Riley, who did reenlist, later brought charges against Bradford in civil court for coercing and threatening him into signing on for another tour. Riley was a gunsmith and blacksmith who regularly made iron hardware for the garrison. Bradford may have tried to persuade a trooper with such vital skills to remain, but it seems out of character for Bradford to use improper means to achieve his reenlistment goals. A jury, however, found for the plaintiff Riley and imposed a fine on Bradford, who probably did not bother to defend himself in court.[2]

Though obviously happy with Caulder's performance of duties, Bradford did not promote him. The commander moved two other riflemen, with less experience and less time in the company, up to corporal and sergeant grades, but not Caulder. Bradford may have suggested to Caulder that the army was a satisfactory career for a man of mixed ancestry especially if the army counted him as a white man and a good soldier. But the major was not to press the issue of color by placing Caulder at a higher rank where his orders to white soldiers would have to be obeyed. Bradford must have certainly considered Caulder a "white" soldier by 1819. What Caulder considered his racial identity to be in 1819 is unclear, but he seemed immersed completely in the army culture.

The army culture, of course, depended primarily on young males mostly disciplined, but sometimes not. That environment could sometimes turn violent with arguments, fisticuffs, and physical attacks. In 1823, a private argued with his peer over a small amount of money while they were hewing logs on fatigue duty. The argument infuriated one of the men, who then turned his axe on his mate and murdered him.[3] Men deserted for a variety of reasons, including for being shunned or teased unmercifully by their peers, treatment that caused some to drink excessively. Some soldiers became drunkards or languished in despair. In his army career, Peter Caulder never spent a day in the stockade and was never, so far as army records reveal, involved in serious scrapes with fellow soldiers or officers. He appeared on the sick roll only once after arriving at Belle Point, was granted a furlough, unusual for enlisted men, sent on duties away from the post, and reenlisted a third time after a break in service. For his third enlistment he received a bonus. Caulder had a few perks: credit at the sutler's store; duties that often took him away from the post routines; and tacit approval from his commanders to work for extra money.

In 1819, Bradford may have sweetened his reenlistment offer to Caulder by indicating that the private would be assigned to guide and hunting duties, providing him with an exemption from the monotonous labor details at the post. Bradford did not hesitate to redeploy Caulder and sent him "roughing it" soon after his reenlistment. The term for a regular soldier going off post on individually directed assignments was "detached duty." In their journals, Nuttall and Bell referred to soldiers used as "guides." By way of contrasting terms, a "scout" referred to a civilian, sometimes a Native American, who was under contract with the army for the same kind of off-post duties that Caulder and other enlisted men engaged in. Thus, Private Caulder guided rather than scouted for the army. In the summer of 1819, Caulder was away from the post, most likely searching for nitrate deposits in the valleys of north Arkansas. This duty might have resulted in an important chance meeting for Caulder. In the spring or summer of 1819, a free black man, David Hall, had reached the Little North Fork of the White River. Hall and his wife, Sarah, emigrants from Bedford County, Tennessee, located some available ground on the left bank of the river, and there they staked a claim. If Caulder met Hall in 1819, it is evident that the two men of color took an instant liking for each other. Within the decade, Caulder joined Hall's family in Marion County as his son-in-law. The close relationship between Caulder and Hall descendants would last for at least seventy-five years, involve three generations, and carry on beyond the boundaries of Arkansas into Missouri.[4]

When Henry Rowe Schoolcraft canoed down the White River in the winter of 1818–19, he spent the night with a woodsman whose name he spelled M'Gary. M'Gary, or McGarrah, pioneered a homestead at the mouth of the Little North Fork five miles above the White River land that David Hall would settle on the next spring. Hall eventually purchased his land from the United States government, but the McGarrah family may have moved on to Fort Smith by then. Schoolcraft described McGarrah and the type of frontier life that he witnessed in such cabins as his along the White River:

> He had a field of several acres under cultivation, where he raised corn, with several horses, cows and hogs. The house was built of logs . . . and the interior of the house . . . far from being either neat or comfortable. . . . Upon the whole, he appeared to live in great ease and independence, surrounded by a numerous family of sons and daughters, all grown up; received us with cordiality, gave us plenty to eat, and bid us welcome as long as we pleased to stay.[5]

By the time Caulder came to know the Halls this description given by Schoolcraft of McGarrah's would have accurately reflected the homestead of David Hall. Caulder no doubt interpreted the efficiency and comforts of the White River log-cabin homes if not the landscapes differently than did Schoolcraft, an Easterner who was critical of the lifestyles and ambition level of backwoodsmen.[6]

In the spring of 1819, increasing boat traffic on the Arkansas River presaged a growing white population. Downpours, the freshets, kept river channels open to keelboats, a few of them carrying supplies to Belle Point and beyond to the trading posts of the Verdigris. Rainfall usually tapered off with the coming of summer, dropping water levels and ending the navigable season. The summer of 1819 was unusual in that respect because in late July, Thomas Nuttall hopped a ride on a keelboat headed upriver from Fort Smith. The boat's owners and operators, Joseph Bogy and William Drope, were familiar to Nuttall and to the riflemen at Belle Point. These two traders made a business of sending bales of furs downstream and bringing manufactured goods back that would be added to their stock of exchange goods at their trading house on the Verdigris River in Osage country.[7]

Bogy and Drope competed with at least three other establishments doing business with the Osages in the Three Forks region. Nathaniel Pryor, his partner Samuel B. Richards, Auguste Choteau, and Hugh Glenn were active traders in and around the Verdigris, and each would at times "keep store" in the confluence known as Three Forks.[8] Added to these trading houses were the itinerant traders. Obviously, commerce with Osages was lucrative and sizable.

Hugh Glenn, a tall, restless man from Cincinnati, had friendships with Fort Smith army officers. That sort of influence helped him gain contracts to supply western outposts and negotiate trading rights with Native Americans in their homelands. Glenn had known Bradford since the two had worked together in St. Louis acquiring supplies and packing the keelboat for the initial voyage to Belle Point. That acquaintance grew into a friendship and business association when the War Department named the energetic Glenn as sutler (an army word for a franchised merchant) for the Fort Smith garrison. He supplied the troops with basics outside army issue and offered a few pleasantries as well. Peter Caulder, the South Carolina–born soldier, and Hugh Glenn, the Ohio merchant, met at Fort Smith and formed a working relationship, probably because of Caulder's chimney-building skills. Caulder, James Turner, and Joseph Clark frequented the store and on occasion ran up hefty charges against their line of credit. Glenn's customers, who included the occasional civilian trapper or fur dealer, often bought now and paid later. The army encouraged that practice by both enlisted men and officers because of the notorious lateness of paymasters. Post sutlers acted as their own bill collectors and were at the pay table when the soldiers stood in line to receive their wages.[9]

Army regulations specified that "the comfort or well-being of the troops" could be increased by the presence of a fair-minded and respectable man of character to conduct the "business of sutling" at remote stations. Glenn had a monopoly at Fort Smith but was supposed to pay an annual fee to the post commander who could use it to finance the relief of widows and orphans and the education of soldiers' children at a post school. The commanding officer could purchase books for a library and maintain a post band with the sutler assessments if the collection became substantial enough. At Fort Smith, it did not. But the store marked Fort Smith's growing and diverse society. In 1820 and 1821 David Stagner, Glenn's store clerk, kept a meticulous ledger of purchases, sales, and credits that reflected the activities of the men and women of the garrison.[10]

The clerk stocked shelves in the tiny store built into a wall of the fort with sundries, lead, cloth, whiskey, and twists of tobacco. When the one-ounce daily ration of spirits was not enough to relax body and mind, the rifleman could buy a round or two over the counter at 12½ cents per shot. Caulder partook of both whiskey and tobacco, hardly vices in those days when most considered whiskey a medicine and tobacco a useful stimulant.

The store carried on a lively trade in cherry bounce, a popular social drink in colonial times. Made with fresh cherries, rock candy, sugar, and brandy, cherry bounce had become in the early nineteenth century a fashionable remedy for monthly female discomforts.[11] At seventy-five cents a quart, it was not a cheap item, maybe used as a gift as well as a medicinal tonic. Martin Turner, James Turner, and Peter Caulder bought several quarts of cherry bounce over a period of time. Caulder also bought buttons, lining, and muslin cloth.[12] Perhaps these purchases indicated Caulder's relationship with a woman at Belle Point. Caulder could have repaid a seamstress or washerwoman with cherry bounce and furs. Perhaps there was more to such a relationship than the business of repairing clothes. William Loving provided his wife, Susan, with the beverage. Bradford allowed a married soldier and his wife to live across the river from Belle Point and farm a small plot of ground held by the post. Most likely it was the Lovings, and if so, it was Susan and her child who were threatened by an Osage war party in 1823. William Loving had enlisted in the Third Rifle Regiment at York, South Carolina, in the same month as Caulder, and the two men served together through Carlisle and Fort Claiborne before coming to Belle Point.[13]

In August 1819, the enlistments of James Turner, Martin Turner, Joseph Clark, and Caleb Cook at last expired. Unlike Peter Caulder, none of these veterans accepted the opportunity for reenlistment. Cook, who had been assigned to the express boat plying correspondence and document pouches between Fort Smith and headquarters in Belle Fontaine, saw his future north of the Ohio and never rejoined Mourning, his wife of seven years whom he had not seen in five. Perhaps accustomed to the equal treatment he received in the army, Cook concerned himself with growing racism and did not want to chance confrontation in South Carolina. He applied for and received a patent for bounty land in Indiana later, but evidently did not send for Mourning to join him. Though Caleb Cook disappeared from the historical record, Mourning successfully applied for a veteran's widow pension in the 1880s while still living in Marion, South Carolina.[14] Martin Turner and James Turner turned to civilian pursuits, but stayed close to Fort Smith. They owned a house and livestock and continued to visit the post store before the arrival of the Seventh Infantry in 1822. The Turners kept their strong friendship with Peter Caulder, and the three sons of Marion County, South Carolina, occasionally pooled their financial resources to pay off bills for one another at the sutler's store. Indeed Martin Turner, four years older than Peter Caulder and from a well-respected black family in Marion County, may have served as a mentor of sorts for Peter Caulder. In key personal decisions such as enlisting in the U.S. Army in 1814 and in homesteading in Izard County, Arkansas, some distance from his bounty land, Peter Caulder followed the actions of Martin Turner.

How did the Turners subsist in Fort Smith after their army paycheck ended? As a private in his time of service, James Turner seemed a likely candidate for assignment to the post garden because of his farming background. After his discharge from the army, James Turner may have been continued to grow corn near the post. Several civilians farmed on garrison lands during Bradford's command, a practice that the major was called on to stop but did not, perhaps because the tillers were former soldiers of his company. From large quantities of sugar purchased in the fall by Caulder, it is likely that someone whom he knew ran a still. The corn that James Turner harvested could have been used to make whiskey and as feed for horses and mules. Martin Turner may well have been a horse trader or teamster, occupations that fitted his background, his status, and his abilities. There were others like him in the area. A free black man, other than Martin Turner, hired on an 1821 expedition to Santa Fe out of Fort Smith as a wagon driver and mule handler.[15]

Both Martin and James apparently found romance in Arkansas and started families. By 1850, nine children with the last name of Turner, orphaned or abandoned by their fathers, had taken up residence with relatives or neighbors in the Hall extended family on the White River.

One of the Marion men, Joseph Clark, took a nine-month break in service over the winter and spring of 1819–20, but reenlisted in Bradford's rifle company on July 4, 1820. Clark may have fortified himself for the reenlisting ceremonies, because the day before, his last as a civilian, he bought a bottle of whiskey at the post store. Auguste Choteau, a trader with the Osages, had landed a whiskey boat in Fort Smith that week. Peter Caulder bought whiskey from Choteau on Thursday, July 6.[16] Military records do not reveal how the garrison celebrated Independence Day in 1820, but arrival of a boatload of spirits may have encouraged a day of song and dance among the riflemen, and Peter Caulder undoubtedly welcomed Clark, his old South Carolina friend, back to the uniform in style. They kept a strong friendship in the coming years and would be transferred to the Seventh Infantry two years later. Caulder and Clark planned their future years together and applied for their bounty lands at the same time. The friends received adjoining tracts of bounty land located in today's Sharp County, Arkansas, on the same day, March 22, 1824. How these pals who had ventured far from their boyhood homes on Catfish Creek must have rejoiced, slapping one another on the back, as they actually became landowners. Gladly, they imagined themselves sharing labor in building neighboring homesteads in Arkansas Territory! But first, more army adventures, trials, and romance awaited Peter Caulder and Joseph Clark.

In late August 1820, Peter Caulder ferried the Arkansas River to Pvt. William Loving's house on the plain across from Belle Point. Probably he spent the night with the Lovings. Susan Loving was eight months pregnant, but she could still set an evening table for her soldier husband and his friend. The next morning, Caulder and his traveling companion, James Turner, reined their horses out of Loving's corral, plunged through the thick canebrakes that lined the banks of the Arkansas, and headed for the more open forests that stretched to the Three Forks region. Caulder was on a furlough granted to him by Capt. James H. Ballard, the new commander of the garrison and its company while Major Bradford attended to military business at Belle Fontaine.[17] Caulder did not carry papers or a pass, but dressed in the uniform of the U.S. Rifles, he anticipated no need to document his absence from the post. Indeed, on several occasions since arriving in Arkansas, Peter Caulder had traveled through strange country alone or with companions. His military bearing, his calmness, his skill with firearms, and his strong frame were always formidable enough to ward off would-be troublemakers in remote regions. Departing Fort Smith on a sweltering day, Caulder looked forward to his first furlough since joining the army, and he had plans to make good use of it. Now twenty-seven and with thoughts of a homestead in his mind, he wanted to earn extra money. The low private's pay did not suffice to build a nest egg. He had gotten his commander's approval to work for additional income. Hugh Glenn wanted help in expanding his trading house on the Verdigris River. Glenn had picked Caulder for the construction job and had offered him fifteen dollars for a month's labor. On this thirty-day furlough, Caulder might triple his income while finding time for a little hunting and fishing along the Grand and Verdigris Rivers.

Caulder had been to the Three Forks region before, of course, with Maj. Stephen H. Long in 1818. But that had been by skiff up the river. He probably had not crossed overland through the region before, and he may have meandered, camping, fishing, and hunting along the way. Caulder had his army rifle with him and his personal stash of gunpowder and gunflints to hunt for game. To fish for catfish, Caulder must have had cheese in mind for bait, having stocked up beforehand on it at the sutler store.[18] He certainly knew how to scout out traces and navigate by stars if necessary to find his way over unfamiliar terrain, but probably was in no particular hurry to reach his destination. At the time, the Osages, upset at recent raids on their horses and villages by the Cherokees, were honing verbal tirades against their old enemies to be performed when the territorial governor James Miller arrived at Claremont's village fifty miles up the Verdigris, a visit rumored to happen soon. Caulder, though wary, expected to be left alone on his trip into the heart of Osage country because he was a rifleman and because the Osages could not afford to jeopardize the council.

After a few days in late August, Caulder arrived at the log house midway between the Grand and Verdigris mouths that served as Glenn's trading headquarters. A grove of magnificent oak trees shaded the house, which was set about two hundred yards above the Arkansas River out of the flood plain. By September 1, 1820, Caulder was well into his task, probably that of constructing a fireplace and chimney, heating and cooking additions to the house. Caulder slept in a wall tent with a rain fly and no doubt intently enjoyed the daily meals of greens, onions, potatoes, and venison cooked by the trading house contingent of Osage women. After laboring during the day, Caulder tossed back a shot or two in the evening. This particular late summertime on the Verdigris constituted what must have been a delightful respite from the army regime for Caulder. Smoking his pipe after dinner and relaxing would have been an ideal time for him to reflect on that winter day in the vicinity three years earlier. Since that trip with Major Long when the location for Fort Smith had been decided, considerable change had come to the frontier, to the army, and to Caulder himself.

What must have his August 1820 conversations with Glenn and Charles Dennis, the trading post interpreter and barkeeper, been like? Did they remark that life on the edges of American civilization was tolerably good? Caulder seemed to be a noncomplaining man who thrived on adventure and serendipity. His fears hardly included imagining a great war over the spread of slavery to the west. But the warpath being trod by Osages and Cherokees must have been a concern. Did the men discuss race or women? A good guess is that their talk kept coming back to arguing the proper qualities of a bear dog or how to choose a good horse. Caulder must have liked the way he was earning money and may have felt secure about a free future in which he made the decisions about his work and his activities. He had never belonged to another man, only to the army, and one day that would be finished service. Glenn presumably spoke of his plans for an upcoming trading expedition to Santa Fe with Jacob Fowler of Cincinnati. Before Caulder's job was finished, Glenn left for Fort Smith, leaving Dennis in charge.

If Caulder built a chimney for Glenn's house, he may have used techniques of stick and mud construction developed in West Africa centuries ago. Such chimneys were common in rural South Carolina communities where Ulster Irish, free black people, and slaves equipped their huts with this sort of rude fireplace.[19] With the time he intended to spend at the Verdigris, Caulder may have set about erecting a stone chimney carefully fitted to be of more lasting quality. But trouble loomed for Caulder on the horizon. Before he completed his building task for Glenn, he was ordered back to Fort Smith.

On Tuesday morning, September 5, 1820, Caulder had an opportunity to exchange banter with the group of Osage women who had risen early and were busily drying deerskins near the trading house. Caulder had stripped to the waist, had laid out his tools, and was engaged in measuring, cutting, and fitting stones for the day's labor, assisted probably by James Turner. At midmorning a party of bedraggled white men on skinny Indian ponies limped into the clearing, interrupting the work of Caulder. The man in the front of the column, accustomed to command, asked Caulder about the house: who owned it and what was available there? Caulder replied that the establishment belonged to Hugh Glenn and pointed out the keeper, Dennis, who had just emerged from the trading house. The stranger dismounted and spoke to Dennis, asking if a man could be hired to guide the party to Belle Point. Dennis responded that he did not have a man for that duty and really one was not needed because the way was easily found. Caulder, who had watched during this conversation, said nothing more and turned back to his work. The leader and spokesman for the party was an army officer, Capt. John R. Bell of the Long expedition, although Caulder and Dennis did not yet know that fact. After a short conversation between themselves, several men swung their horses around and rode back in the direction from which they had come. Bell took a seat near Caulder's tent. While resting there, the captain's gaze fell on a cap and uniform hanging on a post. Recognizing the Rifle Regiment emblems on them, Bell jumped to his feet immediately and hastened inside to question Dennis about the clothing. Dennis told him that the uniform belonged to Peter Caulder, the man working outside.

Bell summoned Caulder and heatedly asked him to what company he belonged. Caulder replied that he was a veteran and assigned to Capt. James Ballard's company. Bell insisted on seeing his "papers authorizing (his) absence from the garrison." Caulder had none and could not convince Bell that he had permission to be at Glenn's. The captain ordered Caulder "to prepare to start with my party in 15 minutes for Belle Point." The private did not argue his case any further, but put on coat and hat and gathered his personal equipment for the journey. The captain appeared to be certain that he had discovered a deserter from Bradford's company. But Bell's soldiers, who had been in pursuit of a runaway horse, returned to the trading house. One of them, Cpl. William Parish "recognized Coulder as one of his old companions [in the Rifle Regiment]." Parish swung down from his horse and greeted Caulder enthusiastically. Their obvious bonding from previous service together, though long ago in South Carolina, broke the tension that had grown with Bell's suspicions.[20] Now, cordiality brought smiles and satisfactions. Even Dennis, who was about to lose a valuable workman and a good listener, became "very civil" and furnished Bell and his men "a dinner of corn bread and honey of which we (Bell's party) partook and relished."[21]

When Captain Bell entered the clearing of Glenn's trading house, he was nearing the end of a long journey from Colorado and the headwaters of the Arkansas River to Fort Smith. Bell served as the journalist of Maj. Stephen H. Long's well-publicized Rocky Mountain Expedition. After four months of exploring the high plateaus of the Platte, Arkansas, and Red rivers in Colorado, Long had split his expedition in two for the downstream return because of dwindling supplies and forage. Long placed Bell in charge of half the expedition that would travel down the Arkansas River to Belle Point, while Long, Edwin James, Titian Peale, two riflemen, and five others of the original party intended to follow the Red downstream. Major Long planned for the two arms of the expedition to reunite at Fort Smith. Long estimated that his party's Red River journey would be longer and more difficult so he had taken the best horses and mules. Making up Bell's command that would take the northern route through Kansas were Lt. W. H. Swift; Dr. Thomas Say, a zoologist; Mr. Samuel Seymour, a landscape painter; Stephen Julian, an interpreter; Corporal Parish; Privates Mord Nowland, Peter Bernard, Robert Foster, and Charles Myers; guide Joseph Bijeau; farrier Abraham Ledoux; and a string of sore back horses. On their journey, rations and trading goods ran perilously low. Game was scare, and the weather was hot. For the month of August, Bell's men labored through scorched Kansas. After a few grim weeks, the men grew gaunt, savoring even the occasional skunk that was killed for their evening meal. Bell, who rode at the head of the column, kept the pace and a journal. Less than ten days out from Belle Point, six days from Three Forks, disaster struck. Disheartened by the starvation and endless chores that had been their lot, Privates Mordica Nowland, Peter Bernard, and Charles Myers on sentry duty for the night waited until the others were sound asleep, stole the only three horses that could still run, and deserted Bell. The recreant riflemen took two rifles and four saddlebags that carried money, clothing, a sextant, manuscripts, a journal, and two vocabularies of Indian languages. The manuscripts collected by the scientist Thomas Say on the five-month expedition detailed Indian customs and manners as well as the zoology and topography of the region covered by the expedition—a wealth of fresh information about environment and ethnology. Unable to pursue the deserters because of the poor condition of their remaining horses, Bell's party slowly continued on "with heavy hearts and sad countenances."[22] Thus, upon arrival at Three Forks, Bell had ample reason to be on the defensive with Caulder. In the end, Caulder's calmness and reputation stood him in good stead with Captain Bell, who paid the private an unusual compliment by including his name in the journal of the expedition. Bell made no mention of Caulder's race.

After hearing of losses and realizing the need of Bell's party to reach its destination in short order, Caulder wholeheartedly agreed to guide the party on to Fort Smith and departed with Bell later in the afternoon of September 6, 1820. The first day, they "met Mr. Glenn's horse which had left him." Bell and Say complained to their journals that the obscure trace and the thick canebrakes caused them to travel about three miles out of the way, blaming the guide. But the missteps occurred probably while Caulder took Glenn's horse back to the trading house.[23] The next day, Caulder picked up a trace that led them out of the canebrakes into a prairie and with the open ground, the group covered twenty-three miles. Caulder may have had one of his hounds with him, and if so, Bell and his men were reminded of Caesar and Buck, the two dogs that had started out with the expedition in June from the Missouri River. The dogs had been boon companions who received special care, including being carried across the saddle, but nevertheless had expired from dehydration in the trek across the "Great American Desert."

On Saturday morning, September 9, Bell's party arrived amidst the yipping of hounds at Private and Mrs. William Loving's farm across from Belle Point. Greeting Susan, whom he knew well, Caulder introduced her to Captain Bell and to his friend Corporal Parish. Seeing a white woman gladdened the men of the expedition, evidence of civilization, which they had been away from for five months. Civilization meant to them a day away from the saddle, beds off the ground, and meals prepared by someone else—hence their excitement. Caulder may have walked the hundred yards from the farm to the ferry landing across from Belle Point. In view of the broad stripes and bright stars of the garrison flag fluttering from its tall pole, Caulder hailed the guard, who promptly sent a scow to transport Bell, his men, and their horses to the south bank. Awaiting the group as the ferry docked, Captain Ballard and Hugh Glenn "politely and hospitably received" them. Captain Bell's command had covered 873 miles down the Arkansas after he left Long, but instead of feeling satisfied by successfully completing all duties assigned, Bell was still dismayed by the desertion and the loss of important manuscripts.[24]

The absence of Long puzzled Bell. Bell had been a critic of some of Long's decisions, but respected the major's knowledge of the country and expected him to be already at Belle Point. While Bell and his men waited, Samuel Seymour sketched two scenes of Fort Smith. The one portrait that survived, painted on a summer day made cool and pleasant by a rain shower, provided a panoramic view of cropland, river, and forest around the fort. It is the sole existing visual evidence of how the fort walls looked in 1820. Seymour's artwork depicts a uniformed rifleman seated in a chair leaning back against the log walls of the fort and a sentry, musket on his left shoulder, marching on the perimeter. In the background of the painting, two soldiers in white shirts and suspenders guide a horse and plow in cultivating a garden plot near the river below the high ground of the fort.[25]

Captain Ballard made sure that Bell's men had quarters. He assigned a soldier to cook them fresh meat and vegetables and another to attend to their wants, which included outfitting the ragged expedition members with new flannel shirts, pantaloons, and hunting frocks from the fort's clothing supply. Hugh Glenn offered credit at his store, which they gladly accepted, assuring the merchant that they would repay Glenn's agent in Cincinnati upon their return trip up the Ohio. The worn-out horses were put out to pasture along the Poteau. Pleased with the red carpet treatment afforded him, Bell noted that the men in his command were "in all respects as comfortable as possible." Bell, Swift, Seymour, and Julian hustled to Glenn's store. Their first purchase was cotton socks. They bought dressed deerskins to make moccasins. Obviously, their feet had suffered on the long trek.[26]

Caulder got by Glenn's store to purchase two pounds of sugar

Peter Caulder in rifleman's uniform and carrying his rifle. Caulder often guided officers through the Ozarks.

ILLUSTRATION BY ERNEST CIALONE.

and a twist of tobacco on credit. Perhaps he had found his friend
Loving across the river in need of sugar to begin the fermentation of
corn or grapes, or maybe Susan Loving was preparing to make jelly.
Caulder would have had to take the boat back across, a transit of at
least an hour, which meant that he went out of his way to accommodate his friends. Perhaps there was another woman in the garrison community close enough to Caulder who might have needed the
sugar. Upon their return, Caulder's friend James Turner suddenly had
a lot of cash. On Wednesday, the day of the parade, the ex-rifleman
cleared his $17.36 bill on the store ledger, the day after Martin
Turner settled his $1.50 bill with Glenn. It is likely that Glenn paid
James Turner a month's salary at one time for providing meat and
wrangling horses at the trading house on the Verdigris.[27]

Excitement at Fort Smith rose even higher the next morning as
the skiff carrying Major Bradford and paymaster Capt. S. W. Kearny
docked at the Belle Point landing on their return from St. Louis.
Now, the troops could be brought up to date on their pay. Kearny
was also the regimental inspector. A parade and inspection was
ordered for the garrison. Noncommissioned officers broke out their
drill manuals. Company musicians rehearsed their marching tunes.
The troops washed tunics, pressed trousers, shined brass, and polished gear. Parades *and* paydays build morale!

Two groups were absent at the formal military ceremonies of
Wednesday, September 13, one just missing the parade. No more
than an hour after it, Major Long and his entire party rode into sight
on the opposite bank, after a "civil" visit with Susan Loving. The
ferry brought the group across, greeted by hurrahs from the riflemen.
Bell noted with satisfaction that Long and his men were in "fine
health" and, unlike the party that arrived first, had been eating well,
having "not," according to Bell, "suffered much for provisions."[28]

The other group that missed the parade and inspection included
Peter Caulder. Still greatly concerned over the deserters and the
missing scientific data, Bell had conferred with Bradford immediately
upon the senior officer's arrival. Bradford caught the urgency of the
matter and responded with prompt action by calling on his most
skilled tracker—Peter Caulder, teaming him with Cpl. Andrew

Samuel Seymour's watercolor of 1820 Fort Smith. Seymour, a landscape painter, accompanied Stephen H. Long on his expedition to the Rocky Mountains.

During a ten-day stay at Fort Smith, Seymour painted two or three scenes of the garrison but the painting pictured is the only one known to exist.

Calhoun and Pvt. Samuel Eaton. With speed essential to pick up the trail of the armed and desperate deserters, the three soldiers left early the next day in company with Hugh Glenn, who accompanied the detachment as far as his house on the Verdigris and there supplied the pursuers with extra mounts and supplies.[29] Caulder, Calhoun, and Eaton knew that they were not in for an easy time. Both the search and the capture, if it came to that, would be dangerous work. Looking for clues and witnesses in Osage villages, the hard-riding Caulder, Calhoun, and Eaton sought to pick up the cold trail of the riflemen-gone-bad. Caulder would have had his hound with him, but even with his nose and a smattering of intelligence tips from friendly Osages, the deserters with their two-week head start eluded their trackers. The exact direction that Caulder, Calhoun, and Eaton took in their pursuit is unknown as is the area that they covered. Bernard was from Pennsylvania. Myers, born in Maryland, enlisted in St. Louis. The likelihood is that the men fled toward the northeast and the anonymity of the cities, having had their fill of the plains. Caulder and his party carried descriptions—Myers was characterized as being a "great talker" with a deep voice. Long-haired Mord Nowland, the tallest and youngest of the three, had deserted the army twice before and had been pardoned each time.[30] His officers thought him a shirker and pathologically unreliable. Bernard had perpetual "blood shot eyes and was slovenly and careless in his dress."[31]

Given the length of Caulder's absence from Fort Smith, almost three months, his search pattern must have been extensive. Bradford advertised in the *Arkansas Gazette*, offering a reward of two hundred dollars for apprehension of the deserters and recovery of the manuscripts.[32] Probably Caulder and his fellow trackers, which may have included an interpreter from Glenn's trading house, told of the reward and sought out information on the fugitives by visiting Indian lodges and white settlements in eastern Kansas and Missouri. To compensate Bradford for his loss of manpower by sending out this detachment, Long transferred his three remaining riflemen, Josiah Verplank, William Parish, and Robert Foster to Ballard's company at Fort Smith. Foster had performed strongly on the expedition and in December won promotion because of it to sergeant.[33] Although

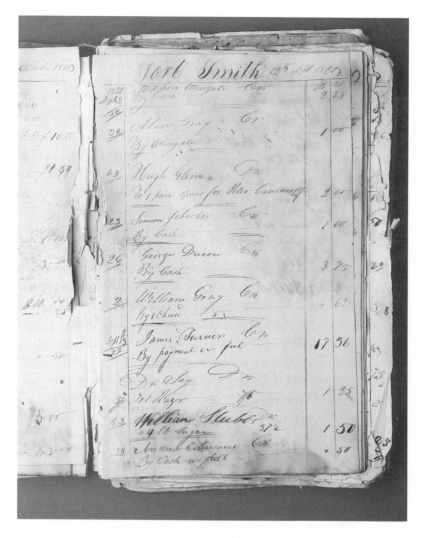

A September 12, 1820, entry from Fort Smith Trader's Ledger showed that Hugh Glenn paid for Peter Caulder's spurs. The sutler added his encouragement to the speed of Peter Caulder as he set off in pursuit of three deserters who had imperiled the Bell party.

the three riflemen from Fort Smith stayed on the manhunt for three months, they did not bring in the recreant deserters. Despite his diligence, Caulder could not recover the manuscripts and journals that his officers wanted returned, but that he himself could not read.[34]

Peter Caulder, Cpl. Andrew Calhoun, and Samuel Eaton, having doggedly pursued the deserters of the Long expedition through the fall finally resigned the chase and made their way back to Fort Smith after New Year's Day, 1821.[35] Caulder and his trail-weary comrades quickly realized that new excitements had replaced those of three months prior generated by the Long expedition. Now, political thunderbolts charged the atmosphere of their home station. Gov. James E. Miller was encamped at Fort Smith, braving the winter housed in a log hut while engaged in an early day form of shuttle diplomacy. He met on several occasions with Clermont in a strenuous effort to arrange a peace agreement between his tribe and the Cherokees. In territorial Arkansas, the Osages and the Cherokees were as recalcitrant in their demands of each other as Palestinians and Israelis seem to be in the modern world and as dangerous. Like the latter two nations today, the rival Indian nations threatened to engulf their region in total war. Bands of warriors from each tribe, never seeking or needing authority from established chiefs, raided, terrorized, and murdered. The cycle of violence between the Osages and the Cherokees injured innocent parties, ruined property, and hamstrung routine life. Arkansas shook.

Organized Indian tribes with their own autonomous territories were not directly under United States jurisdiction. Nevertheless, whites felt in jeopardy, which they were, and insisted that military and territorial officials do something to defuse the powder keg on which they thought they were sitting.

No one was more determined to solve the Osage-Cherokee problems than Miller, a conscientious guardian of the public good. At the battle of Lundy's Lane in the War of 1812, Colonel Miller had been ordered to attack a British battery. Upon being handed his order by his superior officer, he had fastened an eye on the hill where the well-guarded battery was raining down a dreadful fire on American positions and replied somewhat balefully, "I'll try, sir." Miller succeeded in taking the British guns, perhaps going beyond his own expectations, and he became a minor hero of the war. Maybe the battle did not shape Miller into presidential timber, but certainly he proved himself to be gubernatorial caliber and indeed, President Monroe subsequently appointed Miller to the position of territorial governor of Arkansas. His battlefield response became rather famous in America at the time, and Miller adopted it as his motto as Arkansas adopted him and named a county in his honor. But the native of New Hampshire found Arkansas as grueling a challenge as that he had faced at Lundy's Lane. Miller suffered from the heat and the insects, but the stubbornness of the Osages and the Cherokees eventually proved too much even for old "I'll try, sir." The troubles between the tribes continued for another decade.[36]

Miller preferred neutrality and conciliatory negotiation to solve Osage-Cherokee conflicts. Major Bradford thought it best to stay aloof and let the tribes deal with each other. Bradford's actions cast doubt on the standard historical interpretation that Fort Smith was founded for the purpose of keeping peace between the Indians. That does not seem to be the role that the commanding officer understood for himself and his garrison once it was established. Bradford intended to use force against Indians only when they attacked whites on non-Indian territories knowing that the potential power of his troops (he favored sending strong and threatening messages) was more effective in controlling Indian aggression than actually engaging the various war parties. Indeed, Bradford played the right hand. Guerilla capabilities of Indians in Arkansas might have chewed up his small force of riflemen. Besides, the major knew that his superiors would target the Osages in case of warfare, and he had come to believe that not the Osages but the Cherokees were mostly to blame for current troubles.[37] Bradford applied a wider latitude in his responsibilities for himself after the arrival of Ballard. Though he continued to perform his military assignments, he also tended more to personal business and investments. He stayed away from Fort Smith for increasingly long periods of time in 1821. Matthew Lyon, the newly arrived Cherokee factor at Spadra Bayou on the Arkansas River, wanted Bradford to station a squad of riflemen at Spadra for protection of the agency and the Cherokee families near it. Bradford refused the request and later neglected to send word to Lyon about an Osage war party that had passed Fort Smith apparently traveling in the direction of Spadra. Matthew Lyon, no stranger to voicing his opinions, promptly dashed off a "what kind of protection" [is this]? protest note to Bradford and sent a copy on to Secretary of War Calhoun.[38]

Lyon may have had a point. In April, relationships worsened between Osages who wanted to head west for their spring buffalo hunt and their enemies. The Osages were unable to reach a peace accord that would ease their fears of a Cherokee-led attack on their villages while Osage braves were scattered for the hunt such as had happened in 1817. Without a treaty for protection from the Cherokees, Osage chief Clermont could no longer control his violence-prone son, Mad Buffalo.[39] Mad Buffalo, already accused of murdering Cherokees, now raised three hundred warriors for a massive foray deep into Cherokee country. Mad Buffalo's strategy may have been as put poetically by Osage oral traditions, "the lunge of the grizzly to frighten away the prowling panther from his wapiti carcass."[40] A prosaic statement of Mad Buffalo's purpose was to drive the Cherokees back through force of arms, kill as many as he could, and take their horses as prizes. This "big man" leader of scores of angry young Osages intended to stun the army into noninterference, even take munitions from their store, and his first target was the garrison at Fort Smith.

Pvt. Peter Caulder, standing with his rifle at parade rest, watched the opposite side of the river uneasily on Monday morning April 9, 1821. The acting post commander, Lt. Martin Scott, a Vermonter and War of 1812 veteran, had Zacheus Waldo drum the riflemen into formation when his sentries reported seeing Osage warriors infiltrate the shoreline on the west bank. Scott could see through his spy glass that the Osages wore war paint and that they were better armed than ever before. On the fort's parade ground, Caulder stood near his friend and comrade at arms, William Loving, who had come across the river early in the morning to report for duty. Loving had left his wife and child at home on their farm not far from where the Osage braves were milling around on the far bank. Like Caulder and Loving, Lieutenant

Scott tensed over the danger. With Major Bradford and Captain Ballard, his senior officers, absent from the post, Scott faced the most serious test of arms in Fort Smith's short history.

Scott decided that he should parlay with the Osages and sent a boat crew to transport Mad Buffalo and his war chiefs across the river. In a gesture of defiance, the Osages swept by the out-stretched hand of Lieutenant Scott, continuing until they were atop the bluff. There, the bad-tempered leader, seeing the armed riflemen in ranks facing him and the six-pound cannons, hesitated and decided to speak to Scott after all. Mad Buffalo, who may have known of Bradford's absence, tried to intimidate the junior army officer. The Osages needed arms and munitions that the army could supply, he told Scott. The army should ferry the large party and its horses across the river so that they could camp east of the fort. Scott listened to the translations in dismay and turned down all of Mad Buffalo's demands. Convinced of the hostility of the Osages, Scott spoke to the second lieutenant at his side, Morton Keeter, who ordered the drummer to beat out a deployment for the rifle company and gun crews to wheel up the artillery pieces. Private Caulder may have felt a certain pride in his military unit as they snapped to battle stations and prepared to take action if necessary. The rifle company numbered about sixty men. Close to three hundred and fifty Osage warriors opposed them. Among the riflemen were many veterans of the War of 1812, and these men moved smartly and confidently in this confrontation. Awakened to the strength and determination of the garrison, Mad Buffalo broke off his talk with Scott and boated back to join his braves. The family across the river from the fort became a concern. Uproarious barking of dogs warned Susan Loving of trouble. Osage ruffians surrounded the farm where Susan, her infant child, and perhaps another child belonging to a woman of the garrison huddled alone. The eerily painted Indians shouted threats, brandished tomahawks, and waved scalps to terrify the young mother and the children. Susan Loving, a plucky young woman accustomed to taking care of herself, held her ground. No doubt William Loving, Peter Caulder, and their comrades reacted fiercely to the shouts and commotion coming from the farm and had to be prevented from reaching the boats.[41] Tight discipline of his troops in the face of this severe provocation turned out to be a correct approach by Scott, because after about an hour of demonstrating and dust raising, the Osages withdrew without harming the woman, the children, or the farm. The Osages were still furious though and not through with harassing the fort. They began to carry logs out of the canebrakes to assemble rafts on the shoreline. When a few braves crossed the river on their makeshift boats and disappeared into the undergrowth below the fort, Scott ordered the two six-pound cannons to be turned toward the Indians on the far shore who looked to be boarding more of their hastily built rafts. The company artillerists, probably under the direction of Cpl. Bennett Webb, loaded the cannon with canister. Canister charges are used to inflict multiple casualties in the attacking force. A gunner stood by, firing match lit for instant response to the impending amphibious invasion by the Osages. Caulder and the company of riflemen took up firing positions from cover. Fort Smith braced for what appeared to be a certain assault from an enemy, and an enemy with far superior numbers at that. But, Scott's bristling force discouraged Mad Buffalo's band, who retreated from the riverbank. With the attack averted, Scott used the lull to dispatch volunteers, probably including Caulder and William Loving, across the river to bring the woman and the children to safety.

Frustrated by the strong defense of the fort, marauding Osage braves fell instead on a group of Quapaw hunters on the south shore of the Poteau. The Osages ambushed the camp, killing three of the four Quapaws. The survivor fled through the canes and escaped by swimming across the Poteau River. A short distance away, a white hunter maneuvered his canoe, fleeing the Osages who were pursuing him. Sentries in the blockhouse of the fort alerted Scott, who had riflemen to quickly wheel a cannon to face the Poteau in order to protect the escaping hunters. The soldiers and their weapons were primed to rake the Osages in defense of innocent people. The actions of the Osages at the fort, at the Loving farm, and with the Quapaws must have whipped up the emotions of the riflemen. Scott, however, kept his men under firm control and his coolness tempered the hot eagerness that Caulder and the others must have felt. The company's measured responses to the provocations of the day clearly demonstrated the military bearing and the readiness of Bradford's command. Seeing the competently manned firepower trained at them caused the Osages to break off their furious pursuit of the white man, Etienne Vaugine, and the Quapaw brave, both of whom reached the east bank safely.[42] Vaugine and his brother had traded with the storekeeper and the soldiers on a previous mercantile visit to the fort. Knowing and liking the Frenchman, there is no doubt that the troops were but a hair away from triggering a deadly fire on the Osages to protect Vaugine. For the next several days Fort Smith was virtually under siege. Groups of Osages now on the south side of the river hunted in the vicinity of the fort, the sound of their shots and of their signals to one another adding to the daily tension at the fort. Riflemen scouting on the west bank found the Quapaw bodies mutilated beyond the typical scalping of enemy warriors. Their heads were severed. That week, Osage braves killed three hapless Delaware hunters and forced white settlers on Lee Creek to hand over their guns and horses. Word-of-mouth warnings spread quickly down the river. The alarms had elements of truth in it, but like all gossip it had its full share of exaggerations, too. One fleeing settler paddling his canoe downstream as fast as he could shouted that eight hundred Osages had captured Fort Smith. A wild story from a refugee, but certainly, war conditions existed in the Arkansas River valley. The soldiers at the fort were busied with taking care of settlers who had evacuated their farms in seeking protection at the fort. Mad Buffalo's main force had bypassed Fort Smith driving out settlers before them and was riding toward Spadra and the dozens of scattered Cherokee settlements along the river. So great did he deem the peril, Matthew Lyon loaded the Spadra factory's 113 kegs of gunpowder and fifty new rifles into a pirogue and a canoe to move them further downriver.

———————

Within a month's time, however, the temper of war cooled considerably. The Osage braves begin to peel away from Mad Buffalo's band as concerns about their families and the hunt arose to change priorities. Soon, the principal chief of the Osages, Clermont, was once again trying to demonstrate his good faith and make peace with the Cherokees. Clermont had an ally and a strong card to play with the newly established Union Mission, poised to bring civilization to the Osages.[43]

After the siege of Fort Smith, Caulder and the riflemen relaxed a bit, letting down their guard to frequent the post store and reinforce their nerve with a shot or two of whiskey. Perhaps because of stress, Caulder became ill in June, the second and last time that he would go on sick call during his fourteen-year army career. To speed his recovery, Caulder drug himself from his quarters to the sutler's store to buy whiskey. The tiny one-room sutler's store acted as a social center. Soldiers, civilians, visitors, traders, and women bustled about the store every day of the week including Sunday. Conversations over a shot glass surely involved the land bounties that the group of veteran soldiers expected to receive. Joseph Clark, John Brower, Daniel Norman, Martin Turner, and James Turner had filed their applications for 160 acres with the War Department. Surveying of the Arkansas portion of the six million acres that Congress set aside for War of 1812 veterans was not yet underway and the claims would not result in warrants until three years later. But these five as well as other riflemen would eventually receive Arkansas land. An indication that Peter Caulder thought about a career in the army was the fact that he did not join his comrades who apparently stood in line to apply, immediately after their discharge. Peter Caulder applied in December, ten months later than the rest after it became known that the company would be transferred into the Seventh Infantry.[44]

In June 1821, Hugh Glenn's storekeeper, David Stagner, settled the accounts of soldiers in preparation for a change in the sutler's contract in favor of John Rogers and John Nicks. Glenn was being lured to the west.[45] While in Cincinnati, Glenn had arranged a trade venture to Santa Fe in concert with an old acquaintance, a Kentucky gentleman named Jacob Fowler. Fowler with his black servant, Paul, stopped over at Fort Smith in August 1821 before joining Glenn at Three Forks to begin their great wagon trek across the southern plains. Fowler kept a journal that is valuable to historians for its details of the West and for its wonderfully creative spelling. In July, Rogers and

Nicks began their operation. One of their first credit customers was Peter Caulder. He and Susan Loving visited the store on the twenty-first and bought a shot of whiskey. Maybe because of the frightening experiences of April and the desire to forget it, Susan Loving became a regular imbiber at the store, sometimes in company with her husband, and sometimes with Peter Caulder or Adam Lawyer, a young enlisted man who eventually settled in the town of Fort Smith as a civilian. By October, a drinking club had formed that included these friends plus Andrew Calhoun, Joseph Clark, John Inglehart, John Brower, and his wife, Emila. Emila mixed her whiskey with molasses. Occasionally, Joseph Clark joined her in having cocktails, as it were. Thus, John Rogers began his long association with the growing town by making his store more attractive to the women of the post. One wonders if that meant more sweeping of the floor, encouraging less profanity, or even whitewashing the walls as well as serving molasses with the whiskey![46]

White people of various nationalities and language families, blacks both free and slave, and Native Americans of the east and of the plains who spoke different languages frequented the waterways and trails that led to Fort Smith. The ethnically diverse population by 1821 included Martin Turner and James Turner, who owned horses and mules, two of fifty taxpayers in quickly growing Crawford County.[47] With its good water supply, stores, craftsmen, trade goods, crops, livestock, and military presence, Fort Smith beckoned as a natural and exciting gathering spot for travelers, merchants, seekers of fame and fortune. The flag staff, the palisade walls of the fort, the wharf always busy with river traffic and ferries, the huge plain along the river that showed a hundred signs of development, and a number of men and women going about their activities served to quicken the pulse of those just pulling into town. One such visitor, Taylor Polk, a young man from Montgomery County in southwest Arkansas, traveled through "Indian Country" in the early 1820s. While in Fort Smith, he saw an attractive young slave woman. Soon, Polk had purchased the beautiful "brown-skinned" woman named Sally from her Cherokee owner. Polk family oral histories related that for the next few years Sally dwelled in Fort Smith, seeing her master only when he visited. From their liaison, a son, named Peter, was conceived and born in about 1827 probably in Fort Smith. Taylor Polk had a white wife, Prudence Anderson, who bore him three sons. Taylor Polk braved rebuke from Prudence and moved his concubine, Sally, and her infant son, Peter, into a cabin at "the Wilds," the Polk family farm twenty miles below Mount Ida. There, over the next five years Sally and Taylor Polk had two more sons, Frank and John Spencer, both with light features. Their last child, daughter Eliza, had dark skin and other evidence of a strong African genetic strain. The youngest of Taylor Polk's mulatto sons, John Spencer Polk, delivered by Sally in 1833 at the Wilds, is the subject of a family biography entitled *The Seed of Sally Good'n*.[48] Peter Polk and John Spencer Polk, like their brothers, were born into slave status even though their father was a white man.[49]

Sally resided in Fort Smith coincidental with Peter Caulder's years in and around the fort, and since they were both people of color, there is the probability that the two came to know each other. No historical documentation demonstrates such an acquaintanceship, but given names especially among West Africans often are selected to memorialize or honor a person who has established bonds to the parents. It might also be noted that Sally moved to "the Wilds" at about the same time that Peter Caulder left Fort Gibson in May 1827 to homestead in north Arkansas. Peter Caulder may have provided some support to Sally during her time in Fort Smith. At the Washington State Park, an 1820 Rifle Regiment button is on display in the park museum. Such an artifact could have found its way to Hempstead County in many ways. One possibility, however, is that this button was once a memento carried by Sally in remembrance of her halcyon days in Fort Smith.

CHAPTER SIX

Black Yeoman in Arkansas Territory

INDIAN TROUBLES OF 1821 PROMPTED THE SECRETARY OF WAR TO realign troops to ensure order in the West. The Rifle Regiment would be absorbed by larger infantry regiments in order to furnish more manpower for the frontier posts. The reorganization affected Peter Caulder, as the Seventh Infantry was reassigned to Belle Point. Under its commander Lt. Col. Mathew Arbuckle, the Seventh steamed up the Mississippi to the Village at Arkansas. There, because of low water on the Arkansas, Arbuckle transferred his men to keelboats to finish what proved to be an arduous military journey from Fort Scott, Florida Territory, to Fort Smith, Arkansas Territory.

On February 26, 1822, Peter Caulder and his comrades fell out to greet the keelboats loaded with infantrymen who had arrived at the Belle Point landing. The next day, changes in uniform and routines swept over the post. A color guard hoisted the Seventh's regimental flag below Old Glory on the garrison flag pole as the five companies passed in review to the cadence of drums. In a ceremony that signified their transfer, Pvt. Peter Caulder and the riflemen of Bradford's company stood in ranks alongside the musket-toting infantrymen. As historian Edwin Bearss wrote, "the last company of the proud Rifle Regiment was no more."[1]

The 135 newly arrived troops combined with the 70 troops of Bradford's rifle company to significantly increase military presence on the Arkansas frontier. Privates Peter Caulder, Joseph Clark, and Samuel Eaton became a part of Company C of the Seventh Infantry, commanded by Lt. Benjamin L. E. Bonneville. Bonneville was born in France the son of a bookstore owner who had translated Thomas Paine's "Rights of Man." The Bonnevilles counted among their many friends the Marquis de Lafayette, Thomas Paine, Washington Irving,

Robert Fulton, and William Woodruff, founder of the *Arkansas Gazette*. Benjamin graduated from West Point Military Academy in December 1815 at about the same time that twenty-one-year-old Peter Caulder arrived in Louisiana. Six years later, these two reliable army veterans—the officer slowly promoted, the enlisted man not at all—were thrown together for adventures on the Arkansas frontier.

Lt. Col. Mathew Arbuckle acknowledged that Bradford had a tidy, well-managed army post but realized its inadequacy for the two hundred infantrymen who now occupied it. Improvements and additions had to be made, and Arbuckle selected the energetic Bonneville to oversee construction of barracks. Faced with such a task that may have included chimney building, Bonneville came to depend on Peter Caulder. The officer who had transferred to infantry from artillery and the private who had transferred from the rifles gained a working relationship in the Seventh that mirrored the Bradford-Caulder relationship.

Caulder's world soon widened, as did that of Fort Smith. The steamer *Robert Thompson* came chugging up the Arkansas River in March 1822. Long's faulty *Western Engineer* had given way to more reliable shallow draft boats with stern-mounted paddle wheels that could negotiate western rivers. The *Robert Thompson* made the run from Little Rock to Fort Smith in only ten days. Towing keelboats that carried provisions for the fort and with a paymaster on board, the little steamer generated huge excitement as it pulled into the landing, the first of its kind to make it to Fort Smith. Faster freight and faster communication now reduced the isolation, and the anonymity, in which frontier soldiers like Caulder had served. The *Robert Thompson* made two more voyages up the river before low June water slowed her. Governor Miller and Colonel Arbuckle, passengers on the third and last trip of the spring, disembarked just below Fort Smith to finish their journey overland while the little steamer eased its way around the sandbars to Belle Point landing to discharge cargo. With the time of transit between Little Rock and Fort Smith reduced from twenty-seven to ten days, the river became a superhighway.

By the summer of 1822, Peter Caulder saw multiple signs that Fort Smith had changed from the relaxed garrison that Thomas

Nuttall so enjoyed in 1819 and that had welcomed Bell and Long in 1820. From the sixty or so troops in the rifle company, more than two hundred infantrymen now filled the avenues of the post. A tent city spread beyond the palisades. Large fatigue parties marched out to chop down more and more trees further and further away and quarried rocks for building. Work gangs of soldiers set about planting more crops and cutting more hay.

Huge new commissary stores were ordered from the quartermaster. Infantry uniforms and musket ordinance arrived from New Orleans. Fort Smith was to be the main depot of the army if war broke out with Indians in the West.[2] Peace keeping on the frontier had taken on a different meaning. Though Miller and Arbuckle still sought a treaty between the Cherokees and the Osages, white settlement had definitely altered the complexion of the Arkansas frontier and consequently the army's role. The rapidly growing white population mounted pressure on Indian-held lands in Arkansas. Although the government listened to leaders of the tribes about white encroachment and occasionally removed white interlopers, actuality was, as everyone understood, that the army was being beefed up to discourage Indian reprisals against whites.

In donning the thin uniform pants of the infantryman, Pvt. Peter Caulder retained a bit of status as an ex-rifleman. He and other veterans were dispatched for "special frontier missions."[3] Soldiers in other companies viewed such immunity from post routines with a touch of jealousy, but none of the infantrymen in the Seventh could match Caulder's experience or tracking skills in the wilds of Arkansas and Oklahoma. At the end of June, Caulder received his first extended detached duty since joining the Seventh. Bradford, Miller, and Arbuckle had put efforts into arranging a council for the Osage and Cherokee leaders to be held in July at Fort Smith. In late June, Bonneville sent Caulder, Samuel Eaton, and John Brower on a mission, most likely to ride through the Three Forks region and read Osage intentions.

The summer of 1822 brought sweltering weather to the frontier post. Temperatures shot to the high nineties and drought conditions withered the grass, raising concern about the forage and grazing for

Indian ponies that would be needed for attendees of the July conference. Game was nowhere to be found. The hot spell may have encouraged the spirit of confrontation that seemed to grip Fort Smith in 1822. A Captain Woolley and Commissary Officer John Clark feuded and exchanged hot words and threats. Lt. Richard J. Wash thrashed Surgeon Thomas Lawson in a fistfight. On a June morning in 1822, two of Caulder's fellow soldiers on a detail cutting logs had words over money. Pvt. Daniel McGranie had been drinking even before the fatigue party left the post. As Pvt. Benjamin Clark turned to hew a log, McGranie swung his broad axe and almost severed Clark's head from his body.[4] McGranie stood trial for the murder in civil court at Little Rock. The civilian jury acquitted him for reason of temporary insanity and reprimanded him to the stockade in Fort Smith.

A bright spot came when the Grand Council convened at the fort on July 30. After a fortnight of bargaining, posturing, and issuing mild threats, sixteen Little Osage chiefs and sub-chiefs (including Mad Buffalo and Clermont) and four Cherokee leaders (including Wat Webber, who had led the most recent Cherokee slaughtering raid on Osage villages) placed their marks on what amounted to a nonaggression pact between the tribes. Cherokee leaders James Rogers and John Martin, the only literate chiefs in attendance, signed the document with their full names. Governor Miller and Colonel Arbuckle witnessed the treaty along with the agents for both tribes and Reverend Epaphras Chapman of the Union mission to the Little Osages. The tribes disavowed the seeking of armed revenge and agreed to turn over issues to the United States government or their agents for resolve. Exhausted by his labors, weakened by the heat, and bereaved with the sudden death of his young nephew, James Miller, whom he left buried at Fort Smith, the good governor must have thought the treaty to be a capstone for his career as territorial governor and a great spot for a graceful exit from a state that he served well but never learned to like. He departed for good in June 1823 for New Hampshire.

Miller had once written his wife that Arkansans lived on "bread, meat, grease, and coffee." Peter Caulder undoubtedly fared better with his army rations that included vegetables from the post garden. Caulder and his circle of friends, the Lovings, John and Emily Brower, Joseph Clark, and civilians Martin Turner, James Turner, and perhaps Sally Polk shared time together when the soldiers were off duty. Income beyond army pay came from hiring out services, selling pelts and whiskey, and in the case of Susan Loving, taking in washing and sewing. Susan Loving spoke her mind and once refused to pay the store clerk when she thought herself overcharged. She exchanged sewing and washing services to settle her bills at the store. The amount of fatigue work kept the eight washerwomen who had accompanied Arbuckle's Seventh Infantry to Fort Smith busy with uniforms. In addition to washing, one of those women, Anne Miller, had been thought to sell whiskey and female favors to the soldiers. The life of the women matched that of the men in its rigor without some of the benefits provided by the army—clothing for instance. Infantrymen drew cotton and wool overalls and jackets. When soldiers gave away their issue clothing, they had to pay the government out of their pockets. In October 1822, the quartermaster officer docked Peter Caulder for a great coat and a fatigue frock. Perhaps Caulder had lent them out to a friend. Caulder received permission from Bonneville to take a hunting trip in order to accumulate furs and pelts to sell and pay off his bill. Caulder had gained the respect of Bonneville, who allowed him this small perk.

Arbuckle sent Bonneville to Batesville in order to cash a large army draft and bring back the currency to Fort Smith. The government land office there in Batesville was often solvent. An enlisted man guided Bonneville, probably Peter Caulder, who had made the cross-country journey to the White River before. While in Batesville, Bonneville heard complaints from citizens about Cherokee threats, and he decided to tarry in the White River vicinity to determine the intentions of Cherokees there.

The young lieutenant and Private Caulder, if he were with Bonneville as seems likely, were told by whites in Independence County that "there were at least 9,000 [hostile Indians] above them at the forks of the White River" who in several instances "openly robbed the settlers" and threatened their stock. A crafty troublemaker,

Takatoka, stalked the area and Bonneville suspected his intentions of rousing Arkansas Cherokees to action against usurpers. On his return, "passing through the Cherokee nation," Bonneville met with Cherokee chief John Rogers, whom Caulder knew from the Red River trip in 1819. Caulder may have introduced Bonneville to Rogers because something set the stage for a warm exchange between them and a change in attitudes occurred. Takatoka moved his band out of Arkansas and into the Red River valley. Before Bonneville's visit, Arbuckle thought that he might need to "rush soldiers to the White" and had prepared to recall four Seventh Infantry companies from Fort Jesup to Fort Smith (and Jesup commander Lt. Col. Zachary Taylor would have been recalled to Arkansas, explosive because Arbuckle and Taylor were foes, competitive in the army hierarchy).[5] But Arkansas got quieter after Bonneville's self-imposed mission, and the Louisiana detachment of the Seventh Infantry stayed put.[6] Instead, warfare in the Indian Nations arose to monopolize Arbuckle's concerns and eventually cloud Caulder's army career.

Back in Fort Smith for the winter, Peter Caulder kept to his routines for the army that surely included tracking and hunting game animals to help with the post food supply. The deer that he brought in over the back of a pack mule provided soldiers with protein and clothing and moccasin material. Caulder knew how to locate bee trees and gather honey, another valuable commodity. On occasion when his hound treed a mother raccoon in a hollow tree, Caulder might have rescued its young to distribute as pets to soldiers, their wives, or their children.

The sutler store maintained an inventory of dressed deerskins and incurred a lively trade in that particular article useful in so many ways on the frontier. John Nicks and John Rogers, who expanded trade at Fort Smith with the Indian nations, now operated the store and tavern, which had moved to a larger building on the post grounds. Caulder kept the company of the Lovings, John and Emila Brower, Joseph Clark, and Daniel Norman. These old friends, who had stuck together since the Carlisle days, met after duty hours at the store that served as a tavern and in their dwellings. One of their Carlisle companions, David Mullins, died at the fort on March 21,

1822. He was twenty-four when malaria or bloody flux or dysentery (killers of soldiers all) extinguished his short life. Mullins occasionally had enjoyed a shot of whiskey with Caulder, who had known the North Carolina-born Mullins since they joined the Third Rifles together in 1814. Caulder no doubt attended his comrade's burial service maybe even as one of the honor guard of former riflemen who fired a musket salute to Mullins as his casket was lowered into its grave probably in the soldiers' graveyard along the east bank of the Poteau River. Mullins had been a reliable trooper who often joined Caulder in after-duty rounds at the sutler's store and himself anticipated settling on his bounty land in Arkansas, the patent to which he had received in 1820.[7]

At gatherings where songs were sung and a jar of whiskey was passed around, Caulder and his Carlisle mates were joined by ex-riflemen John Inglehart, Andrew Calhoun, Samuel Eaton, and Adam Lawyer. Among this group, enthusiastic conversations about pioneering on bounty lands ensued. Calhoun, like Mullins and Eaton, had already redeemed their warrants for Arkansas land. Even as the soldiers and the women who shared times with them talked, government surveyors and crew tramped through the forests of north Arkansas measuring distances by means of chains and blazing section lines. The surveyor not only marked off lands, but evaluated them as well. His trained eye determined, or was supposed to determine, if the sections were fit for cultivation of crops. Although many surveys were done, the General Land Office was way behind in issuing warrants to some applicants like Caulder and Clark. More than a million acres in Arkansas would be available and with a notification and a warrant number, veterans could appear at a Federal Land Office (there was one in Little Rock and another in Batesville) and receive a patent (original deed) on the one hundred sixty acres set aside for them by an act of Congress. In the winter of 1823–24, Caulder was twenty-nine years old, an unmarried, mature, well-liked, skillful man who had roamed Arkansas Territory as a soldier-guide for six years. But now the army was changing and so was Caulder. Feelings of independence stirred inside him, and perhaps in contradiction, a yearning for a new kind of responsibility.

Caulder and the riflemen who were absorbed into the Seventh Infantry were distinguished and honorable soldiers, and so was their new military unit. But, in 1822, the Seventh Infantry, a regiment with seven companies under the command of Col. Mathew Arbuckle was, typical of the whole peacetime army, beset with personnel and payroll problems. Feuding officers and difficulty in recruiting young men to fill the ranks marred the regiment's effectiveness. To man his companies, Arbuckle sent officers to recruit the Mississippi Valley from St. Louis to Natchez. Recruiters offered steady work and the benefits of a wholesome diet, housing, clothing, and medical care to recent immigrants and to those native-born lads who were seeking an alternative to "unpleasant conditions at home."[8] Still, manpower pickings were slim. The garrison at Fort Smith began to reflect a decline in the work ethic and commitment of enlisted soldiers. Desertions were up, and so were the number of troops on sick call and confined to the stockade. Arbuckle wrote that the "easily available liquor obtained from citizens who have settled near us" made the situation worse. He foresaw better conditions for his garrison if it could be moved further west away from settlement temptations. Only one Carlisle veteran was a noncommissioned officer, Bennett Webb, who had achieved corporal's stripes in 1815. Of the sixty transfers from the Rifle Regiment, only three enlisted men ever ranked higher than private in the Seventh. Caulder, Clark, Loving, and Inglehart were never promoted above the rank of private. Samuel Eaton, once a sergeant under Ballard, lost his stripes.[9] Perhaps in the case of Caulder and Clark, their dark skin and former racial designation precluded promotion to sergeant or even corporal, even if they had aspired to that sort of command position.

Despite the snub of rank, Caulder exercised some privileges after his transfer to the Seventh, based, no doubt, on his skills as a guide, hunter, tracker, and chimney builder. Caulder and his friend Clark were satisfied to be under the command of an officer and gentleman like Bonneville. No doubt Caulder had heard the gossip that Arbuckle wanted to move the regiment further west, a possibility that disturbed the private who had come to find the people and surroundings of Arkansas much to his liking.

The disturbing rumor was about to become true. While Caulder and Bonneville were in the White River country, new troubles with Osage raiders broke out along the Red River. North of the Red, a professional trapper, Curtis Welburn, and his group of seven had joined the Barraque party, made up of two French traders from the Village at Arkansas and their twelve Quapaw hunting partners. Osages, incensed not only because this large group hunted and trapped on their territories, but also flaunted their trespass by laughing, shouting, and singing, stalked and then attacked, killing five of the loudmouths including Welburn. A haggard and bleary Barraque, no longer so merry, straggled into Fort Smith on November 29, 1823, and reported the massacre to Arbuckle. Barraque swore that in addition to those killed and scalped, four more men were missing along with thirty-two horses and four thousand dollars' worth of goods.[10] When such snippets of news about murders of whites reached the enlisted men, they had little doubt about Arbuckle's and the army's intention to insert them into the heart of Osage country. The order to move the garrison west reached Fort Smith on April 2, 1824.

Arbuckle, who was considerate of women fellow travelers, may have allowed Susan Loving and Emila Brower to board one of the two keelboats that carried the regiment's baggage up the Arkansas to the new location. That is, if the soldiers' wives did not remain behind at Fort Smith to tend to what fixed belongings they had acquired. Their husbands, William and John, in company with their two hundred fellow infantrymen started for the Three Forks on Friday, April 9, their goods loaded on wagons and pack horses. Most of the troops went "overland along the well-marked trace that skirted the north bank of the Arkansas." Peter Caulder was not among them. Arbuckle had assigned Bonneville and a skeleton crew of soldiers to stay at Fort Smith, guarding the stores left behind and protecting the near-deserted post. Bonneville had selected Caulder and Eaton to remain along with twelve other soldiers.[11]

Caulder and Eaton, who had been together on the long search for the Bell party deserters, hunted game for the soldiers' table. Caulder did not relish moving further west and may have called on his friendship with Bonneville to prolong his stay at Fort Smith. He may have needed that kind of pull because Caulder would have been valuable to Arbuckle. No one else in the Seventh knew the Three Forks region any better than he did.

Caulder may have had his mind set on the White River hills and looked for an opportunity to go east rather than west. Caulder no doubt questioned Samuel Eaton about the procedure of transferring a bounty land warrant into a deed. Eaton had gotten his patent for Arkansas land in 1820 while on duty with Ballard in Missouri, before these two were transferred to Fort Smith.[12] He outlined the procedure to his friend, which excited Caulder. The prospects of walking on property he could call his own must have dominated Caulder's thoughts in 1824 and punctuated his chats with Lane, Copeland, and Eaton while the soldiers attended to their duties at the near-deserted post.

Peter Caulder became a civilian again on June 4, 1824, a month after his old friend and mentor, William Bradford, had resigned his commission. Having served in the United State Army for two consecutive five-year terms—in the Third Rifles, the Rifle Regiment, and in the Seventh Infantry—Caulder now was granted an honorable discharge declining an invitation to reenlist. Seven days later, his friend John Inglehart joined him as a dischargee. After placing their local affairs in order, the twenty-nine-year-old Caulder and, Inglehart, his forty-year-old white companion from the state of New Jersey, departed Fort Smith, traveling together on horses for a long ride across the territory. Their mood must have been elevated with mustering-out pay in their saddlebags and a spirit of independence infusing their every thought and action. The two men may have split up at Little Rock where Inglehart picked up his warrant for Pulaski County land while Caulder continued on to Batesville.

There, at the land office, Caulder presented his discharge from the army. The clerk had his warrant number on file at the land office. President James Monroe's name appeared on the preprinted form dated March 22, 1824. The warrant allowed the clerk to issue a patent to Caulder for one hundred sixty acres less than a day's ride north of Batesville in what is now Sharp County. Caulder may have

James Monroe

President of the United States of America,

TO ALL TO WHOM THESE PRESENTS SHALL COME, GREETING:

Know Ye, That, in pursuance of the Acts of Congress appropriating and granting Land to the late Army of the United States, passed on and since the sixth day of May, 1812, *Peter Caulder* having deposited in the General Land-office a Warrant in *his* favor, numbered *24899* there is granted unto *the said Peter Caulder* late a *Priv. in Bradford's Co. of Riflemen & to his heirs* — a certain Tract of Land, containing *160 acres* — being the *North West* of Section *twenty nine* of Township *fifteen north* in Range *five West* in the Tract appropriated (by the Acts aforesaid) for Military Bounties, in the Territory of *Arkansas* : TO HAVE AND TO HOLD the said *Quarter* Section of Land, with the appurtenances thereof, unto the said *Peter Caulder* and to *his* heirs and assigns for ever.

IN TESTIMONY WHEREOF, I have caused these Letters to be made patent, and the Seal of the General Land-Office to be hereunto affixed. Given under my Hand, at the City of Washington, this twenty seven day of March in the Year of our Lord one thousand eight hundred and twenty four and of the Independence of the United States of America the forty. eight

By the President,

Commissioner of the General Land-Office.

Peter Caulder's Bounty Land Warrant granting him 160 acres for his service in the War of 1812. Located in the southeast corner of today's Sharp County, Caulder's tract adjoined that of Joseph Clark.

known at that point that Joseph Clark's bounty land adjoined his own and his excitement must have been great. Though he might have felt a tingle in his neck hairs when whites whom he encountered gave him a questioning or hostile glance, Caulder's innate pride-in-self gave him every hope about his future as a yeoman pioneer.[13]

When Caulder reached his land in late summer, he found not the well-watered plain that he may have expected. Today, the only stream that flows across the property that was once his is known as Dry Fork because it vanishes during the summer. Congress had intended to set aside bounty lands that could be cultivated by the claimants. In an age when farms supported the citizenry, a barren tract was worthless. Indeed, the surveyor of Caulder's bounty land had specified in his 1817 report that the "land [is] gently roleing fit for cultivation timber oak & hickory & elm undergroth same (some) hazle & bryars." At first, other than the lack of water, the barrenness of his acreage might have gone unrecognized by Caulder. Sleeping under the stars on his own property, Caulder was no doubt euphoric. He was alone and had only to hunt to feed himself and his hound and find fodder and grain for his horse. He may have chopped enough poles to build a hut and even started digging a well. Caulder had always been a hard worker and knew how to use the raw materials and the tools of the frontier. The region was sparsely populated with no record of any other black people nearby. White neighbors were scarce as well.[14] Caulder would have welcomed seeing Joseph Clark that first summer, but Clark was months away from his discharge and miles and miles away at Cantonment Gibson. By late summer, a combination of loneliness, the lack of water, and the hopelessness of farming on his land may have discouraged Caulder at his homestead. A re-survey of his 160 acres in 1853 by surveyor John Garretson included these remarks: "but no regular survey of the township could ever have been made [because] the land on this line which must have been reported fit for cultivation in order to become military bounty land is rocky & gravelly hills entirely unfit for cultivation under all the circumstances."[15] Caulder, sadly, may have come to a similar conclusion about his bounty land and began to think about greener pastures. One day, he mounted his horse and started west again.

In this summer of his independence, Caulder decided to visit the Little North Fork of the White River where David Hall had settled. Following trails along the river from Batesville north, the ex-rifleman rode up "fingers of civilization." The territory had gained in population, commerce, and civil organization in the seven years since young Henry Schoolcraft had made his 1818–19 winter excursion through the same area and counted only a few cabins while discounting the settlers' lifestyles. Caulder's 1824 route cut through forests still well stocked with wild beasts. Yet, cultivated fields, grazing cattle, men at work logging, and infants playing on cabin porches, telltales of the recurring American story of human encroachment were interspersed upon the wilderness.

As Peter Caulder dismounted at the farmstead of David Hall, he must have felt entirely welcome. The two men of color shared a yeoman's dream of raising a family on land they themselves had cleared, worked, and nurtured, the difference being that Hall was doing just that and Caulder faced a postponement. The North Carolina-born Hall, at age forty-one, was in the prime of life. Muscular, ambitious, and congenial, he set an enviable pattern for all pioneers, white or black, in the White River hills. His pretty wife, Sarah, energetic herself at age twenty-nine, would devote her life to David, to their many children, and to life on the banks of the White. Caulder most likely stayed with the Halls, who would have been harvesting corn and ear marking pigs at that time of year. Caulder, given his long observation of young soldiers, could have immediately recognized the brightness and potential of Hall's strapping eighteen-year-old relative, John. Twelve-year-old David Hall must have followed Caulder about, fascinated with the visitor's rifle and his ability to crease a squirrel out of a tall oak tree without damaging the meat. One day in the future, Caulder named his own first son David. Caulder learned that the rising belles of the Hall family were the precocious twin daughters, Eliza and Margaret. Even at a tender age, Eliza must have flirted a bit with Peter Caulder. The good-natured young man may have teased back. Little Eliza made such an impression that Caulder would forgo romancing anyone else, biding his time until Eliza grew into womanhood. Six years later he would ask for her hand in marriage.

An older sister, Rachel, and a younger one, Harriet, plus two hefty pre-teen boys, Joseph and James, rounded out the Hall family, adding spice and glee to the cabin. After suppertime, the children pelted Caulder with questions and listened in quiet awe to his stories about the army, about the Osages, about exploring, about Fort Smith and the roar of six-pound cannon. David and John Hall accompanied Caulder up the seasonally low river on horseback, scouting out unclaimed lands where a man could clear land, farm, and raise a family. No doubt Peter Caulder inspected Hall's still and the men swapped friendly barbs about the fine art of corn whiskey making. As he wrapped himself in his bedroll at night, the whip-poor-will cry and the lowing of Hall's cattle ranging on the ridge above may have heightened the idyllic feeling that Caulder had about this place and made him realize that despite the disappointment of his bounty land, a pioneering life still held its charm for him.

But the timing was not quite correct. Something was drawing Caulder back to the army. After awhile on the White River, Caulder said his goodbyes and maybe endured a hug from Eliza. He had decided to return to Fort Smith and the Seventh Infantry. The army was something that Peter Caulder knew and it offered him a steady income. The poor bounty land had demonstrated that he had to find land worth improving in order to sustain himself and a family.

Caulder reached Belle Point during the October turn of leaves. When he and his horse, both covered with dust, ambled into the fort, he found a few soldiers still on guard. Bonneville had been transferred to the main body at Cantonment Gibson, replaced by Lt. Thomas Johnston. Caulder made the rounds of the settlement searching for old companions, maybe seeking out Sally Polk to catch up on events of her life. Martin and James Turner apparently were still residing in Fort Smith. Caulder told them about his poor land. He may have contrasted the excellent farm of David Hall with what existed on the bounty lands. Caulder's vivid stories convinced the Turners to visit the White River hill country themselves.

For Caulder, though, the White River would have to wait. On October 3, 1824, he stood before Lieutenant Johnston and took an oath of enlistment for another five-year hitch. Maj. John Rogers paid

Caulder a six-dollar enlistment bonus. Physician C. A. Farley examined Caulder, finding him "free of bodily defects" and "qualified to perform the duty of a soldier."[16] Caulder donned a reissued Seventh Infantry uniform, but he did not immediately travel to Gibson, staying instead at Fort Smith, one of four enlisted men who garrisoned the fort, an arrangement that suited him.

People were moving into Crawford County. In the last five miles of his ride, Caulder passed more than a hundred homesteads. New settlers cut trees to build their lean-tos and start-up huts, while early residents added on to their dwellings and to their cattle herds. Fort Smith horsemen and women may have already established a racetrack to show off fast mounts. Probably a tanner had set up a business for processing cowhides. George Riley, an ex-rifleman, repaired guns and made door hinges and butcher knives in his smithy. The army left a steam-powered sawmill near the Poteau River under the control of John Rogers, who also had the franchise to operate the army's ferry. The sawmill produced boards for building houses, barns, and boats. By 1822, Crawford County had a sheriff, a clerk, and a tax roll with eighty taxpayers. The county clerk, James Wilson, recorded riding horses, carriages, neat cattle, stud horses, and slaves owned by the citizens, and applied a value to each dwelling house depending on its size and location. With no carriages assessed it appeared that no wagon maker had yet established a shop in Fort Smith or that the roads were so bad that carriages were useless. Major Bradford, the biggest taxpayer in the county, paid $11.17 on his thirty-three head of cattle, six horses, and four slaves.[17] Eight years later, the number of county taxpayers had risen to 448, and they paid $717.50 in taxes while the number of slaves jumped from 13 to 198. Steady population growth marked the decade of the 1820s in Fort Smith even as the army left town.

A presidential election with a bewildering array of five candidates confronted voters of the twenty-four states in the fall of 1824. Residents of territories, although under the jurisdiction of the United States government, did not vote in federal elections and as an enlisted soldier and a black man, Caulder did not meet the Arkansas Territory qualifications for voting, anyway. So, he may have had only passing interest in which one of the white men nominated would be elected.[18] The election, though, set off a chain reaction that radically altered the practice of politics in the young country and halted any chance that a free black man like Caulder had of ever voting. With no candidate receiving a majority in the electoral college after it met in December, a majority in the House of Representatives voted for John Quincy Adams, who finished second, as the president-elect.[19] When Adams in turn named Henry Clay, the last-place candidate, as his secretary of state, the Era of Good Feeling in American politics came to an end. Andrew Jackson, the top vote getter, lost the most and was the angriest at the House vote, which he attributed to a "corrupt bargain" between Adams and Clay. Determined to campaign in politics with the same vengeance as he displayed as an Indian fighter, Jackson revolutionized party organization. Free black people like Peter Caulder would be adversely affected.

With the loss of the army garrison, the culture of Fort Smith changed. Civil jurisdiction meant less visibility for the diverse groups that had shared in shaping life at the fort. The black enlisted men, a part of the community, tangibly had temporized local gossip about race and slavery. Now slaves appeared all over the town. Crawford County slave owners did not have the kind of property nor the financial backgrounds that in other parts of the state led to huge plantations and gangs of slaves and ultimately to a "slave society." Nevertheless, a number of townspeople acquired some slaves, enough so that the community began the process of defining itself as white. By 1829, Mark Bean had sixteen slaves, the largest holding in the county, and voters elected him to the Arkansas General Assembly. Benjamin Moore had nine slaves, and Harry A. Quesenberry six to rank two and three on the list of Crawford County's largest slave owners.[20] With fewer free black men, and with more slaves to control, the people of Fort Smith may have been further susceptible to antiblack gossip. Yet evidence of dissent exists, at least among army veterans, to the disrespect whites of the era generally leveled toward blacks. After Adam Lawyer ended his army service, he remained in Fort Smith and lived near the house of John Cooley, a free colored man married to a white woman. The two couples were about the same age and both had young children. Lawyer's two youngsters, no doubt, played with neighborhood boys and girls, including the three mulatto children of Cooley and his wife. John Rogers, the former army officer and land speculator, who signed in Caulder at his 1824 reenlistment and who is referred to by some historians as "the Father of Fort Smith," owned horses, twenty head of cattle, and considerable property. But Rogers used hired hands to help him with the chores of his enterprises and refused to buy slaves for this work. John Hestilow, who had known Caulder since the 1815 Carlisle days, was one of the few ex-riflemen who remained in Fort Smith and became a propertied taxpayer—but not a slave owner.[21] The capable and likeable Peter Caulder and the mulattoes who gathered in Fort Smith may have, for awhile, tempered racist attitudes and kept the community inclusive of dark-skin people.

Over the winter of 1824–25, Caulder rejoined his company at Fort Gibson, reporting once again to Bonneville. Being at Gibson probably did not make him joyous, but Peter Caulder had always been a dependable soldier willing to accept the assignments that fell his way. Bonneville utilized the hunting and scouting skills of Caulder and sent him on "detached services in the vicinity of Fort Gibson." He would soon return again to the Red River valley. Gen. Winfield Scott had recommended that the Seventh Infantry establish a cantonment there to stop slave smuggling and Indian raids. Migration pressure by eastern Indians, Arkansas Cherokees, and whites acted as a catalyst for outbreaks of violence by the Osages and other incoming tribes. Arbuckle complied with Scott's request, naming the newly established cantonment after the army paymaster, Nathan Towson. The strategic post on the Kiamichi necessitated a road connecting it with Fort Smith, the Towson Road. Caulder, who had traveled the route to the Red River, may have lent his knowledge of the terrain to the officers who were planning and mapping the route.

By 1825, Caulder had few close associates left in the army. His mates from Carlisle having one by one been discharged. Many new recruits filled the ranks of the Seventh. One rifleman and friend of Caulder who had remained in the army, Joseph Clark, served far away from Gibson at Fort Jesup near Baton Rouge. Caulder might have

enjoyed the friendship of Bonneville, who kept the plays of Jean
Racine on his bookshelf in his cabin on officers' row at Gibson.
Racine was not at the time translated into English so Bonneville kept
his native language honed by reading a leading playwright of France.
No doubt he enjoyed speaking French to the occasional French trapper on the Arkansas and to the Creoles whom he encountered.[22]
Bonneville, who preferred not to spend time with his fellow officers
at their incessant card games, may have been drawn to Caulder, a
quiet yet adventuresome man. Perhaps Caulder had at times listened
to Bonneville read aloud as the two had traveled through the territorial countrysides. If the two men did have a bond that came from
days and nights spent together on the trail, Bonneville interrupted it
by an extended furlough. In June 1825, Bonneville absented himself
from Gibson for seventeen months. He traveled to New York in order
to join the Marquis de Lafayette for a voyage across the Atlantic to
France, their homeland. Lafayette had been touring the United States
to celebrate the fiftieth anniversary of the American Revolution.
After several months of triumphant but exhausting stagecoach and
steamboat travel to visit virtually all the major cities in this country,
in the summer of 1825 the sixty-nine-year-old French aristocrat and
national hero of two countries sailed for home in the company of Lt.
Benjamin Bonneville.[23]

During Bonneville's absence, Caulder became restless in the
army. The Seventh Infantry at Gibson divided its routines into
mounted patrols, hunting parties, courier services, marches, drill, gardening, logging, quarrying, construction of barracks, road building,
stevedore labor, animal husbandry, manufacturing, supplying water,
grave digging, cooking, and cleaning duties. Caulder's duties probably included patrols, hunting, and quarrying, but he had received
no increase in his monthly pay over the years and still needed credit
from the sutler occasionally. With the labor demands on soldiers'
time at the new post so severe, Caulder probably did not have any
opportunities for extra duties or furloughs to pad his income. In 1827,
Caulder turned thirty-two. Sleeping on the ground became less
enjoyable as his years increased. For small pleasures, Caulder drank
a moderate amount of whiskey, chewed tobacco, and dreamed of the

youthful Eliza and of the fertile lands in the White River hills. In late May 1827, Caulder drastically acted on his dreams.

In April and May 1827 two steamboats each with thirty new recruits, "solid men" the *Gazette* called them, arrived at Gibson to beef up the undermanned regiment. The new men came to a peaceful Fort Gibson. The Osages in the vicinity were on their best behavior. On the sur-face, reenforcements seemed good news, but not enough to overcome the growing dissatisfaction of Peter Caulder with the army. On the night of May 19, 1827, Caulder slipped away from his quarters at the cantonment. He carried his belongings, perhaps his rifle, powder, bul-lets, bedroll, and rations. His career as a guide had taught Caulder how to pack effectively for the trail. At the riverbank, a fellow soldier from C Company, James Aikins, clad in a gray military jacket and trousers, met Caulder in a whispered greeting.[24] From its mooring, Caulder dragged the post mail boat into the water. The two men with hearts pounding, pushed off, scrambled aboard, and took up the paddles to steer the boat to the far side of the fast-moving current of the Arkansas River. Caulder and Aikins had to pass below the sentries. They glided by as soundless as possible, for the two soldiers were unauthorized in their leaving. Caulder's loyal hound may have followed the boat, plunging through the thick cane that lined the riverbank. Caulder and Aikins sped downriver, pushing the skiff with steady oar strokes and perhaps hoisting a sail to take advantage of a westerly breeze. Caulder wanted to put miles behind him and Gibson. On top of deserting, Caulder had left a $11.27 debt to the sutlers, a sum that he knew Nicks and Rogers would not forgive easily.[25]

Caulder's desertion so displeased Colonel Arbuckle that the next day he had his adjutant, Joseph Phillips, write an advertisement and send it to the *Arkansas Gazette*. Arbuckle offered sixty dollars plus expenses for the apprehension and return of these two soldiers. The *Gazette* published the reward notice, alerting the civilian commu-nity.[26] Although desertions commonly occurred at Gibson, Arbuckle posted no reward nor advertised for civilian assistance to return any other wayward soldier. Indeed, troops often "joined from desertion," sometimes in the same month from which they had illegally departed. They simply took a breather from the army.[27] Arbuckle apparently knew that Caulder had determined to runaway permanently. The only other deserters advertised for in the *Arkansas Gazette* were those from the 1820 Bell expedition. Because those three soldiers had stolen horses and valuables and jeopardized an expedition that was already in a perilous condition, Bradford sought civilian help in securing their return as well as sending his own men to search for them. During the War of 1812, army units sent notices of deserters to newspapers in attempting to deal with severe desertion problems. The peacetime army, however, viewed the whole subject differently. Arbuckle's reaction to this desertion is as out of the normal as it was for Caulder to commit the act itself.

Caulder may have anticipated that his unauthorized departure would raise this sort of row. Speeding the skiff downriver through the night, Caulder and Aikins could have reached Fort Smith early on May 20 before their absence went fully noticed at Gibson. Nevertheless, they had to be wary of unwanted attention around the ferry at Belle Point landing. In Fort Smith, Caulder probably went straight to the cabin of Martin Turner to obtain a horse, or he could have called on former army buddies now civilian residents of the town, John Inglehart, Samuel Eaton, or John Hestilow. His old comrades would surely have been helpful in aiding his flight. For Caulder and Aikins to boat beyond Fort Smith would have been their easiest and fastest way of travel, but also would have risked encounter with officers or traders who might be suspicious of two soldiers in a fast-moving skiff. With his self-confident nature, Caulder had calmly mastered hostile questions before and might invent a plausible story to get him by. After a decade in the territory, much of it spent in detached duty beyond the garrison, Caulder might have had a recognizable face to river travelers. Discouraged by the army and now a fugitive from it, Caulder sought a refuge. He headed, probably overland, for the Little North Fork.

...W... Surgery at Little Rock.—His shop is
in the frame building, opposite N. Peay's
tavern, where he may be found unless absent
on professional business.

Little Rock, April 24, 1827.

Cash Store.

...ers have just received by the
Catawba, and opened in the
...ied by Byrne & Overall, an
...ockery & Glass Ware, con-

	Pitchers
s	Enamelled do.
	Painted round Tea
	Pots
	do. Tea Cups and
	Saucers
$	Liverpool blue printed
	Plates
Plates	do. Twifflers
...s	do. Muffins
...	do. Bowls & Pitchers
...rs	do. Ewers & Basins
...	do. Tea Cups and
...eens	Saucers
...nd	Motto Cans, &c. &c.

Decanters; Knob'd & Flint
and plain Wine Glasses; 2
...Ware.
...est Novels; Letter and F.
...uills; a complete assortment
...icines; 10 kegs White Lead;
...se Vermilion; Linseed Oil;
...Porter; 5 do. Newark racked
assorted Wool Hats: Knives
...llocks; Table Spoons, and

...will be sold low for *Cash*,
&c.
...always on hand, at 12½ cents
...S. W. GRAHAM & Co.
June 5, 1827.   23-tf.

...tion of Taxes,

Pulaski County.
...s hereby given, that, pursuant

Sixty Dollars Reward.

DESERTED, from this Post, on the
night of the 19th inst., PETER
CAULDER, and JAMES AIKINS, private soldiers of the 7th Regiment, United
States Infantry.

CAULDER is 52 years of age, five feet
nine inches high, of dark complexion, dark
eyes and hair, born in the State of South
Carolina, and by occupation a farmer.

AIKINS is 24 years of age, five feet ten
inches high, of fair complexion, dark eyes
and hair, born in Pendleton, in the State
of South Carolina, and by occupation a
farmer.

The above reward of SIXTY DOL-
LARS, will be paid for the apprehension and
delivery of the above described deserters
(or THIRTY DOLLARS for either) at this
Post, or to any Officer of the Army. The
Reward to include all expenses attending
apprehension and delivery.

By order of Col. Arbuckle.
JOS. PHILLIPS,
FORT GIBSON,   *Adj. 7th Inf.*
May 20th, 1827.
P. S. It is believed that the above named
deserters passed this Post, down the river,
last night, in a skiff.
May 22, 1827.   23-2w.

Private Entertainment.

THE subscriber, respectfully informs his
old friends and customers, that he has
removed to the house recently occupied by
Col. A. H. Sevier, which he has fitted up for
a house of PRIVATE ENTERTAINMENT, for
the accommodation of Travellers and regular
Boarders, and solicits a share of the patronage
of the public.   N. PEAY.

Arkansas Gazette *advertisement for Peter Caulder and his fugitive partner, James Aikins. The ad appeared on page three of the June 12, 1827, edition.*

CHAPTER SEVEN

Keeper of a "Severe Pack of Dogs"

WE CAN ONLY SURMISE THE REASONS BEHIND PETER CAULDER'S desertion and why Arbuckle resented it more than he did others under his command. Arbuckle knew of the previous characterization of Caulder as a "colored man," but that fact had long been ignored in the frontier army. Still, Private Caulder might have been at some odds with new arrivals to the frontier more geared to color rather than ability in people as a measure. In the late 1820s at Gibson, a tendency toward intolerance may have been underway.

The Seventh at Cantonment Gibson had filled its ranks with young men for whom the War of 1812 resounded but little. Caulder did not outrank these new soldiers and when not on detached duty, he worked shoulder to shoulder with them on fatigue details. Normally in Caulder's case familiarity resulted in respect and friendship. But with younger, more desperate men, being in close quarters could have bred jealousies and led to joking with an edge. A streak of meanness had surfaced among some troops at Gibson. Pvt. Jacob Strickland murdered a fellow soldier at the barracks, a crime for which he stood trial in Little Rock. After his conviction, Strickland went to the gallows, the first person to be executed under the law in Arkansas Territory. Five soldiers at the Cantonment Gibson garrison were hauled to the territorial capital at Little Rock to be tried and convicted for the murder of an Osage. Daniel McGranie, the axe killer imprisoned for almost two years at Fort Smith, was released from the stockade and rejoined his unit at Gibson.[1] Violent behavior among the men coupled with a general laxness in carrying out duty assignments may have pained Caulder, presenting him with a military surrounding far different from that he had known. The men's coarseness may have encouraged more racial insults than before. The community was being redefined. At age thirty-two, Caulder may have realized that the army that he had served in for the past thirteen years was no longer for him. Daily construction work cut into drill time needed by noncommissioned officers to sharpen military bearing of the soldiers, a forfeiture that old-school officers such as George Croghan criticized loudly and frequently.[2] With deteriorating discipline, Caulder's situation became untenable and the two and a half years left on his term seemed much too long. Perhaps a single event such as a stinging rebuke triggered his desertion, but it is more likely that the mood of fellow soldiers and officers toward this formerly esteemed veteran changed into an atmosphere of disrespect. Caulder's decision to go was obviously painful for Arbuckle as it must have been for the private as well.

Downriver at Fort Smith, Caulder made his getaway plans in the company of compatriots and trusted friends. James and Martin Turner, horse owners, were capable of furnishing Caulder with a steed for the overland trip to the Little North Fork. To cross the Ozarks in 1827 was, of course, not an easy task, especially for a fugitive or a person of African ancestry. Caulder, though, knew the trails and the inhabitants. He was aware of hospitable cabins and those to avoid. He had had considerable experience in traveling through isolated country where he had to provision himself. A May ride through the remote areas of the Ozarks would have taken Caulder to where he could find sparkling streams, greening forage for himself and his horse, and game animals out of hiding. A good clip by horse through that landscape might be fourteen to fifteen miles a day, taking a day off occasionally to wait out a downpour or to replenish the food supply.[3] His route may well have taken Caulder to the headwaters of the Buffalo River in today's Madison County.[4] He obviously applied all of his backcountry navigation skills in arriving safely at his destination in what must have been his most perilous journey across Arkansas Territory. Over the two to three weeks of his journey, Peter Caulder no doubt felt stress and may have even wondered a bit about his reception on the Little North Fork. Would his desertion change Hall's opinion of him? Would his notoriety jeopardize the free black community that, after all, depended on obscurity?

Caulder's AWOL partner, James Aikins, was described in the reward advertisement as being of fair complexion and born in Pendleton, South Carolina. Aikins (spelled Akins in the 1822

returns) was twenty-four, eight years younger than Caulder. He probably did not accompany Caulder to the Little North Fork. The two
men split up, because by December 1827, Aikins had decided his best
bet was to return to the army. On the thirteenth of that month, Aikins
"joined from desertion" at Fort Gibson.[5] While planning their bolt,
Caulder and Aikins may have had conversations about journeying all
the way back to their home in South Carolina. Caulder had not seen
his sister Mourning in thirteen years. He fondly remembered her,
though, and later named his second daughter after her. To hatch a
romanticized scheme to return home was one thing, but to carry it out
is quite another. Two men, one of complexion and ancestry that might
attract attention in racially conscious parts and both with posted
rewards on their head, might be asking for trouble on a cross-country
trip through the slave South. Nevertheless, Aikins was absent from
Gibson for six months, long enough to make it to South Carolina and
back. Caulder does not appear on tax records in Arkansas Territory
until 1829. Racial attitudes in Tennessee and Kentucky, through
which the trail from Arkansas to South Carolina would pass, were
blurred enough in 1827, and Caulder, quite used to associating with
white people on more or less equal terms, might never have raised suspicions or brought racial trouble on himself. A return to Marion, however, may well have been beyond the capability of Caulder.

Martin and James Turner had been in and around Fort Smith since
their discharge from Bradford's company in 1819. Both maintained an
account at the Rogers and Nicks store and had established residences
in Crawford County even though their bounty land grants for one hundred and sixty acres lay across the territory in Independence and
Pulaski counties. But, persuaded by Caulder's boldness, the brothers
either joined their friend and relative in his trip across the territory to
the Hall's, or they arrived there shortly afterward. Living free in an
out-of-the-way pioneering community of course had its appeal, but for
the Turners to relocate in north Arkansas well away from Fort Smith
where they had earned a living, and had credit and status, has its mystery as well. Both men had received better than average bounty land,
James Turner's being flat and cultivatable in what is now Lonoke
County near Bearskin Lake. Martin Turner had swapped tracts, and

his exchange acreage in Independence County was well situated near a main road that fit with a business of raising and training horses.[6] One obvious motive for all three men might have been the possibility of gaining wives. David Hall coincidently had several daughters who were coming into marrying age. In fact, the prospects looked so enticing that Martin and James carried or sent word to their relative, John Turner, in Marion, South Carolina. "Come here to Arkansas Territory," they must have proclaimed to young John. "We have found the right place for you!" By 1840, John Turner, free black man in his early thirties, had trekked from South Carolina across the slave South to the mountains of north Arkansas. Settling on the Little North Fork, he married Margaret, Eliza's twin sister, thereby becoming Peter Caulder's brother-in-law.

For eighteen months Caulder's document trail disappeared as he transitioned from soldier to pioneer. With the reward posting, he had to be careful, avoiding figures of authority and places where people who read the *Gazette* might be encountered. Peter Caulder married Eliza in 1829 after her fourteenth birthday advanced her into womanhood as set by the standards of that day. He was in his early thirties and if he harbored any regrets about leaving the army, he did not evince it as he settled on the Little North Fork. The Hall family embraced Caulder, a man of experience and ability. With the happiness of romance and opportunity, he pioneered on land alongside them. In the first year as he courted Eliza, Peter used his estimable skills in carving out a new lifestyle along the White River. He trained another hound or two and ranged into Missouri to hunt deer, elk, bear, and the occasional buffalo. He showed Sarah, Eliza, Rachel, and Margaret the Osage methods of hide curing and tanning that he had witnessed at Three Forks.[7] Poking around in overhangs and caves to chisel out lime for chimney building, he found quality nitrate deposits that he could turn into gunpowder. He taught young David Hall how to line up a target in the sights of a rifle and squeeze the trigger without disturbing the aim. From deep in his saddlebag, Caulder might have produced a set of fiddle strings given to him by Lieutenant Bonneville.[8] The manufacture of a musical instrument would lead to merriment and many lively evenings by the White River. Caulder, Martin Turner, James Turner, and any other War of 1812 veteran who may have visited them in their cabins—John Inglehart, for instance—may have entertained one another with stories turned into folk tunes. The former riflemen could have recounted Jackson's victory at New Orleans. A century and a half later, Jimmy Driftwood, an Arkansas musician raised along the Buffalo Fork, wrote and recorded a hit folk-style song that reflected this famous event.[9]

Other settlers mirrored Caulder's pioneering impulses. When touring the White River, young Henry Rowe Schoolcraft stayed with a family named Wells, who "could only talk of bears, hunting, and the like. The rude pursuits, and the coarse enjoyment of the hunter state, were all they knew." But further downstream at William McGarrah's cabin, which had "a couple of odd volumes of books upon a shelf," Schoolcraft found lively conversation and cordiality with this South Carolina–born frontiersman and his "numerous family of sons and daughters."[10] At the David Hall cabin located a short canoe ride from where Schoolcraft had found the witty McGarrah, Caulder and his remarkable adventures if told could have enlivened conversations. If Schoolcraft, who became an Indian agent in Wisconsin, had had the good fortune to retrace his steps along the White River nine years later, he might have been amazed that he could have asked a resident there about his contact with Washington City and James Madison. Caulder had seen both the city and its first citizen. What about Pennsylvania weather or keelboating from Pittsburgh down the Ohio? Schoolcraft could have compared notes with Peter. Hot Springs? Caulder had bathed there. A six-oared skiff? Yes, with a sail and making ten miles an hour at times! Louisiana and the exotic Caddo Indians and the Red River raft? Caulder could have told stories about them as well as about Mad Buffalo, Clermont, Takatoka, and Arkansas Territory's first governor. Chasing thieving deserters across the wide Missouri? Caulder had done that, too. Not to mention his considerable experiences and yarns about stalking a hound-killing cougar, breaking Osage ponies to the saddle, and conversing with ladies at the sutler's bar that were all part of the life of

Peter Caulder. A visit with the well-traveled Caulder might have relieved Schoolcraft's rather unfavorable look at frontiersmen in Arkansas Territory.[11]

But despite his background, Peter Caulder was starting over in the White River hills. In deserting, he gave up any right to a veteran's pension. He departed Gibson in the skiff with little more than his rifle, his skinning knives, and his saddlebag. He probably had no cash since he left owing money to the sutler's store. His bounty land was forfeited to the state by Lawrence County in 1830 for nonpaid taxes, the fate of a huge percentage of military bounty lands in Arkansas, including those of Martin Turner, James Turner, Joseph Clark, John Inglehart, and John Hestilow. The government's plan to use the bounty land and ex-soldiers to form a buffer between Indians and migrating whites had been stillborned. Most veterans of the War of 1812 never left the east. For the men of Bradford's Company who were already in Arkansas Territory (where a third of the nation's six million acres of War of 1812 bounty lands lay) several negative factors foiled their permanent settling on their bounty land.[12] As in Caulder's case, the soldiers had no choice in the location of their property, no capital to start with, and no local political power.[13] Few veterans sold out in order to raise money to buy elsewhere, though that eventually became a legal option. They simply let it go back to be auctioned off at the county courthouse, the proceeds providing income for the government but not a penny for the original landowner. In an exceptional effort to gain a reasonable tract that he might utilize, Martin Turner traded his original bounty land that lay in a swamp at the White and Black River confluence for a much healthier piece of property only a few miles west of Batesville. But Turner let this choice property slip away for nonpayment of taxes.[14]

Arkansas Territory presented a chance for new starts whether the land was free or not. Congress had passed a preemption act in 1814 during the Madison administration. This law gave a "squatter" the first opportunity to buy the land when it got surveyed, "no matter how flimsy the cabin, nor how small the clearing."[15] Caulder used this method in claiming land on the White River. His cabin would not be flimsy, however. He knew how to build. Caulder was in the prime of life; he was a skilled hunter for the table; and for much of his army career he had performed duties on his own self-initiative.

David Hall, too, had acted on his own initiative in moving west across the Mississippi. Hall and his family and relatives, including John Hall and Thomas Hall, arrived at Bull Shoals in 1819 from Bedford County in central Tennessee. After a long journey to find the right spot, fertile and secluded, and with wife Sarah at his side, Hall surely felt much as did settler Daniel Ashley, who said that he "squatted in the best part . . . [and] was a monarch of all I surveyed."[16] Hall had corn under cultivation by 1828 to feed his livestock and to make whiskey, gradually clearing a large field of the timber that grew huge in the rich bottom soil on the bank of the White River. Over time, the black family's routines evolved from hunting and gathering and rough construction to tending, cultivating, and improving the living quarters, following exactly the same process of settling in as did their white yeoman neighbors.[17] Chores were both the bane and delight of farm children. Each morning in good weather, Hall's daughters toted water from the spring and brought in stove wood before shelling out a tad of corn for the chickens and hunting for the eggs that the hens tried to hide in the corncrib. Sometimes the girls found a pile of feathers left by fox or owl, the aftermath of a pullet feast at the expense of the Hall flock. Sows were kept up in the hog pen when about to farrow, but the rest of the time they fended for themselves in the mast of the surrounding forest despite predators that prowled looking for the tasty domesticated animal. Hall's cattle ranged about making their living on small meadows that dotted the surrounding hillsides. Only his two horses and the mule, his most precious livestock, were fenced in. Black bears, still common, loomed large in many fireside stories and brought fortunate hunters income for prized skins and useful oil. In 1823, Quapaw Indians, their large canoe filled with skin containers of bear oil, came ashore at the present-day site of Memphis to do business with white traders. Martin Turner may have witnessed the rendering of bears on a larger scale at a place known as Oil Trough, just to the north of his bounty land in Independence County. At the Hall farm six miles below the mouth of the Little North Fork, an occasional panther scream or wolf howl scrunched the children deeper into their feather mattresses and rousted hounds from their slumber. In this environment on the boundary of wild country and growing civilization, Peter Caulder sought community and his own hearth.

––––––––––

Peter Caulder's first winter spent on the White River featured colder and wetter weather than normal. In Little Rock, the *Gazette* reported that a week went by without the sun appearing. Rain, sleet, and snow kept water levels high and mail routes impassable. Caulder, nevertheless, pushed himself out of his open lean-to and into the icy mornings to cut down the dormant hardwood trees with which to build a one-room cabin. As was common on the frontier, people traded work and Caulder relished those days when David and John Hall came up the hillside to the crowning knoll, soon to be known as Cawlder Mountain that Caulder selected for a homesite, bringing their stout team to drag in logs. For their new dwellings, Peter Caulder and John Hall constructed chimneys correctly for proper draft and glowing heat. A well-built fireplace produced warmth, light, and good cheer. Travelers enjoyed nothing more than to see white smoke curling from the chimney of a cabin, as the travel journals of Schoolcraft, Meetch, Gerstaecker, and Featherstonehaugh reveal.

Caulder built his cabin in 1828 and cleared a small area for his garden and for a few rows of corn. He seemed to have used his skills as a huntsman and a keeper of hounds to earn a living, selling furs, deerskins, and hides. At Fort Smith, Peter Caulder had built a pirogue and his boat-building expertise was useful to him and his neighbors along the White River. Cherry and locust trees, naturally resistant to rot and water-logging and so best for dugout boats, grew on the benches above the valley. Caulder generated income from the forest and from his building skills. Unlike the Halls, Caulder declined to invest in cattle. Only after his family grew to include several children did he cultivate enough corn to fill his crib for his horses. Caulder, in order to barter his furs or ply his crafts, interacted occasionally with whites in the county.

In February 1829, John Adams, the sheriff of Izard County, made a trip to the Little North Fork to count the population and to assess Caulder and other residents for their property taxes. Sheriff Adams recorded fifteen free black persons on the Little North Fork in his 1829 census. Along with five free black men and six females living in an adjoining township, the Halls, the Turners, and Caulder constituted the entire free black population residing in Izard County.[18] Caulder paid the lowest tax rate in the county for a homestead, about 31 cents, indicating that he had made minimal improvement to his land. At the time, he owned no cattle and only one horse. John Hall, just starting himself, who was unmarried with a tiny cabin and no livestock paid the same amount. David Hall Sr., in contrast, had a $1.37 property tax, a higher assessment than levied on many whites. Martin Turner, new to this region though not to the experience of paying taxes, was assessed at 56 cents, an above-average amount based most likely, as had happened in Crawford County, on the high value of his draft horses.[19] Caulder and Turner probably felt that their role as taxpayers indicated acceptance in their adopted county. Race did not seem an important issue on the frontier. The veterans hunted where and when they wanted, owned firearms, livestock, and dogs, and interacted socially and economically with their white and black neighbors.[20]

Along with acceptance in the community came the opportunity for romance to blossom for Caulder and Eliza. Wedding excitement gripped the Hall family when Peter proposed to his young sweetheart and she responded favorably. Sometime in 1829, probably early in the spring, Peter Caulder, a bachelor for thirty-four years, exchanged the vows of holy matrimony with Eliza. The wedding service is undocumented, but David Hall himself may have officiated. Dallas Tabor Herndon, historian of pioneering Arkansas, wrote that "very seldom did a young couple get married 'on the sly.'" A covered dish feast complete with roasted wild turkey on a platter surrounded by boiled eggs and sweetened with may apple preserves presented the typical fare for hill-folk weddings. The Hall family and Caulder's trusted friends from Marion, South Carolina, Martin and James Turner, joined in the celebration for these two who were "embarking on the sea of matrimony."[21] Indeed, it appears that two other of Hall's daughters, Rachel and Harriet, married Martin Turner and

James Turner at about the same time. All three ex-riflemen set up households in the edge of Izard County. In October 1830, a census marshal, freshly instructed on enumeration procedure, trekked along river trails into a small but vibrant free black community in Little North Fork Township to make his count.

The census marshals categorized individuals who were heads of household as white or in the case of Peter Caulder, Martin Turner, James Turner, David Hall, and John Hall as free colored, basing their evaluation of race on his observation and their reputation. The population of free black persons in Izard County had increased from 22 in 1827 to 26 in 1829 to 32 in 1830. Across the rest of Arkansas Territory, there were only 106 other free colored individuals, by far the least number of free black persons residing in any state or territory and making up less than one-half of 1 percent of the 30,323 people in the territory.[22]

Part of the Little North Fork population increase came in the household of Peter Caulder. Daughter Margaret and infant son David kept Eliza busy inside the small cabin. The naming of the first two Caulder children had honored Eliza's twin sister and her father.[23] Rachel and Harriet, the wives of Martin Turner and James Turner, homesteading near Peter Caulder's cabin, had infants as well, so in the tradition of young mothers everywhere, many evenings were spent cozily together, the sisters talking and laughing about their children while the men followed hounds up the rough hollows that led to the thick forests above the river valley. When not hunting for the table or robbing bee trees that stood in great abundance, Peter Caulder may have pursued the making of gunpowder. On the south side of the White River near the mouth of Jimmie's Creek across from the Caulder and Turner cabins, limestone caves offered a natural ingredient for this manufacturing. When added to charcoal and sulfur, saltpeter found in the caves could create usable gunpowder. Caulder had witnessed the process of making shot and explosives while at Carlisle and no doubt kept himself, his friends, and his Hall in-laws well supplied with ammunition. No one could live on the White River without gunpowder, but other essential compounds were needed, too. Chemical arts applied on the frontier by pioneers included soap making, hide tanning, and whiskey making. Because Caulder hunted, built chimneys, and made gunpowder and boats for a living, his taxes stayed low. Property tax assessments were tied to livestock and farm equipment ownership. Martin Turner's team that he depended on for income cost him dearly. He paid more in annual property taxes than any other free black person except David Hall, who by 1832 had several acres under cultivation along with a number of hogs, cows, and horses.[24]

On the Little North Fork in the early 1830s, the ex-riflemen sustained their family homes much like the household described by traveler Joseph Meetch. Meetch visited the farm of John Magness on Crooked Creek, a man in the vicinity whom Peter Caulder could have come to know as a contemporary. Meetch remarked that Magness had good sense and used less vulgar language than was common. Magness took care in constructing his cabin's chimney from stone, his quality of construction separating it from the usual ones that were thrown together with short sticks and mud.[25] Caulder put the same kind of skill into the building of his cabin that harbored and protected his family for the next thirty years. Pulled high onto a landing below his cabin when not in use, Caulder kept his pirogue for water transportation and to ferry himself across to the south bank of the White, an area with lush canebrakes and plentiful wild game. He prided himself on his ability to trap mink and bag a bear. On the occasions when he led his horse into the yard, a black bear carcass draped across the saddle, family members gathered immediately to help skin, dry, tan, and pound the meat and hide. The Caulder family used every inch of the bear, giving it great utility in frontier home economics. Nothing was wasted. Caulder had a fondness for buffalo robes, and actually a few forest buffalo may have roamed the North Fork and the Buffalo Fork as late as 1832. If so, the Caulders, Turners, and Halls may have emulated the former Osage inhabitants of the area in celebrating a kill and communally processing the beast. For all the tall talk and shooter's braggadocio of White River hill pioneers noted by outside observers from Schoolcraft to Gerstaecker, probably no hunter in the region exceeded the experience, the hounds, and the marksmanship of Peter Caulder, who had once kept a rifle company supplied with bush meat. He took pride in his ability and he was fond of the army and his comrades. But now he felt a different kind of love, a powerful, satisfying love of family and hearth. Peter Caulder's children, especially his oldest son, David, looked up to him with pure devotion.

———————

Most free black people throughout the South stayed well away from politics, Caulder being no exception to that rule. Nevertheless, gossip about slavery, Jackson, and statehood had to catch his attention. The white population was growing steadily along the White River above Bull Shoals. The Indians so prominent in the thoughts and actions of Caulder a decade ago had vanished from his concerns as they had vanished from Arkansas Territory by 1835. Where gossip about Indians had died away, gossip about black people intensified, fueled by alarming news of a murderous slave insurrection in Southampton County, Virginia.

The *Arkansas Gazette* reprinted a list of the fifty-nine white victims killed by Nat Turner and his band. The rampage in Virginia tobacco country that began on August 1831 sent a chill up the back of slave owners and fearful whites. Editorials accused free blacks as conspirators who secretly contributed to the unrest in slave quarters. The *Gazette* reprinted excerpts from *The Confessions of Nat Turner,* a pamphlet by Turner's defense attorney Thomas R. Gray, lengthening the shadow of the revolt.[26] Did Caulder hear of Nat Turner? Eventually, one suspects, though when the news came, people in Izard County apparently did not overreact. The real danger to Caulder and the Halls was not in being driven out by pitchforks and muskets by their white neighbors. The danger was far more insidious and pervasive, although slower in developing. It came in the realm of the mind of white Southerners where attitudes about race were reaching a point of no return. The Virginia legislature engaged in a debate about abolishing slavery as Pennsylvania and New York had done earlier. In those states, the peculiar institution had been eliminated, gradually, but definitely. Some in Virginia, especially those in the mountainous sections, thought their state should emancipate its large slave population. Emancipation there could have had a huge impact on attitudes in her sister slave states, but the Virginia delegates voted to end the debates and slavery remained intact in the Old Dominion. Voluntary abolition by any Southern state became a dead political issue and finished off ambivalence in racial attitudes over most of Arkansas Territory. The number of "boy planters" migrating into Arkansas mostly from Kentucky, Tennessee, and Alabama multiplied as statehood neared. When Arkansas was admitted to the Union in 1836, there was slight doubt that the twenty-fifth state would be a "slave society." Free black people like the Caulders, the Turners, and the Halls would have their days numbered in such a state.

In fact, the Turners, no known relationship to the mystical preacher who led the largest and most violent slave revolt in United States history, had reached a turning point in their pioneering lives in the community. Sometime after 1834, Martin Turner and his younger brother James disappeared from the historical record. Tax records for Izard County are missing for the years 1834–1838. In 1833, the year in which his last child with Rachel, daughter Lydia, would be born, Martin had been assessed a slightly lower amount indicating that perhaps one of his draft horses had died or been injured. James Turner, too, departed the Little North Fork Township, trusting his young wife, Harriet, to care for infant twins, daughters Elizabeth and Fanny, one named after Caulder's Eliza. The absence of these two brothers must have been a major disappointment for Peter Caulder, who had counted on their friendship and support for more than thirty years. It is difficult to imagine that the men intentionally abandoned their families and their comrade of so many years. The Turners had been among the most reliable of Bradford's soldiers, capable, stable, and confident. Martin Turner may have hired out as a teamster on a freight run—by then cotton and logs were being hauled out of upper White River farms on wagons—but no doubt he meant to return. Perhaps they were injured in separate accidents or even in the same misfortune. Perhaps they fell to some sort of unrecorded violent act, though both certainly knew how to take care of themselves. Rachel, presumably Martin's wife, and Harriet, presumably married to James, eventually remarried and had children in their second families. But both did so only after a long period of waiting (or mourning) as single parents. The Turner children by their first marriages continued to live with or near the Hall family until maturity. The story is complicated by John Turner's 1840 entry into the Little North Fork community. The dashing and assertive thirty-five-year-old free black man had been encouraged to migrate from Marion County, South Carolina, to Arkansas for a chance at a more egalitarian society, as was a white emigrant from South Carolina who wrote home that "there is none of this fool aristocracy here [Arkansas] to contend with." Not long after Turner's arrival, he wed Margaret Hall, Eliza's twin sister. Twenty-four-year-old Margaret was not only saved from spinsterhood by the marriage, but was brought into an enduring partnership bound for parenthood and property ownership.

President Andrew Jackson, whom Peter Caulder knew of from stories related by Major Bradford, signed the enactment bill for Arkansas to enter the union in 1836. In the year of Arkansas's statehood, Eliza gave birth to the couple's third child, a daughter that the parents named Mourning in honor of Caulder's sister in Marion. Caulder was, in the tradition of Arkansas hunters-turning-into-farmers, clearing off a small space each autumn, adding to his mountaintop clearing. Pioneers sowed new ground with turnips and the next year fenced it with split rails for more crops, especially corn for the livestock and Irish potatoes for the family.[27] With a growing brood, Peter and Eliza had need of a milk cow and so obtained one from his father-in-law. Perhaps Caulder remembered how well the milk tasted to him as a young soldier once on the Red River. The patriarch of the clan provided a head or two out of his sizable herd of cattle for his sons and sons-in-law to stock their own farmsteads. The Caulder cabin and fields were located above the north bank of the White River, on a bench where Sister Creek flows into the bigger stream. Martin (until he departed) and Rachel Hall Turner lived west of Sister Creek alongside the White River, their twenty acres of cleared ground stretching north away from the stream toward the center of the section. In the winter when trees were bare-limbed, Peter and Eliza could see smoke rising from the Turner chimney or even, when the river gurgled rather than roared, hear the call "Supper is ready!" No one recollects how the creek got its name, but it is certain that the Hall sisters married to the ex-riflemen lived alongside it. There is another Sister Creek that enters the White River from the south directly opposite the northern Sister Creek that ran through the Turner and Caulder homesteads.

Caulder spent much of his time in the forests but never having been a reclusive sort, he must have enjoyed an occasional trip into Marion County villages, Yellville or Flippen Barrens. He may have been reluctant, however, to speak of his army adventures. He did not like to tell war stories apparently. Otherwise, he would have been prone to be quoted by local chroniclers or journalist such as Frederick Gerstaecker, a German-speaking traveler who wandered about Arkansas in the years 1838–41 chronicling stories of the grass-roots people whom he encountered. Gerstaecker hunted and worked his way across the new state and so had many Ozark experiences to write about when he published his account in 1844. Unfortunately and unlike Schoolcraft, Gerstaecker never made it completely up to the White River hills along the Arkansas-Missouri border. He did approach it though. Between Batesville and Oil Trough, he spent a rainy evening in a "sort of tavern" operated by a "free negro." Three white men, one of them a distiller of whiskey named Magnus (or Magness), were having a jovial time around a brightly blazing fire that turned the November chill into comfortable warmth.[28] Gerstaecker wrote nothing more about his host for the night, leaving the tavern keeper's name a mystery. Only one free black man appeared in the 1840 United States Census for Independence County—Lewis Nailer who lived in Washington Township and owned two slaves.

The 1840 Marion County population that included sixty-six free black people appeared more diverse. Within that black community, an adjustment of residences took place when John and Margaret Turner moved in and occupied the original home of David Hall Sr. and Sarah. The patriarch and his wife moved further upstream to a larger tract. David Hall and John Turner eventually patented the lands on which they lived in 1840. In October just as the leaves began to change colors, William Hall Turner became the first addition to the young Turner family. With the birth of William, the black community counted thirty-three children less than ten years old. Eliza Caulder, who had five children of her own, may have midwifed at the birth of Margaret and John's first child, but no doubt the infant boy's entry into the world was made under the watchful eye of Sarah Hall, the most experienced at the art of motherhood. The parents in this community were obviously nurturing and healthy and their babies survived infancy.[29]

Even though patriarch David Hall was nearing sixty and Peter Caulder was forty-five, the average age in the free black community was sixteen. Gatherings of friends and relatives featured groups of toddlers and pre-teens eager to play and to learn. The Hall community's future chronicler, Joseph Hall, a steady source for the tales of Silas Claiborne Turnbo, was seventeen, an impressionable age. In 1840, the Little North Fork free black community sparkled with peals of childhood laughter, a community full of fun and verve and promise.

With youth abounding and with prosperity, confidence, permanency, and growth infused the outlook of the free black population in Marion County. While contemporary observers, who shared a European perspective of proper behavior, depicted Arkansas as dangerous and backward, a closer look at an upper White River hill settlement revealed a community of black and white yeomen.[30] There, marriages lasted, children survived to adulthood, livestock accumulated, assessments rose, and blacks like whites formally acquired the land that they farmed, stepping beyond squatting and preemption.

One noted historian of antebellum Arkansas concluded that 1840s agriculture was "a remarkable success story" in the state, exceeding just the growing of cotton on plantations.[31] The free black settlers of the Little North Fork bore out that conclusion. Sheriffs often missed assessing some of the livestock holdings, and even some of the residents, a chronic problem for historians and statisticians, but steady and surprising material advancement are clearly traced in the existing tax records for the Marion County free black farmers.

The Arkansas territorial legislature split a new county out of Izard County in 1835 and a year later named it for Francis Marion. To Peter Caulder, that must have seemed ironical. Born in Marion County, South Carolina, he had settled in Izard County, named for Arkansas's second territorial governor. That county's namesake, George Izard, was, like Caulder, a veteran of the War of 1812 and a South Carolinian by birth. But now Caulder once again resided in a Marion County. The Swamp Fox proved to be a favorite name for U.S. counties, ranking just behind Washington, Lincoln, and Franklin. Even more ironic, perhaps for Caulder, would have been in learning that Lieutenant Bonneville, his old army officer, had a county in Idaho named in his honor.

By 1840, Marion County boasted six townships, two of them with free black inhabitants—Little North Fork and White River. Those townships bounded each other at a physical feature on the river known to local people as the narrows. A little way above the narrows, Peter and Eliza Caulder homesteaded on Cawlder Mountain, a flat-topped bench above the valley farms of John Hall and a white farmer by the name of George W. Pierson. The founders of the free black community, David and Sarah Hall, who had moved four miles upriver from where they had first settled in 1819, lived on the banks of the White River below Cawlder Mountain. Several other free black homesteaders preempted valley land, drawn to the vicinity, perhaps, by David Hall Sr.'s success and by his daughters. Sarah Bass, a free colored woman, reared her four children in a log cabin a short distance away from Willoughby Hall, a young bear hunting partner of Peter Caulder. James Atkinson, a free colored man who served in the War of 1812, and his wife, a white woman, lived with their one child in a nearby cabin.[32]

Thomas Hall and his prolific wife (the couple had nine children) were about thirty years old in 1840. Listed in Marion County as a colored man, Thomas Hall contested that judgment. From what we may envision as a buckskin pouch secured by a leather thong, he kept a folded letter precious to him that he had carried from his previous domicile in Maury County, Tennessee. On a June day in 1843, he

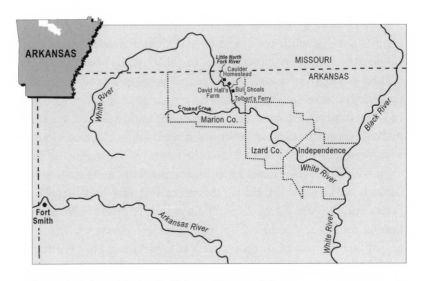

Little North Fork neighborhood of Marion County, Arkansas.
MAP BY TOM PARDISE.

took this letter that attested to his Portuguese descent to the Marion County courthouse where the clerk, Dr. James M. Cowdrey, filed it. His affidavit had been witnessed and notarized originally in 1835, probably inspired by a law that barred free men of color in Tennessee from voting.[33] Those who had been designated as colored men had an opportunity to petition otherwise in order to maintain their citizenry. Hall had done that and now wished to legalize his "whiteness" in Arkansas. Before the decade was out, Thomas Hall pulled up stakes and moved again, this time across the border into Oregon County, Missouri. Hall's protest was never accepted by local authorities in Arkansas or Missouri, but his resistance to the "colored" designation led some in the county to believe that the Marion County Halls were of a mysterious race of people known as "melungeon." The theory went thusly: melungeons were not wholly white, black, or red but a new people. The mixture of these three blood lines had occurred in the isolated southern Appalachians so many generations ago that a distinct race had emerged.[34] Jacob Mooney migrated into the White River hills in 1810 with four dark-skinned "foreigners" who were called "lungeons" by pioneers.

Other mixed marriages had been observed in Marion County. Joseph Coker, a white man, and Ainey, his Indian wife, settled near the White River even before David Hall arrived. As with Hall, Joe Coker established a successful extended family presence. The Cokers thrived on flat lands known as Sugar Loaf Prairie to the west of Little North Fork. Joe Coker's numerous, industrious, mixed-heritage sons built mills and imported slaves to labor in their various enterprises.[35]

David Hall's sons started their own enterprises and families. One son, known as David B. Hall in Missouri after the Civil War, lived below the Bull Shoals narrows. To keep the two David Halls separate on the tax rolls, Sheriff J. B. Everett referred to the father as Sr. and listed the son on the files as "Hall, Jr." John Hall cultivated thirty-nine acres on the White River above the Pace ferry site, but resided downriver on the old home place, a tract of alluvial plain just above the narrows.

Also residing along the White River were Joseph and Absalom Hall, who built hunter's cabins and cleared enough ground for sweet potato patches on riverbank land just above Bull Shoals close to where Hillard Rud resided with his family. Not much is known about Rud, a free black man who disappeared from the historical record even as the settlement expanded in the next decade to include several other free black households. In 1840, the free black community stretched from Rud's cabin at its southernmost point, to Caulder's ridgetop cabin overlooking the mouth of Sister Creek six miles to the north. Most of the year, the river offered a pleasant water route between the home sites. A dip or two of the paddle and a smallmouth bass pulled out of a river that teemed with such fish offered immense satisfaction. A path on the north side of the river linked streamside residents by horse or foot when rains swelled the river. Interspersed in this ribbon of black-owned farms along the White River were white neighbors, those with Irish heritage numbering just slightly more than the settlers of African ancestry. Irish potatoes and African yams, both nourishing root crops, grew well as companions in the gardens of Marion County.

FREE BLACK HEADS OF HOUSEHOLD
IN 1840 CENSUS—MARION COUNTY

*Names of family members, where given,
are reflected back from the 1850 census*

HOUSEHOLD HEAD AND AGE RANGE	AGE RANGE OF SPOUSE AND NAME	MALE CHILDREN UNDER 10 YEARS	FEMALE CHILDREN UNDER 10 YEARS	OTHERS IN HOUSEHOLD AGE RANGE 10–24	OTHERS, AGE RANGE 36 +
Sarah Bass, 36–55	None	2, unknown		2, unknown	1, unknown
Willeby* [Willoughby] Hall, 10–24	10–24, unknown	2, unknown		1, unknown	
Thomas Hall, 24–36	24–36, unknown	5, unknown	3, unknown	1, unknown	
David Hall Sr., 55 +	36–55, Sarah	1, Joseph	1, Mary	4, Henderson, Leonard	
David Hall Jr., 10–24	None				
James Atkenson,* 24–36	20–30 (w), unknown	1, unknown			
John Turner, 24–36	24–36, Margaret	1, William			
Peter Colder* [Caulder], 36–55	24–36, Eliza	1, David	3, Mourning, Susan, one child lost	1, Margaret	
John Hall, 24–36	24–36, Nancy	2, George W., James Irvin	1, one child lost		
Abslum* [Absalom] Hall, 24–26	10–24, unknown	2, unknown	2, unknown	1, unknown	
Joseph Hall, 24–36	10–24, unknown	2, William, Allen	1, Lydia	1, unknown	
Hillard Rud, 36–55	10–24, unknown	2, unknown	1, unknown		
12	**9**	**21**	**12**	**11**	**1**

66 total free black population

* Spelled as on census form by 1840 marshal.

Peter Caulder and his family flourished on the flat-topped bench called Cawlder Mountain. Living close to nature, Caulder, Eliza, and children marveled at such feats as the spectacular meteorite shower of November 12–13, 1833, when a "grand and fearful" night of "falling stars," "fireballs," and "blazing streams of fire" seemed to portend that the "heavens and lower regions were combining together." Two of Caulder's neighbors, John Tabor and Nimrod Teaff, rose from their couches of bear skins and looked out the door to see "hundreds and thousands of stars shooting swiftly down toward the earth." One witness recalled that "the scare among the people lasted several weeks afterward. Prayer meetings were common until the fright among the people died away."[36] Peter and Eliza watched nature in fascination on occasions, such as the spring of 1843 when heavy rains swelled the White River to titanic proportions. Rehashing such natural phenomena split conversation time with rumors about steamboats. As technology improved, powered boats traversed the White River shoals above the site of Tolbert's ferry located at the present-day town of Cotter, and eventually a few were able to mechanically paddle all the way to Forsythe, Missouri. With transportation improvements in a country and era of high birth rates, an influx of new settlers inevitably crowded in on the pioneers, bringing their cast-iron skillets and cooking pots along with boundless energy for homesteading and, not inconsequently, helping to thin out game and fur animals. The White River hills were not quite isolated enough to be immune from national issues, and political news from afar worked its way into the thoughts of Caulder and his neighbors, joining weather and hunting tales as conversational fare.

Statehood had come, making Arkansas the third state located west of the Mississippi to join the Union. That bit of information came to Caulder perhaps casually in a remark made by a visitor. He would have realized, of course, that Arkansas entered the Union as a slave state. If he reflected about progress of civilization, Caulder may have compared conditions upon his arrival in Missouri Territory when he and Long first spotted Belle Point from their skiff. Caulder, like many in the hills, probably regretted that Andrew Jackson retired from office in 1836 and wondered about Martin Van Buren as his successor. It was Van Buren who came to champion free soil, but in

Arkansas laws were passed to safeguard the rising slave society. The Panic of 1837 dropped prices on Caulder's hides. The fall in the economy cast many on the frontier onto times lean enough so that the poor fried rawhide to tide them over the pangs of hunger. Opinions about slavery and Indian removals salted Marion County conversations in the 1830s. The *Arkansas Gazette* had been joined by another newspaper in Little Rock, the *Arkansas Advocate* and the occasional advertisement for fugitive slaves offered an ominous look at the coming decade. Reprinted accounts of Nat Turner and the *Amistad* mutiny warned of dangerous racial unrest.[37]

Yet in the White River hills at the border between north Arkansas and southern Missouri, toleration, frontier isolation, and the presence of mixed families blurred racial lines. Gossip that bent public opinion against free black people in Arkansas towns and in the so-called delta evidently gave way to trust between white and mulatto neighbors in the White River hills where a biracial community defined itself. James Atkinson and his white wife were not the last of mixed marriages. In 1850, at least one other racially mixed couple lived intimately and openly together. No one can say how much the presence of respected people like David Hall Sr., David Hall Jr., John Hall, Peter Caulder, and John Turner had to do in creating a community open to blacks. What is clear is that for three decades Marion County whites tread lightly around questions of racial identity.[38] Warmed by a benign environment, the Halls, Peter Caulder, and the Turners strengthened their hold on their future, improving their property by clearing land, plowing it, and adding livestock. In two decades along the White River, the patriarch David Hall Sr. had prospered. He had forty acres under cultivation, a herd of cattle, a milk cow, a team to plow his field, saddle mounts fast enough to race in local matches, hogs on the range, and most important, his loyal wife and a large number of married children and grandchildren residing with or near him in a land that he chose to live on. When he relaxed, and there is no evidence that he did much of that, and reflected on his accomplishment, he must have glowed just a bit with satisfaction. His eldest son-in-law, Peter Caulder, must have felt much the same way.

———

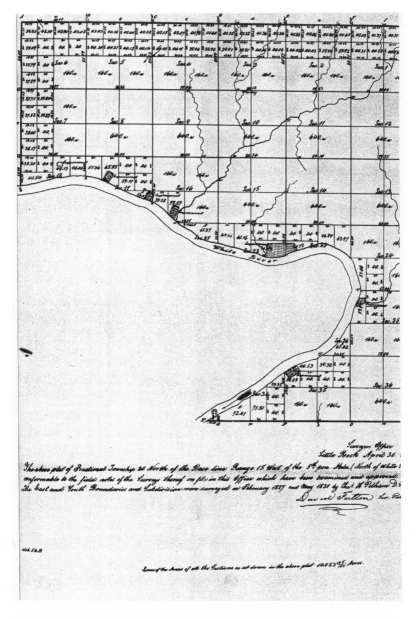

Constructed from surveyor notes of 1827 and 1831, this 1840 map shows Sister Creek flowing into the White River. The cultivated land along the river in section 22 belonged to David Hall Sr., the free black community patriarch. Peter and Eliza Caulder homesteaded above the river valley on Cawlder Mountain in section 15.

By 1841, Peter Caulder still owned but one horse and one cow. His knack for extracting income from the forests continued to be his chief means of supporting his young family. Up the rough hollows and down on the river wherever they congregated, Caulder stalked bulging bucks and fat does. Caulder pitched camp as he had done many times before, sleeping on a bear fur robe, protected from chill winds by doeskin flaps hung across low-slung tree branches. When the trail was cold, Caulder might have settled in to cook his meal, yams and backstrap, over the campfire. As another bear hunter in the area, Thresher Bill Yocum, and his friend Len Coker recalled, "our fare seemed royal to us, for it consisted of both fresh and dried venison, pone bread, bear meat and wild honey."[39] Bear hunters such as the legendary Pete Whetstone of Independence County thrilled to the yelping of his bear dogs, named Fillmore, General Jackson, Sharptooth, and Cherokee. Caulder may have honored some of his former army commanders by naming his hounds "Benjamin" or "'Buckle," or "Old Zach." True hunters found exhilaration at the fight, seeing an old "he-bear" in action. Afterward they feasted on thick fat from his carcass.[40] Always the sharpshooter, Caulder made efficient use of his rifle and his ammunition to take what he needed as a commercial hunter. Entering the decade of the 1840s, Eliza and Peter had four children, the youngest another girl named Susan, perhaps after Susan Loving of Fort Smith days. Their second daughter, Mourning, and ten-year-old David, eyes glistening, were allowed on special nights to accompany their father on coon hunts in favorite woodlands north of Sister Creek. Some nights, David may have ridden in the middle of a pirogue as his father and uncles "fire hunted" from the water.[41]

On the river valley below Cawlder Mountain, John Hall, more of a farmer and less of a hunter than Peter, spent his time cutting timber and building fence for his cattle herd. Livestock trading was his principal means of livelihood. Hall grew corn, wheat, rye, and hay on his meadow along the banks of the White River, transporting the products downstream in November to feed cattle wintering on his second farm at the narrows. A white neighbor, George Washington Pierson, was also expanding his operation and over the years befriended Hall and made remarks about buying a forty that adjoined his own.[42] John Hall, a good businessman, realized that to sell land he must have legal possession. In late February 1848 when the White River rose enough for the pirogues, John Hall set out with David Hall Sr., Pierson, and probably Peter Caulder for the land office in Batesville, one hundred miles down the river. John Hall carried the money to buy the forty next to Pierson (actually it measured 39.11 acres), and another twenty-three-acre bottomland meadow that he already had improved. At the land office, Pierson stepped to the counter just behind John Hall and paid cash for fifty-one acres situated on the left bank of the White River. David Hall Sr. made the third and last of the transactions by these traveling companions at the land office that day. Hall paid cash for seventy-one acres that he had preempted across from the present town of Bull Shoals.[43] The next year, John Hall accepted Pierson's offer on his two parcels, leaving Pierson with a huge tract fronting the White River. The deal was satisfactory to both men and Hall marked his friendship with Pierson by christening his first son, George Washington Hall. Ironically a year later, David Hall sold his seventy-one acres to a white man, John D. Noe.[44]

Caulder, who bought no land but continued to improve his bench farm as he neared the age of fifty in 1843, acquired a second milk cow and another horse, no doubt a mount for his son David, who by now was off on a few of his own pursuits. Young David had three cousins about his age, Jesse Turner, Reuben Turner, and William Hall with whom he fished and hunted squirrels. With canoe, rifle, dog, and horse, David Caulder was brought up wise in the ways of stream, forest, field, and trail, skills that he used to support his own family in Missouri during and after the Civil War. Orphans, run-aways, and sons apprenticed out were common enough on the fron-tier, but not in the Hall-Caulder-Turner extended family. Peter and Eliza Caulder cast strong ties and created a stable environment for their children. Caulder continued to add to his clearing to better accommodate his horses, cows, swine herd, and flock of chickens. He raised tobacco, kept a few sheep, while Eliza tended her vegetable and herb gardens. They may have transplanted wild plum trees from the edge of the forest into an orchard on their elevated homestead.

Apple trees would have fared well on the site that sat some two hundred feet above the water of the White, an uphill walk from the canoe landing. The slope was manageable, similar to that between the Arkansas River and the fort site at Belle Point. Peter, Mourning, and David Caulder, no doubt, hacked out a path to the cabin, carting in large, flat stones for steps, most likely, to negotiate the steeper rises. Caulder hitched his horse or a team of oxen owned by his father-in-law and sledded supplies from the pirogue up to the cabin. Living above the river was worth the trouble to Caulder. He believed that the breezes typical of an upland home site were healthier than the fog or miasma associated with bottomland. He well remembered the epidemics that on occasion swept through the army ranks at Fort Gibson directly adjacent to the river. Besides, Caulder typically roamed to the north and east where rich hunting grounds lay and where he could satisfy not only his instincts, but also his income needs from harvesting furs, skins, and meat of the game animals that inhabited the region.

Peter Caulder gave his name to the plateau on which he settled, a description employed by local residents. In 1898, Mrs. Cassia King related a story to the Ozark scribe, Silas Turnbo, about an 1836 journey undertaken by her family in which they rode their horses along the top of "Cawlder Mountain which is situated not far from where the George Pearson (Pierson) farm on White River is."[45] In 1836, Pierson who eventually came to own a steamboat, lived on the river just to the north of John Hall's place. The upland referred to by Ms. King as Cawlder Mountain where Peter Caulder dwelled with his family is situated two miles south of the Oakland road, overlooking Bull Shoals reservoir and the now inundated George Pierson farmland.

Caulder was atypical of the Hall community, and indeed for the entire African American population in the United States, in being recognized by name in the physical geography of a locale. On some maps today for Baxter-Marion counties, a "Negro Hill" and a "Negro Cemetery" are mentioned, but neither title was related to the Hall family. If geographical titles bypassed the Halls, it was not because the family went unknown and stayed inconspicuous. To the contrary, members of the Hall family gained control of good bottomlands, and their homesteads sat near well-traveled junctures. The mouths of the tributaries to the White River provided guideposts for local navigation and it was in the area of Jimmie's Creek, Sister Creek (both of them), and the narrows (Bull Shoals), all prominent land-marks, that the Halls homesteaded. Caulder's place overlooked the site of Pace's Ferry, a river crossing for pioneers that continued to exist in modern times as an automobile ferry until completion of the dam.[46] Despite this settlement prominence of Caulder, Turner, and the Halls, they were omitted in the reminiscences of early Marion Countians. Given the size of the extended family and its interaction with many whites, that omission is surprising.

Silas Claiborne Turnbo described himself as "nothing more than a poor scribbler." But historians of nineteenth-century Arkansas and Missouri feel fortunate about the primary source material that he left, especially about the Halls.[47] Turnbo's collection of essays refers to the 1819 settlement of the Little North Fork area. Turnbo conducted interviews with "old-time" Ozark hill folk, listening to and writing down hundreds of their stories in his travels in the Arkansas-Missouri border region. Many antebellum memoirs that he collected centered on hunting escapades and encounters with wild animals—folk living on the frontier remembered hearing about the biggest bear, the fat-test deer, the most snakes, the hungriest wolves. Obviously, superla-tive stories (tall tales) were the stuff of frontier conversations and were passed around until everyone knew them by heart.[48] Being widely known because of their constant retelling, these happenings became the oral traditions of the Ozarks. Facts, events, and families that were not discussed, therefore, did not become embedded in this tradition. Evidently then the Hall family or Peter Caulder were not discussed and their story and their integration into the hill-folk culture were left out of the Marion County oral tradition except for Turnbo. The Ozark folk interviewed by Turnbo had stayed put for most of their lives and had survived hardships, epidemics, and the Civil War. They recounted those events that had made the most vivid impressions on them as growing youngsters. Turnbo, born in 1844, had canoed the White River and roamed its banks. He knew the White River hill-folk culture first-hand and loved its people. Though some stories certainly contain errors, where the Little North Fork is concerned at least, Turnbo and his sources are accurate in their topographical descriptions, which fit with modern maps, and in their chronology, which fits, in most cases, with newspaper, census, and tax records. Turnbo came to know Joe Hall, twenty-five years his senior, as they both resided in Pontiac, Missouri, near the turn of the twentieth century. In their meetings, Turnbo gathered a group of stories from Joseph, evidently the most loquacious member of the Hall family. In one of his prefaces to a Joe Hall story entitled, "A Long Time Ago," Turnbo wrote that David Hall Sr., the father of Joe, "was a colored man." Turnbo, an ex-Confederate soldier, admitted that he knew "nothing about their [the Hall's] nationality, but the old settlers, the majority of them, said they were free negroes [sic]."[49]

Remarkably, this is the only time that Turnbo refers to his source's "race" when introducing a Joe Hall story, and even this seems to be a reluctant admission. Joe Hall, too, at least as recounted by Turnbo, kept mum about his origin. The Halls never broadcast their ethnicity nor wore their status on their sleeve. More perplexing is the absence of mention of Negro or colored descriptions in two Turnbo accounts that pitted Willoughby Hall and James Hall against vindictive whites. The Civil War spawned some violent acts among residents of Marion County, a community split by secession, and two of the most bizarre involved these sons of David Hall Sr. Angry whites killed Willoughby Hall and shot James Hall.[50] Yet Turnbo does not indicate that "race" played any part in these attacks. References to black people appear infrequently in his voluminous collection, and except for the Halls, the black people whom he mentioned were slaves. Turnbo tried his hand at Negro dialect writing, proving that he was well aware of cultural differences (his efforts at writing mountaineer dialect is present, but inadvertent), but nevertheless the scribbler treated Joe Hall as a friend, suggesting that he was a reliable source and a good man. Turnbo kept his essays light, without social commentary, and to him obviously, the questions of racial discrimination or racial identification were best left alone.

An early chronicler of the White River and Izard County, Augustus Curren Jeffery, mentioned nothing about the Hall family or about a community of free black people in the part of Izard County that became Marion County. Jeffery was born in a cabin built by his father, Jehoida Jeffery, fourteen miles below the "Calico Rock." Henry Rowe Schoolcraft stayed overnight in January 1819 with Jeffery, five years before Augustus Curren Jeffery was born. His father's stories about the fascinating journalist Schoolcraft may have inspired young Jeffery to produce his own written record of the country and its inhabitants. Historians and genealogists find value in Jeffery's sketches of early settlements on the White River, but he missed writing about the free black community. True, the Halls lived twenty-five miles to the north of Mount Olive, the Jeffery home place, which became the county seat where Jeffery would serve Izard County as its clerk in the mid-1840s. But it is also true that Caulder, the Turners, and the Halls were taxpaying contemporaries in Izard County who must have been known to A. C. Jeffery, at least by hearsay. Again, the omission is puzzling.[51]

Peter Caulder, a self-effacing veteran, told no war stories about himself. He liked being in the background and that is where Joe Hall placed him in his memoirs as given to Turnbo. Hall mentioned "Peter Colder" only once in the surviving stories about his family members and their adventures, calling "Peter Colder" a brother-in-law. Hall said that Caulder "kept a severe pack of dogs to chase bears and panthers with."[52] Caulder had pursued these feared predators since his rifleman days when a panther killed one of his favorite dogs. In addition to the sport associated with keeping panther hounds, Caulder may have earned some income from his surplus pups that could bring a hefty price. A White River bear hunter by the name of Amos Robinson offered Jim Cole "a tolerable good . . . cow for the black pup with white ear," but Cole "laffed" at the offer.

A well-known antebellum Batesville author, Charles Francis Mercer Noland, collected early accounts of bear hunting in the White River valley in letters attributed to Pete Whetstone of Devils' Fork. From Noland's collection, modern historians Ted Worley and Eugene Nolte summarized the incredible spirit of the bear hunt. Bear hunters went on expeditions of up to one hundred miles seeking the fattest bears and the more virulent bear country. Sleeping on mats of skins, hounds leashed for freshness the next day, a heap of logs afire, broiling venison and chunks of bear meat—everyone's favorite —over the coals, swapping stories, a better life seemed hard to imagine for Caulder and other dyed-in-the-wool hunters. On the chase, the mounted hunters trailed the quarry, the bawling hounds exciting the blood of all parties. Finally the quarry was "brought to bay," and sometimes hunters waded in with their knives, unwilling to risk shooting a hound. A he-bear often killed a dog or two, and it was not unknown for a hunter to be killed in the fight as well.[53] There were other reasons for the avocation, too—bear skins sold for one dollar a square yard in Batesville, and the fat could be rendered into the best cooking and lamp oil to be had.[54] Caulder, in a carryover from his days in the military, probably hastened to respond to a distress signal from a neighbor whose livestock on the range was being threatened by a bear or a panther. When "track of a bear had been seen in the vicinity of a settlement, the women and children would 'house up' and 'fear to go out far from their houses.'"[55] A panther attacked a two-hundred-pound sow one night near David Hall's cabin and would have killed the hog had not Hall reached the scene in time. Not too many people wanted anything to do with a ferocious bear. Joe Hall once remarked to Turnbo that he "never had (or wanted) a fight with a wild beast that wore claws," but that his brothers Absalom and Willoughby killed six bears in a cave while the snow was on the ground.[56] Probably these bears were yearlings groggy from hibernation. Hunters armed only with muzzle loaders could find an even match in an adult bear or panther— fast, powerful, and dangerous quarry. The scream of a panther frightened men, women, and children, and as the Turnbo stories reveal, big cats acquired mythical proportions in the minds of many settlers. Peter Caulder, the rifleman and keeper of hounds, assisted white and black farmers in controlling the predators of the forests that watched, and sometimes confronted, them.[57] We might wish that Joe Hall had spoken more to Turnbo about his brother-in-law. What he did say in passing, however, gives us a glimpse to the hunting skill of Peter Caulder and his worth to his community.

One of the most storied and vicious episodes in Marion County history occurred around Shawnee Town or Yellville, the county seat, across one major stream, several tributaries, and a full day's ride from Caulder's farmstead. The Everett brothers migrated into the Crooked Creek area from Kentucky around 1837. Large, tough men, they soon established a reputation for hard drinking and brawling. One of the six brothers, J. B., was elected sheriff and paid visits to the Halls and Caulder to assess the value of their farms and personal property holdings. The Everetts were popular with some, but made their share of enemies with their boisterous habits, one of whom was a Yellville tavern keeper, Hansford "Hamp" Tutt. Tutt found plenty of reasons to challenge the Everetts and their political hold on the county, and a bitter rivalry emerged that entangled friends as well as kin. After a June 1844 fracas in the county seat, "both parties from this time forward generally went armed with large knives, pistols, guns, etc."[58] Like other famous feuds in southern mountains, the "Tutt-Everett War" resulted in public fistfights, shooting from ambush, and murder. Jesse Mooney, later an owner and operator of Tolbert's Ferry on the site of present-day Cotter, became a partisan for the Everetts. After an election day in which Mooney won the office of sheriff, an angered Hamp Tutt struck Mooney in the head with a rock as they fought in the streets of Yellville, knocking him unconscious. Had Mooney not survived the attack, Marion County would have been deprived of its first steamboat owner and operator.[59] In its November 1, 1849, edition, the *Arkansas Gazette* reported on the "Marion County Tragedy" where "much excitement prevails and General Wood [of the Arkansas State Militia] has deemed it necessary to retain a company of seventy-five men at Yellville." The Halls and Caulder certainly knew J. B. Everett and Hamp Tutt as well, but apparently stayed well away from allying themselves with either faction in this countywide feud. The "War" lasted from 1837 to about 1850 when the Everetts and the Tutts had either been killed or had moved on to Texas.

An eyewitness account of those tumultuous early days was written around the turn of the century by a Marion County resident, W. B. Flippin. The black people to whom Flippin referred in his published memoirs were invariably slaves. He made no mention of Caulder or the Halls or Madewells, although he had to have known them or, at the very least, of them.[60]

CHAPTER EIGHT

Flush Times and the Storm

IN THE STATE'S SECOND GUBERNATORIAL ELECTION, ARKANSAS
voters elected Archibald Yell. Yell had migrated to Arkansas from
Bedford County, Tennessee, which lies in the center of the state,
fifty miles south of Nashville. Bedford County was the last Tennessee
home of David and Sarah Hall, the place where their sons David Jr.,
Absalom, and Willoughby had been born. James Henderson Hall,
the son of David Hall's younger sister Rebecca, was born there. David
Hall and Archibald Yell both found Arkansas to their liking. Yell
was a white man, a lawyer, and a restless politician, but nevertheless
had something in common with Peter Caulder as both were veterans
of the War of 1812. Like Maj. William Bradford, Yell had been with
Andrew Jackson at Horseshoe Bend and had caught the Jacksonian
mystique full force. According to his biographer, he participated as
a volunteer in the Battle of New Orleans.[1] Yell was a bombastic
speaker and therefore a popular politician in Arkansas. He once traveled to Marion County in the company of David Walker, the men
competing against each other for a seat in Congress. His friendly
debate with Walker provided so many chuckles and snorts that still-
guffawing citizens began to call their county seat Yellville instead of
Shawnee Town. Yell won that election and recognition in the town's
name, but it was David Walker who acquired properties in Marion
County and helped energize interest in mining around Lead Hill in
the 1850s.[2]

Slaveholders in Arkansas increased in number and in political
power during the 1840–44 period of Yell's administration and with
their heavier clout came anti-black legislation. The General Assembly
passed, and Yell signed into law, an act that infringed further on the
limited rights of free black people. According to the law, free black
persons could not enter the state after March 1, 1843, and those already
residing in the state had to post a five-hundred-dollar bond.[3] The law

was not enforced in Marion County. Had the sheriff wanted to make life hard on Caulder, James Turner, or the Halls or had public opinion insisted that he take action, he might have met resistance from the mulattoes, but no doubt he would have ultimately prevailed. Instead, the sheriff and Marion County people ignored the law as they had bypassed the race of the Halls, Caulder, Turner, and the rest of the free black population before that point. Like most frontier societies, the White River hill folk did not exactly harken to noise from the state capital, even over the matter of race. Indeed, quite the opposite actually occurred. Much to the dismay of Arkansas's "slavocracy" (if they had known), the free black male heads of household in Marion County doubled in number after 1843, with out-of-state immigrants accounting for the growth.

Some free black inhabitants did depart the White River hills after 1840. Not only Martin and James Turner, but James Atkinson, Hillard Rud, and Sarah Bass as well disappeared from county records. Thomas Hall, Henderson Hall, and Leonard Hall moved from Arkansas to Oregon County, Missouri, and then later on to Howell County, Missouri. This branch of the Hall family apparently had reason to be concerned about their negative racial identity in Arkansas. The loss of these individuals and their families drained people and talent from the community. At the same time, new arrivals added to one community of free mulattoes in the county and founded another. Four Madewell families followed a migration pattern like that of the Hall family, from North Carolina to Tennessee to Arkansas. Illinois-born Henley Black, a young free man of color who married Judith Hall, stayed in Arkansas to reside in the extended Hall family after his marriage. Henley and Judith located their cabin, most likely, in a small clearing on a bench above David Hall and gradually expanded their family and their livestock holdings. John Hall's wife, Nancy, was born in Virginia. In time after she and husband had some farming successes, Nancy may have persuaded her aging parents to join her in Marion County. An older couple from Virginia, Charles and Margaret Moore, migrated into the county and set up a household between Yellville and Pyatt. Willis Johnson from Tennessee homesteaded nearby. Johnson's wife, Elizabeth, born in Illinois, may have

FREE BLACK HEADS OF HOUSEHOLD IN 1850 CENSUS— MARION COUNTY

NAME OF ALL HEADS OF HOUSEHOLD WHO WERE CATEGORIZED AS "MULATTO" IN 1850 CENSUS	FIRST YEAR ON MARION COUNTY TAX ROLL 1841–1866	YEARS ON TAX ROLL	STATE WHERE BORN	MOST HEAD OF CATTLE ASSESSED IN ANY ONE YEAR	MOST HORSES ASSESSED	LAST YEAR ON TAX ROLL
1 David Hall Sr.	1841	14	Tennessee	14 (1849)	9 (1841)	1853
2 John Hall	1841	14	Tennessee	22 (1847)	19 (1848)	1859
3 Peter Caulder	1841	11	South Carolina	3 (1859)	2	1859
4 John Turner	1841	11	South Carolina	7 (1849)	3 (1849)	1855
5 Joseph Hall	1841	10	Arkansas	3 (1842)	2	1855
6 David Hall Jr.	1842	10	Tennessee	16 (1859)	3 (1859)	1859
7 Henley Black	1843	10	Illinois	7 (1849)	2	1851
8 Willoughby Hall	1841	9	Tennessee	2	2	1855
9 James Hall	1844	8	Arkansas	5 (1859)	2 (1849)	1859
10 John Dickson	1846	8	Tennessee			1855
11 Absalom Hall	1841	7	Tennessee	2	2	1859
12 John Madewell	1845	6	North Carolina	3 (1848)	3 (1848)	1855
13 James Madewell	1849	5	Tennessee	2	1	1865
14 Thomas Hall	1841	4	Tennessee	2 (1842)	3 (1844)	1844
15 Solomon Madewell	1849	4	North Carolina			1855
16 Francis Nesbit	1853	4	North Carolina			1859
17 Leonard Hall	1846	3	Tennessee	3 (1849)	2 (1849)	1849
18 Charles Moore	1851	3	Virginia			1853
19 Willis Johnson	1851	3	Tennessee			1853
20 Good Madewell	1849	2	Tennessee	1	1	1853
21 Henderson Hall	1846	1	Tennessee	3 (1848)	3 (1848)	1848
22 Rachel Hall Turner	1843	1	Tennessee	0	2 (1843)	1843
23 Clarissa Burns	unknown	unknown	South Carolina	-	-	-

Source: Marion County Tax Record, 1841–1866. Tax records are missing for 1850, 1856, 1857, 1858, 1861, 1862, 1863, and 1864.

accompanied Henley Black from the Prairie State to the White River hill country to find a spouse, even if it meant setting up a home in a slave state. The Moores and the Johnsons settled along Crooked Creek west of the White River in Union Township near the homes of mulattoes Solomon Madewell and John Dickson. A two-day ride prevented frequent contact between this incipient free black community near "Turkey" crossroads and the Caulder, Turner, and Hall families on the White River.[4]

FREE BLACK HEADS OF HOUSEHOLD IN 1830 AND 1840 CENSUS

*In townships that became part of Marion County but **not** enumerated in the 1850 Census*

	NAME OF HEAD OF HOUSEHOLD CATEGORIZED AS "FREE COLORED" IN 1830 OR 1840 CENSUS	FIRST YEAR ON IZARD COUNTY TAX ROLL	YEARS ON TAX ROLL	STATE WHERE BORN	MOST HEAD OF CATTLE IN ANY ONE YEAR	MOST HORSES ASSESSED
1	Martin Turner	1829	3	South Carolina		
2	James Turner	1829	3	South Carolina		
3	Randolph Carter	1829	3	unknown		
4	Hillard Rud	-	-	unknown		
5	Sarah Bass	-	-	unknown		
6	James Atkinson	-	-	unknown		

The assessor for the county did not succeed in placing all county residents on the tax rolls in each year. Probably other duties interfered with his rounds, and potential taxpayers in the more remote nooks were simply omitted. Some county residents may have not had enough property value, no taxable real estate or breeding horses and cattle. Peter Caulder, for example, was not assessed in 1845 or 1846 when he was preempting his land, but maybe not cultivating it, and with little farming equipment or livestock owned. White citizens, too, were occasionally skipped.[5] High water, a new sheriff, a temporary move by a resident, or just a lack of zeal for taxation by a county official might explain the occasional omissions. When Caulder slipped through the net, the county and state did not lose too much revenue since even in his assessed years, his taxes remained among the lowest in the county. A hunter like Caulder might satisfy his tax bill with wolf scalps that became legal tender in Arkansas with the passage of the "wolf scalp bounty" act in 1837.[6] Hogs and chickens, lower maintenance farm animals that Caulder preferred to keep, were not assessed as personal property. Cutting ear marks on his sows and pigs and ranging them on the mast of the surrounding forest might have made more sense to Caulder than the constant management required by herds of cattle or horses. Hams formed a major portion of the food supply at Fort Smith, and it may have been there that Caulder practiced the art of salt curing pork.

John Hall, who farmed below the narrows on good alluvial soil, flat and well watered, steadily increased his holdings in cattle and horses over the years. By 1844, John Hall had a good starter herd of six mother cows. He also had five horses, which included his saddle horse and his team for plowing. With good husbandry practices, his cattle herd increased to twenty-two and his string of horses grew to nineteen.[7] Remarkably, John Hall acquired a slave and probably used him or her in cultivating and harvesting hay and corn fields since his children were still too young for these heavy chores. John Hall, one of two literate mulattoes—James Hall the other—showed the savvy of a businessman. He dealt in livestock and speculated a bit in land, selling a second tract to his white neighbor and friend, George Pierson. Hall returned to the Batesville land office to purchase a forty-acre parcel one and a half miles above Tolbert's Ferry and next to the sixty-one acres owned by David Hall Jr. that is known today as McBee Landing on the White. As the 1850s dawned, John Hall and David Hall Jr. conducted farming operations of above-average scale a mile above present-day Cotter.[8]

John Hall was apparently the only member of the free black community to become a slave owner. Slave owning by free black people violated a legal decision of the Arkansas Supreme Court. But the Marion County sheriff neglected to enforce that ban on John Hall just as he permitted the ownership of firearms, also regulated for free blacks by state law.[9] Caulder and the Halls must have known slaves personally prior to John Hall's acquisition. Caulder may have had a close relationship with Sally, the slave kept in Fort Smith by Taylor Polk. George Pierson, John Hall's friend and Caulder's neighbor, owned a slave. In 1848, the bountiful year that John Hall purchased sixty acres from the government and was assessed $150 property tax for his one slave, there were seventy-three slaves in the county, a number of them held by the mixed-blooded Coker family. The Cokers employed slaves in cutting timber and raising cotton on the tablelands west of the White River.[10]

The cry of gold in California boomed through the Ozarks in 1849, enticing a few Marion County men to join in treks to the west. One Jesse Young, probably a kinsman of John Young who at one time lived near the Halls on the White River, helped form a Marion County company, though Jesse may have aborted his journey to California since he continued to be assessed for taxes in Marion County in the 1850s. Companies of gold seekers formed in many towns, including Clarksville and Harrison, and drew up conduct articles for fellow travelers to sign. Fort Smith was a point of departure for men, and a few women, bound for the gold fields. Wagon trains and pack-mule expeditions searched for good water and sweet grass past the one hundredth meridian along the Santa Fe Trail and more ominously for Marion County Arkansans, via the Utah spur through Mormon country.[11] Black men, free and slave, attached themselves to companies or were attached and became, no doubt, as smitten with the fever as their white traveling companions.[12] The promise land, however, for a number of free black people in Arkansas continued to be the White River hills, one ridge of which near the Caulder and Hall land was so named, Promise Land. In 1849, the communities of mulattoes in Marion County reached new heights of population, property ownership, livestock holdings, and assessed value of personal property. Caulder, Hall, and others paid their county and state taxes each year, including the poll tax, although they probably did not vote or serve on juries. Amidst flush times, enamored with their surroundings, and tuned out to rising anti-black notes in the

Arkansas delta, the Caulder, Hall, Turner, and at least fifteen other free mulatto families framed comfortable and happy lives in the White River hills. The attractions of more liberty or gold awaiting them elsewhere tugged not enough for them to leave Marion County.

Peter Caulder disappeared from the Marion County tax record between 1845 and 1847, as the United States engaged in war with Mexico. Did he reconcile with his old commander and rejoin the army for defense of the country in another national emergency? It is tempting to think of an aging veteran (he would have been around fifty years old) pulled irrevocably down the paths of glory once again, a second act to his army career. Some War of 1812 veterans did shoulder arms in 1846 and win acclaim: Winfield Scott, James E. Wool, and Mathew Arbuckle, for example. But Peter Caulder braced himself against impulses stirred by distant drum and tramping feet. Moreover, the army had not left the door ajar for free black recruits as it did in the preceding war. Instead, army physicians were instructed to inspect recruits for race, implying that African-blooded men would be cast aside, no longer welcomed into the army community. Black men who served with the army during the Mexican-American War did so as musicians and cooks not as riflemen like Caulder and the Turners. Wherever Caulder may have been in 1845 and 1847 when the sheriff missed him in making the appraisal of his property, the ex-rifleman was hardly marching with the Seventh Infantry or any other militia unit.[13] This particular national crisis did not provide an avenue toward more opportunities for blacks. The Mexican War aftermath, in reverse of the emancipation spurt following the Revolutionary War, brought on more racial tension in the United States.[14]

Jacksonian James K. Polk, a wartime president who "supervised every facet of the nation's first foreign war," doubled the area of the United States with his aggressive foreign policy.[15] But, the four monumentally tense years of his first and only term wizened Polk who wanted nothing more in 1848 than to retire to Nashville. With no incumbent running for the presidency, Whigs jumped at the chance to reclaim the office and, true to a tested formula of

Whigdom, nominated a hero of the Mexican War, Gen. Zachary Taylor. Peter Caulder may never have crossed paths with Zachary Taylor, but through friends he knew something about the hard-crusted officer. Bradford, Bonneville, and Caulder's friend Joseph Clark, who had been assigned to Taylor's command at Fort Jesup, must have gossiped to Caulder a bit about the old soldier, revealing a few glimpses. Taylor would be forced by the results of the war to rely on his outspoken nature to lead an increasingly fragmented country. The Treaty of Guadalupe-Hidalgo transferred California and Utah and New Mexico territories to the United States. The resounding U.S. military success and the resulting addition of vast and bewildering landscapes jeopardized, "poisoned" Ralph Waldo Emerson put it, the bonds of union by fueling sectional arguments about the future of slavery and of black people. That chunk of North America gained from Mexico, though indispensable for the nation's destiny, carried a heavy price for its well-being.[16]

A United States stretching from the Atlantic to the Pacific, but internally beset with sectional fault lines greeted the Taylor administration. The *Arkansas Gazette* published a letter calling for secession in 1850. Later in the year, a *Gazette* editorial lauded Crawford County representative Harvey Stewart for introducing a bill in the Arkansas legislature for the removal of all free Negroes from the state. William E. Woodruff added "the sooner the better," and in his paper he labeled free Negroes as "the greatest curse our State labors under" while, ironically, in the same issue he published an advertisement from an entrepreneur desperately seeking to hire five negroes.[17] The removal bill failed in the Assembly and instead its author, Stewart, was removed by the western Arkansas voters. He lasted as representative for only one session. At that point, the majority of Arkansans thought the idea of Union and toleration of free blacks preferable to secession. Union and toleration were ideas that guided the Great Triumvirate, Henry Clay, John C. Calhoun, and Daniel Webster, in the last stages of their noted political careers in piecing together the Compromise of 1850. California, acquired from Mexico, was therefore admitted to the Union as a free state. One of the tradeoffs for the South was congressional approval of the Fugitive Slave Act, which historian Merrill D. Peterson called the "fatal flaw of the compromise."[18] The Fugitive Slave Act had little effect in Arkansas where a professional slave catcher could starve. In Marion County, fugitive slaves were not, evidently, a big problem or a divisive issue, nor were runaways of great significance in the state, even though newspapers carried occasional advertisements for them.[19]

Arkansas newspapers reported, and with its anti-black editorials promulgated, a debate over whether or not free blacks were actually citizens of the United States.[20] The discussion if not the newspapers themselves no doubt reached into the White River hills and may have prompted the mulatto taxpayers to exercise their legal right to purchase and own land to further the impression that they were citizens and therefore members of the state community. During this period, the Halls, John Turner, and Solomon Madewell solidified their position by purchasing land. A legal deed was certainly preferred to claiming squatter rights. Peter Caulder, once a landowner, did not choose to buy or could not afford to buy his homestead on Cawlder Mountain.

Though 1849–50 would have been a propitious point in time for Peter Caulder, or John Turner, or any of the Halls for that matter, to confirm their acceptance by passing for white, none did cross the color line. Perhaps that was impossible, given their local reputations of being mulattoes and having complexion and features that indicated mixed bloodlines. One recorded attempt to cross the color line came with the filing of the affidavit of race by Thomas Hall in 1843, but he was unsuccessful in becoming designated as a white man. Contemporary opinion held that another mixed family, the Cokers, were white although the founding parents, Joe and Ainey, were white man and Indian woman. Joe Coker raised eyebrows in the county when he reputedly took a young Indian woman as his second wife.[21] The Cokers raised eyebrows in other ways in the frontier society as well. The *Gazette* carried a story about a Coker who stabbed an acquaintance to the death across the card table. An early chronicler, William Monks, called one branch of the Coker family "very dangerous men when drinking and the whole county (Marion County) feared them."[22] The Halls lack these kind of local history reminisces and one must wonder how they were referred to by local whites. According to Turnbo, old-timers said the Halls were "free Negroes," but Southern whites almost always termed people of visible African ancestry "nigger." The pejorative term was used deliberately and smugly by whites of all economic classes and all achievement levels. Each and every time it was employed, the illusion of white superiority was conjured, a linguistic dynamic that blacks then as now were acutely aware of. It is possible, but not probable that Marion County settlers referred to Caulder and the Halls in such language. Had they, more might have been made of race in the surviving folk stories. Still, the Halls and Caulders were either not light complexioned enough to pass or they were unwilling to take that step. Turnbo mentioned that Sarah Hall, Eliza Hall Caulder's mother, was "nearly white in color."[23] Perhaps there were too many mulattoes on the White River and they were too well known to suddenly have their African ancestry disregarded by their peers. Whatever their choices or lack of as to racial identity, the Marion County mulattoes continued to live in community with White River hill whites until an episode of violence struck at one of their clan in 1851. Until then, they seem to have avoided the feuds and violence of Marion County, and their good neighbor reputation helped protect them from malice.[24] But the community revamped its racial lines in the decade of the 1850s. The new definition eventually overpowered all the mulatto families' good works and pioneer neighborliness.

James M. Cowdrey, a physician, migrated from South Carolina to Marion County in 1836 and established his medical practice.[25] Cowdrey's wife, Agness, twenty years his junior, bore him seven children to whom she tended while he made house calls, riding his horse for miles to treat the sick and injured.[26] Cowdrey took a salaried job as clerk of the county and so had knowledge of the taxpaying citizens and where they lived. Affable, and unlike many in the medical profession, blessed with superb penmanship, Cowdrey seemed an ideal choice for a census marshal. He, no doubt, dispensed a bit of free medical advice to mothers and children on his census-taking calls. At his home east of Yellville, in early autumn 1850 Cowdrey packed his saddlebags with official preprinted census forms (available from the *Arkansas Gazette*) and set out to count the residents of Marion County. In just two weeks he had reached his sixty-seventh residence, that of John H. Tolbert near present-day Cotter.[27] He enumerated the Tolbert family: John, age twenty-seven; his wife, Adeline, age twenty; and three children, Susan, four; Mary, two; and William, one year old. No one would have forecast that a year later John Tolbert would be dead, murdered some said by one of the mulatto men in Marion County. By Thursday October 25 Cowdrey had reached the farms just north of Bull Shoals and the home of David Hall Sr., where he may have lodged overnight. The next day, Cowdrey rode up to visit Caulder and placed his household on record. Caulder informed the erstwhile physician that neither he nor Eliza could read and write and that, he, Peter Caulder, fifty-five years of age, was born in South Carolina.[28] Caulder and Cowdrey perhaps exchanged pleasantries about their previous homes in the Palmetto state—Catfish Creek and Charleston. Based on what he saw and heard, Cowdrey made two telling judgments about Peter and Eliza Caulder: that their real estate had a value of two hundred dollars, about average for a mountain homestead with cabin, and that both were mulattoes, defined by Arkansas law as a person with one grandparent who was "Negro" or who was "one-fourth or more Negro."[29] Cowdrey made his racial determination about the Caulders, John and Margaret Turner, Henley and Judith Black, and the Halls, a score of households in the county altogether, from his observations of their color and status and with reference to their racial reputation. Just after columns headed *age* and *sex* on the preprinted census form, column six asked for "Color White, black, or mulatto." For each person enumerated in the census, Dr. Cowdrey was required and empowered to mark "w" for white, "b" for black, or "m" for mulatto in this column. The 1850 census was designed by statisticians to be more curious about the population than its forerunners and Cowdrey also listed the profession of the head of household (Caulder's was "farmer"), whether any residents in a household attended school, was married within the last year, or was deaf, dumb, blind, idiotic, a pauper, or a convict. None of the latter categories applied to the Caulders or the Hall families, but column twelve, "persons over 20 years of age who cannot read and write," claimed a check for every adult in the mulatto community, except for John Hall and James Hall. Being illiterate was not unusual in Marion County. Cowdrey checked that column for 45 percent of the heads of households in the county. By December, Dr. Cowdrey completed his rounds and filed his schedules for certification. He marked "b" by no free person in the county, but in his neat script, placed an "m" by the side of 129 men, women, and children, often underlining the letter *m*.[30] Dr. Cowdrey, a decent, well-respected man, thus cast the fate of 129 of his fellow Marion County residents and made official for the third decade in a row the census racial designation of Peter Caulder, David Hall, their wives, their families, and their kinsmen. Nor was racial categorization for the Halls an issue unfamiliar to Cowdrey. He had been the county clerk of Marion County in 1843 when Thomas Hall had brought in his affidavit of race in an effort to be officially noted as a white man of Portuguese heritage. Apparently Cowdrey was not impressed with Hall's affidavit nor was the marshal in Oregon County, Missouri, who continued to classify Hall and his children as mulatto in the 1850 census.[31]

The Hall farms did impress Cowdrey. He evaluated the real estate holdings of David Hall Sr. as worth $1,000 and John Hall's as $2,000, amounts that equaled or exceeded that of locally respected and prosperous white farmers such as that of neighbor John Woods's farm, a larger than average operation in the county that was valued at $2,000. Hall must have had comparable livestock and machinery as Woods, who had $120 of farm machinery, ten horses, fifteen milk cows, four working oxen, thirty beef cattle, seventeen sheep, and sixty hogs. To feed his livestock and family, Woods produced two thousand bushels of corn, thirty bushels of wheat, and one hundred bushels of oats.[32] At the same valuation, John Hall would have had a comparable farm operation, David Hall Sr. about half as much. Down river, Cowdrey visited the farmstead of John Hargrave and evaluated it at $1,000. Dr. Cowdrey had once rushed there to treat Nancy Hargrave, John's wife, for an illness.[33] Hargrave, himself a census marshal in 1840, needed his large family to help him tend such a farm. In addition to six horses, a herd of forty-two steers and heifers, and fourteen milk cows, the Hargraves kept a flock of sheep and sixty hogs. Cowdrey proceeded on to the next household, that of David Jr. and Margaret Hall and children, whom he listed as mulattoes. Cowdrey estimated the value of Hall's sixty-one acres over which ranged his six horses and twelve cows as $350. Margaret Hall informed the census marshal that she had been born in Indiana. Once a year the Halls sheared their thirteen sheep and from the fleece made woolen socks and shirts as did many settlers in Marion County. Ten or twelve sows rooted about the barnyard, swarmed at nursing time by their latest litter of squealing pigs. Cowdrey toured the crib, and David showed him four hundred bushels of Indian corn stored there. Four milch (milk) cows helped nourish David and Margaret's four children that ranged in age from one-year-old Amanda to seven-year-old John R. Margaret churned butter with the excess sweet milk and sold it to nearby tenants. To earn cash, Hall could have worked in the harvests and other heavy farm times for Hargrave. A white tenant, William Slow, who dwelled in a rented cabin next to David Hall in this racially integrated stretch along the White River, hired out to Hargrave and perhaps to Hall, too.[34] Cowdrey listed Slow as Indiana-born. Whether a white William Slow and a mulatto Margaret Hall were kin or just happened to be from the same state is not known. If they were related, it shows that racial classification of husband and wife usually conformed, even though in the case of Spaniard John Brannum, a white man, and his mulatto wife, Harriet Hall, in the same census it did not. Margaret and David Hall Jr. honored close relatives in naming their children. The Caulder, Turner, and Hall families tended to carry names of favorite relatives over into the next generation. David and Margaret's oldest son was named John R.; their second son Irvin, the name of John Hall's second son. The third son born in 1848 was named Marion and their youngest was a daughter they named Amanda, a name shared by Peter and Eliza's youngest daughter. Levi Pierson, father of George Washington Pierson and a widower, married late in life Elizabeth, an older Indiana-born woman. The couple christened their youngest son Marion.[35] The census of 1850 hinted in the very sequence of dwellings at the complexity of relationships that existed between mulatto and white yeoman neighbors. Extended families and intertwined neighbors molded life in the White River hill country. It is clear that whites who pioneered into the White River hills and, over a couple of decades, came to shape opinion and hold office in Marion County, people like George Pierson, John Hargrave, John Magness, John W. Martin, and John D. Noe, interacted on a equal basis with the county's mulatto free persons.[36]

In December 1850, five weeks after Cowdrey's census visit, forty-five-year-old John Turner perhaps in company with his older brother-in-law and close friend Peter Caulder once again took the one-hundred-mile journey down the White River to Batesville. If the men paddled Caulder's pirogue downstream, a five- to seven-day trip, they wit-

WHITE RIVER TOWNSHIP, MARION COUNTY, ARKANSAS, AGRICULTURAL CENSUS OF 1850

Neighbors Adjoining Farm Home of David B. Hall Jr.

DWELLING NO. OWNER OR MANAGER OF FARM	IMPROVED ACRES	UNIMPROVED ACRES	VALUE OF FARM	FARMING IMPLEMENTS	NO. OF HORSES	MULES	MILCH COWS	WORK OXEN	OTHER CATTLE	SHEEP	SWINE	
#28 John Hargrave	45	115	$1,000	$150	6	3	15	2	42	14	60	
#29 David B. Hall Jr.	30	50	$350	$15	5	3	4	2	10	13	60	
#30 William Slow Tenant farmer	-	-	0	$5	2	-	1	-	-	5	20	
Projected land, livestock, and agricultural worth of Peter Caulder in 1850												
Peter Caulder	5	40	$200	$10	3	-	2	-	2	-	40	

nessed more river traffic than ever before. Steamboats now regularly plied the White in winter and spring, hauling goods up to Buffalo Shoals in the southeastern corner of Marion County. There, Missouri traders transferred cargo to their flatboats and continued with trade goods all the way to Forsythe, Missouri, and points in-between. In wintry weather on the water, Caulder and Turner would have worn woolens underneath their buckskin pants and jackets. Turner carried a pouch made of deerskin to encase the deed being held for him by the receiver at the land office. For headwear, Caulder the huntsman might have worn a cap "made of skins of coons or wild cat . . . with the tail hanging down at the back part of the neck."[37] In initiating the patenting process, Turner had journeyed to the land office the previous year to enter $49.98 on the land that his father-in-law David Hall had homesteaded in 1819. This tract on the left bank of

VALUE OF LIVESTOCK	WHEAT BUSHELS	RYE	INDIAN CORN, BUSHELS	OATS	TOBACCO	WOOL	IRSIH POTATOES	SWEET POTATOES	ORCHARD, VALUE OF	BUTTER, LBS.	CHEESE	HAND MANUFACTURES	VALUE OF SLAUGHTER ANIMALS
$850	20	-	1,000	-	-	-	20	50	$5	345	-	$150	$60
$400	20	-	400	-	-	-	10	20	-	200	-	$10	$30
$100	20	-	200	-	-	-	5	12	-	-	-	$10	$30
$200	10	-	400	-	-	-	20	20	$5	200	-	$100	$50

the river included twenty acres of cleared alluvium soil that lay flat and relatively stone free, rich and friable, good for raising corn or cotton. Now the long wait for the land office to churn out the paper was over, and Turner could pick up his legal deed for the very ground that David Hall Sr. had cleared of thick cane and huge gums in 1819, ground on which the pioneer-patriarch had built a cabin and made his whiskey. Ten years later, for some reason Hall Sr. was attracted to a new site four miles upstream and decided to re-settle there. John Hall probably helped Hall Sr. with the move toward the mouth of Sister Creek and maybe even touted the location because he had discovered a likely spot for himself a bit farther up.

Dispersing in the opposite direction at about the same time, young David Jr. settled in on a fertile patch of riverbank land downstream. These moves were expansionist because Hall's son James and his son-in-law John Turner remained to farm the family's original home site just above Bull Shoals. The yeoman Halls were following a classic path of family land aggrandizement well worn by planter families in the Delta and in southwest Arkansas.

James Turner, his wife, Margaret, and James and Salena Hall made improvements on the core farm across the river from which were bluffs honeycombed with limestone caves, favorites of bats and bees and laced with saltpeter. A few miles upstream, David Hall Sr. and Sarah, assisted by sons Joseph and Leonard and son-in-law Henley Black, cleared a substantial swath in the cane-choked bottoms of a seventy-one-acre tract and built their log cabins.

The extended Hall family, like other yeoman families, had become large enough for members to specialize according to their interests. Such branching out by relatives formed a family safety net and was indeed the secret of successful families in the developing frontier society. Joseph Hall, more of a storyteller than an expert hunter, accompanied the men and the hounds, bringing back a wealth of tales about the wilds, some of which he related to Silas Turnbo fifty years later. Willoughby Hall dedicated himself to woodsy pursuits, hunting, fishing, and trapping alongside his brother-in-law Peter Caulder. Their habits were so alike that it seems likely that Willoughby stayed close to Caulder on Cawlder Mountain. The two men spent a good deal of time tracking bears and bringing back deer pelts. But the huntsmen well knew the urgencies of farming, and lent a hand to their more agrarian brothers during the heavy labor occasions of harvest, haying, or curing. Downstream, John Turner and James Hall were helped by Absalom Hall, another huntsman, who lived as a tenant on a bench above them. Though like all Ozark farmers, they at times could attune themselves to the music of the hounds, John Turner and James Hall routinely harnessed the plow horses and cropped large fields. The brothers-in-law had a team of oxen for pulling logs and rocks. They put up a thousand bushels of corn each year, milked five or six cows, the milk from which provided several hundred pounds of butter and cheese. The partners grew rye, wheat, and corn crops for the table and to feed livestock. In the gardens, their wives planted Irish potatoes, yams, and onions.[38]

While Caulder and Willoughby kept their shooting eye sharp by squirrel or turkey hunting, John Hall, David Jr., and Henley Black could be found instead mowing hay with scythes and raking it into stacks to feed cows and horses through the winter. After the planting and harvests, the labors of a yeoman farmer did not end, but changed to cutting timber, clearing and draining more land, and building corrals, cribs, and fences. The surveyor in 1840 had mapped the acreage that John Turner and James Hall had under cultivation. Each year, the ambitious young farmers attempted more improvement, felling trees and cutting drainage ditches to add crop acreage and, it was hoped, add to the yield and to the income. Their plans must have been fulfilled. Their efforts transformed the pioneer homestead into a prosperous, tidy farm, the envy of many a passer-by. After a few years of good harvests of wheat, corn, and rye and steady increases in their herds, Turner had established a farm valued at eight hundred dollars, which in the evaluation codes of the day meant thirty acres of improved land, six or seven horses, fifteen to twenty head of cattle, several milk cows, perhaps a flock of sheep, and forty to fifty hogs.

With decent prices for crops and livestock in 1850, John and Margaret Turner may have discussed an additional investment in land. James Hall's operation was less, his farm being valued at $100. He had ten to fifteen acres under cultivation, a team of horses or oxen, several cattle, and, of course as did everyone else in the county, a number of pigs. With enough money to go ahead with his second land buy, John Turner accompanied by James Hall again traveled south to Batesville in order to acquire title to forty-eight additional acres. Peter Caulder may have gone to paddle the pirogue and hunt game, but twenty-eight-year-old James Hall, though never a man of wealth, had more in mind than merely being along for the ride. While at the land office that day, August 14, 1851, he paid $29.15 in hard-earned cash for 23.32 acres that adjoined John Turner, solidifying the family's claim to 112 acres of choice left-bank property, on which had been located the first cabin of David Hall Sr.[39]

Charles Francis Mercer Noland, recently appointed receiver for the land office, signed the receipts and may have bantered with Turner and Hall about the gold fields. The Batesville *Eagle*, to which Noland contributed stories, had reprinted articles about the route from Fort Smith to California and about the fever that news of gold strikes raised in Arkansans. Noland, a Virginia-educated transplant to the frontier, made one of the earliest contributions to Arkansas literature with his Pete Whetstone letters to a New York magazine, *The Spirit of the Times*. The writer particularly relished the bear hunt and may have asked Turner and Hall about their brother-in-law Peter Caulder in a search for material. Caulder no doubt traveled to Batesville, the best market, to sell his hides, furs, and skins and over the years may have gained notice for his prowess as a hunter. Noland's fictional Whetstone was a "'coon skin frontiersman and 'bar' hunter," much like Peter Caulder. Fent Noland and Caulder may have enjoyed sharing bear stories.[40]

Renewed land buying signaled that the mulatto community on the White River was still on the ascent. Young fathers Henley Black and Francis Nesbit progressed from pioneers to providers, adding stock, filling their lauders, and wresting a satisfactory livelihood from the White River hill country. Like other young wives in antebellum Marion County, Judith Black and Sarah Nesbit processed food for the winter and made clothes. Hardy frontier women like Eliza Caulder and her daughters, Margaret, Mourning, and Susan, worked side by side with the men in keeping the farm. Hitching the team and guiding a jolting plow over rocky fields was considered as much

woman's work as man's. Typically, a woman like Eliza churned butter and spent part of each day sewing, spinning, and baking bread.
Eliza with young children, Moses (Thompson), Amanda, and infant
Stephen to protect while Peter was away for a fortnight on a hunt,
could have kept a loaded musket over the door frame. Peter Caulder's
oldest son David grew to manhood in the community. He married,
built a log cabin for his wife, whose name is unknown, and fathered
a son, James (probably named after Peter's old friend James Turner),
the third generation of Caulders to live in Arkansas.

Absalom Hall had worked here and there for years, living with
family members until he was over forty. Absalom seemed a good catch
to a recently arrived young woman in the community, Martha, who
married him late in the year of 1849. The newlyweds had instant company in their rustic honeymoon cabin smelling of fresh-cut oak as her
younger brother and sister moved in with them. Soon the family
increased naturally with the birth in 1850 of twins, Mary and Clarky.
Martha and her siblings may have been related to the Madewells who
immigrated from Tennessee to the White River hills. The Madewells
were light-skinned mulattoes who ignored, as did Marion County officials, the Arkansas law of 1843 that prohibited free Negroes from
entering the state to live. Four Madewell families founded homesteads
near a crossroads settlement known as Turkey between Yellville and
Pyatt. One of the clan's two patriarchs, Solomon Madewell, patented
his forty-acre homestead. Solomon and his older brother John
Madewell were up in age when they migrated, but apparently were in
good health. Both had young adults and children living with them in
their households. In 1850, Solomon Madewell reported owning two
horses, two milk cows, and five hogs, a farm skimpily stocked by the
standards of the day. His young nephew, Good Madewell, accepted a
horse race challenge from a white neighbor, Jet Chaffin, gambling
that his steed was the fastest. He lost the race and the confidence of
his exasperated wife, Malinda. As Good Madewell paid Chaffin the
stakes, a "rifle gun," Malinda, who probably managed the household
finances, wrung her hands, saying over and again, "I knowed it, I
knowed it, I knowed it." Malinda implored Good to give up horse racing until he was sure that he could win. The agricultural census shows

that the couple had very little to lose. Fortunately, they had support from Good's father, John Madewell.[41] Charles F. M. Noland believed that there were only a few sports worth a man's time: bear hunting, horse racing, and shooting matches in that order. Most Marion County settlers, including the mulattoes, thought about the same. Good Madewell lost a rifle, a heavy bet. In the frontier days when cash was short for everybody, the stakes for a race were often store goods such as trousers, robes, boots, and hats.[42]

With growing prosperity, more machines and implements, and there-fore a bit more free time, organized religious practices in Marion County may have attracted some in the mulatto yeoman communities. At least one camp meeting occurred that was attended by Marion County residents. In such a frontier evangelical setting, the Caulders, Halls, and Madewells surely would have been welcomed. Pioneer Billy Parker recalled that long before the Civil War, Bill Flippin preached on Jimmie's Creek, which was close to the Hall lands. Religiosity must have existed within the Hall family because Dave Hall's son and grand-son, his namesakes, became Baptist preachers in Missouri. When early settlers like the Halls had established themselves well enough and advanced their frontier existence beyond a daily struggle for food, clothing, and shelter, they then could focus on religious services. Between the years 1844 and 1861, for example, Methodist Church membership in Arkansas increased from 9,481 to 24,164. Baptist and Presbyterian denominations had similar growth, and by 1852 at least two churches were underway in Yellville. Two Methodist ministers, Pleasant Bassham and James D. Martin, conducted services in the county. A resident during the antebellum period remembered church houses being "built of hewed timber, floored with puncheons, hewed seats, size of house generally from 18 by 20 to 22 by 25 feet, chinked and daubed. The churches or denominations then were Baptists and Methodist. There didn't appear to be any antagonism or hatred exist-ing between the denominations."[43]

Formal education—book learning—did occur in the Hall family. John Hall, who could read and write himself, had two pre-teen sons

George Washington and James Irvin to attend school, probably the one that opened on Jimmie's Creek. Reuben Turner, an eighteen-year-old who lived with John Hall and was probably the son of James Turner the ex-rifleman, learned to read and write and may have been in charge of rowing a boat across the White River to the small log schoolhouse on Jimmie's Creek. He represented the third generation of mulattoes in Marion County to become a taxpayer.[44] Schoolmaster John Pace may have opened his doors to these children because he depended on tuition and John Hall could afford to pay it. On the way to school, Reuben gathered up Denton, thirteen, and Jackson, twelve, sons of Clarissa Burns and the only other children in the Caulder, Turner, or Hall families to attend a school. Education, even if rudimentary, for free black youngsters in antebellum times ran contrary to norms in the South, but James M. Cowdrey indicated in his census report that the mulatto children had attended school.[45] John Hope Franklin wrote that there was "little doubt that free Negroes were eager to secure an education," and that they certainly were part of the "awakening (to) education in the generation preceding the Civil War."[46] James and John Hall found an opportunity for schooling that they knew would benefit their male children. The Halls's daughters and Clarissa Burns's daughters of school age stayed at home to learn other skills, and so did all the children, male and female, of Peter Caulder. Neither Peter nor Eliza ever learned to read and write, although evidence of a changing world was all around. A professional hunter would have, no doubt, seen these profound changes as soon as anyone. Still, it would be another generation before the Caulder family buckled down into letters. Eventually, Peter Caulder's descendants would master the intricacies of the modern academic world as he had mastered the intricacies of his frontier world.

Cotton prices soared along with the Arkansas slave population in the last decade before the Civil War. In 1850, Marion County farmers planted only twenty-six acres of the "white gold," yet it was, along with timber, furs, and whiskey, a commodity worth enough to be carried out on the steamboats grown common on the White River. The yeoman farmer and his family provided the enormous labor it took to plant, cultivate, pick, and load a thousand pounds of cotton typically produced on a valley farm in the Ozarks, where an acre of good ground yielded a half a bale. Sold at ten cents a pound, the one hundred dollars represented a needed cash income well worth all the work and trouble.[47] In contrast, a Delta plantation could produce two to three hundred bales from premium land and black slave labor. In order to protect such property and their investment in it, Southern planters constructed a mighty political and psychological defense of slavery.

The Gold Rush and the boom in cotton created an irony for the Caulders and the Halls. Having built secure, respected, prosperous, and independent lives amidst the whites of Marion County, the Caulders and the Halls were at the apex of their community and family success on the White River. Entering the decade of the fifties, they were about to come face to face with racial turbulence because of national expansion, cotton wealth, and the slaying of a white man—an incident that involved them. After the Mexican-American War, more vicious anti-black rhetoric, part of the psychological defense of slavery launched by the planters, buffeted the citizenry from articles and editorials in the *Arkansas Gazette* and from endless gossip. In this milieu, an unfortunate event occurred in Marion County that marred relationships between the Hall extended family and their white neighbors.

In September 1851, James Hall and John Turner were returning home from Batesville in great spirits knowing that they were acquiring full legal possession to prized family lands. Their good cheer soured, though, "near Tolbert's ferry on White River ten miles east of Yellville" when James Hall had an encounter and a dispute with John H. Tolbert.[48] Nothing is known of what sparked the violence, but both men were twenty-eight years old when a challenge to one's manhood is difficult to ignore. In the fight, Hall, a "stout, robust, and active" man fatally injured Tolbert, resulting in a charge of murder being brought against Hall. It is not known when or if he were arrested and jailed. In an age when the wheels of justice normally turned a bit faster than today, it seems odd that Hall's trial did not come about until a year later. For his defense, Hall secured the services of William Byers, a prominent Batesville lawyer, and James A. Wilson, an attorney and a wealthy landowner of Marion County.

Byers owned land in Marion County, too, and had in the past conducted business with the mulattoes, once selling John Hall a tract
along the White River. Moreover, Byers was an acquaintance of
Fent Noland, with whom James Hall had spoken while at the land
office to buy his property. John H. Byers, William's brother, and
James P. Spring prosecuted the case for the state. The warm relationship between the opposing attorneys might have tempered any
tendency toward rancorous remarks, which may have worked to
Hall's advantage. Since Arkansas law prohibited free Negroes from
testifying against whites, none of the Halls, Caulder, or James's close
friend and farm partner John Turner took the witness stand. Peter
and David Caulder and other men of the county's free black population may have packed Circuit Judge B. H. Nealey's courtroom at
Yellville to show their support for James Hall and offset the influence
of the Tolberts and their friends who surely gathered as well. The circuit court records for Marion County were destroyed by fire so a transcription of the trial does not exist. As the trial unfolded, Byers and
Wilson succeeded in placing doubt in the minds of the white jurors,
more Tolbert's peers than Hall's. Remarkably, the white jury found
James Hall, a free Negro, not guilty of the murder of John H. Tolbert,
a well-known and well-liked white man.[49]

Two Little Rock newspapers, the *Whig* and the *Arkansas Gazette*,
reported the jury's decision and referred to James Hall as a "free
negro" but did not editorialize about the case. William E. Woodruff,
editor of the *Gazette*, took a strong stand against free Negroes living
in the state, but despite his vilification of them, the northern-born
editor was committed to the principle of due process for Negroes. On
one reported occasion, a mob dragged a slave jailed for murdering a
white in Arkansas to a hanging tree. The *Gazette* adamantly opposed
mob rule and demanded that the law deal severely with those who
lynched the man.[50] In Marion County, whites may have been agi-
tated after the Hall trial but there evidently was no mob vengeance.
Even so, the carryover from the trial disturbed the delicate equilib-
rium for the mulattoes in Marion County. The gap in taxation for
1852, the year of the trial, clearly shows the rise in tensions and the
struggle of the Halls to pay for James Hall's defense.

Quite unlike the preceding years when up to eighteen mulattoes had been assessed by the county sheriff, in 1852 not a single member of the Hall extended family appeared on the tax record. Moreover, John Turner, who had just purchased the White River lands that formed the core of the Hall settlement in Marion County, sold it in June 1852 to John W. Martin, a Yellville merchant. Probably the cash was needed to pay attorney fees and court costs for James Hall, Turner's close friend, relative, and farm partner. People associated with the Halls through marriage—Peter Caulder, David Caulder, Henly Black, and Francis Nesbit—also were omitted from the tax rolls. James Hall moved off the river onto seventy-two acres of bench land (just to the west of today's Promise Land Church) that Absalom Hall had probably occupied. Hall may have moved there until passions cooled. On the mountain farm, he could caretake Absalom's cabin and more easily avoid travelers on the White River. Across Sister Creek, James Hall could see Cawlder Mountain (Caulder's name is spelled Cawlder in the 1849 tax record) and the smoke rising from Caulder's chimney. Caulder, who continued to preempt his land rather than purchase it, may have liquidated some of his livestock to help with trial expenses and had so little to declare that the sheriff ignored him.

Six of the Halls resurfaced on the tax rolls by 1855 and Caulder returned by 1859, his last year of paying taxes in Arkansas. The trial had been successful from the Hall point of view in acquitting James, but it took a few years for the family to recover from the expense of it. The old home place sold after the trial was never recovered for the family. The slaying of Tolbert generated enough local animosity that relationships changed, and in most cases physical locations changed, too. The majority of Marion County citizens might have been fair minded enough to believe that justice had been served, but not all of them were. Tolbert left a young wife, three children, and some irate family members and friends. Their time for revenge against James Hall came during the Civil War.[51]

At the turn of the century, Silas Turnbo solicited details of the Tolbert killing from Peter Keesee, a contemporary of the Halls and Tolberts. Turnbo fashioned a sort of Ozark comic opera based on what Keesee had told him. In his piece, "Dodging Bullets," Turnbo related that James Hall, a brother of Willoughby Hall and a son of Dave Hall, "killed John Tolbert near Tolbert's ferry on White River ten miles east of Yellville." During the Civil War, "some of Mr. Tolbert's friends captured the murderer and taken [sic] him to the foot of [T]hree [B]rothers in what is now Baxter County." There intending to execute Hall, the men shot at James Hall, but he rolled, jumped, and whirled about so that the shooters inflicted only flesh wounds. Hall "deceived his enemies by falling on his face . . . and they believed he was dead." To check, the avengers pecked Hall's forehead with a sharp rock, but he did not flinch, and the men, satisfied that they had carried out their intention, rode away without burying Hall "for they had rather the wolves devour his body." The feigning Hall revived himself and crawled into the bushes. That night he climbed down the rocky hollow of Sister Creek and along the edge of the White River until he reached what had been his and John Turner's place. There, in his father's old farm, Hall "was seen on the following day using his tongue pretty lively."[52]

Turnbo's rendition of what must have been an event that inspired rounds of gossip, which was by no means confined to Marion County, confirmed there were whites who would be happy to apply vigilante justice to the Halls. Turnbo used the term *murderer* in the story and his concluding statement about Hall and his tongue, though meant to be humorous, has a cutting tone. Just the same, Turnbo refused to type Hall as a free Negro in his story, though the two contemporary newspaper accounts did so. Part of Turnbo's reticence to involve race in his stories might have resulted from his apparently close relationship with Joseph Hall, one of his sources whom he may have spent a good deal of time with at Pontiac, Missouri. Similarly, Turnbo had a nonracial slant to the mutilation of Willoughby Hall, Peter Caulder's friend and hunting companion. In a story entitled, "How the Man Willoughby Hall Was Scalped," Turnbo described another revenge shooting of one of the Hall family.[53]

Obviously, animosities did build up in Marion County but a concerted local movement to force the Caulders, the Turners, and the

Halls from their ancient homes yet may not have come about and is not a part of traditional county lore. Friendships with respected and influential whites such as George Pierson, William Byers, John Martin, and John Hargrave formed a line of defense. Marion County had already seen too much violence and too much mixing of blood lines to overreact to a single incident, even though that happened to be the killing of a white man by a member of the free Negro Hall family. Although life would never return to what was normal before 1852, mulatto families stayed in the county for another eight years, continuing to raise children and tend their agricultural interests. In fact, at the age of forty-six in 1853, John Hall acquired more property along the White River. In February, he made his third trip to the Batesville Land Office and paid $49.62 for 39 acres on the right bank of the White River in Marion County. Hall also purchased adjoining lands from the Batesville attorney William Byers. In all, he had title to 129 acres of prime land that lay across the river from today's town of Cotter directly below the Highway 62 bridge.[54]

A clear separation of Marion County's two mulatto communities is outlined in the deed and tax records of the 1850s. The Turkey settlement stayed intact and as normal had their property assessed in 1852 and 1853. However, in 1854 the Madewells disappeared from the roll, never to fully reinstate themselves as county taxpayers. At the same time, ironically, the Halls and Peter Caulder made a return as tax-paying property owners. Free mulattoes in both Marion County clusters may have felt that their hold on Arkansas lands was becoming tenuous as they heard rumors emanating from the Arkansas River valley that newspapers and some legislators wanted a law passed driving their category of people out of the state. But that was old news, based on well-worn complaints against free Negroes in Little Rock where occasional black mettle annoyed dogmatic whites. Before the Hall-Tolbert affair changed the attitudes in Marion County, no one, not Caulder nor the Halls, took legislative expulsion as a serious threat. After all, settlement in the upper White River hills of Arkansas had been multicultural since the Cherokee arrival. The large Coker extended family was mixed-race people, and their presence must have created a more tolerant atmosphere for darker-skinned people.

The numerous Cokers kept a good portion of the slaves in Marion County. Joe Coker's eighteen slaves, all but one of whom was female, constituted the largest holding in the county. Marion County free blacks outnumbered slaves in the 1850 census, 129 to 126.[55] In no other county in Arkansas did this proportion occur, and far from feeling uneasy about free blacks in general, Marion County whites had little to fear from slave uprisings nor did they gossip about runaway slaves.[56] Moreover, Caulder and the Halls, or the Cokers for that matter, had no real cultural differences with their fellow Marion County residents of Scotch-Irish or English heritage. Their homesteads, their vocations and avocations, their methods of parenting, their recipes, and their socioeconomic class mirrored that of their white counterparts in the White River hills. Dissimilar ways and interests, often the stuff of suspicion, were not apparent; common interests and common preparation, the stuff of trust, were. No strange cultural habits or language barriers divided Caulder and the Halls from the Piersons or the Woods or the Hargraves or other long-term settlers who multiplied into extended families along the White River. The mulatto men and women had valuable skills to provide for a county short on population. Caulder hunted bears, sold honey, and could build a chimney or a pirogue upon demand. John Hall raised and sold good horse flesh, and may have learned farrier arts from Martin Turner that he could apply when his neighbors needed it.[57] Good Madewell raced his colt. Dave Hall Sr. made whiskey, ranged sows, and cured bacon and hams. Joe Hall fire hunted from a canoe and entertained with tales of his woodland adventures. Copperheads and panther screams frightened the mulattoes just as they did the whites; the Halls had shooting accidents and they drowned. In a hundred ways, the Caulders, Halls, Turners, and Madewells proved, without being self-conscious, that they belonged to the White River hill community. Whites, in turn, defined the community to include this vigorous and harmonious segment of dark-skinned people.

Arkansas had the lowest percentage of free black people as measured against whites than any other of the slave states. Yet the size, independence, and endurance of the two free black clusters in Marion County reveal the benevolent effect that a convergence of frontier-hill-western cultures had in structuring and *preserving* a unique racial situation. In the White River hills, black and white people were not natural enemies. Anti-black Southerners may have preferred to ignore successful free black enclaves living in harmony with white neighbors, but their existence demonstrated that racial attitudes and relationships were not uniform across the Southern states in the antebellum period. Other examples existed in the South. Vernon Burton in a study of the Edgefield, South Carolina, free black community concluded "that on the eve of war which would lead to the freedom of all blacks, the barriers in Edgefield District between whites and blacks were not so formidable as historians have thought."[58] With a similar conviction, the noted historian C. Vann Woodward held that *despite* the old regime's insistence on white superiority, racial boundaries in the South were *neither uniform nor rigid* because slavery did not breed segregation, rather integration (italics added) and free blacks were so small in number that their segregation had little relevance.[59] Groups in Crawford County (Fort Smith) and in Little Rock came closer to the normal pattern of "quasi-free" existence defined by John Hope Franklin or "slaves without masters" described by Ira Berlin. But in the Arkansas lowlands at the convergence of two great rivers, another cluster of free black people in Desha County defied antebellum norms and manifested a high degree of independence and showed its acceptance into a larger riverside community.

At least ten free black families plus several mixed households resided near Napoleon, a flourishing and quaintly cosmopolitan nineteenth-century river town. Napoleon eventually disappeared as the mighty Mississippi changed channels and cut off land approaches. Today, nothing remains of the settlement except a few forgotten grave markers hidden under a tangle of vegetation on an uninhabited island. In its heyday, Napoleon was a storied town, called by one investigator of the past, the "Port Said of the Mississippi river of the 1800's." Located at the mouth of the Arkansas River, where it empties into the Mississippi, Napoleon became a well-publicized entrepôt for shippers and travelers into and out of Arkansas. Schedules of the packet steamboats from Vicksburg to Napoleon and from Napoleon to Little Rock ran in Little Rock newspapers. A developer laid out town lots in Napoleon for resident boat captains, ironworkers, and machinists. Free black laborers carted cargo in and out of floating warehouses at the Napoleon wharf.[60] So professional was the population and so accepted were the free black families who lived in the vicinity of Napoleon that a town ordinance allowed the black men to serve on slave patrols, a nocturnal drudgery for civilized whites, an unabashed power trip for mean-spirited whites, but an unusual "public service" request for blacks in plantation country. Such policing duty performed by them, of course, refuted the oft-repeated argument of anti-black Southerners that free blacks by nature and by habit conspired with slaves against whites. But no one bothered to publicize this action or make it a part of gossip that would undermine the edifice of white superiority. In 1850, the Desha County population included some seventy free black people. Innocent of rebellion and hardworking, these folk came to feel the bitter effects of the removal law of 1859 just as Peter Caulder and the free blacks of Marion County did.[61]

CHAPTER NINE

Sojourning in Southern Missouri

THE FREE BLACK COMMUNITIES IN MARION COUNTY NEVER RECOVERED completely from material loses coincident with or tied to the James Hall murder trial. Psychological damage, no doubt, had been inflicted as well. In late 1851 or early 1852, perhaps for the first time in his Arkansas life the veteran Peter Caulder felt grave concern for the safety of his family and may have moved across the line into Missouri. The yeoman had become a stranger and a sojourner. Caulder kept a low profile after the murder trial, avoiding tax men and pro-Southern antagonists, especially those who might look askance at his rifle and hounds. Caulder knew that a challenge to his prized possessions would result in someone's death, and to the seasoned soldier, discretion was the better part of valor. He skipped fur markets at Batesville and Yellville and any friction with rowdies that his presence in the towns may have sparked. In these uncertain times he could earn more and make himself more useful to his neighbors and therefore that much less vulnerable by building chimneys and pirogues and manufacturing gunpowder than by selling bales of deerskins. Caulder spent less time listening to "music in the forest leaves." Game was harder to find and travel a bit riskier after 1852.[1] White River hill people were scarcely immune to dreadful news from outside or to the hateful emotions that the news evoked. In domino fashion across the nation, one spectacular and brutally divisive event followed another in the years coincidental with the James Hall tragedy. Harriet Beecher Stowe outraged Southern whites with her melodramatic portrayal of slave life in *Uncle Tom's Cabin*. Personal liberty laws in Massachusetts and Wisconsin defied the Fugitive Slave Law, incensing Southerners. However, the arrest of fugitive slave Anthony Burns in Boston, a center of the abolition movement and presumed a safe haven for escaped slaves, shocked Northerners. The Kansas-Nebraska Act of 1854 evoked a storm of Northern protest, which in turn spun out a reform political movement, the

Republican Party. The new party's candidates for Congress attracted droves of Northern voters eager to block the extension of slavery into western territories and, while at it, to extirpate Mormonism. Abraham Lincoln and William E. Seward, Republican Party hopefuls from Illinois and New York respectively, made widely reported speeches warning that the country could not stand divided and that conflict was irrepressible. Their ominous messages repelled Southerners and accelerating the country's fragmentation.

Plantation owners shaped Southern public opinion and established a "thoroughgoing consensus among all of white society." That applied even in Arkansas, whose "frontier society energized by hyper-democracy" and extreme individualism should have cancelled such uniformity, but did not.[2] With yeomen firmly in the orbit of the planters, virtually all white Arkansans hailed as good news the Supreme Court decision in the Dred Scott case, *Scott v. Sandford* (*1857*), that terminated Federal jurisdiction in restricting slavery. Chief Justice Roger B. Taney wrote the majority opinion stating that black people, free or slave, were not citizens of the United States. Noncitizens could not bring suit for their freedom or for anything else in a federal court.[3] A prescient (or presumptuous) editorial in the *Arkansas Gazette* had declared in 1845 that "free negroes and mulattoes are not citizens."[4] Encouraged by the ruling of the high court, anti-black legislators in Arkansas dusted off their bill to cleanse the state of free Negroes and mulattoes and pushed it through the General Assembly. In February 1859, after years of trying, planters and friends at last had sufficient votes in the assembly to pass an act banishing free blacks from Arkansas soil. The ban would take effect on January 1, 1860. Though proposed by Virginia legislators in 1832, the legal soundness of expulsion remained in question, Arkansas being the only state to enact such a law.[5]

In the spring of 1859, J. W. Methvin, clerk of Marion County, unaware of or unconcerned about the removal act passed in Little Rock, duly assessed the personal and real property of Peter Caulder and six other mulatto heads of households in the Little North Fork. John Madewell remained for a while longer at Turkey Crossroads after his brother Solomon had died. The younger mulattoes, Good and

James Madewell along with Willis Johnson, John Dickson, and Charles Moore had left Marion County by 1853.[6] Solomon's widow, Elizabeth, stayed despite the expulsion law, keeping household and farm going with the help of her teen-age children. The sudden absence of most Turkey Crossroads mulattoes repeated the action of the Halls in 1852, who, ironically, had returned or resurfaced. The sheriff may have ridden out to Cawlder Mountain to make his call on Peter Caulder, or the aging veteran may have come to town for the purpose of assessing his property. Besides the horse, he owned three cows that he would pay taxes on, the last time that he would do that in Arkansas. By this last year of their residence in the county, David B. Hall Jr. had become the largest mulatto property owner, having an appraised real estate and personal property value amounting to $1,035, which was well above the county average for farms.[7] Hall Jr. owned a herd of cows, a saddle horse, and a plow team, most of which had probably been passed on to him by his father, David Hall Sr., who had died at age seventy, before the evacuation took place. Death spared the patriarch the final agony of hearing the sheriff's grim instruction to leave lands that he had settled in 1819. The senior Hall was buried near his second homestead on the White River.

Expelling the free mulattoes as required by state law may have been slowed by local indifference, but that changed with the action of John Brown at Harper's Ferry in October 1859. Opinions about Brown's violence and the threat of insurrection spewed from tens of thousand of tongues. Anti-black gossipers had a field day for months, and no doubt Caulder and the Halls were singled out. Sheriff I. M. Stinett, by reputation a brave man with a fast horse, must have been the point man for the unpleasant task of informing the Halls, Blacks, Caulders, and Nesbits that if they did not leave the state by January 1, 1860, they would be arrested, without warrant, and sold twenty days later "at the court house door to the highest bidder."[8] Peter and Eliza Caulder may or may not have heard this ignominy with their own ears, but the message was clear. By fall of 1860, they no longer resided in the state of Arkansas. They, their small children, their grown son David and his young family, David B. (Jr.) and Margaret Hall, John and Nancy Hall, James and Salena Hall, John and Margaret Turner,

Absalom and Martha Hall, Henley and Judith Black, Francis and Sarah Nesbit packed their belongings on to wagons, carts, and horses for a Mormon-like exodus from the land of their hearths and birthplaces. Discarding what could not be carried, they gave up their homesteads on the White River.

Willoughby Hall hiked to a new site further up the Little North Fork across the state line in Ozark County, Missouri. Young cousins and third-generation mulattoes of Arkansas, Reuben and Jesse Turner, who traveled light because they had few possessions anyway, mounted their horses and rode out of the state of their birth. By January 1, 1860, the Arkansas law for the removal had forced away the free black taxpayers on the White River. The Madewells, Dicksons, and Johnsons had preceded the Halls and Caulders in the flight. Across the state, vulnerable free black householders were forced to flee from their homes. Arkansas's free black population dropped from 734 to 144 in a single year. At least 590 people, including potential leaders for the freed men in Arkansas, went to live in other states and territories. In the case of Marion County, none returned permanently to Arkansas.[9]

Fort Smith had been a home to free black people since the army posting of Peter Caulder and his mulatto comrades. In 1850, ninety-two free black men and women resided in Crawford County (Sebastian County had not yet been created) earning their living mostly as laborers, washers, or servants. With the removal law, these folks, except for six females who remained in white households, packed their belongings and moved across the border into Indian Territory. The Crawford County evacuation was second only to Marion County in numbers.[10] Napoleon's free blacks, joined by a group of Little Rock exiles, traveled, probably by steamboat, upriver to Ohio, which they reached on January 3, 1860. As "homeless strangers in . . . the icy North," these Arkansas refugees composed a testimonial to their trials, entitled "An Appeal to Christians Throughout the World." The eloquent letter recounted the tragedy of innocent people who were "driven from the homes of our childhood." Certainly no sympathy attached itself in the home state as the *Arkansas True Democrat* continued its roast of "an unfortunate class" and smugly commented that "the law has proven itself to be one of the very best on our statute book."[11]

Contrary to the people from Napoleon and Little Rock, Peter Caulder and his friends migrated unheralded, issuing an appeal to ease their plight probably never entering their mind. They trekked northward, but not so far as the free soil states, only into Missouri. Southern Missourians held slaves and in the boot heel, cotton plantations dominated the economy. Even in the hill counties that bordered Arkansas, secessionists tended to be in the majority. Missouri was not a paradise for free blacks—an 1847 Missouri statute barred free black or mulatto emigration into the state. Evidently that law was roundly ignored in Ozark County, which bordered Marion County, for its free black population jumped from zero to forty-three by 1860.[12]

The White River and its tributaries offered a convenient and familiar waterway for Caulder to reach a new home in Missouri. The tier of counties just over the boundary held much in common with the northern Arkansas environment that Peter and Eliza Caulder knew best. Thomas Hall, a friend of Caulder's, had moved to Oregon County (the part that became Howell County in 1851), Missouri, a decade earlier and may have offered advice about where and how to settle. Most mulattoes from Marion County quietly moved no further than southern Missouri. Eight mulattoes did remain in Marion County. They were Solomon Madewell's widow, Elizabeth, her fifteen-year-old son, Solomon, and three daughters who lived independently and apparently undisturbed at Turkey Crossroads. Her twenty-year-old daughter, Elizabeth, lived with whites Edmund and Sena Fraley. Her twenty-three-year-old son, Reuben, lived in the household of Nancy Railsback. Reuben helped the forty-six-year-old white widow manage her large farm and her six children. Cousin Charles Madewell had lived with John and Sarah Magness for ten years. But after the Civil War began, even this determined group migrated to Benton County, Missouri.[13]

The Arkansas removal statute had a loophole for free blacks who wanted to stay in the state above all risks. The law permitted a free black person about to revert to slave status to choose his or her master. Had the Marion County mulattoes stayed put and worked out an arrangement with white neighbors willing to serve as ostensible "masters," they might have been spared at least loss of property if not humiliation. An addendum to the removal act, passed in 1861 by the General Assembly, delayed implementation of the eviction until after January 1, 1865. By that time, the fortunes of war would have rendered removal a moot point. Lands of the Halls, John Turner, and Solomon Madewell might have been saved to their ownership.[14]

For Caulder and the Halls, however, migration, though an unfortunate reality, did not mean capitulation. With the coming of the Civil War, the ex-Arkansans took a firm stand for union and against the secessionists who had imposed the racial discrimination that had resulted in the loss of their farms. Most Arkansas citizens believed that union and slavery were both possible, and people in Marion County joined those in Carroll, Newton, and Searcy counties to pass a regional resolution begging that Arkansas should stay in the Union. Perhaps some Unionists around Yellville, like those in Little Rock, took to wearing a blue cockade in their hats in to signify sentiment for the Union.[15] In accordance with this dream of Union first, a majority of delegates to the statewide convention of February of 1861 voted down the ordinance to secede.

It was only a lull before the storm. Confederate artillery fired on Fort Sumter on April 12, 1861, and President Lincoln responded in kind to the military escalation. He called for troop quotas from each of the states (an act of Northern "mendacity" according to Arkansas governor Henry M. Rector) "to suppress combinations too powerful for ordinary means." The Lincoln administration's resolve to quell the rebellion by force of arms effected a reconvening of the Arkansas convention to reconsider secession. The second time around, delegates voted 65 to 5, amended to 69 to 1, to secede. On May 6, 1861, Arkansas stepped out of the United States and into the Confederacy.[16] Two weeks after the secession, James R. Dowd organized a company of Confederate volunteers at Yellville, ninety men strong.[17] The rebellion quickly fractured the White River hill white society when the schism turned deadly.

Most whites in the county were Southern sympathizers. A scholar who studied the effects of civil strife on the Arkansas-Missouri border concluded that "civilians in the Ozarks during the Civil War experienced as bitter and protracted an ordeal as any people of the Trans-

Mississippi . . . whole communities ceased to exist and their former residents became fugitives."[18] As in hill country and mountain communities throughout the South in the 1860s, choices such as "the
Confederate Army or Hell" were forced on the populace by secessionist
officials who now held the power of civil law. Pro-Confederate organizations passed resolutions proclaiming that "every Union man should
show his colors in favor of the South or be hung as high as Hamen."[19]
Conscription into the Confederate army or arrest and sentencing to
jail were but two of the milder punishments for Unionists. Paralleling
the free mulatto flight of a year earlier, white Unionists who had been
neighbors of Peter Caulder and James Hall streamed toward Rolla or
Cape Girardeau. With lines drawn, hostile feelings escalated. Guerrilla
units and paramilitary bushwhackers raided, looted, and took reprisals
in undocumented, but bloody and inhumane actions. For those who
remained, be they Unionist or secessionist, the "struggle for supremacy
and revenge" became an everyday fact of life. In his article, "Inside
Wars," the historian Michael Fellman described the awful numbing of
Missouri-Arkansas people, whose values and sensitivities were buffeted
by four years of surreal horrors—thundering of hooves, battering down
of doors, and shooting of men without a twinge of conscience.[20]

The document trail of Peter Caulder ended with his tax assessment in 1859 when he would have been sixty-four years old. In his
military career, he had experienced hardships and armed engagements,
but the removal of his family from Arkansas and the ensuing Civil War
were his grimmest days. During the relocation of his family, he may
have continued to provide for and protect them in the brutal times
when food was scarce and cutthroats roamed the countryside. There
were plenty of rustlers, night riders, bushwhackers, and horse thieves
for the old veteran to use his trusty rifle and martial skills against.
He and Eliza had four daughters, Margaret, Mourning, Susan, and
Amanda, all of whom had grown into womanhood.

Caulder's teen-age son, Moses Thompson Caulder born in 1845,
accompanied his uncle Henderson Hall to Rolla, Missouri, and then
on to Fort Scott, Kansas. Moses enlisted in the Fourteenth Kansas
Cavalry on September 1, 1863, the day that he turned eighteen, skirt-
ing the race issue by declaring that he was born in the Osage Nation.

His recruiters pried no further and the determined, dark-complexioned young man was issued a horse, a uniform, and a carbine. He served twenty-one months with the Fourteenth, including a tour in Fort Smith.[21] His younger brother, Stephen, underage for such military glamour even though eager for it, had to settle for staying near his mother, Eliza, guarding the family's cows as they pastured and fending off his nephew James Henry Caulder, born in 1856, the first of David Caulder's sons. Certainly the close-knit Caulder family relied on one another in the 1860s as they had for years on the frontier. In the midst of racking personal and social strife, David Caulder's first wife, whose name was never revealed in the historical record, birthed a child, Adeline, in 1862 with the midwife assistance of Eliza.

Sometime during the Civil War and in some place determined by the misfortunes of that war, David Caulder buried his father, Peter. He grieved the death of his father and his wife and his aunt Margaret Hall, who died in 1862. These sorrows and the fact that he now had the responsibility for five dependent children and his mother influenced David Caulder to set out with his family for a refugee camp at Cape Girardeau, Missouri. Once there, six feet seven inch tall David enlisted in the Twelfth Cavalry of the Missouri State Militia. The young private may have come to know a fellow cavalryman, Eldridge Hill, who had married Matilda Cato in Bollinger County in February 1860. Two years later in Cape Girardeau, Eldridge Hill fell ill with measles following a mission to the Arkansas border country and in a few days died. He left a pregnant wife who gave birth in May to a daughter she named Missouri. She did not remain without support for too long. On November 12, 1863, Pvt. David Caulder, now thirty, married the young war widow.[22] While Caulder patrolled southern Missouri with his cavalry unit, his young wife, Matilda, and his mother, Eliza Hall Caulder, cared for her young granddaughter Mary, the infant Missouri Hill, and the young Caulder siblings, Amanda and Stephen. Thus in Missouri, the Caulder family expanded by forging new kinship bonds with the Cato family, some of whom were classed as free black people.[23]

One historian noted that in Arkansas *the* war was fought with "ambushes, midnight raids, often with civilians treated as combatants and neighbors turned predators." In no section of the state were these fratricidal-type conditions any worse than on the Arkansas-Missouri border "where the families of Confederates and persecuted Unionists, many of them reduced to flight across the border, lived cheek by jowl."[24] Caulders, Halls, and Turners were unflinching Union men because of their racial identity and their wrenching experience with Arkansas's slavocracy. They assisted Federal units in military operations, and if they had happened to have been in the wrong place at the wrong time and fell into the hands of guerrillas settling scores, any one of the free black men would have been hanged.[25]

The Confederate government saw value in the Ozarks for its minerals and as a manufactory of gunpowder for its armies. Agents and money from Richmond arrived in Marion County to exploit for this purpose the saltpeter caves along the White River.[26] Gen. Samuel R. Curtis, commander of Federal forces in Missouri and Arkansas, sought to disrupt this gunpowder supply for the enemy with raids from north of the border.[27] Willoughby Hall, protégé of Peter Caulder, volunteered to guide the Union army on its dangerous raids into Arkansas. On one such mission—called "scouts" by Federal officers—in November 1862, Hall, described by the commander of the scout as "an excellent woodman," stealthily guided a forty-man unit of the Fourteenth Missouri State Militia Cavalry under the command of Capt. Milton Burch through dense, trackless forests toward the caves in the White River bluffs that he had roamed in his youth.[28] As the soldiers passed across a stretch of George Pierson's farm that had once belonged to Willoughby's relative John Hall, they discovered a Confederate raider named John McClure on the place. In pouring rain, Hall and the militiamen fired upon and killed McClure as he tried to get away and warn the Confederate encampment. Continuing the march, Burch took the guard by surprise at Bean's Cave, capturing the twenty-three-man detachment and their horses. Willoughby Hall helped Burch's men destroy six thousand dollars' worth of saltpeter that the Confederates had readied for shipment and "5 buildings, 1 engine, 26 large kettles, 6 tanks, blacksmiths' and carpenters' shops and tools." Brig. Gen. E. B. Brown lauded the success, made the more remarkable because "a large force of the enemy was encamped within a few miles of the works." All of Burch's men returned from this scout safely.

Willoughby Hall knew a couple of the captured rebels, "Mun" Treat and Henry Ray, Marion County men who were consigned to a determent camp at St. Louis. To make matters worse, Ray collapsed and died on a sidewalk in St. Louis as the prisoners of war were marched through the city. Burch inferred in his official report that much of the credit for the surprise in the attack went to Willoughby Hall.[29] Confederate sympathizers in Marion County blamed him rather than credited him.

Local rebels knew that Willoughby and James Hall were helping the Union army and were on the lookout for them. In 1863, Bill Cain and Hugh McClure, John's father, probably acting on a tip about Hall's whereabouts, led a company of secessionist guerillas up the Little North Fork and surprised Willoughby Hall and Jim Gilliland in a barn. Opening fire, Cain's men wounded both Unionists. Cain's men captured and later released Gilliland, whom they recognized as a Federal soldier out of uniform, but poured shots at Willoughby Hall as he made "a desperate effort to escape with his life." A bullet in the shower of lead fired at him found its mark, felling Hall into a branch by the barn. At that point, Hugh McClure, who thought that Hall helped kill his son on the November night of the raid on Bean's Cave, "ran forward with knife . . . and scalped him . . . while Hall was in the agony of death." McClure exhibited Willoughby Hall's scalp to parties that the raiders met on their return to Arkansas, then he tossed it into a hollow stump on the Flippin-Yellville road.[30]

Turnbo refrained from mentioning Willoughby's "race" in this story, but he recounted McClure's brutality toward Hall in graphic terms. McClure "caught the dying man by the hair," cut a three-inch square of skin and hair, "then jerked and peeled it off." Later according to Turnbo, McClure retrieved the scalp from the stump, salted it, and nailed it up at his home on Clabber Creek. Capt. William R. Piland, an officer of volunteers in the federalized Missouri State Militia Cavalry, observed after the war that he did not blame McClure for killing Hall since he had helped kill his son, but the scalping was "barbarous and horrible in the extreme."[31] White men resorted to such irrational treatment of an offender's corpse for the most hated of enemies.[32] Piland's statement on McClure's action seems curiously even-handed and may indicate his wish to bury the past hatreds between neighbors, especially if the mutilated man happened to be a black man.

As in the case of Moses Caulder in the Kansas militia cavalry, David B. Hall Jr. was apparently sworn into the Missouri militia cavalry as a white man. Hall Jr. at the age of forty-four in February 1862 preceded David Caulder's enlistment by volunteering for service with the Twelfth Missouri State Militia Cavalry. Like his brothers James and Willoughby Hall, Hall Jr. faced hostile fire. At a skirmish in Bollinger County he was shot in his left leg. Hall Jr. limped to a nearby home only to be captured by Confederate raiders. Hall Jr. was exchanged and sent to the U.S. Army hospital at Jefferson Barracks near St. Louis to recover from his wound. While there, the widower met and married a young Irish immigrant, Mary Ellen Norman.[33]

Reuben Turner, who lived in the house with John and Nancy Hall in 1850, had mounted his horse and left Arkansas before the war. On February 17, 1864, a Reuben Turner from Zanesville, Ohio, enlisted as a private in the Eighty-second Ohio Infantry, serving eighteen months until July 24, 1865. After his discharge from the Grand Army of the Republic, this Reuben Turner, younger by sixteen years than the Reuben Turner born in Marion County and most likely his son, settled in Bollinger County, Missouri, indicating a family connection.[34]

In 1860, James Hall, whose killing of John Tolbert contributed to the demise of the free black communities in Marion County, moved up the Little North Fork into Ozark County, Missouri. James Hall was mentioned in a Unionist memoir as "loyal to [his] country in the dark days when it tried men's souls to be loyal." Surviving the hostilities and the revenge unleashed during the war, James Hall had no love lost for secessionists when the fighting was done. Neither did a "Mr. [Leonard] Hall" of neighboring Howell County, a relative of pioneer David Hall Sr. In a public meeting in the spring of 1866, Leonard Hall announced that "if any loyal man kills a rebel and has to leave the country, I will furnish him a good horse to ride off on." As it happens, a man named Frederick Baker murdered the Finleys, an elderly Howell

County couple and their grown daughter, who had been Rebels but lived as quiet and peaceful citizens following the surrender of Confederate forces. Leonard Hall made good on his word, however, and furnished the murderer with a good horse, saddle, and bridle. Baker escaped and Hall was arrested and charged with being an accessory to murder before the fact. But Leonard Hall "took a fever" and died in 1867 before he went to trial. The Union man whose grudge against the Rebels contributed to his own demise was buried in the Evergreen Cemetery in Howell County. Baker was never captured.[35]

David Caulder deemed it prudent in the last months of the war to venture back into the hills west of Cape Girardeau in hopes of finding a place to relocate. Caulder's young wife, Matilda, apparently had convinced him that their best bet was to settle in the southwest corner of Bollinger County near her birthplace. The refugees arrived at an unclaimed, forested, well-watered spot just a few miles from the village of Zalma. Happy once again to be peaceful and independent, the Caulders launched into building a homestead. The couple soon had a child, a son whom they named Peter. Matilda became pregnant again, and in January 1868 gave birth at home to the couple's second son, Henry. Two years later, a third child was born, a girl named Salena Anna Caulder, probably in memory of Salena Hall, the wife of David's uncle, James Hall. Salena was six months old when the assistant marshal came about in September of 1870 to take the first census since the American Civil War. Under the racial category, the marshal placed a "B" by the name of each member of the Caulder household signifying that they were a black family.[36]

David Caulder's uncle and dear friend David B. Hall Jr. built his cabin a short distance up the road.[37] Hall Jr. and his second wife, Mary Ellen, soon had a son whom they named David. Later in life, this son would be known in Bollinger County as Reverend Dave Hall. His father, also taking up the cloth after the war, known in Arkansas as David B. Hall Jr., came therefore to be known in Bollinger County as David B. Hall Sr. Hall Jr. crossed the race line by the fall of 1870. This 1870 census was the first to ever record any member of pioneer David Hall's family as other than black, colored, or mulatto in the racial category. The advantages of passing as white were obvious to the former Arkansan.

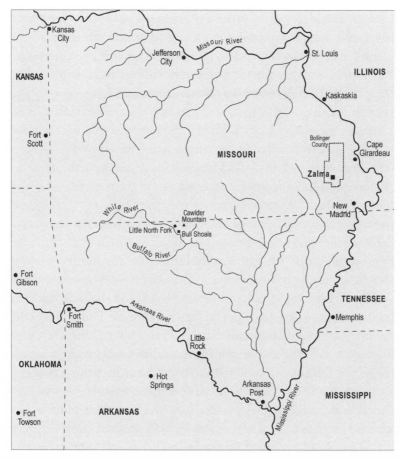

Bollinger County, Missouri. David Caulder relocated the family from Cawlder
Mountain to Cape Girardeau during the Civil War. In 1864, he moved with his
new wife, Matilda Cato, to her family's home near Zalma. Both Caulder and
David B. Hall Jr. homesteaded in Bollinger County on land that they patented. The
Hall Cemetery in which members of the Caulder family, David B. Hall Jr. and his
son Reverend Dave Hall, are buried is located three miles southwest of Zalma.
MAP BY TOM PARDISE.

The Caulders and the Halls had lost much by being on the wrong side of the color line despite their *always* being integrated into their surrounding community. Hall's postwar passing connoted a sensible way to maintain a normal relationship with his rural white neighbors.[38] The Caulders may have been reluctant to cross over and thereby deny their African heritage. In fact, they affirmed their close relationships with black families such as the Catos through marriage and living in proximity. To not pass as white may have been a conscious decision by David Caulder even if he had opportunity to do so. He surely treasured the stirring adventure stories that his father had told him of Martin Turner, James Turner, Caleb Cook, and Joseph Clark. Pride in knowing how his father and his comrades, soldiers of color and elite riflemen, served their country during a perilous war and built Fort Smith in the heart of Indian country ran deep within him. Boyhood memories of the White River woods, cabins, and fields led David Caulder to trust his mixed-racial heritage and perhaps yearn for a return to the lifestyle enjoyed by the close-knit mulatto community before the Hall-Tolbert trial and the Civil War destroyed it. To cross the color line, David could have reasoned, might also have caused him to shortchange some of his most precious memories, and what acceptance or convenience could be worth that? David and Matilda Caulder may have had another child, a son Charles born in 1875, a year before David's death in 1876.[39]

Moses Caulder, David's younger brother who had served in the Kansas cavalry, married Mary Ann Nelson, a white woman in Ozark County, Missouri, in 1876 and the two had six children. Although generally accepted as white, some in southern Missouri had their doubts about the ancestry of Moses, who had a reputation within his family as being a womanizer. Perhaps that was why he was shot and killed on the streets of West Plains on January 4, 1900, by a woman of his acquaintance, Cora Belle Gilliland. The local newspaper wrote that Moses Caulder was "a turbulent character who claimed to be Portuguese."[40]

Peter Caulder had never patented his preempted homestead above the White River on Cawlder Mountain, so the family had no legal claim on property. But David B. Hall Jr. had purchased his property at the Batesville Land Office and had then been forced to abandon it after the 1859 law passed the state assembly. He retained title to the acres that he had patented in 1850.[41] Conceivably, he could have returned to Arkansas when the new state constitution took effect in 1864, or any time afterward, and reclaimed the land that had been expropriated from him by a state government that acted under authority of the abrogated 1836 constitution.

No member of the Hall-Caulder-Turner extended family was ever compensated for the lands that they had cultivated, lands now submerged below Bull Shoals Reservoir.[42] Pioneer David Hall's remains and probably those of other members of the extended family who had been buried in the family plot at the core farm were disinterred by the Corps of Engineers and reburied on high ground adjacent to the Promise Land cemetery in Marion County. On top of a stone wall, a score of undated, nameless, weathered wooden markers lay today as eerie reminders of long-deceased pioneers who once plowed fields, hunted bears, raised children, and lived not only racially integrated but dependent upon one another along the banks of the White River.[43]

Gradually, southern Missourians and northern Arkansans regained stability and security after the Civil War. In Bollinger County no less than in Ozark and Marion counties across the state line from each other, rural residents operated postage stamp farms with minimal capital, garnering cash from sale of a few feeder livestock or commodity crops to local markets. At the very heart of such

Shortly after noon Thursday Belle Gilliland shot and killed Mose Calder, a turbulent character who claimed to be a Portuguese. He was drinking and quarrelsome and insisted on getting into the house. She refused him admittance and he persisted, cursing and threatening her. She emptied the contents of a revolver into him. It occurred at a house where several loose characters live, in the north part of town, near the powder house.

West Plains newspaper article reporting the demise of Civil War veteran Moses Caulder.

Americana were family, neighbors, church gatherings, livestock, corn and hay crops, and acoustical music. The Caulders and Halls were enthusiastic practitioners in this culture and they found toleration, even social acceptance in Bollinger, Ozark, and Howell counties as they had in Marion County before the war. These families seem to have assimilated comfortably into the rural white world, at last finding community.

Epilogue

MY WIFE, PEGGY, AND I REACHED THE PAPE STORE ON THE UNPAVED
main street of Zalma, Missouri, in the summer of 2001.[1] Inside, we
spotted a likeness of the Reverend Dave Hall and his wife, Dora,
amongst old photographs hung here and there on the store wall. The
reverend, seated in a familiar pose of the time, had large hands resting on his knees, a huge handlebar mustache, impish eyes, and skin
tones just dark enough, at least in the tintype reprint, to suggest
mixed ancestry. Dora, in hat, stands resolutely to the side and slightly
behind the fifty-eight-year-old preacher. The couple, childless themselves, framed a young girl, Caltha Prather, daughter of a McKinley
Prather, an orphaned boy raised by the Halls. We were shown the
photographs in the store by Dolores Abernathy Jackson, related by
marriage to Dora Hall. Ms. Jackson gave us directions to the Hall
Church cemetery situated southwest of Zalma just off rural road "E."
She warned of ticks and chiggers on the walk in. The barbed-wire-
bounded cemetery stands fifty yards off the road in a roughly cut
clearing obscured by scrub oaks and briar patches. A granite monu-
ment dedicated to the brief life of infant Mamie D. Calder, May 29,
1893, to January 11, 1894, caught our eye. Mamie was the daughter
of William H. Caulder and Mary J. Young Caulder, and most likely
the great-granddaughter of Peter Caulder. A few feet away, a sand-
stone tombstone rises from the hardscrabble ground, hand engraved
—"Rev Dave Hall 1862–1930," the third generation of the Hall
family to bear the David first name. Somewhere in this cemetery lies
the unmarked grave of Reverend Dave Hall's father, the man known
in his Arkansas home as David B. Hall Jr., a battle veteran who preceded his son in pulpits of Bollinger County and who died in 1892.
His wife, Mary Ellen, survived him for six years. Thus, amidst third-
growth woodlands of southern Missouri can be found the final resting place of a son and a grandson, indeed the namesakes, of David
Hall, patriarchal pioneer of the White River hills.[2] Dave B. Hall Jr.
pronounced the wedding vows exchanged between his niece, thir-
teen-year-old Salena, and the groom George W. Pape. Matilda,

Salena's mother, had to "assent" to the marriage since Salena was under the age of eighteen. On the death of David Caulder, Salena, his daughter, had been adopted and raised in the Hall home. The wedding ceremony took place in "widow Calder's" home in Bollinger County, well after the death of her husband. The oldest son of Peter Caulder had died on December 3, 1876, in Bollinger County at the age of forty-five.[3]

David Caulder's oldest surviving son, James Henry Caulder, wed Caroline Berry on March 10, 1887. David B. Hall conducted the ceremony in which William Henry Caulder wed Mary Josephine Young on January 18, 1888.[4] Through the turn of the century, after the death of David B. Hall Jr., his son, widely known as the Reverend Dave Hall, continued to shepherd his father's General Baptist congregation. Reverend Dave's fifty-year tenure in the pulpit, his sense of humor, his theatrical instincts, and his compelling voice elevated him to near legendary status in the community.[5]

Descendants of Peter Caulder married into local families and established themselves in communities across southern Missouri, though only a smattering of documents survived to illustrate their activities. Peter Thomas Caulder and his wife, Sarah R., acquired forty acres in rural Bollinger County, logged and farmed, and then in the 1890s sold the land and moved to Cape Girardeau. Peter Caulder, grandson of the rifleman, and his wife, Sarah, thereupon disappeared from the Missouri record.[6]

Moses (Thompson) Caulder, Peter's second-oldest son and veteran of the Fourteenth Kansas Cavalry, purchased one hundred and sixty acres two miles northeast of Pontiac in Ozark County, Missouri, less than a day's ride from his birthplace in Arkansas. To finance the purchase, Moses and his wife, Mary Ann Caulder, previously had bought and sold land near Gainesville, a speculation in which they made a small profit. In another real estate venture, the couple sold forty acres southeast of Pontiac, land now bordered by Bull Shoals Lake, to James D. Turnbo, relative of Silas Claiborne Turnbo.

Near Moses and Mary's home, his uncle Joseph Hall farmed corn and cotton. Hall operated his farm with the help of "Brown" Hall, and by 1878 had gained enough equipment and livestock to cultivate

The Reverend Dave Hall and his wife, Dora. Hall, grandson of free black patriarch David Hall, pioneer on the Little North Fork, was the third generation of Halls to bear the name David. Reverend Dave's father was David B. Hall Jr.

Photograph of William Henry Caulder, probable grandson of Peter Caulder, taken in 1927. At the time, William Henry was about sixty-one years old and had been married to Mary Josephine Young for thirty-nine years. The couple had eleven children.

Ida Caulder, right, and her brother Jim, who never married, are shown in 1969 photograph along with the children of Dolores Abernathy Jackson, a neighbor and friend of the Caulders and Halls in Bollinger County. Jim and Ida Caulder are perhaps the great-grandchildren of Peter Caulder.

twenty acres of corn and thirteen acres of cotton. Hall had a team with which he plowed and which pulled the wagonload of cotton that he took to Ray's gin at Noe's ferry near his old home site in the fall of 1878. Joe Hall rode about southern Missouri and northern Arkansas on "Star," a tall, sorrel gelding. Joe Hall, or his wife, milked two cows, one of them a nine-year-old "read cow [with] bauld face." Hall ducked the census marshal in 1870 maybe because he split his time between the two states and because he was leery of the racial typing that he knew went with the census. Despite being officially invisible, Joe Hall lived the typical Ozark County farmer's life after the war, taking his responsibilities seriously and gaining trust from his Missouri neighbors. Silas Turnbo, an ex-Confederate who knew of Hall's ancestry, commented that Joe Hall "was intelligent and peaceable and . . . his accounts of early times can be relied on as truthful."[7] After he retired from the life of a plowman near the end of the century, Joe sat in his rocker, chuckling at images from the past. Sometimes, too, those reflections saddened him and tears may have welled in his ancient eyes. Joe Hall supplied the wandering Silas Turnbo with a score of whimsical tales of the frontier involving his father and brothers.[8]

———————

A few members of the Madewell family who had been categorized as mulatto in 1850 did return to Arkansas. In 1885, Christina (Cresa), the daughter of Solomon Madewell, patented forty acres, and in 1905 Martha E. Madewell, widow of John Madewell, who was the son of Goodman Madewell, purchased one hundred sixty acres of the original homestead. The elderly Solomon Madewell died before the 1859 expulsion, but his relatively young widow Elizabeth kept the family together. Elizabeth refused to leave Marion County in 1859, sticking it out for awhile in the family homestead with her teen-age children and Cresa, her oldest daughter. Two nephews, Reuben Madewell and Charles Madewell, stayed put as well. The young men lived with whites in separate households. None of the Madewells was enslaved according to the initial threat to do so in the expulsion law, but with the war impending and with an increasing number of guerrillas pillaging the hills and valleys of Arkansas, they sought refuge in Benton

County, Missouri. There in the confusion of dislocation, they managed to cross the color line.

Passing, however, as most of the Marion County mulattoes seemed to have done during and after the Civil War, was not without risks and not always permanently accomplished. In the post–Reconstruction era, white Americans took the color line seriously. A classic example of the perils of passing occurred in Omaha, Nebraska. There in 1919 through court action, a husband sought to annul his marriage to Clara McCary, an attractive, fair-haired young woman, because he had discovered that she had "negro blood in her veins." The husband, Francis P. Dwyer, may have had a misguided attitude, but his charge was correct. The blue-eyed Clara, who had a blue-eyed three-year-old son, surely did have African ancestry. Clara was the daughter of Douglass P. McCary, once a resident of Natchez, Mississippi. The McCary family, one generation removed from slavery, along with William Johnson, a barber and noted free man of color, with their friends made up "the aristocracy of the free black population" of Natchez.[9] The trial embarrassed the McCary family and showed the incredibly hostile white attitudes in the nation when mulattoes including those formerly of Marion County, Arkansas, were making their transition across the race line.

Two of Peter Caulder's relationships by marriage, James Henderson Hall and James Henderson Hall Jr., also went to court on account of "race" in the postwar years. In 1880, James Henderson operated a typical farm in Howell County, Missouri, that included sixty-five acres of crops, meadows, pastures, orchards, and vineyards. Pigs and sheep complemented the diet and the income. He maintained five milk cows and a herd of twenty beef cattle. Despite James Henderson's thrifty farm, his war service (he drew a four-dollar a month pension for war injuries), and the fact that his wife, Sarah Collier, was the daughter of a well-to-do white farmer, gossip swirled in the community that the Halls were Negro. They were categorized as mulattoes in the census of 1880, and their grandchildren were barred from the public school. Determined to rebuff the rumors and establish his "whiteness," James Henderson Hall took the school authorities to court. With a change in venue, Hall won his case by

Circa 1896 photograph of Hall farm home one-half mile north of Hall School and
Church, Bollinger County, Missouri. The young man holding the horses is most
likely Charles Caulder and a descendant of Peter Caulder. The man with a fiddle is
James Benton Randolph. To his right is his pregnant wife, Dora, David B. Hall
Jr.'s youngest daughter. The children are Ernie and Julietia. Dora, granddaughter
of patriarch David Hall, holds her infant son, Adoph. The porch roof is purposely
slanted to funnel water by drainpipe into a cistern.

"declaring and proving" that his children were of Portuguese and Indian descent.[10]

His son, James Henderson Hall Jr., had by that time moved to Muskogee, Oklahoma. Hall, like his father, had a "swarthy complexion," and his white neighbors supposed him to be Negro. He was ostracized and his children were not allowed to attend white schools. Faced with an unendurable situation, Hall asked to be tried in court on the charge of having Negro blood. His request was granted and a day in court followed. The municipal judge and jury heard evidence that included family records and testimony from witnesses called in from Missouri and returned a verdict that he was a "man of untainted Caucasian blood."[11] The grandfather of James Henderson Hall Jr. was Thomas Hall, an 1840s resident of the White River hill community who carried the affidavit attesting to his Portuguese heritage. Hall had filed this document in Arkansas and Missouri, but with no effect on the census marshals, all of whom through 1870 continued to categorize him as mulatto on their records. However, his affidavit, first notarized in 1830 Maury County, Tennessee, finally paid off in changing the racial status of his descendants.[12] James Henderson Hall's court action to gain equality may have marked the last of racial obstacles to be faced by descendants of Peter Caulder and David Hall.

Peter Caulder's lifelong identity as a man of color hardly stifled his achievements. The Caulder family and their mulatto friends and relatives of the Little North Fork succeeded, by virtue of their goodwill, their determination, and their sustaining home and hearth, in creating a unique and powerful heritage for their descendants, their state, their region, and their nation. Their lives amply demonstrate the ludicrousness of racial categorization and give evidence of the agency of free blacks that existed within the antebellum frontier society. Through their story and others like them, a fuller understanding of the meaning of "race" in the history of the country could proceed. The author of a classic study of free blacks in Virginia stated in the beginning of his book that "public opinion in Virginia . . . was always hostile to the free Negro. . . . they should be expelled or their number kept as small as possible." Ironically much of the author's subsequent presentation of the latitude of domiciles and activities accorded to or claimed by free black farmers in Virginia seemed to contradict his opening statement.[13] Toleration for free black people who looked and acted white certainly manifested itself in rural venues such as Marion County, Arkansas, and Edgefield, South Carolina. These communities, and perhaps there were others as well in the South, temper the widely accepted view that "free Negroes were segregated and inclined to be urban." That might have been the case in other slave states, but in Arkansas as in South Carolina, most antebellum free blacks "lived in rural areas not urban centers." Peter Caulder and his Marion County friends and relatives integrated themselves into the overall community in which they lived and were far from being continually humiliated by whites. Until the eve of secession, when they were proven to be sojourners, these free black farmers lived in harmony and seemed to have been incorporated into the community of Marion County whites.[14]

Appendix A

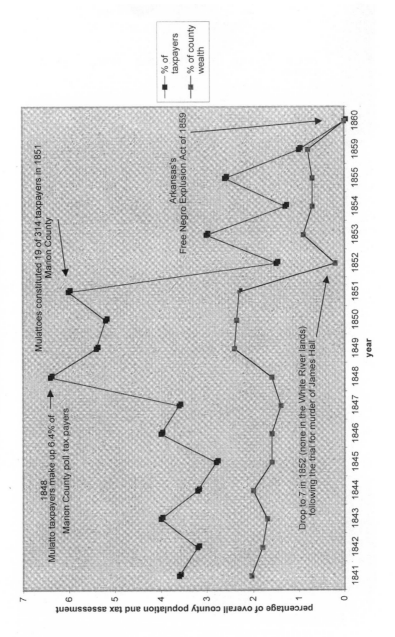

Mulatto Tax Record in Antebellum Marion County

Mulattoes constituted 19 of 314 taxpayers in 1851 Marion County

1848
Mulatto taxpayers make up 6.4% of Marion County poll tax payers

Arkansas's
Free Negro Explusion Act of 1859

Drop to 7 in 1852 (none in the White River lands) following the trial for murder of James Hall

% of taxpayers

% of county wealth

percentage of overall county population and tax assessment

year

Lands Patented by Marion County Mulattoes

*(All land patents below were issued by Batesville
Land Office and all were cash entries)*

PATENTEE (AGE AT PURCHASE DATE)	DATE OF PURCHASE	LOCATION	DESCRIPTION	ACRES	REMARKS	DISPOSITION	DOC #
David Hall, Sr. (66)	Nov 1, 1849	Marion County	SNE Sec 22 T20N R15W	71.13	Left Bank of White River	Sold to Noe, Oct 1, 1850	3213
John Hall (42)	Nov 1, 1849	Marion County	SWNE Sec 17 T20N R15W	39.11	Left Bank of White River	Sold to G.W. Pierson, 1852	3210
John Hall (42)	Nov 1, 1849	Marion County	NESE Sec 17 T20 R15W	23.08	Left Bank of White River	Sold to G.W. Pierson, 1852	3212
David Hall, Jr. (35)	Oct 1, 1850	Marion County	NWNE Sec 23, T19N R15W	61.22			3738
John Turner (45)	Dec 5, 1850	Marion County	SWNW Sec 35 T20N R15W	39.99	Left Bank of White River		3916
Solomon Madewell (69)	March 1, 1855	Marion County	NWSW Sec 2 T18N R17W	40.00			6617
John Hall (48)	June 15, 1855	Marion County	SESE Sec 14 T19N R15W	39.7			6013
James Hall (33)	March 1, 1856	Marion County	NE 1/4 Sec 34 T20N R15W	23.32	Left Bank of White River	Original Hall homesite	5000
John Turner (51)	March 1, 1856	Marion County	NNW Sec 35 T20N R15W	48.53		Original Hall homesite	5001

Livestock Owned by Marion County Mulattoes

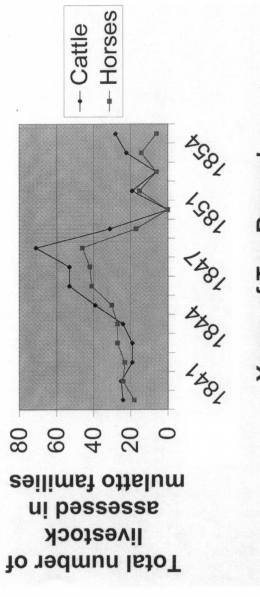

Total number of livestock assessed in mulatto families

80 — 60 — 40 — 20 — 0

1841 1844 1847 1851 1854

Years of Tax Record

- Cattle
- Horses

MARION COUNTY RESIDENTS IN ORDER OF FARM VALUE, 1850

HOUSEHOLD/ TWN	NAME (AGE IN 1850) OCCUPATION MULATTOES (M) IN BOLD	PRESENT ON CENSUS		1850 CENSUS DATA								
		1840	1860	NO. IN HOUSE-HOLD	STATE OF BIRTH	FARM CASH VALUE	MACHINE/ IMPLEMENT CASH VALUE	LIVE-STOCK CASH VALUE	TOTAL HORSES, MULES, CATTLE, SWINE, SHEEP	TOTAL BUSHELS, CORN, RYE, AND WHEAT	IRISH POTATOES/ SWEET POTATOES BU	COTTON, SLAVES WOOL OR TOBACCO LBS
1	145/SL	Jacob Nave (31) Farmer	÷	No	6	Tn	$5000 500a	$150	$565	88	400	0	0	1
2	143/SL	Edward Coker (49) Farmer	÷	÷	2	Tn	$4000	$200	$2070	262	2400	10	12 lbs Wool	5
3	200/ Union	Nancy Tutt (30) Widow	÷	÷	11	Tn	$3500 225a	$200	$1785	225	2200	100		1
4	157/SL	William P. Coker (40) Farmer	÷	÷	6	Tn	$3000 200a	$150	$780	109	2000			6
5	8/	Michael Yokum (51) Farmer	÷	÷	5	Tn	$3000							5-8
6	357/ Union	James A. Wilson (29) Atty at Law	No	No	4	NC	$2500 200a	$100	$650	89	3120			1
7	146/SL	Thornton Medlock (36) Farmer	No	No	8	Ky	$2500 235a	$8	$160	37	300		30 lbs Wool	unk
8	54/ Union	Moses Ray (50) Farmer	No	÷	9	Va	$2400 570a	$400	$1342	235	8700		50 bales Cotton	No

| | | 1850 CENSUS DATA | | | | | | | | | | |
HOUSEHOLD/ TWN	NAME (AGE IN 1850) OCCUPATION MULATTOES (M) IN BOLD	PRESENT ON CENSUS 1840 / 1860	NO. IN HOUSE-HOLD	STATE OF BIRTH	FARM CASH VALUE	MACHINE/ IMPLEMENT CASH VALUE	LIVE-STOCK CASH VALUE	TOTAL HORSES, MULES, CATTLE, SWINE, SHEEP	TOTAL BUSHELS, CORN, RYE, AND WHEAT	IRISH POTATOES/ SWEET POTATOES BU	COTTON, WOOL OR TOBACCO LBS	SLAVES
9	106/NF	**John Hall (M) (43)** Farmer	÷ / No	8	Tn	$2000							
10	32/SL	Joseph Coker, Sr. (63) Farmer	No / ÷	5	NC	$2000 298a	$75	$395	93	600	20		6-8
11	65/WR	Ewing Summers (40) Farmer	No / No	5	Mo	$2000 165a	$75	$765	153	1400	55	25 lbs Wool	2-4
12	15/PR	Michael Young (39) Farmer	÷ / No	9	Tn	$2000 280a	$100	$817	178	2700	130	60 lbs Wool	No
13	113/	Ewing Hogan (55) Farmer	÷ / No	5	SC	$2000							
14	192/ Union	John Wood (35) Farmer	No / ÷	9	Tn	$2000 320a	$120	$1130	136	2130		100 bales Cotton	No
15	202/ Union	William J. Wood (39) Farmer	÷ / ÷	9	Ga	$2000 100a	$2000	$660	93	1100	40	30 lbs Wool	1-3
16	312/Pr	Joel King (60) Farmer	÷ / ÷	6	Va	$2000 155a	$100	$645	128	1600			No

No.	Dwelling/Family	Name (Age) / Occupation					Birthplace	Real Estate	Pers. Est.	Value				Product	
17	319/ Union	Michael Mathis (32) Blacksmith	÷	No	7		Tn	$2000 120a	$100	$305	81	400			1-2
18	41/ Union	Daniel Wickersham (25) Millerite	No	÷	2		Ky	$1500 55a	$160	$155	8	500			1-2
19	173/ Blythe	Hardin Coker (29) Farmer	No	No	6		Tn	$1500 180a	$25	$670	48	1200	62		4
20	218/	Thomas Wilson (36) Millerite	No	÷	5		Tn	$1500							No
21	213/ Union	Jesse Wickersham (29) Carpenter	No	No	2		Ky	$1500 160a	$15	$100	10	250	12		No
22	201/ Union	Calvin Coker (28) Farmer	No	No	3		Ala	$1500 163a	$100	$775	199	240	100	Orchard	No
23	20/ Union	John Hurst (43)	÷	÷	7		Ky	$1500 140a	$125	$658	183	1350	10	50 lbs Wool	1-4
24	43/ Union	Elizabeth Wood (44)	÷	÷	8		Unk	$1500 80a	$100	$635	114	1500	30		No
25	95/NF	David Hall, Sr. (M) (67)	No	÷	5		NC	$1000							No
26	21/WR	William Flippin (33) Farmer	÷	No	9		Ky	$1000 225a	$50	$412	92	1000	80	25 lbs Wool	No
27	38/ Union	James Wickersham (25) Farmer	÷	No	5		Ky	$1000 160a	$100	$533	88	700		30 lbs Wool	No
28	44/ Union	John Wickersham (31) Cabinet Maker	No	No	5		Ky	$1000 1½a	$125	$35	25		18		No
29	46/ Union	John H. Swafford (36) Farmer	No	No	7		NC	$1000 220a	$25	$126	29	289		15 Cotton	No

HOUSEHOLD/ TWN	NAME (AGE IN 1850) OCCUPATION MULATTOES (M) IN BOLD	PRESENT ON CENSUS		NO. IN HOUSE-HOLD	STATE OF BIRTH	1850 CENSUS DATA							
		1840	1860			FARM CASH VALUE	MACHINE/ IMPLEMENT CASH VALUE	LIVE-STOCK CASH VALUE	TOTAL HORSES, MULES, CATTLE, SWINE, SHEEP	TOTAL BUSHELS, CORN, RYE, AND WHEAT	IRISH POTATOES/ SWEET POTATOES BU	COTTON, WOOL OR TOBACCO LBS	SLAVES
30 52/ Union	William A. Wood (43) Farmer	÷	÷	10	Tn	$1000 160a	$100	$847	266	750	40	Orchard	No
31 66/WR	William Hurst (33) Farmer	No	÷	2	Tn	$1000 114a	$25	$430	60	750	20	30 lbs Wool	No
32 67/WR	John H. Tolbert (27) Farmer	No	No	5	Ar	$1000 100a	$15	$365	22	1250	20	Orchard	No
33 79/ Union	Thomas Jefferson (51) Farmer	No	÷	7	Va	$1000 245a	$50	$545	97	1250	12		2
34 301/Pr	William Davis (41) Farmer	No	÷	6	Tn	$1000 160a	$100	$200	51	350	30	150 lbs Tobacco	No
35 305/Pr	Fielding Wilbourn (45) Farmer	÷	No	10	Ga	$1000 120a	$100	$675	59	765			No
36 307/Pr	Richard Langdon (42) Farmer	No	No	8	Va	$1000 120a	$120	$1835	142	1550	20		No
37 362/ Union	James M. Cowdrey (55) Physician	No	÷	9	SC	$1000 80a	$30	$1350	108	650			No
38 206/WR	John S. Tolbert (32) Farmer	No	÷	5	Ill	$1000 95a	$100	$410	66	1080	50		No

No.	Code	Name (age)	Occupation				State								Orchard
39	233/WR	John Hargrave (54) Farmer		÷	÷	5	NC	$1000 160a	$150	$850	140	1000	70		No
40	259/Pr	William Goodall (40) Farmer		÷	No	15	Ga	$1000 110a	$100	$550	100	1225	20	12 lbs Wool	No
41	267/ Blythe	James Magness, Jr. (61) Farmer		÷	÷	8	SC	$1000 470a	$125	$1700	215	1625	60	50 lbs Wool	1
42	280/Pr	John Reeves (60) Farmer/Miller		No	÷	6	SC	$1000 85a	$140	$400	92	460			No
43	140/SL	William E. Coker (28) Farmer		No	÷	3	Ar	$1000 185a	$100	$1090	130	1200		10 lbs Wool	6-7
44	151/SL	David/John McCord (22/25) Farmer		No	÷	7	Ind	$1000 195a	$150	$1195	152	1650	70	12 lbs Wool	No
45	175/ Blythe	Eli Young (67) Farmer		÷	÷	5	Va	$1000 215a	$80	$270	59	556		20 lbs Tobacco	No
46	189/ Blythe	John Magness (27) Farmer		No	÷	7	SC	$1000 240a	$125	$450	60	150		40 lbs Wool	No
47	144/SL	Lewis Clarkson (47) Farmer		No	No	10	Ky	$1000 235a	$100	$360	80	500			No
48	197/ Union	Jesse Hudson (47) Farmer		÷	÷	7	SC	$1000 120a	$200	$400	52	850			No
49	26/Pr	William Riggins (42) Farmer		No	No	9	NC	$1000 240	$100	$545	56	460	25		No
50	347/	William Moorland (60) Farmer		÷	No	5	Tn	$1000 90a	$10	$440	65	200			No
51	107/NF	George Pierson (35) Farmer		÷	÷	11	Ohio	$1000							No

HOUSEHOLD/ TWN	NAME (AGE IN 1850) OCCUPATION MULATTOES (M) IN BOLD	PRESENT ON CENSUS 1840	1860	NO. IN HOUSE- HOLD	STATE OF BIRTH	FARM CASH VALUE	MACHINE/ IMPLEMENT CASH VALUE	LIVE- STOCK CASH VALUE	TOTAL HORSES, MULES, CATTLE, SWINE, SHEEP	TOTAL BUSHELS, CORN, RYE, AND WHEAT	IRISH POTATOES/ SWEET POTATOES BU	COTTON, SLAVES WOOL OR TOBACCO LBS
52 98/NF	John Turner (M) (45) Farmer	÷	No	7	SC	$800						No
53 350/	John Moorland (40) Farmer	÷	No	5	Tn	$800	$8	$210	65	400		No
54 Union	David Stinett	÷	÷			$800 160a	$25	$766	89	1040	40	12 lbs Wool	1-3
55 28/ Union	Samuel Railsback (33) Farmer	No	÷	6	Ky	$800 107a	$300	$294	74	316	65	40 lbs Wool	No
56 293/ Blythe	James Ezekiel Young (36) Farmer	No	—	6	Ky	$800 70a	$20	$262	40	650		15 lbs Wool	No
57 296/Pr	John Marshall (42) Farmer	÷	No	10	Tn	$800 80a	$75	$310	60	540	200	No
58 156/SL	Joseph Coker, Jr. (26) Farmer	No	÷	6	Ar	$800 95a	$100	$1050	92	1940		4
59 141/SL	William Holt (50) Farmer	No	÷	5	Va	$800 160a	$75	$710	135	1400	30	60 lbs Wool	No
60 34/Pr	William Ryalls (48) Farmer	÷	÷	15	NC	$800 130a	$100	$546	74	1050	30	100 lbs Wool	No

#	Ref	Name (Age) / Occupation												
61	163/WR	Thomas H. Flippin (31) Farmer	÷	No	3	Ky	$800 110a	$100	$835	109	1600	170	40 lbs Wool	No
62	149/SL	William Coker (81) Patriarch, Farmer	÷	÷	2	Va	$800 176a	$100	$610	69	600	70	45 lbs Wool	No
63	186/NF	Nimrod Teaff (47) Black and Gun Smith	÷	No	11	Pa	$600							
64	234/WR	David B. Hall, Jr. (M) (35) Farmer	÷	No	6	Tn	$350 80a	$15	$400	94	400	30		No
65	100/NF	Peter Caulder (M) (55) Farmer	÷	No	9	SC	$200							
66	96/NF	Joseph Hall (M) (25) Farmer	÷	No	8	Ar	$200							
67	190/Blythe	John Madewell (M) (70) Farmer	No	No	8	NC	$200 40a	$12	$480	87	1025	25	10 lbs Wool	No
68	194/Union	James Madewell (M) (34) Farmer	No	No	4	Tn	$200 40a	$6	$150	23	318	40		No
69	205/WR	Thomas S. Williams (45) Farmer	÷	÷	9	Ky	$200 34a	$50	$550	96	300	45	Orchard	No
70	51/WR	Jackson Dean (24) Farmer	No	÷	3	Ga	$200 100a	$30	$245	61	600	50	15 lbs Wool	No
71	63/Union	William Elkins (43) Farmer	No	÷	7	NC	$200 50a	$10	$175	21	300		15 lbs Wool	No
72	137/SL	Sylas Loveall (30) Farmer	No	No	5	KY	$200 30a	$5	$250	38	200	40		No
73	97/NF	James Hall (M) (27) Farmer	÷	No	4	Ar	$100							No

| | | PRESENT ON CENSUS | | 1850 CENSUS DATA | | | | | | | | |
HOUSEHOLD/TWN	NAME (AGE IN 1850) OCCUPATION MULATTOES (M) IN BOLD	1840	1860	NO. IN HOUSEHOLD	STATE OF BIRTH	FARM CASH VALUE	MACHINE/IMPLEMENT CASH VALUE	LIVE-STOCK CASH VALUE	TOTAL HORSES, MULES, CATTLE, SWINE, SHEEP	TOTAL BUSHELS, CORN, RYE, AND WHEAT	IRISH POTATOES/SWEET POTATOES BU	COTTON, SLAVES WOOL OR TOBACCO LBS
74 62/WR	Washington Morris (34) Farmer	÷	No	7	Ky	$100 34a	$9	$290	45	130	10	No
75 178/ Blythe	Elijah Wood (28) Farmer	No	÷	5	Tn	$100 40a	$7	$111	27	308		No
76 150/SL	Lemuel Coker (29) Farmer	No	No	3	Ar	$100 40a	$8	$210	41	150		12 lbs Wool No
77 93/NF	Henley Black (M) (36) Farmer	No	No	5	Illinois	$100						No
78 104/NF	Francis Nesbit (M) (37) Farmer	No	No	6	NC	$100						No
79 196/ Union	Willis Johnson (M) (25)	No	No	3	Tn	$100 100a	$10	$40	5	120		No
80 193/ Union	Solomon Madewell (M) (64) Farmer	No	No	9	NC	$50 40a	$3	$55	9	200	15	No
81 210/ Union	John Dickson (M) (31) Farmer	No	No	7	Tn	Tenant	$10	$375	62	385		No
82 195/ Union	Charles Moore (M) (66) Farmer	No	No	3	Va	Tenant	$20	$130	45	500		No
83 99/NF	Absalom Hall (M) (44) Farmer	÷	No	6	Tn	Tenant						No

Appendix B

Marion County Free Black Tax Record

1841

TAXPAYER, AGE	POLL TAX	LAND/ACRES (VALUE)	HORSES (VALUE)	CATTLE (VALUE)	PROPERTY VALUE	COUNTY TAX*	STATE TAX*
		Little North Fork mulatto community					
1 Caulder, Peter, 46	yes		1 (40)	1 (10)	$50		
2 Hall, David B., Jr., 26	yes		2 (150)	2 (20)	$170		
3 Hall, David, Sr., 58	no		9 (450)	8 (80)	$530		
4 Hall, John, 34	yes		2 (150)	7 (70)	$220		
5 Turner, John, 37	yes		1 (50)	2 (25)	$75		
6 Hall, Willoughby, 24	yes		1 (60)	1 (10)	$70		
7 Hall, Joseph, 21	yes		1 (50)	2 (20)	$70		
8 Hall, Thomas, 51	yes		1 (50)	1 (10)	$60		
9 Hall, A. [Absalom], 35	yes		-	-	-		
9 Totals for Marion County mulattoes			**18 ($1,000)**	**24 ($245)**	**$1,245**		

*County and State taxes assessed not available (n/a) for 1841.

1841 Marion County had 219 poll-tax payers; 536 horses ($27,130); 1,104 cattle ($13,226); mules n/a; jacks and jennies n/a; 23 slaves ($10,900); sawmills n/a; distilleries n/a. Total assessed property value: $63,603. County tax assessed: $537. State tax assessed: $79.50.

Mulattoes constituted 4.1 percent of county taxpayers and owned 18 horses, 3.3 percent of the county's horses; 24 cattle, 2.1 percent of the county's cattle; no slaves out of 23 in the county and had $1,245 in property assessment, 2 percent of the county's wealth.

Marion County White Neighbors and Acquaintances of Caulder and the Halls

1841

TAXPAYER, AGE	POLL TAX	LAND/ACRES (VALUE)	HORSES (VALUE)	CATTLE (VALUE)	PROPERTY VALUE	COUNTY TAX*	STATE TAX*
1 Cowdrey, James, 46 (county clerk)	yes		2 (100)	4 (40)	$140		
2 Hargrave, John, 45 (neighbor of David B. Hall Jr.)	yes	160a ($480)	4 (300)	6 (70)	$850		
3 Hogan, Young, 53	yes		1 (65)	2 (25)	$90		
4 Pierson, George W., 26 (neighbor of John Hall)	yes		1 (200)	2 (20)	$220		
5 Pierson, Levi, 51	yes		2 (80)	4 (60)	$140		

*These taxes not available for 1841.

237

MARION COUNTY FREE BLACK TAX RECORD

1842

Sheriff: J. B. Everett; Clerk: James M. Cowdrey

	TAXPAYER, AGE	POLL TAX PD.	LAND/ACRES (VALUE)	HORSES (VALUE)	CATTLE (VALUE)	PROPERTY VALUE	COUNTY TAX**	STATE TAX**
	Little North Fork mulatto community							
1	Calder, William,* [Peter] 47	yes		1 (40)	1 (10)	$50		
2	Hall, David, Jr., 27	yes		1 (75)	2 (20)	$95		
3	Hall, David, Sr., 59	yes		8 (320)	5 (50)	$370		
4	Hall, John, 35	yes		6 (300)	13 (130)	$430		
5	Turner, John, 38	yes		2 (60)	1 (10)	$70		
6	Hall, Willoughby, 25	yes		1 (55)	2 (20)	$75		
7	Hall, Joseph, 22	yes		3 (100)	1 (10)	$110		
8	Hall, Thomas, 52	yes		2 (80)	-	$80		
8	**Totals for Marion County mulattoes**			24 ($1,030)	25 ($250)	$1,280		

*Clerk miscopied Caulder's first name; William is the previous given name on the roll.

**These taxes not available for 1842.

1842 Marion County had 248 poll-tax payers; 547 horses ($26,973); 1,020 cattle ($11,819); 7 mules ($575); jacks and jennies n/a; 32 slaves ($14,830); 3 sawmills ($2,500); 2 distilleries ($225). Total assessed property value: $71,843.50. County tax assessed: $614.33. State tax assessed n/a.

Mulattoes constituted 3.2 percent of county taxpayers and owned 24 horses, 4.3 percent of county's horses; 25 cattle, 2.4 percent of county's cattle; no slaves out of 32 in county; and owned $1,280 in assessed property, 1.8 percent of county's wealth.

MARION COUNTY WHITE NEIGHBORS
AND ACQUAINTANCES OF CAULDER AND THE HALLS

1842

TAXPAYER, AGE	POLL TAX	LAND/ACRES (VALUE)	HORSES (VALUE)	CATTLE (VALUE)	PROPERTY VALUE	COUNTY TAX*	STATE TAX*
1 Cowdrey, James M., 47 (Assistant Census Marshal in 1850)	yes		3 (100) 1 jenny (100)	5 (50)	$250		
2 Hargrave, John, 46 (Neighbor of David Hall Jr.)	yes	80a ($480)	8 (400)	7 (90)	$970		
3 Hogan, Young, 54	yes		n/a	n/a	n/a		
4 Pierson, George W., 27 (Accompanied Halls to Batesville land office)	yes		-	3 (30)	$30		
5 Pierson, Levi, 52 (Neighbor of Halls and Caulder)	yes		n/a	n/a	n/a		
6 Teaff, Nimrod	yes		2 (100)	2 (20)	$120		

*These taxes not available for 1842.

Marion County Free Black Tax Record

1843

Sheriff: Thomas D. Wood; Clerk: James M. Cowdrey

	TAXPAYER, AGE	POLL TAX PD.	LAND/ACRES (VALUE)	HORSES (VALUE)	CATTLE (VALUE)	PROPERTY VALUE	COUNTY TAX	STATE TAX
	Little North Fork mulatto community							
1	Colder, Petter, [Caulder, Peter] 48	yes		2 (50)	2 (20)	$70	$1.01¼	$0.08¼
2	Hall, Absalom, 37 (listed, but not taxed)	yes		-	-	-	-	-
3	Hall, David, Jr., 28	yes		2 (100)	3 (30)	$130	$1.23	$0.16¼
4	Hall, David, Sr., 60	yes		3 (300)	5 (5)	$350	$1.51¼	$0.43¼
5	Hall, John, 36	yes		6 (300)	6 (60)	$360	$2.10	$0.45
6	Black, Henley, 29	yes		1 (30)	1 (10)	$40	$0.90	$0.05
7	Turner, John, 39	yes		1 (35)	1 (10)	$45	$0.91	$0.08¼
8	Hall, Willaby, [Willoughby] 26	yes		1 (50)	1 (10)	$60	$0.93¾	$0.06¼
9	Adkinson, James, 48	yes		1 (40)	-	$40	$0.90	$0.05
10	Hall, Rebecca,*	no		2 (100)	-	$100	$1.37½	$0.37½
11	Hall, Rachel,* 27	no		2 (75)	1 (10)	$85	$1.31½	$0.31½
11	**Totals for Marion County mulattoes**			**21 ($1,080)**	**20 ($155)**	**$1,235**	**$12.19**	**$2.04**

*First and only appearance on tax roll.

1843 Marion County had 270 poll-tax payers; 661 horses ($30,705); 1,217 cattle ($11,557); 24 mules ($1,415); 8 jacks or jennies (n/a); 29 slaves ($11,300); 1 sawmill ($1,000); 1 distillery ($150). Total assessed property value: $73,066. County tax assessed: n/a. State tax assessed: $92.99.

Mulattoes constituted 4.0 percent of county taxpayers and owned 21 horses, 3.1 percent of county's horses; 20 cattle, 1.6 percent of county's cattle; owned no slaves of 29; owned $1,235 in assessed property value, 1.7 percent of county's wealth.

Marion County White Neighbors
and Acquaintances of Caulder and the Halls

1843

TAXPAYER, AGE	POLL TAX	LAND/ACRES (VALUE)	HORSES (VALUE)	CATTLE (VALUE)	PROPERTY VALUE	COUNTY TAX	STATE TAX
Cowdrey, James M., 48	yes		3 (100) 1 jenny (50)	5 (40)	$190	$1.46	$0.25
Pierson, George W., 28	yes		2 (110)	2 (20)	$130	$1.23	$0.16
Hargrave, John, 47	yes		6 (250) 1 mule (50)	10 (90)	$870	$4.01	$1.08
Hogan, Young, 55	yes		'	'	'	'	'

Marion County Free Black Tax Record

1844

Sheriff: Thomas D. Wood; Clerk: Thomas F. Austin

	TAXPAYER, AGE	POLL TAX PD.	LAND/ACRES (VALUE)	HORSES (VALUE)	CATTLE (VALUE)	PROPERTY VALUE	COUNTY TAX	STATE TAX
	Little North Fork mulatto community							
1	Callder, Peter, 49 [Caulder]	yes		2 (55)	2 (20)	$75	$1.08¼	$0.09¾
2	Hall, James, 21*	yes		1 (50)	-	$50	$0.93¾	$0.06¼
3	Hall, David, Jr., 29	yes		2 (100)	2 (16)	$116	$1.18½	$0.14½
4	Hall, David, Sr., 61	yes		9 (450)	6 (60)	$510	$2.65	$0.65¾
5	Hall, John, 37	yes		6 (300)	5 (40)	$340	$2.02½	$0.42½
6	Black, Henley, 30	yes		2 (60)	2 (16)	$76	$1.03½	$0.09½
7	Turner, John, 40	yes		1 (50)	1 (8)	$58	$0.96¾	$0.08¾
8	Hall, Absalom, 38	yes		1 (50)	-	$50	$0.93¾	$0.06¼
9	Hall, Thomas, 54	yes		3 (120)	1 (8)	$128	$1.20	$0.16¾
9	**Totals for Marion County mulattoes**			**27 (1,290)**	**19 (168)**	**$1,403**	**$12.02**	**$1.80**

**First appearance on tax roll.*

***1844** Marion County had 284 poll-tax payers; 609 horses ($24,859); 1,305 cattle ($11,803); 15 mules ($570); 8 jacks or jennies ($670); 30 slaves ($11,500); 2 sawmills ($1,500); 1 distillery ($150). Total assessed property value: $67,211. County tax assessed: n/a. State tax assessed: $86.94.*

***Mulattoes** constituted 3.2 percent of county taxpayers and owned 27 horses, 4.4 percent of county's horses; 19 cattle, 1.4 percent of county's cattle; owned no slaves out of 30; owned $1,403 in personal property value, 2 percent of county's wealth.*

Marion County White Neighbors
and Acquaintances of Caulder and the Halls

1844

TAXPAYER, AGE	POLL TAX	LAND/ACRES (VALUE)	HORSES (VALUE)	CATTLE (VALUE)	PROPERTY VALUE	COUNTY TAX	STATE TAX
Cowdrey, James M., 47	yes		4 (100) 2 jennies (100)	15 (120)	$320	$1.95	$0.40
Pierson, George W., 29	yes		2 (80)	1 (8)	$88	$1.08	$0.11
Hogan, Young, 56	yes		-	2 (18)	$18	$0.81	$0.02
Hogan, Ewing, 49	yes	1-20-16 208a 2 slaves ($700)*	4 (160)	20 (240)	$1,874	$7.74	$2.34
Hargrave, John, 48	yes	13-19-14 80a (240)	5 (230) 1 mule (50)	10 (98)	$858	$3.96	$1.07

Slaves valued in a range of $300–$500 in this year.

Marion County Free Black Tax Record

1845

Sheriff: Jesse Mooney; Clerk: William Barrett

	TAXPAYER,* AGE	POLL TAX PD.	LAND/ACRES (VALUE)	HORSES (VALUE)	CATTLE (VALUE)	PROPERTY VALUE	COUNTY TAX	STATE TAX
	Little North Fork mulatto community							
1	Hall, James, 22	yes		1 (25)	1 (5)	$30	$0.86	$0.03¾
2	Hall, David, Jr., 30	yes		3 (150)	3 (18)	$168	$1.36	$0.21
3	Hall, David, Sr., 62	yes		8 (200)	5 (25)	$225	$1.59	$0.28
4	Hall, John, 38	yes		10 (350)	12 (60)	$410	$2.28	$0.51
5	Hall, Joseph, 25	yes		1 (30)	1 (6)	$36	$0.88½	$0.04½
6	Black, Henley, 31	yes		1 (50)	1 (6)	$56	$0.96	$0.07
7	Hall, Abram, [Absalom] 39	yes		2 (40)	-	$40	$0.90	$0.05
7	**Totals for Marion County mulattoes**			24 (805)	35 (120)	$925	$7.93½	$1.15¾

*Peter Caulder does not appear on the tax roll in this year, nor does John Turner.

1845 Marion County had 251 poll-tax payers; 567 horses ($18,306); 1,379 cattle ($9,655); 12 mules ($445); 8 jacks or jennies ($1,040); 38 slaves ($12,850); 3 sawmills ($1,800); 0 distilleries; 0 tanneries; 1 pleasure carriage ($60). Total assessed property value: $62,655. County tax assessed: $422.54. State tax assessed: $78.12.

Mulattoes constituted 2.8 percent of county taxpayers and owned 24 horses, 4.2 percent of county's horses; 35 cattle, 2.5 percent of county's cattle; no slaves out of 38; had $925 in assessed property, 1.5 percent of county's wealth.

Marion County White Neighbors and Acquaintances of Caulder and the Halls

1845

TAXPAYER, AGE	POLL TAX	LAND/ACRES (VALUE)	HORSES (VALUE)	CATTLE (VALUE)	PROPERTY VALUE	COUNTY TAX	STATE TAX
Cowdrey, James M., 50	yes		2 (100) 3 Jennies (150)	11 (61)	$311	$1.92	$0.39
Pierson, George W., 30	yes		1 (30)	3 (15)	$45	$0.92	$0.05
Hogan, Young, 57	yes		1 (25)	1 (5)	$30	$0.86	$0.03
Hargrave, John, 49	yes	13-19-14 80a 18-19-13 80a (480)	5 (200) 1 mule (30)	10 (70)	$780	$3.67	$0.97
Talburt [Tolbert], John H., 22	yes	18-19-15 100 a	5 (125)	5 (35)	$463	$2.48	$0.57
Teaff, Nimrod, 42	yes		2 (50)	4 (20)	$90	$1.01	$0.08
Slow, William, 35	yes		-	2 (9)	$9	$0.78	$0.01

Marion County Free Black Tax Record

1846

Sheriff: Jesse Mooney; Clerk: William Barrett

TAXPAYER,* AGE	POLL TAX PD.	LAND/ACRES (VALUE)	HORSES (VALUE)	CATTLE (VALUE)	PROPERTY VALUE	COUNTY TAX	STATE TAX
Little North Fork mulatto community							
1 Hall, James, 23	yes		1 (40)	1 (5)	$45	$0.92	$0.05½
2 Hall, David B., Jr., 31	yes		3 (60)	3 (15)	$75	$1.04	$0.09¼
3 Hall, David, Sr., 63	yes		8 (160)	7 (35)	$195	$1.49	$0.24
4 Hall, John, 39	yes		7 1280)	12 (120)	$400	$2.25	$0.50
5 Hall, W. [Willoughby], 29	yes		2 (60)	5 (35)	$95	$1.10¾	$0.12
6 Hall, Joseph, 26	yes		1 (30)	2 (10)	$40	$0.90	$0.05
7 Hall, Lineas [Leonard], 22	yes		2 (55)	2 (10)	$65	$1.00	$0.08
8 Hall, Henderson	yes		1 (30)	1 (5)	$35	$0.88	$0.04
9 Black, Henley, 32	yes		1 (50)	1 (6)	$56	$0.96	$0.07
10 Hall, Abram [Absalom], 40	yes		2 (50)	2 (10)	$60	$0.97	$0.07½
Turkey mulatto community							
1 Dickson, John, 27	yes		1 (10)	3 (15)	$25	$0.84½	$0.03
2 Madewell, John, 66	yes		2 (40)	3 (15)	$55	$0.95½	$0.07
12 **Totals for Marion County mulattoes**			31(495)	42 (280)	**$675**	**$13.19¼**	**$1.93¼**

*Peter Caulder does not appear on the tax roll for this year, nor does John Turner.

1846 Marion County had 230 poll-tax payers; 503 horses ($15,506); 1,245 cattle ($8,206); 14 mules ($620); 7 jacks or jennies ($960); 42 slaves ($13,900); 3 sawmills ($1,400); 0 distilleries. Total assessed property value: $63,050. County tax assessed: $405.81. State tax assessed: $78.73.

Mulattoes constituted 2.8 percent of county taxpayers and owned 31 horses, 6.2 percent of county's horses; 42 cattle, 3.4 percent of county's cattle; no slaves out of 42; had $675 in assessed property, 1.0 percent of county's wealth.

Marion County White Neighbors
and Acquaintances of Caulder and the Halls

1846

TAXPAYER, AGE	POLL TAX	LAND/ACRES (VALUE)	HORSES (VALUE)	CATTLE (VALUE)	PROPERTY VALUE	COUNTY TAX	STATE TAX
Cowdrey, James M., 49	yes		2 (75) 3 Jennies (200)	5 (30)	$305	$1.89	$0.38
Pierson, George W., 31	yes		4 (120)	6 (30)	$150	$1.31	$0.19
Hogan, Young, 58	yes		1 (30)	1 (5)	$35	$0.88	$0.04
Hargrave, John, 50	yes	13-19-14/80a 18-19-13/ 80a (480)	5 (250)	11 (95)	$865	$4.09	$1.08
Talburt [Tolbert] John H., 23	yes	18-19-15 101a (303)	-	-	$303	$1.14	$0.38
Teaff, Nimrod, 43	yes		3 (70)	5 (25)	$95	$1.11	$0.12
Slow, Edwin [William E.], 36	yes		1 (10)	1 (6)	$16	$0.81	$0.02

247

Marion County Free Black Tax Record

1847

Sheriff: Jesse Mooney; Clerk: William Barrett

	TAXPAYER,* AGE	POLL TAX PD.	LAND/ACRES (VALUE)	HORSES (VALUE)	CATTLE (VALUE)	PROPERTY VALUE	COUNTY TAX**	STATE TAX
	Little North Fork mulatto community							
1	Hall, David, Jr., 32	yes		6 (150)	10 (40)	$190	$1.47½	$0.47½
2	Hall, David, Sr., 64	yes		8 (200)	10(64)	$264	$1.66	$0.66
3	Hall, John, 40	yes	(508)	14 (280)	22 (78)	$358	$2.27	$1.27
4	Hall, Willoughby, 30	yes		2 (50)	1 (7)	$57	$1.14½	$0.14½
5	Hall, Joseph, 27	yes		1 (25)	2 (10)	$35	$1.08¼	$0.08¾
6	Hall, Leonard, 23	yes		2 (50)	2 (10)	$60	$1.15	$0.15
7	Hall, Thomas, 57	yes		2 (50)	23 (15)	$115	$1.28	$0.28
8	Black, Henley, 33	yes		4 (60)	1 (4)	$64	$1.16	$0.16
9	Turner, John, 43	yes		2 (35)	3 (12)	$47	$1.11¾	$0.11¾

Turkey mulatto community

1	Dickson, John, 28	yes	2 (60)	6 (30)	$90	$1.22½	$0.22½
2	Maidwell [Madewell], John, 67	no	2 (50)	5 (20)	$70	$1.17	$0.17
3	Maidwell [Madewell], James, 31	yes	1 (15)	2 (10)	$25	$1.07	$0.07
12	**Totals for Marion County mulattoes**	(508)	46 (1,025)	87 (300)	$1,325	$15.80	$3.81

Peter Caulder does not appear on the 1847 tax roll.   **County tax rates based on flat poll tax of $1 charged to each male between the ages twenty and sixty together with ¼ cent per $10 of assessed real and personal property value.*

1847 Marion County had 279 poll-tax payers; 710 horses ($18,159); 1,776 cattle ($10,428); 12 mules ($460); 9 jacks or jennies ($750); 71 slaves ($23,900); 2 sawmills ($800); 1 distillery ($89). Total assessed property value: $87,305.78. County tax assessed: $499.29. State tax assessed: $219.99.

Mulattoes constituted 4.3 percent of county taxpayers and owned 46 horses, 6.5 percent of county's horses; 87 cattle, 4.9 percent of county's cattle; no slaves out of 71; had $1,325 in assessed personal property, 1.5 percent of county's wealth.

Marion County White Neighbors
and Acquaintances of Caulder and the Halls

1847

TAXPAYER, AGE	POLL TAX	LAND/ACRES (VALUE)	HORSES (VALUE)	CATTLE (VALUE)	PROPERTY VALUE	COUNTY TAX	STATE TAX
Cowdrey, James M., 52	yes		2 (60) 3 (150)	11 (60)	$270	$1.67	$0.67
Pierson, George W., 32	yes		9 (200)	12 (96)	$296	$1.74	$0.74
Hogan, Young, 59	yes		2 (40)	2 (10)	$50	$1.12	$0.12
Hargrave, John, 51	yes	13-19-14 18-19-14 160a (780)	6 (180) 1 mule (30)	18 (100)	$1,099	$3.72	$2.72
Tolbert, John H., 24	yes	18-19-15 101 a (503)	-	-	$503		
Teaff, Nimrod, 44	yes		3 (75)	6 (30)	$105	$1.26	$0.26
Bass, William	yes		1 (25)	4 (35)	$60	$1.15	$0.15
Slow, William, 37	yes		1 (15)	1 (8)	$23	$1.05	$0.05

Prominent Marion County Slave Owners

1847

TAXPAYER, AGE	POLL TAX	LAND/ACRES (VALUE)	SLAVES (VALUE)	HORSES (VALUE)	CATTLE (VALUE)	PROPERTY VALUE	COUNTY TAX	STATE TAX
Coker, Joseph, 60	yes	1-19-15 298a	17 slaves (4600)	3 horses (75)	16 cows (76)	$5,935	$15.83	$14.83
Coker, Wm., Sr., 78	no	31-21-18 80a	3 slaves (900)	3 (90)	6 (40)	$1,270	$3.17	$3.17
Coker, Edward, 46	yes	14-21-18 95a	4 slaves (2,000)	6 (300) 3 jacks (150)	75 (375)	$4117	$11.29	$10.29
Coker, Joseph, Jr., 23	yes	5-18-18	4 (1,100)	3 (300)	7 (45)	$2,155	$6.38	$5.38

Statement by County Clerk William Barrett on tax receipts in the county: "[It is] useless to enter in the caption of each page the following items to wit: town lots, household furniture over $200, pleasure carriages, money loaned at interest, capital in steam boat ferries and toll bridges, value of gold watches and jewelry of every kind, and capital invested in manufactories because there were none of said articles subject to taxation in Marion County."

MARION COUNTY FREE BLACK TAX RECORD

1848

Sheriff: Jesse Mooney; Clerk: James M. Cowdrey

	TAXPAYER, AGE	POLL TAX PD.	LAND/ACRES (VALUE)	HORSES (VALUE)	CATTLE (VALUE)	PROPERTY VALUE	COUNTY TAX*	STATE TAX
	Little North Fork mulatto community							
1	Caulder, Peter, 53	yes		1 (30)	2 (10)	$40	$1.10	$0.10
2	Hall, James, 25	yes		1 (50)	2 (10)	$60	$1.15	$0.15
3	Hall, David, Jr., 33	yes		1 (30)	2 (10)	$40	$1.10	$0.10
4	Hall, David, Sr., 65	yes		5 (125)	8 (32)	$157	$1.39¼	$0.39¼
5	Hall, John, 41	yes	1 slave (150)	19 (550)	18 (88)	$788	$2.97	$1.97
6	Hall, Absalom, 42	yes		1 (25)	2 (10)	$35	$1.08¾	$0.08¾
7	Hall, Willoughby, 31	yes		2 (60)	1 (5)	$65	$1.16¼	$0.16¼
8	Hall, Joseph, 28	yes		2 (40)	4 (20)	$60	$1.15	$0.15
9	Hall, Leonard, 24	yes		2 (45)	3 (10)	$55	$1.14	$0.14
10	Hall, Henderson [Henry], 18	yes		3 (100)	3 (15)	$115	$1.28	$0.28
11	Hall, Thomas, 58	yes		2 (50)	2 (10)	$60	$1.15	$0.15
12	Black, Henley, 34	yes		4 (60)	3 (12)	$72	$1.18	$0.18
13	Turner, John, 44	yes		1 (30)	6 (24)	$54	$1.13½	$0.13½
	Turkey mulatto community							
1	Maidwell [Madewell], James, 32	yes		1 (30)	2 (10)	$40	$1.10	$0.10
2	Maidwell [Madewell], John, 68	yes		1 (30)	2 (10)	$40	$1.10	$0.10
3	Dickson, John, 29	yes		1 (30)	2 (10)	$40	$1.10	$0.10

16 Totals for Marion County mulattoes   1 (150)   45 (1085)   60 (266) $1516 $20.29 $5.29

*County tax based on flat poll tax of $1 plus 1/4 cent per $10 assessed property value.

1848 Marion County had 299 poll-tax payers; 800 horses ($23,637); 1,644 cattle ($10,741); 12 mules ($525); 12 jacks or jennies ($950); 73 slaves ($26,800); 4 sawmills ($2,400); 2 distilleries ($150). Total assessed property value: $101,684. County tax assessed: $554.13. State tax assessed: $255.14.

Mulattoes constituted 5.3 percent of county taxpayers and owned 45 horses, 5.6 percent of county's horses; 60 cattle, 3.6 percent of county's cattle; one slave, 1 percent of county slaves; $1,516 in assessed personal property, 1.5 percent of county's wealth.

Marion County White Neighbors and Acquaintances of Caulder and the Halls

1848

TAXPAYER, AGE	POLL TAX	LAND/ACRES (VALUE)	HORSES (VALUE)	CATTLE (VALUE)	PROPERTY VALUE	COUNTY TAX	STATE TAX
Cowdrey, James M., 53	yes		2 (60) 5 jennies (250)	11 (50)	$360	$1.90	$0.90
Pierson, George W., 33	yes		9 (200)	12 (96)	$296	$1.74	$0.74
Hogan, Young, 60	yes		7 (175)	8 (40)	$215	$1.53	$0.53
Hargrave, John, 52	yes	160a (780)	6 (210)	19 (120)	$1,100	$3.77	$2.77
Tolbert, John [John H.?], 25	no	18-19-15 103a (550)	-	-	$550	$1.37	$1.37
Teaff, Nimrod, 45	yes		3 (75)	5 (40)	$115	$1.28	$0.28
Slow, Edwin [William E.]	yes		1 (35)	1 (5)	$40	$1.10	$0.10
Bass, William	yes		1 (25)	4 (35)	$60	$1.15	$0.15

MARION COUNTY FREE BLACK TAX RECORD

1849

Sheriff: Jesse Mooney; Clerk: T. E. Wilson

TAXPAYER, AGE	POLL TAX PD.	LAND/ACRES (VALUE)	HORSES (VALUE)	CATTLE (VALUE)	PROPERTY VALUE	COUNTY TAX	STATE TAX
Little North Fork mulatto community							
1 Cawlder, [Caulder], Peter, 54	yes			-	-	$1.00	-
2 Hall, James, 26	yes		2 (50)	2 (7.50)	$57.50	$1.14	$0.14
3 Hall, David, Jr., 34	yes		5 (150)	20 (100)	$250	$1.62	$0.62
4 Hall, David, Sr., 66	no	22-20-31/ 71a ($225)	7 (145)	14 (70)	$440	$1.10	$1.10
5 Hall, John, 42	yes	17-20-15/ 23a & 39a ($356) 1 slave (150)	16 (320)	3 (100)	$926	$3.31	$2.31
6 Hall, Absalom, 43	yes		1 (25)	2 (7)	$32	$1.08	$0.08
7 Hall, W. [Willoughby], 32	yes		1 (100)	2 (10)	$110	$1.27	$0.27
8 Hall, Joseph, 29	yes		2 (40)	3 (15)	$55	$1.13	$0.13
9 Hall, Leonard, 25	yes		2 (50)	3 (18)	$68	$1.17	$0.17
10 Black, Henley, 35	yes		2 (70)	7 (35)	$105	$1.26	$0.26
11 Turner, John, 45	yes		3 (75)	7 (35)	$110	$1.27	$0.27

Turkey mulatto community

1	Madewell, [John], 69	no	3 (40)	5 (30)	$90	$0.2 ½	$0.22½
2	Madewell, Good, 26	yes	1 (10)	1 (5)	$15	$1.03	$0.03
3	Madewell, James, 33	yes	1 (30)	2 (10)	$40	$1.10	$0.10
4	Johnston [Willis], Davis, 25	yes	1 (25)	5 (40)	$65	$1.16¼	$0.16¼
5	Dickson, John, 30	yes	3 (90)	5 (25)	$115	1.28¾	$0.28¾
16	**Totals for Marion County mulattoes**		50 (1220)	81 (507.5)	**$2,478.5**	**$20.15½**	**$6.15½**

1849 Marion County had 296 poll-tax payers; 720 horses ($23,267); 1,724 cattle ($11,540); 12 mules ($550); 13 jacks ($950); 65 slaves ($27,065); 2 sawmills ($1,150); 1 distillery ($40). Total assessed property value: $102,145. County tax assessed: $551.33. State tax assessed: $255.33.

Mulattoes constituted 5.4 percent of county taxpayers and owned 50 horses, 6.9 percent of county's horses; 81 cattle, 4.7 percent of county's cattle; one slave, 1.5 percent of county slaves; had $2,478.50 in assessed personal property, 2.4 percent of county's wealth.

Marion County White Neighbors
and Acquaintances of Caulder and the Halls

1849

TAXPAYER, AGE	POLL TAX	LAND/ACRES (VALUE)	HORSES (VALUE)	CATTLE (VALUE)	PROPERTY VALUE	COUNTY TAX	STATE TAX
Cowdrey, James M., 54	yes	40a; (500)	2(100) 4 jennys (400)	4 (80)	$1,080	$3.70	$2.70
Pierson, George W., 34	yes	17-20-18 51a; (500)	9 (225)	21 (116)	$841	$3.10	$2.10
Hogan, Young, 61	yes		1 (25)	1 (5)	$30	$1.07	$0.07
Hargrave, John, 53	yes	18-19-13 80; 13-19-14 80a (600)	3 (105) 2 mules (70)	2 (100)	$875	$3.18	$2.18
Talbert [Tolbert, John H.], 26		18-18-15 100a (500)	3 (103)	6 (49)	$6.54	$2.63	$1.63
Teaff, Nimrod, 46	yes		3 (75)	8 (40)	$115	$1.28	$0.28
Brannon, John	yes		1 (10)	-	$10	$1.02	$0.02
Bass, William	yes	-	2 (10)	-	$10	$1.02	$0.02

MARION COUNTY FREE BLACK TAX RECORD

1851

Sheriff: William Wood, Jr.; Clerk: Thomas F. Austin

TAXPAYER, AGE	POLL TAX PD.	LAND/ACRES (VALUE)	HORSES (VALUE)	CATTLE (VALUE)	PROPERTY VALUE	COUNTY TAX	STATE TAX
Little North Fork mulatto community							
1 Caulder, Peter, 56	yes		1 (50)	2 (16)	$66	$1.14½	$0.13½
2 Hall, James, 28	yes		2 (50)	3 (25)	$75	$1.18	$0.15
3 Hall, David B., Jr., 36	yes	NWNE 23-19-15/ 61a ($381)	5 (200)	8 (56)	$637	$2.57	$1.36
4 Hall, David, Sr. 68	no	22-20-14/ 71a ($225)	6 (150)	14 (66)	$441	$1.10	$0.86
5 Hall, John, 44	yes	17-20-15/ 23a & 39a ($250) 1 slave $160	18 (450)	16 (80)	$940	$3.32	$1.86
6 Hall, Willoby [Willoughby], 34	yes		2 (50)	-	$50	$1.12	$0.10
7 Hall, Joseph, 31	yes		2 (60)	2 (12)	$72	$1.18	$0.14
8 Hall, William, 19	yes		1 (15)	-	$15	$1.03	$0.03
9 Hall, Abner [Absalom], 45	yes		1 (20)	2 (10)	$30	$1.07	$0.06
10 Black, Henley, 37	yes		2 (100)	5 (35)	$135	$1.33	$0.27
11 Turner, John, 46	yes	SWNW 35-20-15/ 59.9a $170	2 (50)	6 (30)	$250	$1.62	$0.50
12 Turner, Reubin, 19	no		1 (25)	-	$25	$0.06	$0.03
13 Turner, Jesse, 19	no		1 (25)	-	$25	$0.06	$0.03

continued on following page

Turkey mulatto community

1	Madewell, S. [Solomon] H., 65	no	4 (100)	5 (49)	$149	$1.36	$0.27
2	Madewell, Riley, 24	yes	1 (40)	-	$40	$1.10	$0.08
3	Madewell, James, 34	yes	-	-	-	$1.00	-
4	Madewell, George, 23	yes	1 (20)	-	$20	$1.05	$0.04
5	Madewell, John, 71	no	2 (40)	7 (28)	$68	$0.17	$0.15
6	Dickson, John, 32	yes	4 (190)	6 (55)	$245	$1.67	$0.49
7	Johnston, [Johnson] Willis, 26	yes	-	2 (20)	$20	$1.08	$0.04
8	Moore, Charles, 67	yes	1 (50)	-	$50	$1.12	$0.10
21	**Totals for Marion County mulattoes**		54 (1,625)	76 (477)	$3,353	$24.19	$6.59

1851 *Marion County had 314 poll-tax payers; 758 horses ($26,625); 1,903 cattle ($15,144); 15 mules ($820); 11 jacks ($1,075); 82 slaves ($35,085); 3 sawmills ($1,600); 1 distillery (n/a). Total assessed property value: $146,557. County tax assessed: $682.96. State tax assessed: $295.66.*

Mulattoes *constituted 6.9 percent of county taxpayers and owned 54 horses, 7.1 percent of county's horses; 79 cattle, 4.2 percent of county's cattle; owned one slave, 1.2 percent of county slaves; had $3,353 of total valuation, 2.4 percent of county's wealth.*

MARION COUNTY WHITE NEIGHBORS
AND ACQUAINTANCES OF CAULDER AND THE HALLS

1851

TAXPAYER, AGE	POLL TAX	LAND/ACRES (VALUE)	HORSES (VALUE)	CATTLE (VALUE)	PROPERTY VALUE	COUNTY TAX	STATE TAX
Bassham, Pleasant*, 38	yes		3 (150)	8 (90)	$240	$1.54	$0.44
Cowdrey, James M., 56	yes	41 a; 40a; (800)	5 (90) 7 jennys (525)	14 (100)	$1,515	$4.81	$3.03
Pierson, George W., 36	yes	17-20-18 51a; (200)	8 (280)	42 (332)	$812	$3.78	$2.22
Hogan, Young, 63	yes		1 (50)	2 (10)	$60	$1.15	$0.12
Hargrave, John, 55	yes	18-19-13 80; 13-19-14 80a (600)	4 (135) 1 (40)	28 (180)	$955	$3.38	$1.91
Tolbert, John H., 28	yes	11-18-15 43a 13-19-15 61a (1,000)	3 (110)	4 (60)	$1,170	$3.92	$2.43

*New county resident, Methodist minister.

Marion County Free Black Tax Record

1852

Sheriff: John Wood; Clerk: Thomas F. Austin

TAXPAYER, AGE	POLL TAX PD.	LAND/ACRES (VALUE)	HORSES (VALUE)	CATTLE (VALUE)	PROPERTY VALUE	COUNTY TAX	STATE TAX
*Little North Fork mulatto community**							
Turkey mulatto community							
1 Madewell, Solomon, 67	no		1 (15)	3 (26)	$41	$0.10¼	$0.08¾
2 Madewell, George, 24	yes		1 (25)	2 (15)	$40	$0.85	$0.08
3 Johnston, [Johnson] Willis, 27	yes		-	-	-	$0.75	$0.25
4 Moore, Charles, 68	yes		1 (50)	-	$50	$0.87½	$0.10
5 Madewell, John, 72	yes		2 (55)	5 (35)	$90	$0.97½	$0.18
6 Madewell, Wm. Riley, 25	yes		1 (35)	1 (6)	$41	0.83¼	$0.08¾
6 Totals for Marion County mulattoes			**6(180)**	**11 (82)**	**$266**	**$2.33**	**$0.48**

* No mulattoes were assessed for taxes in the Little North Fork township in 1852.

1852 Marion County had 470 poll-tax payers; 900 horses ($34,722); 2,295 cattle ($20,797); 27 mules (n/a); 13 jacks (n/a); 92 slaves ($39,285); 4 sawmills ($2,100), 4 distilleries ($355). Total assessed property value: $185,847. County tax assessed: $839.63. State tax assessed: $369.37.

Mulattoes constituted 1.35 percent of county taxpayers and owned 6 horses, 0.7 percent of county's horses; 11 cattle, 0.5 percent of county's cattle; no slaves; and had $266 in assessed property value or 0.1 percent of county's wealth.

1852

TAXPAYER, AGE	POLL TAX	LAND/ACRES (VALUE)	HORSES (VALUE)	CATTLE (VALUE)	PROPERTY VALUE	COUNTY TAX	STATE TAX
John W. Martin acquired these tracts from John Turner in 1852	yes	SW pt. 25-20-15 39.99 a NE pt 34-20-15 29.15 a NW/2 35-20-15 48.53 a ($552)	1 (20) 2(100)	52 (520)	$1,200	$6.75	$4.78
John D. Noe Purchased this tract from David Hall, Sr.	yes	S pt. NW/4 22-21-15 71.13a ($1,000)	1 (45)	11 (86)	$1,221	$3.80¼	$2.44
Bassham, Pleasant, 39	yes	40 a ($200)	4 (150)	13 (77)	$427	$1.81	$0.85
Cowdrey, James H., 57	yes		2 (80) 7 jennys (500)	16 (130)	$1,500	$3.37	$2.10
Friend, Peter, 39	yes		2 (100)	7 (70)	$170	$1.17	$0.34
Hargrave, John, 56	yes		7 (500)				
Teaff, Nimrod, 49	yes		6 (150)	13 (104)	$254	$1.38	$0.85

MARION COUNTY FREE BLACK TAX RECORD

1853

Sheriff: Isom Stinnett; Clerk: Thomas F. Austin

TAXPAYER,* AGE	POLL TAX PD.	LAND/ACRES (VALUE)	HORSES (VALUE)	CATTLE (VALUE)	PROPERTY VALUE	COUNTY TAX	STATE TAX
Little North Fork mulatto community							
1 Hall, David, Sr., 70	no	($483)	4 (115)	7 (80)	$678	$0.48	$0.48
2 Hall, John, 46	yes	23-19-15/61a David B. Hall Jr. former owner 13-19-15/29a ($850) Wm Byers former owner	7 (280)	8 (90)	$853	$3.03	$2.13
3 Hall, Joseph, 33 [perhaps James Hall]	yes		1 (30)	3 (24)	$54	$1.05	$0.13½
4 Nesby [Nebsit], Francis, 40	yes		1 (30)	-	$30	$0.97½	$0.07½
5 Turner, John, 48	yes	35-20-17/71a ($263)	2 (40)	1 (10)	$313	$1.65¼	$0.78¾
6 Turner, Rheuben [Reuben], 21	yes		1 (25)	-	$25	$0.96 ¼	$0.06¼
Turkey mulatto community							
1 Madewell, Solomon, 68	no		2 (15)	3 (29)	$44	$0.11	$0.11
2 Madewell, Good, 30	yes		1 (25)	1 (10)	$35	$0.98¾	$0.08¾
3 Madewell, John, 73	no		2 (55)	7 (88)	$143	$0.35	$0.35
4 Madewell, James, 17	yes		1 (45)	2 (16)	$61	$1.03¼	$0.13¼

#	Name						
5	Madewell, William R., 26	yes	-	4 (32)	$32	$0.78	$0.08
6	Dickson, John, 34	yes	4 (210)	2 (30)	$240	$1.50	$0.60
7	Johnston, Willis, 28	yes	2 (80)	5 (50)	$130	$1.23½	$0.32½
8	Moore, Charles, 69	yes	2 (50)	-	$50	$0.90	-
9	Madewell, Charles, 19	yes	-	-	-	$0.90	-
10	Madewell, Samuel, 19	yes	1 (25)	-	$25	$0.96¼	$0.06¼
16	**Totals for Marion County mulattoes**		31 (970)	43 (459)	$2,713	$16.88	$5.38

*Peter Caulder did not appear on the tax roll for this year.

1853 Marion County had 530 poll-tax payers; 1,022 horses ($43,750); 2,867 cattle ($29,890); 31 mules ($1,835); 15 jacks ($2,150); 126 slaves ($57,150); 4 sawmills ($2,100), 4 distilleries ($355). Total assessed property value: $283,171. County taxes assessed: $1,188.13. State taxes assessed: $709.44.

Mulattoes constituted 3.0 percent of county taxpayers and owned 31 horses, 3.0 percent of county's horses; 43 cattle, 1.5 percent of county's cattle; no slaves; and had $2,713 of total assessed property, 0.9 percent of county's wealth.

MARION COUNTY WHITE NEIGHBORS
AND ACQUAINTANCES OF CAULDER AND THE HALLS

1853

TAXPAYER, AGE	POLL TAX	LAND/ACRES (VALUE)	HORSES (VALUE)	CATTLE (VALUE)	PROPERTY VALUE	COUNTY TAX	STATE TAX
Bassham, Pleasant,* 40	yes						
Cowdrey, James M., 58	yes	41a; 40a; (800)					
Pierson, George W., 38	yes	17-20-18 51a; (200)	3 (150) 2 mules (150)	33 (365)	$1,605		
Hargrave, John, 57	yes	18-19-13 80; 13-19-14 80a (600)	3 (150) 4 mules (200)	28 (162)	$1,100	$3.68	$2.78
Teaff, Nimrod, 50	yes		5(125)	9 (90)	$215	$1.43	$0.53
Hall, Jno (a white John Hall?)	yes		1 (60)	2 (40)	$100		

Pleasant Bassham missing this tax year.

MARION COUNTY FREE BLACK TAX RECORD

1854

Sheriff: Isom Stinnett; Clerk: Thomas F. Austin

TAXPAYER,* AGE	POLL TAX PD.	LAND/ACRES (VALUE)	HORSES (VALUE)	CATTLE (VALUE)	PROPERTY VALUE	COUNTY TAX**	STATE TAX**
		Little North Fork mulatto community					
1 Hall, David, Sr., 71	no		3 (130)	8 (115)	$250		
2 Hall, John, 47	yes	NE 33-19-15/ 61.22 a E/4 13-19-15/ 29.45 a ($700)	7 (350)	10 (100)	$1,150		
3 Hall, James, 31 (noted as Administrator, probably of Peter Caulder's land)	yes	NWNE 10-20-15/ 72.59a ($250)	2 (75)	1 (10)	$335		
4 Hall, Willoughby, 37	yes		-	6 (50)	$50		
5 Hall, Joseph, 34	yes		2 (80)	4 (65)	$145		
6 Neisby, Frank, [Nesbit, Francis] 41	yes		1 (30)	-	$30		
		*Turkey mulatto community***					
7 Turner, John, 49	no	35-20-17/ 71a	1 (25)	2 (25)	$550		
7 Totals for Marion County mulattoes			17 (750)	33 (405)	$2,610		

265

*Peter Caulder did not appear on the tax roll for this year.

**Tax amounts not included on individual record for 1854.

***No mulattoes were assessed for taxes in the Blythe-Union townships in 1854.

1854 Marion County had 544 poll-tax payers; 927 horses ($48,698); 2,621 cattle ($35,214); 15 mules ($1,210); 17 jacks ($2,395); 132 slaves ($67,080), 3 sawmills, 1 distillery, 1 pleasure carriage. Total assessed property value: $367,559. County taxes assessed: n/a. State taxes assessed: $918.31.

Mulattoes constituted 1.3 percent of population of county taxpayers and owned 17 horses, 1.8 percent of county's horses; 33 cattle, 1.3 percent of county's cattle; no slaves; and had property assessed at $2,610, 0.7 percent of county's wealth.

MARION COUNTY WHITE NEIGHBORS
AND ACQUAINTANCES OF CAULDER AND THE HALLS

1854

TAXPAYER, AGE	POLL TAX	LAND/ACRES (VALUE)	HORSES (VALUE)	CATTLE (VALUE)	PROPERTY VALUE	COUNTY TAX*	STATE TAX*
Bassham, Pleasant, 41	yes	9-17-18 40a(150)	4 (250)	9 (125)	$575		
Cowdrey, James M., 59	yes	3-18-16 160 a; (1,000)	3 (200) 8 jennies (1,000)	14 (160)	$2,360		
Pierson, George W., 39	yes	19-20-15 51 a 17-20-15 65a 18-20-15 88a 21-20-15 61 a	-	-	-		
Hargrave, John, 58	yes	18-19-13 80; 13-19-14 80a (600)	-	-	-		
Hall, Jno	yes		1 (60)	2 (40)	$100		
Noe, John D.	yes	s/2, w/4 22-21-15 71.13 a se/4 nw/4 32-20-15 46.78 a	1 (50)	42 (416)	$1,557		

*Tax amounts not included on individual record for 1854.

Marion County Free Black Tax Record

1855

Sheriff: William M. Brown; Clerk: Thomas F. Austin

TAXPAYER,* AGE	POLL TAX PD.	LAND/ACRES (VALUE)	HORSES (VALUE)	CATTLE (VALUE)	PROPERTY VALUE	COUNTY TAX	STATE TAX
		Little North Fork mulatto community					
1 Hall, David, Jr. 40	no		2 (30)	6 (60)	$90	$1.47½	$0.22
2 Hall, John, 48	yes	No description, 129a ($600)	5 (250)	11(225)	$1,075	$3.67½	$2.68
3 Hall, James, 32	yes		2 (50)	1 (10)	$60	$1.15	$0.15
4 Hall, Absalom, 49	yes		1 (45)	-	$45	$1.11¼	$0.11¼
5 Hall, Wiloby, [Willoughby] 38	yes		-	5 (50)	$50	$1.12½	$0.12½
6 Hall, Joseph, 35	yes		1 (40)	4 (50)	$90	$1.22½	$0.22½
7 Nesbit, Francis, 42	yes		-	-	-	$1.00	-
8 Turner, John, 50	yes		3 (75)	3 (30)	$105	$1.26¼	$0.26¼
9 Turner, Jesse, 23	yes		-	-	-	$1.00	-
10 Black, Henley, 41	yes		3 (135)	9 (120)	$255	$1.63¾	$01.63¼
11 Hall, William, 23	yes		1 (50)	1 (8)	$58	$1.14½	$0.14½

Turkey mulatto community

1 Madewell, Solomon, 69	yes	SW/4 2-18-17 40a ($150)	1 (20)	2 (30)	$200	$0.50	$0.50
2 Madewell, Lewis, 22	yes		1 (50)	-	$50	$1.12½	$0.12½
3 Madewell, John G.	yes		1 (30)	1 (15)	$45	$1.21¼	$0.21¼
4 Madewell, James, 39	yes		2 (80)	4 (55)	$135	$1.33¾	$0.33¾
5 Dickson, John, 36	yes	SW/4 NE/4 35-19-17/ 40a ($120)	7 (315)	15 (125)	$560	$2.40	$1.40
16 Totals for Marion County mulattoes			**30 (1170)**	**55 (788)**	**$2,818**	**$22.33½**	**$8.09½**

*Peter Caulder did not appear on the tax roll for this year.

1855 Marion County had 622 poll-tax payers; 1,112 horses ($56,877); 3,096 cattle ($39,070); 44 mules ($3,175); 17 jacks ($2,222); 136 slaves ($71,850), 4 sawmills ($1,330), 1 distillery ($100), 1 tannery ($150), 5 pleasure carriages ($265). Total assessed property value: $409,894. County taxes assessed: $1,652.61. State taxes assessed: $1,027.25.

Mulattoes constituted 2.6 percent of county taxpayers and owned 30 horses, 2.7 percent of county's horses; 55 cattle, 1.8 percent of county's cattle; no slaves; and had $2,818 in property value, 0.7 percent of county's wealth.

Marion County White Neighbors
and Acquaintances of Caulder and the Halls

1855

TAXPAYER, AGE	POLL TAX	LAND/ACRES (VALUE)	HORSES (VALUE)	CATTLE (VALUE)	PROPERTY VALUE	COUNTY TAX	STATE TAX
Pierson, George W., 40	yes	17-20-15 51.63 a 17-20-15 65.95 a ($455.80)					-
Hall, Jno, (white John Hall)	yes	1 (60)	2 (40)	$100	$1.15	$0.15	
John Hargrave, 59	yes	W/2 NW/4 18-19-13 80a E/2 NE/4 13-19-13 80a ($800)	2 (120) 1 mule (100)	24 (250)	$1,270	$4.17½	$3.17½
McClure, William	yes		-	-	-	$1.00	-
Noe, John D.	yes						
Bassham, Pleasant, 42	yes	SE/4 SW/4 9-17-18 40a ($400)	4 (250)	7 (90)	$340	$2.85	$1.85
Hogan, Young, 67							
Cowdrey, James M., 60							

MARION COUNTY FREE BLACK TAX RECORD

1859

Sheriff: Isom M. Stinnett; Clerk: J. W. Methvin

TAXPAYER, AGE	POLL TAX PD.	LAND/ACRES (VALUE)	HORSES (VALUE)	CATTLE (VALUE)	PROPERTY VALUE	COUNTY TAX	STATE TAX	SPECIAL TAX
Little North Fork mulatto community								
1 Caulder, Peter, 64*	no		1 (50)	3 (75)	$125	$0.31	$0.21	$0.31
2 Hall, James, 36	yes		1 (50)	5 (40)	$90	$1.23	$0.15	$0.22
3 Hall, David, Jr., 44 (probably inherited David Hall Sr.'s cattle)	yes	N/2 SW 19-19-14/ 80a Spt SE 4-19-14/ 25a N/2 NE 16-19-14/ 80a ($640)**	3 (180)	16 (215)	$1,035	$3.59	$1.72	$2.54
4 Hall, John E., 52	yes	/442a ($1,500)	6 (350)	18 (180)	$2,030	$6.07	$3.38	$5.08
5 Hall, Absalom, 53	yes		-	2 (45)	$45	$1.11	$0.07	$0.11
6 Black, Henley, 45	yes		2 (60)	3 (30)	$90	$1.23	$0.15	$0.23
7 Nesbit, Francis, 46	yes		-	3 (40)	$40	$1.10	$0.06	$0.10
Turkey mulatto community								
1 Madewell, Lewis, 26 (only Madewell remaining on tax roll)	yes		1 (20)	-	$20	$1.05	$0.03	$0.05
8 **Totals for Marion County mulattoes**			**14 (710)**	**50 (625)**	**$3,475**	**$15.69**	**$5.77**	**$8.64**

* Last tax roll appearance of Peter Caulder or any Caulder in Marion County, Arkansas.   **Incorrectly marked as section 15 on tax roll.

1859 *Marion County had 763 poll-tax payers; 1,234 horses ($80,853); 3,917 cattle ($52,826); 73 mules ($5,575); 19 jacks ($1,845); 188 slaves ($120,675); 4 tanyards ($1,250); 3 pleasure carriages ($325). Total assessed property value: $708,135. County taxes assessed: $2,543.91. State taxes assessed: $1,187.67. Special tax assessed: $1,770.35.*

Mulattoes *constituted 1 percent of population of county taxpayers and owned 14 horses, 1 percent of county's horses; 50 cattle, 1 percent of county's cattle; no slaves; and had $3,475 in property assessed, 0.5 percent of county's wealth.*

Marion County Whites Associated with Mulatto Residents

1859

TAXPAYER, AGE	POLL TAX	LAND/ACRES (VALUE)	HORSES (VALUE)	CATTLE (VALUE)	PROPERTY VALUE	COUNTY TAX	STATE TAX	SPECIAL TAX
Hall, John (white John Hall)	yes		1 (60)	-	$60	$1.15	$0.11	$0.15
Cowdry, James M., 64	no	/120a (1,200) City lot (800)	7 (400) 7 jennies (600)	20 (240)	$3,240	$8.10	$5.40	$8.10
Noe, John D., (purchaser of David Hall land)	yes	/188a ($2,000)	9 (495) 1 mule (130)	45 (495)	$3,140	$8.83	$5.23	$7.85
McClure, John (killed by Willoughby Hall during the Civil War)	yes		4 (200)	-	$200	$1.50	$0.33	$0.50
Hargrave, John, 63								
Bassham, Pleasant, 46								
Pierson, George, 44								

MARION COUNTY FREE BLACK TAX RECORD

1860

Sheriff: Isam. M. Stinnett; Clerk: J. W. Methvin

TAXPAYER, AGE	POLL TAX PD.	LAND/ACRES (VALUE)	HORSES (VALUE)	CATTLE (VALUE)	PROPERTY VALUE	COUNTY TAX	STATE TAX
		*Little North Fork mulatto community**					
		*Turkey mulatto community**					

o **Totals for Marion County mulattoes**

*No mulattoes assessed for taxes in 1860.

1860 Marion County had 751 poll-tax payers; 1,212 horses ($85,735); 3,941 cattle ($75,224); 81 mules ($7,231); 20 jacks and jennies ($2,975); 176 slaves ($123,300). Total value of property: $676,753. County taxes assessed: $2,443.53. State taxes assessed: $1,136.91. Special taxes assessed: $1,364.60.

Mulattoes constituted none of 751 taxpayers in 1860.

1860

TAXPAYER, AGE	POLL TAX	LAND/ACRES (VALUE)	HORSES (VALUE)	CATTLE (VALUE)	PROPERTY VALUE	COUNTY TAX	STATE TAX
Hall, John	yes						
Cowdrey, James M., 65	yes						
Pierson, George W., 45	yes						
Cummins, P. D.	yes						
Coker, Edward	yes						
Martin, John W.	yes	/166.87 a 2 slaves					
Hogan, Young,							
Hargrave, John, 64							
Bassham, Pleasant, 47							

Appendix C

CAULDER FAMILY TREE

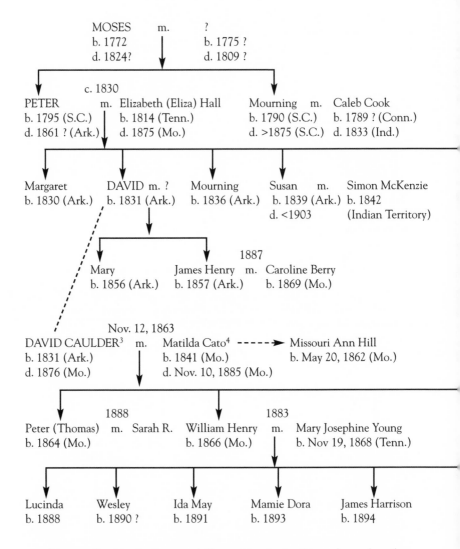

1. Moses enlisted in the Fourteenth Kansas Cavalry in 1863 and served until the war's end. He migrated back to Missouri where he married Mary Ann Nelson in 1876.

2. Hiram M. Caulder served as a sailor aboard the USS *Kansas* in 1910. He is listed as white. Hiram's birth on December 26, 1888, was recorded in the family Bible. Mary Ann Nelson Caulder submitted the page to the pension office to support her claim as the widow of Moses Caulder. Other names on the page include John Bias who is found in the 1870 Washington County, Arkansas, census.

3. After the death of his first wife, David Caulder joined the Twelfth Missouri

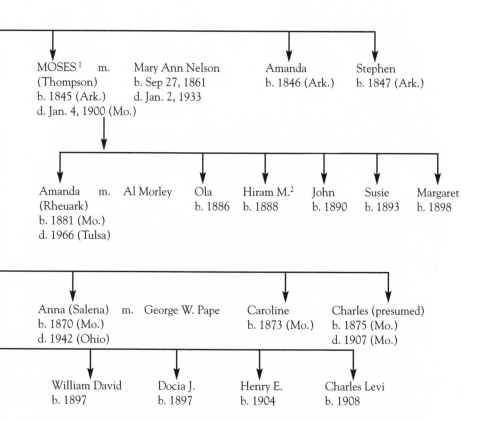

MOSES [1]   m.   Mary Ann Nelson   Amanda   Stephen
(Thompson)   b. Sep 27, 1861   b. 1846 (Ark.)   b. 1847 (Ark.)
b. 1845 (Ark.)   d. Jan. 2, 1933
d. Jan. 4, 1900 (Mo.)

Amanda   m.   Al Morley   Ola   Hiram M.[2]   John   Susie   Margaret
(Rheuark)   b. 1886   b. 1888   b. 1890   b. 1893   b. 1898
b. 1881 (Mo.)
d. 1966 (Tulsa)

Anna (Salena)   m.   George W. Pape   Caroline   Charles (presumed)
b. 1870 (Mo.)   b. 1873 (Mo.)   b. 1875 (Mo.)
d. 1942 (Ohio)   d. 1907 (Mo.)

William David   Docia J.   Henry E.   Charles Levi
b. 1897   b. 1897   b. 1904   b. 1908

Cavalry (Federal) and married the widow of his fellow soldier Eldridge Hill of
Bollinger County. Hill and his wife Matilda Cato had three children. Only Missouri
survived the war. After the death of David Caulder, David B. Hall Jr. adopted her.

4. Matilda Cato married Elbridge Hill in Bollinger County on March 15, 1860.
Anderson George conducted the ceremony, and the couple had twins named
Missouri and Columbia born on May 20, 1862. Columbia died as an infant.
Elbridge Hill died at Cape Girardeau while in the service of the Twelfth
Missouri Cavalry (Federal).

HALL FAMILY TREE

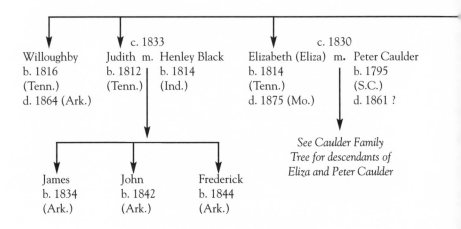

Family of David Hall who migrated to Arkansas with him

Thomas J. Hall   m.   Louisa J.   Absalom (Abram) Hall   m.   Martha
b. 1790 (Tenn.)   b. 1810 (Il)   b. 1806 (Tenn.)   b. 1832 (Tenn.)
d. 1888 (Mo.)

Willoughby   Judith m. Henley Black   Elizabeth (Eliza) m. Peter Caulder
b. 1816   b. 1812   b. 1814   b. 1814   b. 1795
(Tenn.)   (Tenn.)   (Ind.)   (Tenn.)   (S.C.)
d. 1864 (Ark.)   d. 1875 (Mo.)   d. 1861 ?

c. 1833   c. 1830

*See Caulder Family
Tree for descendants of
Eliza and Peter Caulder*

James   John   Frederick
b. 1834   b. 1842   b. 1844
(Ark.)   (Ark.)   (Ark.)

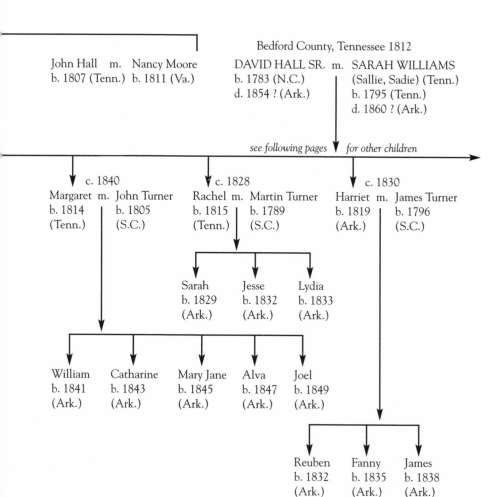

Bedford County, Tennessee 1812

John Hall   m.   Nancy Moore
b. 1807 (Tenn.) b. 1811 (Va.)

DAVID HALL SR. m. SARAH WILLIAMS
b. 1783 (N.C.)   (Sallie, Sadie) (Tenn.)
d. 1854 ? (Ark.)   b. 1795 (Tenn.)
                      d. 1860 ? (Ark.)

see following pages   *for other children*

c. 1840
Margaret m. John Turner
b. 1814   b. 1805
(Tenn.)   (S.C.)

c. 1828
Rachel m. Martin Turner
b. 1815   b. 1789
(Tenn.)   (S.C.)

c. 1830
Harriet m. James Turner
b. 1819   b. 1796
(Ark.)   (S.C.)

Sarah   Jesse   Lydia
b. 1829   b. 1832   b. 1833
(Ark.)   (Ark.)   (Ark.)

William   Catharine   Mary Jane   Alva   Joel
b. 1841   b. 1843   b. 1845   b. 1847   b. 1849
(Ark.)   (Ark.)   (Ark.)   (Ark.)   (Ark.)

Reuben   Fanny   James
b. 1832   b. 1835   b. 1838
(Ark.)   (Ark.)   (Ark.)

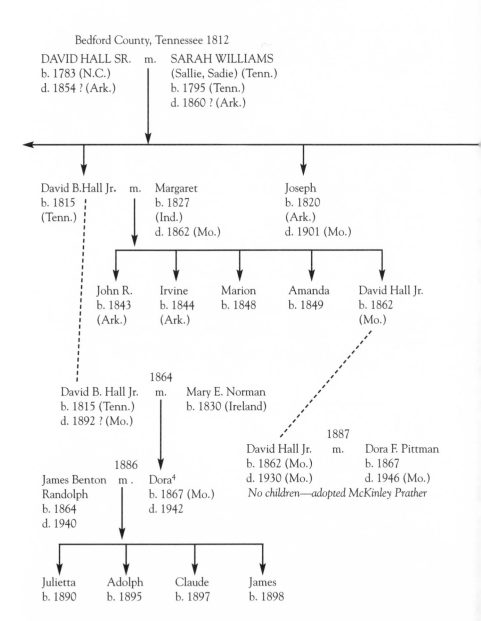

Bedford County, Tennessee 1812

DAVID HALL SR.   m.   SARAH WILLIAMS
b. 1783 (N.C.)   (Sallie, Sadie) (Tenn.)
d. 1854 ? (Ark.)   b. 1795 (Tenn.)
                                      d. 1860 ? (Ark.)

David B.Hall Jr.   m.   Margaret   Joseph
b. 1815   b. 1827   b. 1820
(Tenn.)   (Ind.)   (Ark.)
                                  d. 1862 (Mo.)   d. 1901 (Mo.)

John R.   Irvine   Marion   Amanda   David Hall Jr.
b. 1843   b. 1844   b. 1848   b. 1849   b. 1862
(Ark.)   (Ark.)   (Mo.)

                        1864
David B. Hall Jr.   m.   Mary E. Norman
b. 1815 (Tenn.)   b. 1830 (Ireland)
d. 1892 ? (Mo.)

                                                            1887
                                    David Hall Jr.   m.   Dora F. Pittman
                     1886   b. 1862 (Mo.)   b. 1867
James Benton   m .   Dora[4]   d. 1930 (Mo.)   d. 1946 (Mo.)
Randolph   b. 1867 (Mo.) *No children—adopted McKinley Prather*
b. 1864   d. 1942
d. 1940

Julietta   Adolph   Claude   James
b. 1890   b. 1895   b. 1897   b. 1898

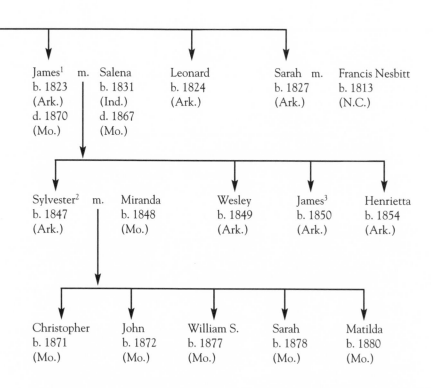

James[1] m. Salena
b. 1823   b. 1831
(Ark.)   (Ind.)
d. 1870   d. 1867
(Mo.)   (Mo.)

Leonard
b. 1824
(Ark.)

Sarah m. Francis Nesbitt
b. 1827   b. 1813
(Ark.)   (N.C.)

Sylvester[2] m. Miranda
b. 1847   b. 1848
(Ark.)   (Mo.)

Wesley
b. 1849
(Ark.)

James[3]
b. 1850
(Ark.)

Henrietta
b. 1854
(Ark.)

Christopher
b. 1871
(Mo.)

John
b. 1872
(Mo.)

William S.
b. 1877
(Mo.)

Sarah
b. 1878
(Mo.)

Matilda
b. 1880
(Mo.)

1. Accused killer of John Tolbert (1851).

2. Brought lawsuit against Howell County, Missouri, School District 422 in 1888 for denial of admission of children enumerated above on account of race.

3. Signed affidavit as first cousin of Moses Caulder in widow's pension claim, dated February 12, 1902. Address Cotbus P.O., Howell Co., Mo.

4. Dora Hall, half-sister to David Hall Jr. married James Benton Randolph. The couple occupied the Hall homestead after the death of David B. Hall Jr. in 1892. They appear in the 1896 photograph along with their three children and a man holding the horses. He is most likely Charles Caulder, presumed youngest son of David and Matilda Caulder.

NOTES

Introduction

1. According to the 1870 census for Bollinger County, Missouri, David Caulder was black. David B. Hall Jr., counted in Arkansas as a mulatto, was listed as white in 1870. U.S. Bureau of the Census, The Ninth Census of the United States: 1870 (Washington, D.C., 1870), Missouri, Bollinger County, Wayne Township, Schedule 1, Population, dwelling #103.

CHAPTER ONE: Catfish Creek

1. Department of Commerce and Labor, Bureau of the Census, Heads of Families, *First Census of the United States: 1790*, State of South Carolina (Washington, D.C.: Government Printing Office, 1908).

2. Hendrik Booraem, *Young Hickory: The Making of Andrew Jackson* (Dallas, Tex.: Taylor Trade Publishing, 2001).

3. Michael Kammen, *People of Paradox: An Inquiry concerning the Origins of American Civilization* (Ithaca, N.Y.: Cornell University Press, 1990), 57. Kammen paraphrases Ortega y Gasset in a portion of this quotation.

4. Walter Edgar, *South Carolina: A History* (Columbia: University of South Carolina, 1998), 131.

5. Joel Williamson, *New People: Miscegenation and Mulattoes in the United States* (New York: Free Press, 1980), 50–51; Ruth Polk Patterson, *The Seed of Sally Good'n: A Black Family of Arkansas, 1833–1953* (Lexington: University of Kentucky Press, 1985), 52–53. Patterson explained that the term *mulatto* itself reflected the distaste of whites for mixed marriages. Mulatto being derived from the Spanish word for mule, the inference is that offspring of "unnatural" couplings are "biologically incomplete." Patterson writes that "of course, all mulattoes were 'kin' to white folk."

6. George Milligen Johnston, *A Short Description of the Province of South-Carolina* (1763), reprinted in Edgar, *South Carolina*, 63.

7. Paul Finkelman, "The Crime of Color," *Tulane Law Review* 67 (June 1993): 2096. Finkelman wrote that "South Carolina was committed to a system of slavery from the moment of its settlement." Virginia, by contrast, developed its views on the role of black people in slavery and indentured service in piecemeal fashion over a long period of time.

8. Booraem, *Young Hickory*, 17. Booraem's chapter on "The Carolina Irish" detailed the habits and characteristics of the ethnic group that dominated Carolina backcountry population.

9. Edgar, *South Carolina*, 5; Chinua Achebe, *Things Fall Apart* (New York: Fawcett World Library, 1969), Reprint Paperback Edition, 35. Yams, like okra, are gifts from Africa to the culinary fare of South Carolinians, white and black.

10. Finkelman, "The Crime of Color," 2101.

11. Arkansas governor Orval Faubus used the specter of inevitable "Negro" assaults on white schoolgirls to justify his actions regarding Little Rock Central High School in 1957. A large percentage of the white population in Arkansas bought that bogus sales pitch. See particularly Phoebe Godfrey, "Bayonets, Brainwashing, and Bathrooms: The Discourse of Race, Gender, and Sexuality in the Desegregation of Little Rock's Central High," *Arkansas Historical Quarterly* 62 (Spring 2003): 43–45.

12. See, for example, the speech of Georgia congressman Henry M. Turner delivered in the U.S. House of Representatives on September 3, 1868, reprinted in Herbert Aptheker, ed., *A Documentary History of the Negro People in the United States: From the Reconstruction Years to the Founding of the N.A.A.C.P. in 1910*, vol. 2 (New York: Citadel Press, 1968; 4th pbk. ed.), 569–71.

13. Kammen, *People of Paradox*, 94. Kammen documents the divided mind of Americans. "In America, henceforth, there could be no singular Society—only societies conceived by communities of unlike-minded men." See also Ira Berlin, *Slaves without Masters: The Free Negro in the Antebellum South* (New York: Pantheon Books, 1974).

14. Williamson, *New People*, 17. Williamson wrote that though chary about free blacks after the Vesey plot in 1822, the white population did not turn on mulattoes in their midst. The author also contrasted the feeling in Virginia, "where the animus against free mulattoes of any sort began early" and that in South Carolina, where the feeling was "strikingly soft on free mulattoes of the upper echelons through the 1840's."

15. Peter Caulder, Martin Turner, and James Turner were paid the same rates as white volunteers. Muster Rolls for War of 1812 Militia, South Carolina Department of Archives and History, Columbia, South Carolina.

16. Act of December 4, 1820 in *Seven Statutes at Large of South Carolina*, note 4, 459. William Faux, "Faux's Memorable Days in America, 1819–1820," in *Early Western Travels, 1748–1846*, ed. Reuben Gold Thwaites (Cleveland, Ohio: Arthur H. Clark Company, 1905), Vol. 11, Pt. I (1819), 103.

17. *First Census of the United States:* 1790, State of South Carolina.

18. *Second Census of the United States:* 1800, South Carolina, Liberty County, Marion District, 806; *Third Census of the United States:* 1810, South Carolina, Liberty County, Marion District, 79–85; *Third Census:* 1810, South Carolina, Liberty County, Kershaw District, 407, 796, 803, 806. Ironically, the namesakes of Reuben Turner and Moses Caulder, two young men of the Marion County, Arkansas, free black community, passed for white in 1863 in order to join Union Army regiments.

19. Faux, "Faux's Memorable Days in America," 100.

20. Edgar, *South Carolina*, 188.

21. Equity Roll #607, South Carolina Department of Archives and History, Columbia, South Carolina.

22. See Paul G. Faler, *Mechanics and Manufacturers in the Early Industrial Revolution: Lynn, Massachusetts, 1780–1860* (Albany: State University of New York Press, 1981), 9–10, 81–82. This study of trades and part-time artisans concentrates on New England, but has application to the situation of manufacturing in the rural South as well.

23. W. W. Sellers, *A History of Marion County* (Columbia, S.C.: R. L. Bryan Company, 1902), 24. A book useful for detail about early life on the South Carolina frontier.

24. Ibid. John "Buck Swamp" Bethea drove one hundred calves north to market each spring.

25. Williamson, *New People*, 19. In 1835, South Carolina district judge William Harper ruled that "The condition of the individual is not to be determined solely by distinct and visible mixture of negro blood, but by reputation, by his reception into society, and his having commonly exercised the privileges of a white man." Helen T. Caterall, ed., *Judicial Cases concerning American Slavery*, 5 vols. (Washington, D.C.: Carnegie Institute of Washington, 1926–37), 2:269.

26. Folder from the Darlington County Historical Society, Darlington, South Carolina, containing photocopies of the brief of *Charles Powers, Et Al. v. James A. McEachern, Administrator, Et Al. (1875)*, and a photocopy of subpoena issued by *State of South Carolina* for Martin W. Turner of Marion County, dated August 30, 1873. Equity Roll #607, South Carolina Department of Archives and History, Columbia, South Carolina.

27. *First Census of the United States: 1790*, South Carolina; *Third Census of the United States: 1810*, South Carolina. The Caulder family followed a tradition in carrying on given names from generation to generation. Moses Caulder would have a grandson named Moses, who served with the 14th Kansas Cavalry during the American Civil War. The Hall and Turner families shared this tradition of continuing forenames through succeeding generations.

28. In 1822, South Carolina prevented free black sailors from entering the state with "An Act for the Better Regulation and Government of Free Negroes and Persons of Color, and for Other Purposes," Act of December 21, 1822, in *Statues at Large in South Carolina*, note 4, 461.

29. Pension File of Mourning Calder Cook, Pension Claim #5459, RG 94, National Archives and Records Administration, Washington, D.C.

30. *First Census of the United States: 1790*, South Carolina; *Second Census of the United States: 1800*, South Carolina.

31. Faux, "Faux's Memorable Days in America," 99–100. Though criticized by London newspapers for his exaggerations and his apocryphal style of writing, Faux's account of his stay on Sullivan's Island seems plausible enough.

32. Jimmy Calder, Marion, South Carolina, personal interview with the author at Calder Farms, Marion, South Carolina, March 17, 2000.

33. Patrick C. T. White, *A Nation on Trial: America and the War of 1812* (New York: John Wiley and Sons, 1965). The vote in the House of Representatives was 79 to 49; in the Senate, 19 to 13. White wrote that "a solid core of Senators were strongly opposed to war with Britain." Americans were deeply divided over the issue, and many politicians thought naval reprisals a preferable response to British provocations. However, all of the South Carolina congressmen voted for the war declaration, a unanimity that existed among only sister (and lightly settled) states of Georgia, Kentucky, and Tennessee.

34. *Annals of Congress*, Twelfth Congress, First Session, I, 426.

35. Two fine accounts of the War of 1812 are Donald R. Hickey, *The War of 1812: A Forgotten Conflict* (Chicago: University of Illinois Press, 1989), and John R.

Elting, *Amateurs, To Arms: A Military History of the War of 1812* (Chapel Hill, N.C.: Algonquin Books, 1991). Hickey describes the maritime pressure and diplomatic failures that bring Madison to recommend war against Britain. Elting details the shape of the army, its leadership, manpower, and equipment at the outset of the war. Since by far the bulk of manpower came from militia units rather than regular army battalions, professional military leaders worried that the tradition of short, fixed terms for militia volunteers might interfere with success on the battlefield. Their fears were well grounded.

36. Merrill D. Peterson, *The Great Triumvirate: Webster, Clay, and Calhoun* (New York: Oxford University Press, 1987), 19.

37. Ibid., 4 , 18. Calhoun, Henry Clay, and Daniel Webster met in Congress in May 1813. Andrew Jackson, political foe of all three, derisively labeled them, "The Great Triumvirate" because of their supposed collusion in gaining control of Congress.

38. Michael E. Stauffer, *South Carolina's Antebellum Militia* (Columbia: South Carolina Department of Archives and History, 1991), 1.

39. War of 1812 Compiled Service Records, Microfilm Series M602, Roll 36 (CAS-CAZ), Record Group 94, National Archives and Records Administration, Washington, D.C. Caulder is referred to as "colored man." War of 1812, Index to Military Service Records for Soldiers Serving from South Carolina, Microfilm Series M652, Roll 2, RG 94, National Archives, Washington, D.C.

40. Mark Edward Lender, "The Social Structure of the New Jersey Brigade," in *The Military in America: From the Colonial Era to the Present*, ed. Peter Karsten (New York: Free Press), 30–36.

41. Elting, *Amateurs, To Arms*, 9.

42. Muster Rolls for War of 1812 Militia, South Carolina Department of Archives and History, Columbia, South Carolina; *Biographical Directory of the House*, 3: 720–21, SC Archives; *Third Census of the United States: 1810*, Georgetown District, 363, 213; *Fourth Census of the United States: 1820*, Georgetown District, 66. John Keith, the son of a medical doctor, served a number of terms in the South Carolina Senate and General Assembly. In addition to his appointment as major in the Fifth Regiment of the state militia, Keith was a member of legislative committees on judiciary, military affairs, agriculture, inland navigation, high roads, bridges, and ferries; he headed a commission to establish a ferry across the Pee Dee River, presided over the Georgetown Library Society, and was an elected trustee of South Carolina College. Like in most South Carolina tidewater plantations, John Keith's slaves probably worked under the task system, which allowed a bit more flexibility for slaves who gained some free time to pursue their own interests.

43. John K. Mahon, *American Militia in the 1790's* (Gainesville: University of Florida Press, 1960), 22.

44. Ibid.; War of 1812 Compiled Service Records, Microfilm Series M602, Roll 36. According to a note on the Company Pay Roll in the Compiled Service Records, Alexander Lane was entitled to receive Caulder's three months' pay. Martin Turner had substituted for John Manning and earned a like amount. For regulations and organizational charts of South Carolina militia, see Michael E. Stauffer, "South Carolina's Antebellum Militia" pamphlet of the South Carolina

Department of Archives and History (1991). A complete list of War of 1812 engagements as well as a significant bibliography of those engagements are found in John C. Fredriksen, *Free Trade and Sailors' Rights: A Bibliography of the War of 1812* (Westport, Conn.: Greenwood Press, 1985).

45. *Encyclopedia of South Carolina: A Reference Guide to the Palmetto State* (NewYork: Somerset Publishers, 1993), "Governors," 87–88.

46. John C. Fredriksen, "Thomas A. Smith," John A. Garraty and Mark C. Carnes, ed., *American National Biography* (New York: Oxford University Press, 1999), 295–96; Letter from Thomas Adams Smith to General Flournoy, dated February 24, 1813, in Thomas Adams Smith Papers, Western Historical Manuscript Collection, University of Missouri, Columbia. Smith wrote of his capture of Bolegg's Town and Negroe Town. In the former, according to his account, Smith's men burned three hundred and eighty-six houses, destroyed fifteen hundred bushels of corn, captured three hundred horses and four hundred head of cattle, and stole two thousand deerskins. Smith wrote his superiors that the hammocks (swamps) were "extensive tracts of fertile land covered with thick shrubbery," (that afforded) "a safe retreat to Indians, and therefore require much caution to penetrate them safely."

CHAPTER TWO: Rifleman

1. W. W. Sellers, *A History of Marion County* (Columbia, S.C.: R. L. Bryan Company, 1902), 24.

2. J. C. A. Stagg, "Enlisted Men in the United States Army, 1812–1815: A Preliminary Survey," *William and Mary Quarterly*, Vol. 43, No. 4, 1986, 626. On page 628, Stagg wrote that all "recruits described as 'colored men' enlisted in the last six months of 1814 and in early 1815, on which basis it is possible to suggest that at least 280 to 370 blacks may have been in the ranks by the end of the war." Stagg cited letters from the adjutant general in drawing the conclusion that by 1814 the War Department unequivocally endorsed the recruitment of blacks, but no other soldier in the Third Rifle Regiment appear to be among the number that he cited.

3. Walter Lord, *The Dawn's Early Light* (New York: W. W. Norton and Company, 1972), 214. Lord's account of the British invasion force, the capture of Washington, the attack on Fort McHenry and Baltimore, and the Battle of New Orleans remains the definitive scholarship of the British offensive in the War of 1812. His well-written account illuminates day-by-day events and decisions by British commanders during the invasion.

4. *DeBow's Review* 29 (1860), 580. In 1740 James Oglethorpe's force of six hundred soldiers, rangers, volunteers, and Indians landed on the southern bank of the St. Johns River. Aided by supplies and reenforcements (pioneers) from South Carolina, Oglethorpe, in obedience to orders, invaded Florida, then held by Spain. Oglethorpe's goal was to take the Castillo de San Marcos—the massive Spanish fortress—at St. Augustine. He was unsuccessful.

5. Edward S. Farrow, *Farrow's Military Encyclopedia: A Dictionary of Military Knowledge* (New York: Self-published, 1885). Farrow, an instructor of tactics at

West Point, wrote that "These pioneers march at the head of the regiment and the senior among them commands as corporal." (But none of the mulattoes from Marion were ever promoted to corporal.) Col. H. L. Scott, an inspector-general of the U.S. Army, in his *Military Dictionary* published in 1864 summarizes the role of the pioneers as "Soldiers . . . furnished with saws, felling axes, spades, mattocks, pickaxes, and bill hooks. Their services are very important, and no regiment is well fitted for service without pioneers completely equipped." A general order issued by the secretary of war and reprinted in the *Daily National Intelligencer* of March 3, 1815, mentions the pay scale for enlisted men and includes specialty descriptions such as sappers, miners, bombardiers, and drivers. Peter H. Wood in *Black Majority: Negroes in Colonial South Carolina, from 1670 through the Stono Rebellion* (New York: Alfred A. Knopf, 1974) concluded that herding, clearing, and logging work was the fundamental work of the first slaves in Carolina. "Slaves fenced off necks of land for pastures, built pens for calves, and erected shelters for hogs; they branded new animals, hunted for strays, and ferried stock to and from the numerous island preserves. There was employment in butchering, barrel-making, and salt-gathering, and in packing and loading the meat for export." This was the work experience that the Caulder and Turner family may have had in Marion County and afterward for their army units.

6. Captains T. J. Robeson and W. Coles' Company, Muster and Receipt Rolls, Third Rifles 1814–15, Volume 205, Textual Records, Record Group 94, National Archives and Records Administration, Washington, D.C.

7. Baltimore *Niles' Weekly Register*, October 27, 1814. Pennsylvania-born Herekiah Niles (1777–1839), a vigilant and politically oriented newspaperman in the mold of Benjamin Franklin, founded the *Niles' Weekly Register* in 1811. Published in Baltimore and reprinting news items from other contemporary news-papers, *Niles* provides modern historians with a weekly sampler of the news and gossip of early nineteenth-century America.

8. Washington, D.C. *Daily National Intelligencer*, February 23, 1815. The Rifle Regiment adjutant inserted the names and descriptions of deserters in this daily newspaper. The advertising, which included the notice about rewards, exact descriptions of most of the deserters, and what citizens could do to return the men to the army, ran for ten consecutive editions. The advertisements were dropped only when the treaty of peace arrived in Washington city.

9. Captains T. J. Robeson and W. Coles' Company, Muster and Receipt Rolls, Third Rifles 1814–15, Volume 205, Textual Records, RG 94, National Archives, Washington, D.C.

10. *Niles' Weekly Register*, December 31, 1814, 216.

11. *Niles' Weekly Register*, February 4, 11, 18, and 25, 1815.

12. *Niles' Weekly Register*, Volume 7 Supplement, 149–50; Lord, *The Dawn's Early Light*, 180–81. Lord supplies the daily weather patterns during the invasion of Washington and the bombardment of Fort McHenry.

13. Letitia Woods Brown, *Free Negroes in the District of Columbia, 1790–1846* (New York: Oxford University Press, 1972), 11.

14. Ibid., 142–48. Brown's final chapter, "The Life of Free Negroes," indexes names and gives occupations of many of the city's black population.

15. Jack D. Foner, *Blacks and the Military in American History* (New York: Praeger Publishers, 1974), 25.

16. Records of the Adjutant General's Office, 1780s-1917, Confidential Inspection Reports, 1812–1826, Box 1, June 23, 1812, RG 94, National Archives, Washington, D.C. This once-confidential report written by Alexander Smyth, acting inspector general of the army, clarified the fact that under the Act of 1812, "men of color may be enlisted." Smyth stated in his memo that he "recommends the measure of authorizing the enlistment of colored men as musicians."

17. Foner, *Blacks and the Military in American History*, 26. Foner is convinced that positive attitudes toward blacks changed quickly into negatives. He specifies a memo from the War Department probably issued soon after the Treaty of Paris, in which the statement appeared that "a Negro is deemed unfit to associate with the American soldier" (27). That intolerant attitude was obviously not army-wide, however, as the decision to retain mulattoes at Carlisle within the Rifle Regiment demonstrated.

18. *Niles' Weekly Register,* May 27, 1815, printed letters sent out by the secretary of war regarding the impact of the Military Peace Establishment Act on the army. The full report covers several pages in the newspaper. On page 233, the secretary comments that the number of regimental officers would be reduced from the current 2,055 to 450, field officers from 216 to 39. The two ranking officers under the act would be Maj. Gen. Jacob Brown and Maj. Gen. Andrew Jackson, commanders of the army Division of the North and the Division of the South, respectively. Winfield Scott was retained as a brigadier general.

19. Thomas G. Tousey, *Military History of Carlisle and Carlisle Barracks* (Richmond, Va.: Dietz Press, 1939), 169. Hardworking and capable though they might be, a streak of defiance against central authority and its demands ran through Pennsylvania farmers, too. During Gen. Edward Braddock's campaign against the French in 1754, only with the intervention of Benjamin Franklin could the British general persuade local farmers to give up their stoutest wagons and strongest teams needed for his strike at what he had thought to be the common enemy. In George Washington's first term, a broad band of settlers on the frontier refused to pay federal imposts on their home-distilled products and resisted revenuers who were sent to collect the tax from them. Alexander Hamilton, secretary of treasury and leading Federalist theorist, urged President George Washington to take strong action against these backwoods whiskey makers who were defying the federal government. Washington, an advocate of reliable government revenues since the Revolution when his ragtag Continental Army went unpaid by a broke Continental Congress, determined to put down the so-called whiskey rebellion. Governors of mid-Atlantic states heeded his call for strong federal action and responded with militia levies. An army to break the whiskey rebellion mustered at the barracks of United States troops near the village of Carlisle where a 150-man regular army training cadre was stationed. On October 4, 1794, Washington rode his horse into the camp as New Jersey and Philadelphia troops stood aligned before their tents in a silent, awestruck, reception to the father of the country. The president, accompanied by Secretary Hamilton, reviewed the line and then tipped his hat to the troops, a show that touched off cheers and huzzas

from the men and officers in return. Washington appeared to be well pleased at the "cheerful subordination of citizens to the call of their chief for the support of law and order." Washington spent a few days overseeing drill of the men and their preparation to break resistance to federal authority by rebellious whiskey men. Departing Carlisle Barracks on October 12 for Pittsburgh, Washington's militia army found no opposition in western Pennsylvania, many of the rebels already having struck out for the newly opened Ohio frontier. A few leaders were arrested. Most were given amnesty. The antigovernment, anti-tax movement attenuated. For a sympathetic portrayal of the Westerners, see Thomas P. Slaughter, *The Whiskey Rebellion: Frontier Epilogue to the American Revolution* (New York and London: Oxford University Press, 1986).

20. Tousey, *Military History of Carlisle and Carlisle Barracks*, 172–75.

21. Captains T. J. Robison and W. Coles' Company, Muster and Receipt Rolls, Third Rifles, 1814–15, Volume 205, Textual Records, RG 94, National Archives, Washington, D.C.; Col. William E. King, who was replaced by William S. Hamilton on May 17, 1815, as the ranking officer at Carlisle, signed this order.

22. Letter from John Adams to Abigail Adams, dated June 17, 1775, reprinted in *Documents of the American Revolution*.

23. Inspection Roll of Walter Coles Company of the Third Rifle Regiment, Captains T. J. Robison and W. Coles' Company, Muster and Receipt Rolls, Third Rifles, 1814–1815, Volume 205, 1–2, RG 94, National Archives, Washington, D.C.

24. *Daily National Intelligencer*, February 11, 1815; Coles' Company Muster and Receipt Rolls, 1.

25. *Daily National Intelligencer*, August 14, 1815. Up the Mississippi from St. Louis, commissioners William Clark, Ninian Edwards, and Auguste Chouteau met in council with Sioux, Shawnee, Delaware, and Maha chiefs. Sauk and Kickapoo refused to send head men, which indicated their "unfriendly disposition." Those two tribes were warned by Clark that if their chiefs did not appear within thirty days, the result would be war. The Pottawatomie chiefs came reluctantly to the council.

26. *Daily National Intelligencer*, August 16, 1815.

27. *Daily National Intelligencer*, September 6, 1815.

28. W. S. Hamilton, Lt. Col. Rifle Regiment, Orders, Carlisle Barracks, July 22, 1815, published in *Daily National Intelligencer*, August 16, 1815. Brevet Lieutenant Colonel Chambers at Detroit, Brevet Lieutenant Colonel Selden, Brevet Major Bradford, and Brevet Major Birdsall are all mentioned by name as respective commanders. *Registers of Enlistments in the United States Army, 1798–1914*, Microfilm Series M233, Roll 3, Entry #4186, RG 94, National Archives, Washington, D.C.; Bureau of Land Management, General Land Office Records, RG 49, Serial # IL5280, Patentee Name: Moses Caulder, Issue Date: 12/22/1818.

29. Roger L. Nichols, *The Missouri Expedition, 1818–1820: The Journal of Surgeon John Gale with Related Document* (Norman: University of Oklahoma Press, 1969). Gale accompanied General Atkinson as he transported his Rifle Regiment up the Missouri River on keelboats in 1819. His entry for September 24, 1819,

reads "Discharging of Fire arms . . . from the flotilla except by special permission or in obedience to established signals is in future positively prohibited. The unfortunate occurrence of today, in the death of one of the Riflemen, is a melancholy instance of the necessity of a rigid compliance with this regulation."

30. *Registers of Enlistments in the United States Army, 1798–1914*. M 233, Roll 3, Volumes 5 and 6 (C) Entry #4541, RG 94, National Archives, Washington, D.C.

31. Francis Paul Prucha, *Broadax and Bayonet: The Role of the United States Army in the Development of the Northwest, 1815–1860* (Lincoln: University of Nebraska Press, 1953).

32. Muster Rolls for Fort Claiborne, Louisiana, April 1816, October 1816, December 1816. Rifle Regiment Returns, July 1815–December 1818, Box 139, Flattened Records, RG 94, National Archives, Washington, D.C.; Harold D. Moser, et al., eds., *The Papers of Andrew Jackson: Guide and Index to the Microfilm Editions* (Wilmington, Del.: Scholarly Resources, 1987), 425–26. Jackson wrote to William H. Crawford, secretary of war, urging an early decision in the William Bradford–Joseph Selden dispute. Smith's letter on the quarrel is on Microfilm 566–89, March 28, 1816, RG 94, National Archives, Washington, D.C.; see also Library of Congress Microfilm DLC-20, letter dated June 12, 1816, for Bradford's comment on settling the dispute.

CHAPTER THREE: Stranger at Belle Point

1. The French phrase *Prairie du Chein* meant Prairie of the Dogs and referred to a small group of Indians who followed Chief Dog and inhabited the fertile plain at the forks of the Ouisconsin and Mississippi rivers. In 1817, Maj. Stephen H. Long wrote that "this family or band has become extinct," victims of intertribal warfare. Stephen H. Long, "Voyage in a Six-Oared Skiff to the Falls of the Saint Anthony in 1817," *Collections of the Minnesota Historical Society*, Volume II, 1860–1867 (Ann Arbor, Mich.: University Microfilms, Inc., 1958), 64.

2. John C. Fredriksen in John A. Garraty and Mark C. Carnes, *American National Biography* (New York: Oxford University Press, 1999), 295–96. At least two officers on that march from Plattsburg became geographical names in Arkansas, Fort Smith and Izard County. C. Fred Williams, S. Charles Bolton, Carl H. Moneyhon, and LeRoy T. Williams, *A Documentary History of Arkansas* (Fayetteville: University of Arkansas Press, 1994), 23.

3. Letter from Lt. James Gaddey to Gen. Thomas A. Smith dated June 20, 1816, in Thomas Adams Smith Papers, Western Manuscript Collection, University of Missouri, Columbia; Roger L. Nichols and Patrick L. Halley, *Stephen Long and American Frontier Exploration* (Norman: University of Oklahoma Press, 1995), 21–40, chronicled Long's unusually quick rise in military rank.

4. Letter from Stephen H. Long to Brig. Gen. T. A. Smith, dated October 15, 1817, in Smith Papers, Western Manuscript Collection; The last sentence in the letter is: "Please give my best respects to Mrs. Smith. . . ."

5. Annie Heloise Abel, "History of Events resulting in Indian Consolidation West of the Mississippi," American Historical Association, *Annual Report*, 1906, I,

241. Henry Putney Beers in *The Western Military Frontier, 1815–1846* (Gettysburg, Pa.: Times and News Publishing Co., 1935), 56, wrote that "The Louisiana territorial act of March 26, 1804 authorized the President to secure an exchange of Indian lands east of the Mississippi for reservations west of that river where the Indians were to be under the protection of the United States Government."

6. Grant Foreman, *Indians and Pioneers: The Story of the American Southwest before 1830* (New Haven, Conn.: Yale University Press, 1930).

7. Morris S. Arnold, *Colonial Arkansas, 1686–1804: A Social and Cultural History* (Fayetteville: University of Arkansas Press, 1991), 62, 116, 119.

8. John Joseph Mathews, *The Osages: Children of the Middle Waters* (Norman: University of Oklahoma Press, 1961), 408.

9. Ibid., 112–17.

10. C. A. Weslager, *The Delaware Indians: A History* (New Brunswick, N.J.: Rutgers University Press, 1972), 362–63. Weslager describes the forlorn experiences of Delaware Indians who came to live on the White River in Missouri and Arkansas. A more cheerful tale of the Delawares is about a chief named Johnny Cake who invited whites to celebrate the Green Corn Dance festivities. One white neighbor, John Tabor who had the first cabin in the Flippin Barrens, "helped drag several slain bufflo (*sic*) down to the Indian village for the occasion. Some of the animals were roasted for the dance, and the rest were dried for future use." Duane Huddleston, Sammie Rose, and Pat Wood, *Steamboats and Ferries on the White River* (Conway: University of Central Arkansas, 1995), 6. A fine account of the Delaware's "Walking Purchase" may be found in H. W. Brands, *The First American: The Life and Times of Benjamin Franklin* (New York: Doubleday, 2000), 222–23.

11. Letter from Trimble to Calhoun dated August 7, 1818, Adjutant General's Office, Old Records Divison, RG 94, National Archives, Washington, D.C.

12. Mathews, *The Osages*, 383. Mathews, a capable if somewhat biased historian of the Osages, wrote poetically of this situation regarding white renegades killed by respectable Osage warriors only to have their actions in self-defense misinterpreted by white authorities: "The 'Flanders' knives" of the Little Ones (Osages) was the only agency that could effect such a transformation (that is turning the white bad guys into victims by virtue of their being scalped)."

13. Foreman, *Indians and Pioneers*, 55. Foreman detailed the uncertain situation of the southeastern Indians in the decades preceding removals.

14. Bradford, a Kentuckian, had been promoted temporarily to major, breveted as the army put it, because of his stellar battlefield performance during the War of 1812. Bradford, who enlisted in the militia on July 6, 1812, took a bullet in the leg in action against the British in Ohio on May 5, 1813. He had been part of a Kentucky militia advance guard that had arrived just in time to help Maj. Gen. William Henry Harrison's besieged force stave off a British and Indian attack at an earthen and log fortification named Fort Meigs. After the enemy assault broke up, Harrison, though still without the main body of Kentuckians, pursued the British anyway. Harrison's small force was turned back in a skirmish in which Bradford received the wound to his leg. Nothing is known about Bradford's convalescence, but the little major recovered sufficiently to join the

regular army infantry and accompany Andrew Jackson in the campaign against the Creeks in Alabama the next year. Bradford's deeds in directing artillery fire at the March 27, 1814, Battle of Horseshoe Bend earned him a letter of commendation from the general. That campaign, one of Jackson's most important, created somewhat of a bond between the young, tough major and the older, tough general, an acquaintance that made Bradford feel comfortable enough to visit Jackson at the Hermitage, bringing a horse as a gift. Bradford on a few occasions during his military career jumped the chain of command and wrote directly to Jackson, whom he may have considered his mentor. That correspondence included a long letter written to General Jackson soon after Bradford arrived at Belle Point in 1817. *Registers of Enlistments*, Entry #7622; Donald R. Hickey, *The War of 1812: The Forgotten Conflict* (Urbana: University of Illinois Press, 1989), 134–36, explained the battle of Fort Meigs and Gen. Green Clay and his twelve hundred Kentuckians who arrived to relieve Gen. William Henry Harrison's besieged force. Major Bradford had his seniority over Maj. Joseph Selden confirmed in February 1817.

15. Glenn, who would show up six months later at Camp Smith in a keelboat with the first resupply for Bradford, had experience in supplying the riflemen at Fort Snelling and Fort Crawford. He was an acquaintance of General Smith.

16. Francis B. Heitman, *Historical Register and Dictionary of the United States Army, From its Organization, September, 1789 to March 2, 1903* (Washington, D.C.: Government Printing Office, 1903); Returns of the First Rifle Regiment, 1817–1821, April 1817, Microfilm 40, Fort Smith National Historic Site, Fort Smith, Arkansas. Bvt. Maj. Joseph Selden would stopover at Cape Girardeau, too sick to continue on to Belle Fontaine. Three years later, the Virginia-born officer would retire from the army at age sixty-two. The military cantonment at Natchitoches was named Fort Selden in his honor, apparently superceding its former title, Fort Claiborne.

17. Letter from Thomas A. Smith to Colonel Robert Butler, dated September 7, 1817, Smith Papers, Western Manuscript Collection.

18. *Niles' Weekly Register*, November 8, 1817.

19. Thomas Nuttall, *Journal of Travels into the Arkansa Territory During the Year 1819, with Occasional Observations on the Manners of the Aborigines*, ed. Reuben Gold Thwaites (Cleveland, Ohio: Arthur H. Clark Company, 1905), 71. Nuttall's Journal has been edited and published more recently by Savoie Lottinville, the work that will be cited hereafter. Thomas Nuttall, *A Journal of Travels into the Arkansa Territory During the Year 1819*, ed. Savoie Lottinville (Norman: University of Oklahoma Press, 1980).

20. Letter from Thomas A. Smith to Maj. William Bradford, dated January 3, 1818, Smith Papers, Western Manuscript Collection. Bradford had been cautioned about a lack of medical attention for the expedition by General Smith, who said he had "strong fears that it would never be in my power to send you a (medical) officer."

21. Microfilm Return for Bradford's Company, December 31, 1817, RG 94, National Archives, Washington, D.C. Of the fifty-six privates who formed Bradford's first command at Belle Point, twenty-eight soldiers joined him at the

mouth of the Ohio. This small body had a few new recruits, but mostly consisted of men from Baton Rouge formerly commanded by Selden. Earlier historians may not have recognized that there were two separate groups of riflemen who combined at Arkansas Post to make up Bradford's company that founded Fort Smith and thus inaccurately described the ill soldiers as those being transferred from Natchitoches.

22. *Niles' Weekly Register*, January 6, 1818. A news report mentioned that the Ohio rose rapidly thirty feet in only three days in the autumn of 1817. Heavy rains and flooding were as bad as low water in creating bacterial concentrations in rivers and tributaries used for drinking water. In 1820, a promising settlement on the Kentucky bank of the Ohio was abandoned because low water in the rivers led to a deadly epidemic among the populace.

23. Letter from Maj. Stephen Long to Gen. Thomas A. Smith, dated October 15, 1817, Smith Papers, Western Historical Manuscript Collection.

24. John James Audubon, "Audubon's America," in *Arkansas, Arkansas: Writers and Writings from the Delta to the Ozarks, 1541–1969*, ed. John Caldwell Guilds (Fayetteville: University of Arkansas Press, 1999), 143.

25. See *Arkansas Gazette*, November 20, 1819, for a good contemporary description of the land and crops surrounding the Village of Arkansas.

26. S. Charles Bolton, *Territorial Ambition: Land and Society in Arkansas, 1800–1840* (Fayetteville: University of Arkansas Press, 1993), 17–19. Professor Bolton provides a well-documented and well-written account of various settlements in early Arkansas. His primary sources included John B. Treat's letters, which appeared in Clarence Edwin Carter, ed., *Territorial Papers of the United States: Territory of Arkansas, 1819–1836* (Washington, D.C.: Government Printing Office, 1953–54). Apparently, the Quapaw were down to about seventy warriors when Bradford and Caulder entered the state.

27. Morris S. Arnold, *Colonial Arkansas, 1686–1804: A Social and Cultural History* (Fayetteville: University of Arkansas Press, 1991), 70. Arnold wrote that "a person spending only a day in the last decade of the eighteenth century at the fort and village would almost certainly have heard at least five languages spoken — French, Spanish, German, English, and Quapaw — and probably another Indian tongue or two."

28. Edwin Bearss in his unpublished typewritten manuscript "Fort Smith 1817–1838" (a bound copy is available at the Fort Smith Public Library) maintained that General Smith gave up on the new recruits as being unfit for this sort of duty in the perceived heat and insects of Arkansas. He ordered instead a detachment that was ascending the Mississippi from Baton Rouge and Natchitoches to meet Bradford at Arkansas Post. This interpretation does not quite square with the reports sent back to Belle Fontaine while Bradford and Long were en route to Arkansas Post. The *Registers of Enlistments* duty notations for individual soldiers who arrived at Belle Point on December 25, 1817, infers that a cadre of riflemen, including Peter Caulder, came upriver with Maj. Joseph Selden from Louisiana as far as Arkansas Post where they were detached to await Bradford.

29. Many travelers referred to the hunting economy of Arkansas. One who mentions the trade in "bear's oil and tallow" between Arkansas and New Orleans

was British officer Philip Pittman in *The Present State of the European Settlement on the Mississippi, 1770* (Gainesville: University of Florida Press, 1973), 40.

30. Dorothy Jones Core, "Marie Longuedoc," 16 *Grand Prairie Historical Society Bulletin* 10, 12, 1973 as cited in Arnold, *Colonial Arkansas*, 201.

31. Ted Ownby, *Subduing Satan: Religion, Recreation, and Manhood in the Rural South, 1865–1914* (Chapel Hill: University of North Carolina Press, 1990), 13.

32. Microfilm Return for Bradford's Company, Rifle Regiment, December 31, 1817; Roberta Burns Hofmann, "Sergeant Balthazar Kramer," *Frontier Research* (June 1985): 4, 151–54. Hofmann is the great-great-great-great-granddaughter of Balthazar and Elizabeth Kramer. Elizabeth Kramer applied for a pension and as proof of her husband's military service produced two letters to her from him, the last written in October 1822 and mailed from Fort Smith. The pension was denied.

33. Maj. Stephen H. Long, "Voyage in a Six-Oared Skiff to the Falls of Saint Anthony in 1817," *Collections of the Minnesota Historical Society*, Vol. 2, 1860–67 (St. Paul: Minnesota Historical Society, Reprint, 1889), introductory note by E. D. Neill, 56.

34. Ibid., 8–9.

35. Roger L. Nichols and Patrick L. Halley, *Stephen Long and American Frontier Exploration* (Norman: University of Oklahoma Press, 1985), 51–54. The authors used Long's travel descriptions in chronicling his habits, his leadership, and the daily routines that he followed while on expedition. They concluded that Long's preference for speedy transits over precise measurements "reduced his contributions as an explorer." One gathers that Long was extensive rather than intensive where exploration was concerned.

36. Bradford listed these men as being "on command," a military euphemism for temporary duty away from the unit. Microfilm Return for Bradford's Company, December 31, 1817, RG 94, National Archives, Washington, D.C.

37. Long, "Voyage in a Six-Oared Skiff," 34.

38. Ibid., 82.

39. Long was born on December 30, 1784, on a New Hampshire family farm. His father had served in the Continental Army during the Revolutionary War. Stephen Long would have been near his thirty-third birthday on his voyage up the Arkansas in 1817.

40. Long to Smith, dated May 12, 1818. Letters Sent Book, 96, War Department, Files, Western Department, RG 94, National Archives, Washington, D.C.

41. Hofmann, "Sergeant Balthazar Kramer," 154. Balthazar Kramer never recovered and as an invalid had to be discharged from the army. Bradford wrote the War Department trying to gain for him a pension. Despondent because he was unable to travel back to Kentucky to rejoin his family, Kramer stayed in the Fort Smith hospital as a disabled veteran until his death on December 5, 1823.

42. Thomas James, *Three Years among the Indians and Mexicans*, Milo Milton Quaife, ed. (New York: Citadel Press, 1966), 115. General James led an expedition from St. Louis to Santa Fe in 1821. He passed through Fort Smith in June 1821 where he enjoyed the hospitality of Bradford and his wife. When James departed, Bradford presented him with a barrel of onions which James was "not to broach

until we had killed our first buffalo, when we were enjoined to have 'a general feast in honor of old Billy Bradford.' His kindness made a deep impression on us."

43. Ibid. Thomas James remarks that Bradford was a "stern-looking man, an excellent disciplinarian, and a gallant officer," 115. There is little doubt that his men were loyal and trusting of his command.

44. *Niles' Weekly Register*, September 27, 1817, a letter signed by nine Cherokee chiefs outlined events of Osage treachery. It was commonly thought in the East because of such publicity that Osage Indians were bloodthirsty. Their reputation for savagery was well established by French and Spanish witnesses before the United States purchased their territories.

45. Long, "Voyage in a Six-Oared Skiff," 42. Long had his men do the same sort of night floating on his skiff run up the Mississippi the year before.

46. Bradford was well satisfied with Daniel Norman's work and his promise. Bradford promoted him to sergeant on January 1, 1818, a week after his arrival at Belle Point. Microfilm Return for Bradford's Company, January 31, 1818, RG 94, National Archives, Washington, D.C.

CHAPTER FOUR: Army Guide

1. William Dunbar and George Hunter camped at some hot springs from December 9, 1804, until January 8, 1805. Dunbar reported to President Jefferson that "the hot springs themselves are indeed a great curiosity; the temperature of their waters is from 130 to 150° of Farheneits' [sic] thermometer." Dunbar's original journal is in the Ouachita Baptist University archives. Long mentioned the journal of Dunbar and may have had a copy with him.

2. Edwin James, *Account of an Expedition from Pittsburgh to the Rocky Mountains* (Philadelphia: H. C. Carey and I. Lea, Chestnut Street, 1823), Vol. 2, 171–72, republished in 1966 by University Microfilms, Inc., of Ann Arbor, Michigan; Bearss, unpublished manuscript, 21–22: Richard G. Wood, "Stephen Harriman Long at Belle Point," *Arkansas Historical Quarterly* 13 (Winter 1954): 338–40.

3. Roger L. Nichols and Patrick L. Halley, *Stephen Long and American Frontier Exploration* (Norman: University of Oklahoma Press, 1995), 56–57. Letter from Stephen Long to Thomas A. Smith dated May 12, 1818. Photocopy in I-105 file, Fort Smith National Historic Site.

4. Inspection Return of Capt. William Bradford's company, February 28, 1818. Flattened returns, textual records, RG 94, National Archives, Washington, D.C. Bradford listed Caulder, Cole, Sloan, Watkins, and Martin Turner as being "absent on command." The March 1818 return is missing, and these enlisted men returned to Belle Point in time to be marked present on the April return.

5. Letter from William Bradford to Andrew Jackson dated January 1, 1818, Jackson Papers, 7020, Library of Congress.

6. John R. Bell, *The Journal of Captain John R. Bell: Official Journalist for the Stephen H. Long Expedition to the Rocky Mountains, 1820*, ed. Harlin M. Fuller and LeRoy R. Hafen (Glendale, Calif.: Arthur H. Clark Company, 1957), 48.

7. *American State Papers*, Indian Affairs, Vol. 2, 557.

8. Juliet E. K. Walker, *Free Frank: A Black Pioneer on the Antebellum Frontier*

(Lexington: University of Kentucky Press, 1983).

9. *Niles' Weekly Register*, March 27, 1819. The bill with which Congress established a separate "Arkansaw" Territory in the southern part of Missouri territory included a rider introduced by New York representative Taylor that "the further introduction of slavery be prohibited" and that all slave children born in Arkansas after its admission to the Union should be freed upon attaining age twenty-five. Taylor's bill failed in the House of Representatives by one vote.

10. Merrill D. Petersen, *The Great Triumvirate: Webster, Clay, and Calhoun* (New York: Oxford University Press, 1987), 284–85. Although on record repeatedly as anti-slavery, Henry Clay was bothered about emancipation without colonization. He opposed a society filled with free blacks, whom Clay thought of as degraded, vicious, and dangerous members of the race. Petersen quoted Clay's remark about free blacks as being society's "most troublesome element." The full title of Clay's colonization brainchild was the American Society for Colonizing the Free People of Color in the United States.

11. Billy D. Higgins, "Origins and Fate of the Marion County Free Black Community," *Arkansas Historical Quarterly* 54 (Winter 1995): 429–30.

12. John C. Inscoe, ed., *Appalachians and Race: The Mountain South from Slavery to Segregation* (Lexington: University of Kentucky Press, 2001), 5–6, 74.

13. *Niles' Weekly Register*, November 15, 1817.

14. *Niles' Weekly Register*, July 4, 1818, 321.

15. "Boy Planters" is a term used by Donald P. McNeilly to refer to the sons of established planters east of the Mississippi who sent sons with slaves to set up plantations in newly opened Arkansas delta lands. Donald P. McNeilly, *The Old South Frontier: Cotton Plantations and the Formation of Arkansas Society, 1819–1861* (Fayetteville: University of Arkansas Press, 2000), 69–70.

16. Petersen, *The Great Triumvirate*, 285. To curry votes north of the Ohio in his 1824 presidential campaign, Henry Clay emphasized his dislike of slavery and pointed out his numerous legal, pro bono representations of slaves in legal efforts to make them free men.

17. An opponent of the soldier-farmer concept was U.S. Army colonel George Croghan. In the 1820s and 1830s Croghan inspected frontier forts and made his reports to the Army Command writing at one point that the policy has sunk the proud soldier into a "troop of awkward ploughmen." Francis Paul Prucha, ed., *Army Life on the Frontier: Selections from the Official Reports Made between 1826 and 1845 by Colonel George Croghan* (Norman: University of Oklahoma Press, 1958), 6.

18. Edwin James, *Account of an Expedition from Pittsburgh to the Rocky Mountains*, Vol. 1, 167.

19. Long, "Voyage in a Six-Oared Skiff," 48, 51.

20. Ibid., 58. At Fort Crawford, soldiers "were compelled to get their fuel at the distance of two or three miles from the garrison, and in many instances to draw it home by hand."

21. Microfilm Returns for Bradford's Company, March 31, 1818 through November 30, 1818, RG 94, National Archives, Washington, D.C. These returns indicated detached duty assignments of Caleb Cook.

22. Prucha, *Army Life on the Western Frontier*, 64.

23. Fort Smith Trader's Account Book of May 1820 to June 1821. Entry dated August 26, 1820, Gilcrease Museum Archives, Tulsa, Oklahoma.

24. Bell, *The Journal of Captain John R. Bell*, 284.

25. Fort Smith Trader's Account Book of May 1820 to June 1821, August 26, 1820, in Gilcrease Museum Archives, Tulsa, Oklahoma.

26. Thomas Nuttall, *A Journal of Travels into the Arkansa Territory During the Year 1819*, ed. Savoie Lottinville (Norman: University of Oklahoma Press, 1980), 312–16.

27. Brian Fagan, *The Little Ice Age: How Climate Made History, 1300–1850* (New York: Basic Books, 2000), 201–3. Across Western Europe and in thousands of similar scenes in North America, tree felling cleared vast tracts of forests. "The pioneer agricultural explosion . . . was the first human activity that genuinely altered the global environment." Global warming resulted, which in turn formed favorable conditions for industrialized agriculture in the next century.

28. Fred W. Allsopp, "History of the Arkansas Press," reprinted in Dallas Tabor Herndon, *Annals of Arkansas* (Hopkinsville, Ky., and Little Rock, Ark.: Historical Record Association, 1947), 79. Woodruff, a young man with an idea and one year's apprenticeship, persuaded two boatmen to tie their pirogues together to transport him and his second-hand screw printing press over the final leg of his journey. In this style, Arkansas's first printer came the distance from the mouth of the White River to the village where he would establish the *Arkansas Gazette*.

29. Eleven months separated their arrivals at Arkansas Post, Nuttall walking by path into the village of twenty houses on January 22, 1819, and Woodruff stepping ashore from his pirogues on December 19, 1819.

30. Nuttall, *A Journal of the Travels into the Arkansa Territory During the Year 1819*, 159.

31. Ibid. Nuttall's account of his separation from Bradford's riflemen gave him an opportunity to detail a week in the life of a squatter in the Arkansas backwoods.

32. Ibid., 167–68.

33. Ibid., 166–69. Nuttall wrote about the excitement of this impromptu side trip from his planned itinerary, his separation from Bradford and the detachment, his stay with a hospitable family in the wilds, and his satisfaction in the number of plant species that he cataloged. S. W. Geiser, "Thomas Nuttall's Botanical Collecting Trip to the Red River, 1819," *Field and Laboratory* 24 (April 1956): 43–61.

34. Nuttall, *A Journal of the Travels into the Arkansa Territory During the Year 1819*, 168.

35. Prucha, *Army Life on the Western Frontier*, 95. Vermilion, a pigment made from red crystals of mercury (cinnabar), was a favorite, even revered substance of Native Americans, who used it extensively as a red dye for not only wood and leather objects but for toning skin as well.

36. Bell, *The Journal of Captain John R. Bell*, 98–99.

37. Nuttall, *A Journal of the Travels into the Arkansa Territory During the Year 1819*, 171–72.

38. Letter from John C. Calhoun to William Bradford at Belle Point dated

September 9, 1818, in War Department, Secretary's Office, Letters Sent, Indian Affairs, D, 211, Microfilm No. 15, Roll 4, RG 94, National Archives, Washington, D.C.

39. Nuttall, 171–73. While in Washington, D.C., Major Bradford wrote an affidavit dated March 25, 1824, explaining his actions on the Red River to Congressman Elisha Conway of Arkansas Territory. Bradford wrote that he ordered those intruders without crops in the field to leave immediately, an order which he claimed that they obeyed. Those settlers with crops growing in the field, he gave until October to vacate. Captain Combs, the commanding officer at Natchitoches, was not so lenient. Operating in the Red River under a similar order, Combs, in some instances, burned houses and destroyed crops of the white settlers to force them out of the territory. Letter dated March 25, 1824, from William Bradford in *American State Papers*, Volume II, Indian Affairs, 557.

40. Geiser, "Thomas Nuttall's Botanical Collecting Trip to the Red River, 1819," 46.

41. Nuttall, *A Journal of the Travels into the Arkansa Territory During the Year 1819*, 183.

CHAPTER FIVE: Fort Smith

1. Inspection Return of Bradford's Company, September 1819. Flattened Muster Rolls and Returns, 15W-1: Map Case #15, Drawer #1, Box 144, Riflemen, January 1819–January 1821 (Companies A–C), RG 94, National Archives, Washington, D.C.

2. Little Rock *Arkansas Gazette*, April 2, 1822.

3. Edwin Bearss, "Fort Smith 1817–1824," 15, undated and unpublished manuscript available at the Fort Smith Public Library. Bearss, the Fort Smith National Historic Site's start-up historian, compiled his military history of nascent Fort Smith by scrutiny of post returns and drawing from the earlier works of Grant and Carolyn Foreman.

4. Hall Cemetery, small, overgrown, and barely accessible, in southern Bollinger County, Missouri contains gravesites of Hall and Caulder family members.

5. George E. Lankford, "'Beyond the Pale': Frontier Folk in the Southern Ozarks," in *The Folk: Identity, Landscapes, and Lores*, University of Kansas Publications in Anthropology, no. 17, ed. Robert Smith and Jerry Stannard, (Lawrence: University of Kansas, 1989), 53–70. Lankford traced leapfrogging settler James McGarrah to this area and suggested that he is the same man as Henry Schoolcraft's M'Gary.

6. Milton D. Rafferty, ed., *Rude Pursuits and Rugged Peaks: Schoolcraft's Ozark Journal, 1818–1819* (Fayetteville: University of Arkansas Press, 1996), 98. Henry Rowe Schoolcraft's subsequent career on the Michigan frontier was recognized by having a county in Michigan named for him.

7. Thomas Nuttall, *A Journal of Travels into the Arkansa Territory During the Year 1819*, ed. Savoie Lottinville (Norman: University of Oklahoma Press, 1980), 107–50.

8. Grant Foreman, "Nathaniel Pryor," *Chronicles of Oklahoma* 7 (June 1929): 152–63. Pryor, a veteran of the Lewis and Clark Expedition, married an Osage woman. The couple "kept a little trading establishment a mile and a half above the mouth of the Verdigris." Nuttall had met Pryor and Richards in March 1819 while descending the Arkansas with "cargoes of furs and peltries, collected among the Osages" and was impressed that "the former [Pryor] was one of those who had accompanied Lewis and Clarke (*sic*) across the continent." Nuttall, *A Journal of the Travels into the Arkansa Territory During the Year 1819*, 108.

9. Elliott Coues, ed., *The Journal of Jacob Fowler* (Lincoln: University of Nebraska Press, 1970). Preface and additional notes by Raymond W. and Mary Lund Settle and Harry R. Stevens, 14. Prucha, *Army Life on the Western Frontier*, 103.

10. Fort Smith Trader's Account Book for 1820–21, Gilcrease Museum Archives, Tulsa, Oklahoma. The Fort Smith trader's store sold thread, sewing material, and cloth to soldiers and to the women of the fort. Mending his uniform and keeping it neat enough for the occasional muster inspection was part of Caulder's army life. Cutting trees, clearing briars, hewing logs, digging postholes, chipping rock—"fatigue" duties—ripped and shredded uniforms of the pioneering riflemen. Col. George Croghan commented on the heavy toll that clearing land and building roads took on military dress. He noted that soldiers so assigned had to draw extra clothing at their own expense, something that Peter Caulder did. In the 1850s, Gen. Albert Sydney Johnston warned his men of the "toil, privation, and hardships incident to frontier service." Certainly, Major Bradford warned his men of the same conditions at Fort Smith.

11. According to a description dated March 14, 2002, provided by Thomas A. Wing, park ranger, Fort Smith National Historic Site, the recipe for cherry bounce called for blending the ingredients and letting stand in a crock or glass-topped apothecary jar, shaking or stirring occasionally. If black cherries could be substituted, then bounce could have been made in Fort Smith. An English observer in 1787, William Attmore, noted that it was "very much the custom in North Carolina to drink Drams of some kind or other before Breakfast; sometimes Gin, Cherry-bounce, Egg Nog &c" implying that Cherry-bounce was an alcoholic drink. William Attmore, *Journal of a Tour to North Carolina*, ed. Lida Tunstall Rodman, *James Sprunt Historical Publications*, 17, No. 2 [1922], noted in Booraem, *Young Hickory*, 191.

12. Fort Smith Trader's Account Book for 1820–21, June 14–July 6, 1820, Gilcrease Museum Archives, Tulsa, Oklahoma.

13. *Registers of Enlistments of the U.S. Army, 1798–1914*, Microcopy 233, Roll #16, 1798–May 15, 1815, (I-M), Entry #850, RG 94, National Archives, Washington, D.C.; Bearss and Gibson, *Fort Smith*, 30.

14. Pension File of Mourning Caulder Cook, Widow Claim #4950, War of 1812 Pension Records, Record Group 49, National Archives, Washington, D.C.

15. Josiah Gregg, "Commerce of the Prairies," in *Early Western Travels*, ed. Reuben Gold Thwaites (Cleveland, Ohio: Arthur H. Clark Company, 1905), 101–2. Josiah Gregg was a Santa Fe trader and journal keeper who made eight expeditions across the Great Plains in the early nineteenth century. In 1839

Gregg set out from Van Buren with fourteen wagons loaded with $25,000 worth of choice goods pulled by teams of oxen and mules. One of his teamsters was a "free mulatto."

16. Fort Smith Trader's Account Book for 1820–21, June 14–July 6, 1820, Gilcrease Museum Archives, Tulsa, Oklahoma.

17. Arkansas Post *Arkansas Gazette*, December 12, 1819.

18. Fort Smith Trader's Account Book, July 16, 30, and 31, 1820. Caulder and James Turner bought powder, gunflints, and cheese on credit. He probably intended to pay off the store bill out of his earnings from Glenn.

19. Booraem, *Young Hickory*, 6–8. The author includes a bibliographical essay on studies of the Ulster Irish in colonial South Carolina.

20. *Registers of Enlistments of the U.S. Army, 1798–1914*, Microcopy 233, Roll #10, 1798–May 15, 1815, (P-R), Entry #68, RG 94, National Archives, Washington, D.C. Parish had enlisted in the Third Rifles on September 24, 1814, at Cheraw, South Carolina, and had marched north with Caulder. Both were eighteen years old at the time and were off on the adventure of their lives. After the war, Parish was assigned to Birdsall's Company, Rifle Regiment, deployed on the northwest frontier.

21. John R. Bell, *The Journal of Captain John R. Bell: Official Journalist for the Stephen H. Long Expedition to the Rocky Mountains, 1820*, ed. Harlin M. Fuller and LeRoy R. Hafen (Glendale, Calif.: Arthur H. Clark Company, 1957), 269–70; Inspection Return of Capt. James H. Ballard's Company at Fort Smith, August 31, 1820, RG 94, National Archives, Washington, D.C. The August 1820 return shows that Peter Caulder was on furlough confirming his story to Bell. No other enlisted man was on furlough in that return. Most likely, the man with Peter Caulder was James Turner. He may have had rifleman's issue clothing that led Bell to believe that there were two soldiers. Turner resided in Fort Smith, was a close and longtime friend of Caulder, and had stocked up on similar items at the post store at the same time before the furlough that Caulder had. Bell spells Caulder as Coulder, a spelling sometimes used by the army and by county officials. Grant Foreman, guided by Bell's suspicions, wrote that the captain came across "two deserters" at Glenn's Trading Post and forced them to return to Fort Smith with him.

22. Ibid., 257.

23. Ibid., 270. Caulder would have been the only man in the party who could have recognized the horse as being Glenn's.

24. Ibid., 276.

25. Seymour's original watercolor painting of Fort Smith is in the Academy of Natural Sciences. A large replica of the portrait is on display at the Fort Smith Historic Site. The park ranger, Tom A. Wing, interviewed in August 2002, stated that the soldier on guard duty appeared in the painting to be shouldering a musket rather than a rifle, which was about twelve inches shorter. Bradford's quartermaster had an inventory of both types of weapons for issue. In Wing's opinion, Seymour oriented his painting of the fort to reflect the view to the northwest of the fortification. The Arkansas River would therefore be to the left of the field that the agricultural soldiers are tending.

26. Fort Smith Trader's Account Book, September 9, 12, and 13, 1820.

Cotton socks were among the most expensive items at the sutler's store, selling for $1.25 per pair. Dressed deerskins, used to make moccasins, cost $1.00 each.

27. Fort Smith Trader's Account Book, September 9, 12, and 13, 1820.

28. Ibid., 279–81.

29. Ibid., 280. Bell noted that "Glenn and three soldiers in pursuit of *the* deserters (italics mine) set out for the Trading house where they will be reinforced and proceed." In the Post Return for October 31, 1820, these three soldiers are named as "on command in pursuit of deserters." Inspection return for Bradford's Company, October 31, 1820. Flattened Muster Rolls and Returns, 15W-1: Map Case #15, Drawer #1, Box 144, Riflemen, January 1819–January 1821 (Companies A–C), RG 94, National Archives, Washington, D.C. Edwin James, who was with Stephen Long, mentioned in his journal that less than a day out from Belle Point, Long's group heard gunshots. A bit later, Hugh Glenn visited the Long camp bringing "coffee, biscuits, a bottle of spirits, etc." The "party of men accompanying Mr. Hugh Glenn on his way from Fort Smith to the trading house at the mouth of the Verdigris" were not named by James nor was their mission mentioned. Long and Caulder would, of course, have known each other from their earlier travels together. Edwin James, *Expedition to the Rocky Mountains*, Vol. II, 171.

Caulder and his mates were still on detached duty for the December 31, 1820, return, indicating that the pursuers conducted a prolonged attempt to bring back their quarry. It is notable that Bradford had only fifty-eight enlisted men in his company and some had been detached "cutting [a] road from Fort Smith to Missouri" and another to cultivate crops with which to trade Indians and white civilians for horses, leather, and beef.

30. *Registers of Enlistment*, Microcopy 233, Roll #17, Entry #223, Mordecai Nolen (Nolan, Nowlin). The spelling of Nowland's named varied from return to return. His record includes a number of "sick in quarters" references.

31. Little Rock *Arkansas Gazette*, October 7, 1820. The *Gazette* carried the reward notice for three weeks, once on the front page.

32. Little Rock *Arkansas Gazette*, October 14, 1820.

33. Muster Roll of James H. Ballard's Company, Rifle Regiment, December 31, 1820. Flattened Muster Rolls and Returns, 15W-1: Map Case #15, Drawer #1, Box 144, Riflemen, January 1819–January 1821 (Companies A–C), RG 94, National Archives, Washington, D.C. Lonnie J. White, "James Miller: Arkansas' First Territorial Governor," *Arkansas Historical Quarterly* 19 (Spring 1960): 21–22.

34. Bell was especially distraught about losing the manuscripts and journals, rating the theft as surpassing "the most abominable acts of villinany [sic] recorded in any history." Bell, *The Journal of Captain John R. Bell*, 256. From Fort Smith on September 19, Captain Bell set out for Cape Girardeau, Missouri. He and the expedition naturalist, Edwin James, traveled to Washington, D.C., by separate routes. In the capital city, these veterans of the Long expedition spent months refurbishing and editing their journals for publication. James's work eventually encompassed two volumes, incorporating his notes, the manuscripts of Thomas Say, and the geographical observations of Stephen Long. Bell and James presented modern readers with rich sources about life and times beyond the Missouri

when Native Americans still controlled the Great Plains. Both men wrote well and their fascinating details about Indians and the natural environment of the Arkansas River basin and how the party provided for basic needs while on the trail intrigues even casual readers today. Bell and James's published accounts became fundamental reading for their contemporaries who wanted professionally gleaned knowledge of the west. Both the military officer and the scientist continued to lament the stolen manuscripts that contained so much of value for their (and our) understanding of the natural and human environments of the Arkansas and Canadian River basins.

35. Muster Roll of James H. Ballard's Company, Rifle Regiment, December 31, 1820. Flattened Muster Rolls and Returns, 15W-1: Map Case #15, Drawer #1, Box 144, Riflemen, January 1819–January 1821, Companies A–C, RG 94, National Archives, Washington, D.C.

36. White, "James Miller: Arkansas' First Territorial Governor," 22.

37. Clarence Edwin Carter, ed., *Territorial Papers of the United States: Territory of Arkansas, 1819–1836* (Washington, D.C.: United States Government Printing Office, 1953), xix, 308, William Bradford to Secretary of War John C. Calhoun dated August 1821.

38. Edwin Bearss, "Fort Smith 1817–1824," 140; *Territorial Papers*, XIX, 331–33, Matthew Lyon to William Bradford, April 10, 1821. During the John Adams administration, Matthew Lyon had been jailed for his unflattering published comments about the president and the federal government.

39. Clermont's Osage language name was *To-Wo'n Ga-Xe*, which translated to Arrow-Going-Home. He was the Hunkah (townbuilder) of the Little Osage. His son's name was *Tse-To-Gah Wah-Shi'n-Pische*, translated to Bad-Tempered-Buffalo and known to whites at the time as Mad Buffalo. John Joseph Mathews, *The Osages: Children of the Middle Waters* (Norman: University of Oklahoma Press, 1961), 432–33.

40. Mathews, *The Osages*, 468.

41. A few months before, the party of Stephen Long approached the cabin of the Loving family located "not ten rods from the ferry." Edwin James of the expedition party had been impressed by the mannerisms of the "young woman who came to the door and attempted to silence the clamor of the dogs." She treated the "uncouth" appearing men with "civil" good humor. Edwin James, *Account of an Expedition from Pittsburgh to the Rocky Mountains*.

42. Letter from Martin Scott that appeared in the Little Rock *Arkansas Gazette*, May 12, 1821; Mathews, *The Osages*, 470–71; *Niles' Weekly Register*, June 30, 1821. Bearss, "Fort Smith 1817–1824," 141–45. After his narrow escape, Etienne Vaugine made it back to Little Rock by June to pick up mail that awaited him at the post office and to wish his brother, Francis Vaugine, success in his campaign to become the Pulaski County delegate to the Territorial Legislature.

43. Little Rock *Arkansas Gazette*, June 16, 1821.

44. Entry for Joseph Clark, Warrant Number 24, 554; Entry for John Brower, Warrant Number 24,558; Entry for Daniel Norman, Warrant Number 24,560; Entry for Martin Turner, Warrant Number 24,559; Entry for James Turner,

Warrant Number 24,557; Entry for Peter Caulder, Warrant Number 24,899; Bounty Land File, RG 49, National Archives, Washington, D.C.

45. Thomas James, *Three Years Among the Indians and Mexicans*, 117–18. James encountered Glenn and Bradford at what is now the town of Pryor, Oklahoma, in September 1821. Glenn was about to set out for Santa Fe with Fowler, twenty men, and twenty wagons. Glenn carried a license to trade with Indians effected by William Bradford as commandant of Fort Smith.

46. Nicks and Rogers Account Book, 1820–22, Microfilm Roll, Arkansas History Commission, Little Rock, Arkansas, Entries of Brower and Clark, October 1821.

47. Crawford County Records, Tax Records, 1821–1851, Microfilm Roll 22, Arkansas History Commission, Little Rock, Arkansas. Martin Turner paid $1.62 in taxes (including the poll tax) and James Turner $1.00.

48. Ruth Polk Patterson, *The Seed of Sally Good'n: A Black Family of Arkansas, 1833–1953* (Lexington: University of Kentucky Press, 1985), 16–17.

49. Ibid., 136–37. Descendants of Peter Polk lived in Fort Smith and in Newport, Arkansas, in recent times. Many documented stories exist regarding the children of slave women and white slave owners, including the detailed life of Virginia-born educator and abolitionist John Mercer Langston. See William L. Cheek and Aimee Lee Cheek, *John Mercer Langston and the Fight for Black Freedom, 1829–1865* (Urbana: University of Illinois, 1989). One of the most remarkable such episodes in Arkansas involved the largest landholder in Chicot County, Elisha Worthington. By 1860, Worthington owned 543 slaves. He had two children, James W. and Martha W. Mason, born out of his long-term relationship with a slave woman. Martha, the daughter with whom old Elisha lived until his death in 1873, fought legal battles in an effort to retain part of Redleaf and Sunnyside plantations in her name. Willard B. Gatewood Jr., "Sunnyside: The Evolution of an Arkansas Plantation," in *Shadows over Sunnyside: An Arkansas Plantation in Transition, 1830–1945*, ed. Jeannie M. Whayne (Fayetteville: University of Arkansas Press, 1993).

CHAPTER SIX: Black Yeoman in Arkansas Territory

1. Edwin C. Bearss and A. M. Gibson, *Fort Smith: Little Gibraltar on the Arkansas* (Norman: University of Oklahoma Press, 1969), 54. The authors detailed the Seventh Infantry's reassignment and are especially attentive to Arbuckle's pre-Fort Smith command.

2. Woolley to Hook, April 9, 1822, War Department File, Quartermaster-General Letters Received, RG 94, National Archives and Records Administration, Washington, D.C.; Gaines to Arbuckle, May 15, 1822, War Department File, Western Department, Letters Sent, Book 97, RG 94, National Archives.

3. Bearss and Gibson, *Fort Smith*, 59.

4. Ibid., 86.

5. Letter from Benjamin L. E. Bonneville to Mathew Arbuckle, dated December 3, 1823; Carter Jr., *Territorial Papers*, XIX, 571.

6. Ibid. Zachary Taylor stayed in Louisiana long enough to acquire a planta-

tion and a number of slaves, an unusual investment for an army officer. His plantation never made profits, and Taylor while president favored admitting California to the union as a free soil state. His son Robert, however, was a Confederate general in the Trans-Mississippi theater.

7. Entry for David Mullins, Warrant Number 22402, Bounty Land Files, RG 49, National Archives.

8. Bearss and Gibson, *Fort Smith*, 76–77.

9. Inspection Returns for Seventh Regiment of *U.S.* Infantry, Fort Smith, Arkansas Territory, February 28, 1822, lists Sergeants Oliver Carter and Henry Thompson and Cpl. Adam Lawyer as the only transfers, besides Webb, to receive the rank as noncommissioned officers in the Seventh Infantry. The rest of the riflemen transferred over as privates, and none was ever elevated above that rank while in the Seventh Infantry.

10. Ginger L. Ashcraft, "Antoine Barraque and His Involvement in Indian Affairs of Southeast Arkansas, 1816–1832," *Arkansas Historical Quarterly* 32 (Fall 1973): 227–28. Arbuckle to Gaines, December 3, 1823, in Carter, *Territorial Papers*, XIX, 570–71.

11. Inspection Returns, Seventh Infantry, Fort Smith, Arkansas Territory, April 30, 1824, War Department, Western Department Reports Received File, RG 94, National Archives.

12. Entry for Samuel Eaton, Warrant Number 22217, Bounty Land Files, RG 49, National Archives. In recent times, the Bureau of Land Management has digitized the bounty land records allowing ready access to researchers. For example, Samuel Eaton may be referenced at *www.glorecords.blm.gov* using his warrant number, his name, and the territory in which he applied, Arkansas.

13. The philosopher-historian William Durant described the "secret pride in self" that sustained the lowliest serf in medieval Europe, giving him hope and a trust in the future that belied his disadvantages and his station in life. According to Durant, common people naturally possess that pride, and Caulder certainly had little reason to distrust his own future.

14. Census for Arkansas Territory on January 1, 1823, Little Rock *Arkansas Gazette*, June 17, 1823. The population for Independence County was 2,014. Twenty-two were free colored persons and most of these were David Hall's family.

15. "Compared Copy of Field Notes of Township 16 North, Range 5 West," Book #1375, Bundle #12, 1574, Commissioner of State Lands, Little Rock, Arkansas.

16. Reenlistment document of Peter Caulder dated October 3, 1824. Bounty Land Files, RG 94, National Archives, Washington, D.C.

17. Crawford County Tax Record 1821–1851, Microfilm Roll 22, Arkansas History Commission, Little Rock, Arkansas.

18. The Arkansas Territorial General Assembly had franchised free white males who were at least twenty-one years of age, had resided in the territory for one year before the election, and had paid his territorial taxes. When Bradford ran for the state assembly in 1823, he received 252 votes in Crawford County to Conway's eight. Little Rock *Arkansas Gazette*, August 19, 1823. The only other county in Bradford's column was Lawrence with a 38–0 return. A letter published

in the *Arkansas Gazette* encouraged enfranchising soldiers who presumably would turn out in large numbers to vote for their commander in this election. Ibid., Letter from Pike, April 15, 1823.

19. Little Rock *Arkansas Gazette*, December 28, 1824, gave the completed 1824 Electoral College tabulation by state. The announcement of the House vote in favor of John Quincy Adams appeared in the Washington, D.C. *Daily National Intelligencer* on February 8, 1825, and in the *Arkansas Gazette* on March 15, 1825, after the inauguration of Adams.

20. Crawford County Tax Record, 1821–1851, Microfilm Roll 22, Arkansas History Commission, Little Rock, Arkansas.

21. Ibid.; *Fifth Census of the United States*, 1830: Arkansas, Crawford County.

22. Samuel Solomon, ed., *The Complete Plays of Racine* (New York: Modern Library, 1967), I, xliv.

23. Little Rock *Arkansas Gazette*, November 7, 1825. Michael de la Bedoyere, *Lafayette, A Revolutionary Gentleman* (New York: Scribner's and Sons, 1934). Bedoyere stated that Gilbert Motier de Lafayette was born on September 6, 1757. The tendency in the eighteenth century was to spell the name as one word, rather than the proper La Fayette. Bodoyere lists Lafayette's itinerary: 1824: New York to Providence to Boston to Albany, Washington, and Richmond. That was "but a trifle compared with the schedule for 1825." That rigorous agenda included travel to the Carolinas to Mobile to New Orleans and a thousand miles up the Mississippi to St. Louis. Perhaps the general considered visiting Fort Smith in order to see Bonneville. Edith H. Lovell, *Benjamin Bonneville: Soldier of the American Frontier* (Bountiful, Utah: Horizon Publishers and Distributors, 1992), 42.

24. James Akins (Aikins) had arrived with the Seventh Infantry at Fort Smith in 1822. Aikins reenlisted from desertion on December 13, 1827. Microfilm 127, Inspection Returns for the Seventh Infantry, December 1827, RG 94, National Archives, Washington, D.C.

25. Little Rock *Arkansas Gazette*, June 12, 1827. Accounts of Nicks and Rogers, 1827, Folder #2, Gilcrease Museum, Tulsa, Oklahoma. Microfilm 127, Inspection Returns, Seventh Infantry, May 30, 1827, RG 94, National Archives, Washington D.C., Microfilm Roll 27, Fort Smith National Historic Site.

26. Little Rock *Arkansas Gazette*, June 12, 1827.

27. Microfilm 127, Inspection Returns for the Seventh Infantry, April through October 1827.

CHAPTER SEVEN: Keeper of a "Severe Pack of Dogs"

1. Little Rock *Arkansas Gazette*, June 24, 1828. The public hanging of Strickland in Little Rock drew a large crowd. McGranie had been returned to the army after a Little Rock jury in a civil trial for murder acquitted him of the ax slaying on grounds of insanity. A twenty-four-month stay in the stockade must have restored his senses because the army released McGranie from confinement and sent him back to duty. In 1825, he reenlisted in the Seventh Infantry. Clarence E. Carter, Jr., *Territorial Papers*, XX, 543; Microfilm 127, Seventh Infantry Returns, July 1825, RG 94, National Archives, Washington, D.C.

2. Francis Paul Prucha, *Army Life on the Western Frontier, Selections From the Official Reports Made Between 1826 and 1845 by Colonel George Croghan* (Norman: University of Oklahoma Press, 1958), 134. Prucha wrote Croghan had the attitude that "soldiers should be soldiers, not workmen."

3. Milton D. Rafferty, ed., *Rude Pursuits and Rugged Peaks: Schoolcraft's Ozark Journal, 1818–1819* (Fayetteville: University of Arkansas Press, 1996).

4. Caulder may have referred to that waterway as the Buffalo Fork of the White River, which had banks of "rich alluvium and . . . much resorted to by hunters on account of the abundance of game it affords." Rafferty, *Rude Pursuits*, 102. If that were his route, Caulder would have passed by the cabin of John Brisco, "who had just settled on the river near Jasper." See Dwight Pitcaithley, "Settlement of the Arkansas Ozarks: The Buffalo River," *Arkansas Historical Quarterly* 37 (Autumn 1978): 203–22. Pitcaithley mentions the free black families of the Little North Fork, 220–21.

5. Microfilm 127, Seventh Infantry Returns, RG 94, National Archives, Washington, D.C.

6. Crawford County Tax Record, 1821–1851, Microfilm Roll 22, Arkansas History Commission, Little Rock, Arkansas.

7. Frederick Gerstaecker, *Wild Sports in the Far West* (New York: John W. Lovell Company, no date), 365. Gerstaecker undertook a "living off the land" excursion to the White River in 1838. He described in detail many activities and practices of backwoods people in Arkansas including the Indian method of curing deerskins.

8. Lovell, *Bonneville*, 86.

9. Brooks Blevins, *Hill Folks: A History of Arkansas Ozarkers and Their Image* (Chapel Hill: University of North Carolina Press, 2002), 248–49. Blevins describes Jimmy Driftwood's inspiration for and the marketing of his renowned song, *The Battle of New Orleans*.

10. Rafferty, *Rude Pursuits*, 55.

11. Schoolcraft's 1818 travel journal into Arkansas and his insistence on reporting crude and backward behavior in Arkansas to the exclusion of all else has received welcomed criticism from George E. Lankford in "'Beyond the Pale,': Frontier Folk in the Southern Ozarks," in Robert J. Smith and Jerry Stannard, eds., *The Folk: Identity, Landscapes and Lores*, University of Kansas Publications in Anthropology, No. 17 (Lawrence: University of Kansas, 1989).

12. About 6,600 warrants were issued to War of 1812 veterans for Arkansas bounty lands. In 1830, less than 1 percent of the grantees resided on their bounty lands. Katheren Christensen, ed., *Arkansas Military Bounty Lands—War of 1812* (Hot Springs: Arkansas Ancestors, 1971).

13. The congressional legislation creating bounty lands exempted those lands from taxes for three years. The Arkansas Territorial General Assembly passed an act providing for taxation of all bounty lands. Land Use Folder, WPA, Writers Project, summary by Lucy Crooks, "Land Grants, Military Bounty," dated May 29, 1941, in the Arkansas History Commission.

14. Little Rock *Arkansas Gazette*, August 26, 1829, Sale of Lands for Taxes, Independence County.

15. Dallas T. Herndon, *Centennial History of Arkansas* (Chicago, Ill., and Little Rock, Ark.: S. J. Clarke Publishing Company, 1922), 184.

16. Donald P. McNeilly, *The Old South Frontier: Cotton Plantations and the Formation of Arkansas Society, 1819–1861* (Fayetteville: University of Arkansas Press, 2000), 13–21.

17. McNeilly combs through early settlers' accounts of land that they encountered and activities that they engaged in for a revealing look at Arkansas Territory's development. The quote from Daniel Ashby appeared in Malcolm J. Rohrbough, *The Land Office Business: The Settlement and Administration of American Public Lands, 1789–1837* (New York: Oxford University Press, 1968), 200.

18. Sheriff's Census of Izard County, 1829, Arkansas History Commission, Little Rock, Arkansas.

19. Izard County Tax Record, 1829–1866, Microfilm Roll 16, Arkansas History Commission, Little Rock, Arkansas.

20. Pitcaithley, "Settlement of the Arkansas Ozarks: The Buffalo River," 204, 221.

21. Dallas T. Herndon, *The Annals of Arkansas, 1947* (Hopkinsville, Ky.: Historical Record Association, 1947), I, 113.

22. Little Rock *Arkansas Gazette*, November 23, 1831.

23. The naming patterns of the Caulder and Hall families followed well-established folkways. Forenames of parents and grandparents were perpetuated in each generation. Peter Caulder named a daughter Mourning after his sister and a son Moses after his father. David Caulder, himself named after Eliza's father, named a son Peter, and so on. In the case of the Hall family, James and David are repeated often enough to ensure survival of favorite family forenames as well as to sow confusion for later-day historians and genealogists. See David Hackett Fischer, *Albion's Seed: Four British Folkways in America* (New York: Oxford University Press, 1989), 306, 686, for a discussion of "naming ways" of eighteenth- and nineteenth-century Americans.

24. Izard County Tax Records, 1829–1866, Microfilm Roll 16, Arkansas History Commission, Little Rock, Arkansas.

25. Joseph Meetch, Diary of Travels in Arkansas, 1826–27, University of Arkansas at Little Rock Archives, h. 4. cited by S. Charles Bolton, *Territorial Ambition: Land and Society in Arkansas, 1800–1840* (Fayetteville: University of Arkansas Press, 1993), 33.

26. Little Rock *Arkansas Gazette*, September 28, 1831, January 11, 1832.

27. Gerstaecker, *Wild Sports in the Far West*, 142.

28. Near where Gerstaecker encountered the distiller in the tavern home, the present village of Magness now sits. The next day, a sober "Magnus" accompanied Gerstaecker as the two hunted a bear.

29. *Sixth Census of the United States, 1840: Arkansas, Izard County.*

30. Bolton, *Territorial Ambition*, 32–34.

31. Ibid., 38.

32. Sarah Bass evidently left Marion County in the 1840s and never appeared on the tax rolls for Izard County or Marion County (some mulatto women did). A free colored man, Josuha Bass, is listed in the 1840 Pulaski County census. The name similarity creates a possible link between the free black population of Little

Rock and that on the White River. James Atkinson may have also been a veteran of the War of 1812. Several James Atkinsons appear in the *Registers of Enlistment* for soldiers who joined before 1815. None of them was assigned to Bradford's Company at Fort Smith and none of them is described as "colored." A James Atkinson appears on the list of bounty land recipients for Arkansas, Warrant Number 25595. That veteran exchanged his warrant for a patent on 160 acres in Independence County in 1824, the same year as Caulder and Martin Turner patented their bounty land in the same area of the state.

33. "Proof of Race and Rights of a Free Private Citizen" affidavit from Maury County, Tennessee, filed by Thomas Hall on September 19, 1835, and again in Marion County, Arkansas, on June 26, 1843. Deed Book for 1890, Howell County Circuit Clerk Records, West Plains, Missouri. After his move to Missouri, Hall filed the affidavit in Oregon County on February 13, 1850. The affidavit was filed again on May 5, 1890, after Thomas Hall's death, which occurred on December 30, 1888, at his home in Howell County. Thomas Hall's "proof of race" affidavit, however, did not deter Missouri census marshals in 1850, 1860, 1870, and 1880 from typing him as "mulatto," meaning that they always considered him primarily of African descent.

34. For existing documentation on Melungeon people and a good, if biased, presentation of the case for a separate race, see N. Brent Kennedy and Robyn Vaughan Kennedy, *The Melungeons: The Resurrection of a Proud People* (Macon, Ga.: Mercer University Press, 1977). Coincidentally, a common surname of Appalachian "Melungeon" families is Hall. From Kennedy's book, 129: "In the year 1810, Baxter County, Arkansas saw the arrival of frontiersman Jacob Mooney, who came to barter and among other vocations, smelt silver ore into bars for trade with the Indians. Mooney had four dark-skinned men assisting him, whom the oldtimers could not categorize as Negro, Indian, or White. They were called, simply, 'lungeons,' and Mooney was apparently ostracized for cohorting with these 'foreigners.'" Also, *The History of Baxter County, Arkansas*, Centennial Edition (Mountain Home, Arkansas, 1972).

35. Earl Berry, *History of Marion County* (Little Rock, Ark.: International Lithographing Company, 1977). Blevins, *Hill Folks*, 16, 21, 278.

36. Mary L. Kwas, "The Spectacular 1833 Leonid Meteor Storm: The View from Arkansas," *Arkansas Historical Quarterly* 53 (Autumn 1999): 312–24. Kwas concluded from reports of contemporary and modern observers that "on the night of November 12–13, 1833 the Leonid meteoroid stream produced over north America what was probably the most spectacular display in recorded history . . . modern estimates suggest that there were as many as 50,000 to 150,000 meteors visible per hour." Silas Claiborne Turnbo, "How the Great Meteoric Shower Was Seen and Felt in Hall County, Georgia," and "More about Yellville and the Early Residents There and Vicinity," Springfield-Greene County Library Turnbo Collection, Springfield, Missouri.

37. Little Rock *Arkansas Gazette*, September 28, 1831, January 11, 1832.

38. Silas Claiborne Turnbo, "A Long Time Ago," v. 21, 19 in Heiskell Collection, University of Arkansas at Little Rock, Little Rock, Arkansas. See also James F. Keefe and Lynn Morrow, *The White River Chronicles: Man and Wildlife on the Ozark Frontier* (Fayetteville: University of Arkansas Press, 1994), for selected

Turnbo stories drawn from the Springfield-Greene County Library Turnbo Collection. That collection holds the original handwritten stories. The University of Arkansas at Little Rock archives holds typewritten copies of Turnbo's Ozark manuscripts, as part of their J. N. Heiskell Collection. Desmond Walls Allen extracted material from the eight hundred or so Turnbo stories in the Heiskell Collection to publish a ten-volume series, entitled *Turnbo's Tales*. Today, Turnbo's stories are accessible in Keefe and Morrow's book, Allen's paperbound volumes, in bound volumes at the Springfield-Greene County Library, or at the internet address: http://thelibrary.springfield.missouri.org/lochrist/turnbo.html. Hereinafter references to Turnbo stories are by title and accessible in bound copy at the Springfield-Greene County Library as well as accessible online from their web site.

39. Turnbo, "Desperate Struggle between Two Bucks."

40. Ted Worley and Eugene Nolte, eds., *Pete Whetstone of Devil's Fork: Letters to the Spirit of the Times* (Van Buren, Ark.: Press Argus), 4, 5, 144, 115.

41. Turnbo, "Meeting an Angry Catamount." An "old time hunter" described a delicious-tasting deer that he killed in that area as having "a layer of pure fat an inch thick over . . . its body."

42. George W. Pierson at times had his surname spelled Pearson in the tax record and on the census.

43. Batesville Land Office Track Book, 2-2-34, Part I, vol. 7, 43, document #3212, Cash Entry for John Hall; document #3213, Cash Entry for David Hall, RG 49, National Archives and Records Administration, Washington, D.C.

44. Batesville Track Book 2-2-34, Cash Entry Nos. 3210, 3211, 3212, and 3213 dated February 28, 1848. John Hall, George Pierson, and David Hall Sr. received their patents on November 1, 1849. Marion County Tax Records, 1841–1866, Microfilm Roll 12, Arkansas History Commission. In 1852, John D. Noe begins to be assessed for the 71.13 acres patented by David Hall. A deed from David and Sarah Hall to John D. Noe, dated October 1, 1850, was recorded in the Marion County Court House on January 14, 1949.

In 1852, George Pierson began to be assessed by the county for both tracts patented in 1849 by John Hall.

45. Turnbo, "An Interesting View of a Wild Bear."

46. The Arkansas Highway Department map for Marion County, 1936, shows the location of Pace's Ferry just below the mouth of Sister Creek that connected Oakland and Flippin.

47. For an excellent account of the life and writing times of Turnbo, see Lynn Morrow, "I Am Nothing but a Poor Scribbler," in *White River Valley Historical Quarterly* (Spring 1991).

48. Of course, Turnbo was not the only recorder of tall tales in Arkansas. See also James R. Masterson, *Tall Tales of Arkansas* (Boston: Chapman and Grimes, 1943); and Norris W. Yates, *William T. Porter and the Spirit of the Times: A Study of the BIG BEAR School of Humor* (Baton Rouge: Louisiana State University Press, 1957).

49. Turnbo, "A Long Time Ago."

50. Turnbo, "Dodging Bullets" and "How the Man Willoughby Hall was Scalped."

51. Dale Hanks, ed., *Historical and Biographical Sketches of the Early Settlement of the Valley of White River Together with a History of Izard County by A. C. Jeffery* (Richmond, Va.: Jeffery Historical Society, 1973). Jehodia Jeffery, A. C.'s father, became well enough known as a legislator and judge in antebellum Arkansas that news of his death in Izard County was carried in the statewide newspaper; Little Rock *Arkansas Gazette*, December 5, 1846.

52. Turnbo *Tales*, "Panther Stories," 73.

53. Charles F. M. Noland, *Pete Whetstone of Devil's Fork: Letters to the Spirit of the Times*, ed. Ted R. Worley and Eugene A. Nolte (Van Buren, Ark.: Press-Argus, 1957), iv–v.

54. Batesville *News*, March 17, 1842. Caulder might have preferred to trap otters. Their skins brought $1–$3 a piece compared to the 25 cents brought by top raccoon and fox furs.

55. Vicki Roberts, "Marion County As She Was In 1836, Adapted from the *Mount Echo* Articles by W. B. Flippin, ca. 1899." (1996)

56. Turnbo, "A Midnight Attack of a Panther on a Bunch of Hogs."

57. Turnbo writes stories of "wild country then overrun with wild animals" and "huge beasts." A good example of the dangers of panthers, at least in the minds of even fearless settlers, can be found in his story, "A Mixture of Stories in One Chapter," in Desmond Walls Allen, ed., *Turnbo's Tales*, " Schools, Indians, Hard Times and More Stories," 29–31.

58. Berry, *History of Marion County*.

59. Duane Huddleston, Sammie Rose, and Pat Wood, *Steamboats and Ferries on White River: A Heritage Revisited* (Conway: University of Central Arkansas Press, 1995), 193.

60. W. B. Flippin wrote an account of the Tutt-Everett War in 1876. Flippin's original manuscript is in the Trimble Collection at the Arkansas History Commission; a version was published by the Yellville *Mountain Echo* in 1899. Flippin, for whom the town of Flippin is named, migrated into Marion County in 1837.

CHAPTER EIGHT: Flush Times and the Storm

1. William W. Hughes, *Archibald Yell* (Fayetteville: University of Arkansas Press, 1988), 21.

2. Marion County Tax Record, 1841–1866. Walker owned mineral-rich lands in Prairie Township near the town of Lead Hill. He was a nonresident owner throughout the 1850s when a mining boom in Marion County occurred.

3. Clyde W. Cathey, "Slavery in Arkansas," *Arkansas Historical Quarterly* 28 (Spring 1944): 72–73. Luther P. Jackson, *Free Negro Labor and Property Holding in Virginia, 1830–1860* (New York: Appleton-Century Corporation, 1942), 5. Jackson comments on the "hostility toward the free Negro in Virginia" as measured by the numerous legal restrictions on their rights continuously being invented by lawmakers. This legislative stance carried into Arkansas. But in Virginia as in Arkansas, actual enforcement of these restrictive laws varied greatly from locale

to locale within the state.

4. U.S. Bureau of the Census, *The Seventh Census of the United States: 1850* (Washington, D.C., 1850), Schedule 1, Population, Marion County; Marion County Tax Record, 1841–1866, Microfilm Roll 12, Arkansas History Commission, Little Rock, Arkansas.

5. Marion County Tax Record, 1841–1866.

6. Dallas T. Herndon, *Annals of Arkansas, 1947: A Narrative Historical Edition, Revising, Reediting and Continuing "A Centennial History of Arkansas* (Hopkinsville, Ky.: Historical Record Association, 1947), 132–33.

7. The livestock figures for Hall are according to the tax record. Sheep and pigs were not assessed for taxes.

8. Batesville Land Office Track Book, 2–8–34, Part I, Vol. 8, 31, Document #3738, Cash Entry for David Hall, RG 49, National Archives. See Appendix A for comparison of seventy-five farmers in 1850 Marion County.

9. Jacob Trieber, "Legal Status of Negroes in Arkansas before the Civil War," Arkansas Historical Association *Publications*, 3 (Fayetteville, 1911), 176. Florence R. Beatty-Brown, "Legal Status of Arkansas Negroes before Emancipation," *Arkansas Historical Quarterly* (Spring 1969): 28, 6. The prohibition against free Negroes owning slaves came through a state supreme court ruling rather than by legislation. Arkansas had a small free Negro population and rarely could any of them afford a slave. An exception to the rule was Josiah Weddington's son at Lakeport Plantation in Chicot County, who was a de facto owner and operator of one of the state's largest plantations. See *Gould's Digest*, chapter 153, Article III, section 27, 947, for the restriction against free Negroes owning guns or ammunition.

10. Blevins, *Hill Folks*, 283 (fn) mentions that the Cokers and other large slaveowners in the Ozarks held by far more women than men as slaves.

11. At least three men from Marion County, William Prewitt, John Prewitt, and Lawson A. McIntire, joined the ill-fated Fancher wagon train to California in 1857. They, along with 117 other men, women, and children, were killed by Paiute Indians and Mormons at Mountain Meadows in southwest Utah on September 11, 1857. Will Bagley, *Blood of the Prophets: Brigham Young and the Massacre at Mountain Meadows* (Norman: University of Oklahoma Press, 2002), 66.

12. Pricilla McArthur, *Arkansas in the Gold Rush* (Little Rock, Ark.: August House, 1986), 226–35. McArthur has assembled the rosters of twenty-five groups that departed Fort Smith in 1849 and 1850 by wagon or pack mule train. To become a member of certain companies, prospects had to sign an agreement that they would supply themselves with minimum provisions and transportation.

13. A detailed account of the military organizations and events of the war can be found in Richard Bruce Winders, *Mr. Polk's Army: The American Military Experience in the Mexican War* (College Station: Texas A&M Press, 1997). Winders, historian and curator of the Alamo in San Antonio, contrasts the personalities, methods, and ambitions of Taylor and Scott. Winders hardly mentions Archibald Yell and the Arkansas Mounted Regiment, and black soldiers not at all. According to Melvin Sylvester of the B. Davis Schwartz Memorial Library at the C. W. Post Campus of Long Island University, black soldiers served in the

First Regiment of Volunteers, New York; the Fourth Artillery; and the Ninth, Tenth, Eleventh, and Thirteenth Infantry regiments during the Mexican-American War. Richard Bailey, author of the forthcoming "They Too Call Alabama Home: African American Profiles, 1800–1998," identified James H. Alston, later of Tuskegee, as a drummer in the Mexican War.

14. Herbert Aptheker, ed., *A Documentary History of the Negro People in the United States*, Vol. 1 (New York: Citadel Press, 1968), 4th ed.

15. Sam W. Haynes, *James K. Polk and the Expansionist Impulse*, 2d ed. (New York: Addison Wesley Longman, 2001), 208.

16. Winders, *Mr. Polk's Army*.

17. Little Rock *Arkansas Gazette*, February 22, 1850; November 8, 1850.

18. Merrill D. Peterson, *The Great Triumvirate: Webster, Clay, and Calhoun* (New York and Oxford: Oxford University Press, 1987), 475.

19. Most fugitive advertisements in the *Arkansas Gazette*, the *Arkansas Banner*, and the *Arkansas Advocate* were illustrated with a woodcut icon of a top-hatted black man with a bundle tied to a stick over his shoulder, a nonthreatening caricature to be sure and almost a nonserious one. The slave population of Arkansas in 1850 was 47,100 with 21 reported fugitives. In 1860, the figures were 111,115 slaves of which 28 were recorded as fugitives. *Miscellaneous Statistics, Seventh Census, 1850*, and *Eighth Census, 1860* (Washington, D.C.: United States Government Printing Office, 1864), 338. In his meticulous study of the planter class in Arkansas, Donald P. McNeilly mentions that "thousands (of slaves) fled into the Arkansas night." A metaphor, of course, because the reality is as McNeilly mentions a few sentences later, slaves "knew there was nowhere to run." One of the few scholarly analyses of fugitive slaves in Arkansas was presented in Paul D. Lack, "An Urban Slave Community: Little Rock, 1831–1862," *Arkansas Historical Quarterly* 41 (Autumn 1982): 258–87. Donald P. McNeilly, *The Old South Frontier* (Fayetteville: University of Arkansas Press, 2000), 152.

20. The Taney court ruled tangentially and adversely on the question of free status for blacks who lived in the North. Southerners shouted at one another that they could now drive slave coffles to Kansas or Nebraska, or for that matter to southern Illinois.

21. Turnbo, "The Drowning of Sam Johnson." Turnbo described the wife of George Hogan as a "daughter of Joe Coker and had Indian blood in her veins." George Hogan kept a slave or two, probably women, most of the years before the war. Blevins, *Hill Folks*, 16.

22. William Monks, *The History of Southern Missouri and Northern Arkansas* (West Plains, Mo.: West Plains Journal Co., 1907), 26. Monks referred to two branches of the Coker family, one group of Coker's sons having an Indian mother who resided most of the time in the "Nation" and her sons switched back and forth from Marion County to Oklahoma. Monks wrote of these half-Indian Coker men: "They had killed three or four men and if the authorities attempted to arrest them, they defied them, and would go to the Nation and remain awhile."

23. Turnbo, "A Long Time Ago." The history of an Arkansas legal case of skin tones, racial identification, and the quandary that light-complexion mulattoes with European features caused in a slave society based on color and race can be found in

Robert S. Shafer, "White Persons Held to Racial Slavery in Antebellum Arkansas," *Arkansas Historical Quarterly* 44 (Summer 1985): 134–55.

24. The Tutt-Everett War and outbreaks of violence in Marion County drew statewide attention in 1849 and 1850. See Monks, *The History of Southern Missouri and Northern Arkansas*, 24–26, for his version of the war and newspaper accounts in the Little Rock *Arkansas Gazette*, September 13 and 20 and November 1, 1849.

25. John C. Calhoun, after some schooling in the Palmetto state, led his class at Yale. A local story, probably apocryphal, had it that Cowdrey attended the same South Carolina school as Calhoun. Cowdrey served as Marion County clerk from 1840 to 1844.

26. *Seventh Census of the United States: 1850*, Schedule 1, Population, Marion County, 334. Obviously proud of their states, the Cowdreys named their second daughter Arkansas and their last Carolina. Joining the secessionists, Dr. Cowdrey was assigned as surgeon to Col. William Mitchell's Fourteenth Arkansas Infantry. The War Between the States caused the total destruction of his home and personal property.

27. Cowdrey's list of Marion County households numbered 363. His own household was number 362.

28. Given the distances involved between home sites and the fact that Cowdrey invariably listed five or six households on each day, he could have relied on reports from heads of families who gathered at a central location like the house of David and Sarah Hall. The census act allowed that latitude in stating that "the assistant marshals shall make the enumeration by actual inquiry at every dwelling house, or by personal inquiry of the head of every family, and not otherwise." The Caulders lived in a more difficult place to reach, probably an hour's ride away from the Halls. Another possibility is that families gathered in one spot for Cowdrey to interview. He certainly missed a few in the community, including the mulatto Leonard Hall. The enumerated agricultural data for North Fork Township has not survived, an unfortunate loss since that is the township where most of the Halls and Peter Caulder dwelled. The last reported township on the record is White River and it did include David Hall Jr. (as well as Cowdrey's holdings). But White River and Blythe are not copied in Cowdrey's handwriting. Perhaps he became ill before he could finish or he ran into a deadline and assigned White River agricultural census to an assistant. Agricultural data on the Madewells, Dicksons, Moores, and Johnsons were recorded as they resided in Union Township.

29. *Arkansas Revised Statutes* (1838), Chapter 103, Section 1, 584; *Gould's Digest*, Chapter 76, Section 1, 553. See also Beatty-Brown, "Legal Status of Arkansas Negroes before Emancipation," *Arkansas Historical Quarterly* 18 (Spring 1969): 28, 11.

30. *Seventh Census of the United States: 1850*, Schedule 1, Population, Marion County, 635.

31. Ibid. Thomas Hall affidavit filed in Marion County, June 26, 1843. *Seventh Census of the United States: 1850*, Schedule 1, Population, Oregon County, Missouri, District #65, household #225.

32. *Seventh Census of the United States: 1850*, Schedule 4, Agricultural

Manuscript, Marion County, Union Township, entry number 17 for John Wood.

33. W. B. Flippin, "Marion County as She Was When Settled in 1836," Yellville *Mountain Echo*, May 9, 1899. Gladys Horn Brown's transcription of Flippin's reminensces of Cowdrey, who came to Yellville in 1836, include this delightful account of a verbal faux paus by an Eastern sophisticate: Dr. Cowdrey was "called to see a patient, who now lives in Baxter county, then Marion, by the name of Hargrave, the wife of John Hargrave, an early settler, a man of some means and a good citizen. The doctor went to the patient, but after examining the case, said he had forgotten to bring any Nitre with him, and the case needed the drug, and he could not treat the case as he wished without. Hargrave said he would send a boy after it, if he knew where to send, the doctor told him he had the drug at home, but it was about fifteen or eighteen miles from Hargraves to where the doctor was living. The boy was told to hurry, so he did not spare his horse. When he returned the doctor opened the paper containing the Nitre, as the doctor called it, and the boy saw it said, it looks like salt petre. The doctor, replied, that is what some people call it, and the old man Hargrave said, there is plenty of salt petre here. So there was a ride of thirty miles at least, because the doctor failed to call Nitre salt petre." Other early inhabitants had fond memories of Cowdrey, such as this statement by Polly Ann Haskett in Turnbo's "Recollections of Early Days in Marion County, Arkansas as Told by a Lady Contributor": "Dr. Cowdry was well known along White River from Batesville to the Mo. state line as an honest and an able physician and had a host of friends. Sometimes he was known to visit the sick 75 miles distant."

34. *Seventh Census of the United States: 1850*, Schedule 4, Agricultural Manuscript, Marion County, White River Township, 53–54.

35. Ibid., 626, 642. The practice of reissuing favorite given names in the extended family was not confined to the mulattoes along the White River. Marian and Lester Burnes, *Early Days of Marion County* (Ozark, Mo.: Dogwood Press, 1992), 31, "The Coker family used the same given names in each family, making it very difficult to identify them. . . ."

36. Noe, Martin, and Pierson bought land from the Halls. Hargrave lived next door to David Hall Jr., and they no doubt shared labor with each other at critical times as their wives shared mutual concerns about raising a family. John Magness accepted Charles Madewell, a mulatto, into his household.

37. Turnbo, "Recollections of Early Days in Marion County, Arkansas as Told by a Lady Contributor." William Monks, The *History of Southern Missouri and Northern Arkansas* (West Plains, Mo.: West Plains Journal Co., 1907), mentioned that fox furs were made into hats often worn by the pioneers and hunters.

38. *Seventh Census of the United States: 1850*, Schedule 4, Agricultural Manuscript, Marion County. Although the manuscript census and exactly what was produced on John Turner and James Hall's farm is missing, the marshal valued their farms at $800. The production that appears is typical for a Marion County farm of that magnitude.

39. Batesville Track Book, Cash File #5000 for James Hall and Cash File #5001 for John Turner, RG 49, National Archives and Records Administration, Washington, D.C.

40. Charles F. M. Noland, *Pete Whetstone*, xii, xiii.

41. The elder Madewell owned seven horses, two milk cows, fifteen steers and heifers, nineteen sheep, and thirty-five hogs. *Seventh Census of the United States:* Schedule 4, Agricultural Manuscript, Marion County, Union Township, Entry #38.

42. Turnbo, "A Little Horse Race." Marion County Tax Record, 1849, Manuscript Roll 12, Arkansas History Commission. *Seventh Census of the United States: 1850:* Schedule 4, Agricultural Manuscript, Marion County, Blythe Township, Entries #33 and 34. Ted Worley and Eugene Nolte, eds., *Pete Whetstone of Devil's Fork: Letters to the Spirit of the Times* (Van Buren, Ark.: Press-Argus, 1957).

43. Martin may have truly been a man of spirit without regard for material possessions. Landless, he paid rent for his cabin with the sweat of his brow and owned a single horse and a milk cow, the bare minimum for pioneer subsistence. Nancy Britton, *Two Centuries of Methodism in Arkansas, 1800–2000* (Little Rock, Ark.: August House Publishers, 2000), 339, 377. Walter N. Vernon, *Methodism in Arkansas, 1816–1876* (Nashville, Tenn.: Parthenon Press, 1976), 67. The description of church house construction is drawn from William Monks, *A History of Southern Missouri and Northern Arkansas: Being an Account of the Early Settlements, the Civil War, the Ku-Klux, and Times of Peace* (West Plains, Mo.: West Plains Journal Co., 1907), 14. *Seventh Census of the United States,* 1850, lists the ministers in Marion County. Baptist, Methodists, and Presbyterians made up about 90 percent of church members in antebellum Arkansas, although the Church of Latter Day Saints under the leadership of Joseph Smith Jr. in far west Missouri sent eloquent missionaries to Arkansas in the 1830s and 1840s who "baptized entire families and congregations." See Will Bagley, *Blood of the Prophets: Brigham Young and the Massacre at Mountain Meadows* (Norman: University of Oklahoma Press, 2002), 20.

44. Marion County Tax Record, Microfilm Roll 12, Arkansas History Commission for years 1851, 1853, and 1855. Reuben Turner, who lived until age eighteen in John Hall's household, appeared on the tax roll for 1851 and 1853, assessed for owning one horse. He disappeared afterward, indicating that he may have migrated before the expulsion law. His double first cousin and exact contemporary, Jesse Turner, probably the son of Martin Turner, appeared only on the 1855 tax roll.

45. *Seventh Census of the United States: 1850,* Marion County, 316.

46. John Hope Franklin, *From Slavery to Freedom: A History of Negro Americans,* 3d ed. (New York: Alfred A. Knopf, 1967), 230.

47. See Brooks Blevins, *Hill Folks: A History of Arkansas Ozarkers and Their Image* (Chapel Hill: University of North Carolina Press, 2002), 31–34, for an informed summary of cotton growing in the eastern Arkansas Ozark counties.

48. Turnbo, "Dodging Bullets."

49. William Byers, who was forty-one years old at the time of the Hall trial, was born in Pennsylvania and raised in Ohio. During the Civil War, at the time of the Federal occupation of Batesville, Judge William Byers signed a loyalty oath and in 1866 tried to take his seat in Congress as an elected delegate under Presidential Reconstruction. He was denied the seat, but his testimony revealed his knowledge of and association with free Negroes before the war and he quoted the old law on legal competency of free Negroes and mulattoes in court.

"Testimony of Willaim Byers of Batesville Before the Joint Committee on Reconstruction." Washington, D.C., February 2, 1866. Reprinted in the *Independence County Chronicle*, Vol. 46 No. 1 (January 2005): 55–62.

50. Little Rock *Arkansas Gazette*, July 13, 1846.

51. Little Rock *The Whig*, November 4, 1852, and Little Rock *Arkansas Gazette*, November 5, 1852. Marion County Tax Record, 1841–1866, Microfilm Roll 12, Arkansas History Commission for 1848–1859. The years 1850 and 1856–58 are missing records.

52. Turnbo, "Dodging Bullets."

53. A good discussion of Turnbo's biases can be found in Nan Thompson Ernst, "Scenes from the Southern Frontier: Silas Claiborne Turnbo's Stories of the Ozarks," unpublished M.A. thesis, George Washington University, 1989, and available at the University of Arkansas at Little Rock Archives and Special Collections Department.

54. Batesville Track Book 24, 109, Land Entry Files, Cash Entry #6013; Marion County Tax Record, 1853. This acreage was the SE quarter of the SE quarter of Section 14, Township 19N, Range 15W.

55. Brooks Blevins, *Ozark Hill Folk*, 278 fn 31.

56. Some counties had fewer slaves than Marion County, but none had more free blacks. Eight counties, Drew, Izard, Lafayette, Madison, Pike, Polk, Searcy, and Van Buren had no free blacks in their 1850 population.

57. The 1850 census lists only thirteen blacksmiths in Marion County. None of the Halls claimed to be blacksmiths or ply any other trade but farming.

58. Vernon Burton, "The Antebellum Free Black Community: Edgefield's Rehearsal for Reconstruction," *Furman Review* 5 (Spring 1974): 24. Burton's dissertation is on this subject.

59. C. Vann Woodward, *The Strange Career of Jim Crow*, 2d rev. ed. (New York: Oxford University Press, 1966), 16–17.

60. Little Rock *Arkansas Gazette*, October 11, 1850. The Goad Company of Napoleon advertised that it had "procured another Wharf-boat at their landing which is capable of storing 800 tons of freight and is fitted up with a comfortable cabin suitable to entertain 50 persons." In the same issue, owners advertised the Arkansas River Packet Ship, *P. H. White*, a "staunch, fast-running low water steamer" that will "ply as a regular packet between Napoleon and Fort Gibson."

61. *Seventh Census of the United States:* 1850, Schedule 1, Population, Desha County, 1–15. T. L. Hodges, "Possibilities for the Archaeologist and Historian in Eastern Arkansas," *Arkansas Historical Quarterly* 2 (March 1943): 156–60; Dallas T. Herndon, "A Little of What Arkansas Was Like a Hundred Years Ago," *Arkansas Historical Quarterly* 3 (Summer 1944): 97–124.

Chapter Nine: Sojourning in Southern Missouri

1. After years where advertisements placed by fur and hide buyers listing market prices for furs in Natchez and New Orleans routinely appeared, the Batesville *News* and the Batesville *Eagle* ran fewer such notices. By the mid-1850s, in the White River hill country, agriculture, shipping, and mercantilism overshadowed hunting and gathering products in local importance and in local

interest. The Marion County Tax Record for 1852–1855 shows no listing on the roll for Peter Caulder or for Willoughby and Absalom Hall, who like Caulder sometimes hunted rather than farmed for a livelihood. Although they may have remained in the county, they may have had no taxable property.

2. Donald P. McNeilly, *The Old South Frontier: Cotton Plantations and the Formation of Arkansas Society, 1819–1861* (Fayetteville: University of Arkansas Press, 2000), 180. McNeilly concluded his interpretation with the observation that the "crowning achievement" of Arkansas planters was their success in getting Arkansas society to define *freedom* "as the right to own slaves."

3. In *Dred Scott v. Sandford* (March 6, 1857) the United States Supreme Court under the leadership of Chief Justice Roger B. Taney ruled that Dred Scott, a Negro slave, was not a citizen of the United States and not eligible to bring suit in a federal court. With the ruling the court had in effect declared unconstitutional the provision in the Missouri Compromise that permitted Congress to prohibit slavery in the territories. See Don E. Fehrenbacher, *The Dred Scott Case: Its Significance in American Law and Politics* (New York: Oxford University Press, 1978).

4. In 1837, Missouri legislators had named a new county formed on the Arkansas border in honor of Roger B. Taney. Andrew Jackson elevated Secretary of Treasury Taney to the Supreme Court as a reward for his loyalty in transferring federal funds from the Bank of the United States to state banks that Jackson favored.

5. Ira Berlin, *Slaves without Masters: The Free Negro in the Antebellum South* (New York: Pantheon Books, 1974). Margaret Ross insisted that "Mississippi passed a law expelling free Negroes before the Arkansas law was passed." Little Rock *Arkansas Gazette*, November 16, 1959. For connection between the Dred Scott ruling and the Arkansas "Act for Removal," see Don E. Fehrenbacher, *Slavery, Laws and Politics: The Dred Scott Case in Historical Perspective* (New York: Oxford University Press, 1981), 237.

6. Solomon Madewell, the namesake of his father born in 1844 before the family left Tennessee for the White River hills, appeared as a white head of household in the 1870 Benton County, Missouri, census.

7. Marion County Tax Record, 1841–1866.

8. Act No. 151, "An Act to Remove the Free Negroes and Mulattoes from this State," February 12, 1859, *Acts of the General Assembly of the State of Arkansas, 1859*, 175–78. Sheriff Stinett had trouble in serving warrants to the Cokers and may have brought several deputies with him to face the Hall family with this notice. See the tale "Indians Chase a Sheriff Ten Miles" about Stinett's problems with the mixed-blooded Coker brothers in William Monks, *A History of Southern Missouri and Northern Arkansas*, 26–27.

9. Little Rock *Arkansas Gazette*, November 6, 1858, Secretary of State Census, *Eighth Census of the United States: 1860*.

10. *Seventh Census of the United States: 1850*, Schedule 1, Population, Crawford County. The county's free black population was broken down into forty-two males and fifty females; Fort Smith's free blacks included eleven males and nineteen females.

11. New York *Weekly Anglo-African*, February 4, 1860, and February 11, 1860;

Little Rock *Arkansas True Democrat*, March 7, 1860.

12. Donnie E. Bellamy, "Free Blacks in Antebellum Missouri, 1820–1860," *Missouri Historical Review* 67:2 (1973): 205. Bellamy concluded that free blacks were surrounded by hostile attitudes that made them feel unwelcome. Evidently these attitudes were suspended in the south-central counties as Civil War approached and white Missouri Unionists saw free blacks as potential allies. *The Seventh Census of the United States: 1850* and *Eighth Census: 1860*. Enumeration for free blacks are missing for Howell and Oregon counties in the 1860 census.

13. U.S. Bureau of the Census, *The Eighth Census of the United States: 1860*, Schedule 1, Population, Marion County, Union Township, dwellings number 41 and 42.

14. *Acts of the General Assembly of the State of Arkansas, 1859*, "An Act to Remove the Free Negroes and Mulattoes from this State," February 12, 1859.

15. Little Rock *Arkansas Gazette*, December 15, 1860; January 12, 1861. The meeting of pro-Union supporters from the north-central counties met at Bluff Springs.

16. Carl Sandburg, *Abraham Lincoln: The Prairie Years*, Vol. 2 (New York: Harcourt Brace and Company, 1926). Sandburg quotes Lincoln upon his leaving Springfield, Illinois, for his inauguration: "Friends, no one who has never been placed in a like position can understand my feelings at this hour nor the oppressive sadness I feel at this parting." While Caulder and the Halls endured great suffering and loss just before and during the war triggered by Lincoln's election, in the end they gained full citizenship; C. Fred Williams, S. Charles Bolton, Carl H. Moneyhon, LeRoy T. Williams, eds., *A Documentary History of Arkansas* (Fayetteville: University of Arkansas Press, 1984), 92–96. Regarding secession, "most Arkansans in the spring of 1861 took the advice of the *Gazette* and adopted a wait-and-see attitude." Governor Rector in recommending secession to the General Assembly on December 21, 1860, mentioned Mr. Lincoln as being an embodiment of northern fanaticism and a "staunch endorser of the 'Helper' book." David Walker of Fayetteville, the president of the convention and an absentee taxpayer in Marion County, asked for unanimity of delegates, and four Unionists from the mountain counties switched their vote for the final count. Isaac Murphy of Madison County did not and left the state to join the Federal army.

17. Dowd's men became Company E, Fifth Regiment, Arkansas State Troops, July 11, 1861, under command of Col. Thomas Pleasant Dockery. As part of Brig. Gen. Nicholas Bartlett Pearce's brigade, the Fifth Regiment took part in the Battle of Wilson's Creek, Missouri, August 10, 1861, where the regiment suffered casualties of three killed and eleven wounded. Of those, Dowd's company suffered five wounded. All of the state troops were mustered out of service in late August and early September 1861, releasing the volunteers to return to their homes and organize companies for Confederate service. Most of Dowd's company subsequently enlisted in Confederate service. Several served in the Twenty-seventh Arkansas Infantry Regiment, CSA. This information was furnished courtesy of an online site created and copyrighted by Edward G. Gerdes.

18. John F. Bradbury Jr., "'Buckwheat Cake Philanthropy': Refugees and the Union Army in the Ozarks," *Arkansas Historical Quarterly* 57 (Autumn 1998): 233.

Scholars have recently taken notice of the impact of the Civil War on Arkansas people, their families, and their communities. Almost all studies further substantiate, and detail, the dreadful material and human losses suffered by the folk during the four years of the Civil War. For particularly revealing studies, see William Richter, "'Oh God, Let Us Have Revenge': Ben Griffith and His Family during the Civil War and Reconstruction," *Arkansas Historical Quarterly* 57 (Autumn 1998): 233–54; Daniel E. Sutherland, "Guerillas: The Real War in Arkansas," *Arkansas Historical Quarterly* 52 (Autumn 1993): 257–85; Kenneth C. Barnes, "The Williams Clan: Mountain Farmers and Union Fighters in North Central Arkansas," *Arkansas Historical Quarterly* 52 (Autumn 1998): 286–317; Bobby L. Lovett, "African-Americans, Civil War, and Aftermath in Arkansas," *Arkansas Historical Quarterly* 54 (Autumn 1995): 304–58; and Randy Finley, "'This Dreadful Whirlpool' of Civil War: Edward W. Gantt and the Quest for Distinction," in Randy Finley and Thomas A. DeBlack, ed., *The Southern Elite and Social Change: Essays in Honor of Willard B. Gatewood Jr.* (Fayetteville: University of Arkansas Press, 2002), 53–72. A memoir that demonstrated much of the chaos and dislocation of the Civil War in Marion County is William Monks, *A History of Southern Missouri and Northern Arkansas* (1907). Silas C. Turnbo collected a number of reminiscences about the war years from Ozark residents.

19. Monks, *A History of Southern Missouri*, 46–47.

20. Michael Fellman, "Inside Wars: The Cultural Crisis of Warfare and the Values of Ordinary People," 187–99, in Daniel E. Sutherland, ed., *Guerrillas, Unionists, and Violence on the Confederate Home Front* (Fayetteville: University of Arkansas Press, 1999). Ted Worley, "The Arkansas Peace Movement," *Journal of Southern History* (1958).

21. Military Service Records File of Moses Colder, Company I, 14th Kansas Cavalry, RG 94, National Archives, Washington, D.C. Caulder's military records show two birthplaces for the enlistee, Osage Nation and Cherokee Nation. In reality, he was born in Marion County, Arkansas, in September 1845.

22. Pension File of Mary Nelson Hall, widow of David B. Hall, Certificate No. 339234, Box No. 38968, Bundle No. 24, RG 49, National Archives, Washington, D.C. Letter from Rosetta Pope to James Houck, dated July 1, 1974, a copy of which is in the possession of the author. A brief description of David Caulder by his gradnddaughter Rosetta appears on page 4 of the handwritten letter.

23. Caulder and Cato heads of households are found in adjoining dwellings in 1870 and 1880 Bollinger County censuses. Sixteen-year-old Henry Caulder lived in the household of Louisa Cato in 1880 and Mary J. Caulder and her daughter-in-law Emma Cato dwelled together for at least ten years. A number of Cato heads of household in the 1880 Bollinger County census are listed as white while only James Cato is black. In contrast, most Catos in Cape Girardeau are listed as black in the 1880 *U.S.* Census.

24. Sutherland, "Guerillas," 257.

25. Ibid. Woodcut illustrations in this anthology portray the terrors and tragedies of the Civil War on civilians in divided loyalty locales throughout the South. The Arkansas-Missouri border country was certainly not the only internecine battleground as Sutherland's collection of essays so wonderfully reveal.

26. James J. Johnston, "Bullets for Johnny Reb: Confederate Nitre and Mining Bureau in Arkansas," *Arkansas Historical Quarterly* 49 (Summer 1990): 124. Johnston opens his study with this statement: "At the beginning of the Civil War Richmond viewed the Arkansas niter deposits as a valuable war resource and, beginning in the summer of 1862, it expended manpower and funds to develop these resources." See also Brig. Gen. E. B. Brown's report to General Curtis dated December 18, 1862, O. R. Part I, 34, 159.

27. Ibid. The Confederate army sent the hardware and a detachment to Bean's Cave to begin gunpowder manufacture. The cave was situated on a bluff directly across from the land owned by John Turner and James Hall. Acting on orders from Brig. Gen. Samuel Curtis, in April 1862 an eight-man detachment from the Third Illinois Cavalry stationed in West Plains, Missouri, led by Col. Lafayette McCrillis "crossed over (the White River) in canoes from opposite the works . . . and destroyed the operation" (137). Willoughby Hall, Absalom Hall, or David Caulder might have guided the Illinois cavalrymen in this successful raid.

28. *U.S. War Department, The War of the Rebellion: A Compilation of the Official Records of the Union and Confederate Armies* (Washington, D.C.: Government Printing Office, 1880–1891), Series I, Vol. XXII, Part I, 159–61. Hereinafter referred to as the O.R. Burch credits Willoughby Hall with guiding the detachment through the worse of weather and terrain to their successful launch of a surprise attack on the Confederate gunpowder works in Bean's Cave. Thomas Jerome Estes, "Early Days and War Times in North Arkansas," from a series of articles written for the Yellville *Mountain Echo* in 1914. Estes, a contemporary source, wrote that the Federal troops who destroyed the powder works were "led or piloted by a free negro, Willoughby Hall."

29. O.R., Brig. Gen. E. B. Brown's report to General Curtis dated December 18, 1862, O.R. Part I, 34, 159.

30. Turnbo, "How the Man Willoughby Hall Was Scalped." Bill Cain lived on Jimmie's Creek and knew the Halls from before the war. Later Cain was killed in action "in a hollow that empties into Jimmie's Creek." Turnbo, "A Few Names of Men Who Were Slain in War Days."

31. Piland's comment about the killing of Hall by McClure, made to Peter Keesee, who then related it to Silas. This was a strangely weak condemnation about a rebel act against one of his own partisans.

32. Turnbo, "How the Man Willoughby Hall Was Scalped."

33. United States Bureau of the Census, *Missouri Veterans Census: 1890,* Special Schedule, Ozark County, Bridges Township, S. D.: 4, E. D.: 148, 4, Microfilm 123–30; Bollinger County, Wayne Township S.D.: 2 E. D.: 9a, 11.

34. Ibid. Bollinger County, Lorance Township, S. D.: 2, E. D.: 6, 3.

35. Monks, *A History of Southern Missouri,* 186–89, 194. Robert Gilliland, father of Jim Gilliland, Willoughby Hall's companion at the time of his death, was mentioned as an unswerving loyalist of Ozark County along with Hall.

36. U.S. Bureau of the Census, *The Ninth Census of the United States,* 1870, Missouri, Bollinger County, Wayne Township, dwelling 103.

37. John R., Irvine, Marion, and Amanda Hall disappeared from the southern Missouri historical record.

38. Whites might feel that black people who passed for white did so without support from other black people. Far from meeting resistance inside the black community, many black people felt as though it was necessary for those blacks light enough to pass to do just that. See the comments of black Seattle newspaper editor Horace Cayton about the operation and objectives of "turning white" from a black person's viewpoint in Willard B. Gatewood Jr., "The Perils of Passing: The McCarys of Omaha," *Nebraska History* (Summer 1990): 67.

39. In order to cut down on embarrassment and risks of being discovered when permanently crossing over, blacks often determined to break cleanly with their relatives and former close friends.

40. West Plains *Howell County Gazette*, January 5, January 12, and January 26, 1900; Pension file of Mary A. Caulder, widow of Moses Caulder, Certificate No. 553339, Can No. 48132, Bundle No. 20, RG 94, National Archives, Washington, D.C. The Gilliland family had known and associated with the Halls and Caulders since the Marion County, Arkansas, years. In filing affidavits for Mary A. Hall to collect a widow's pension, James Hall mentioned his cousin's habit of "taking up with and running with lewd women" as did T. J. Hall a lifelong friend of Moses.

41. The same is true for John Hall's 39.7-acre tract that he patented from the government in 1855.

42. A white John Hall appeared as a Marion County landowner after the war, but he may not have been the prosperous mulatto of the 1850s who carried the same name. New Deal mega dam experts calculated that the White River narrows would be a good place for a barrier that could generate electricity and control floodwaters. Putting the concept into action in 1947, the Army Corps of Engineers first had to search out legal ownership of lands to be inundated by a reservoir. A title insurance company concluded that David Hall Sr. and his heirs had never alienated their patent to the seventy-one acres on the White River. That finding just happened to be incorrect because David Hall Sr. and Sarah had conveyed that property to John D. Noe in October 1850 for $425. The deed was recorded in retrospect, but there is no doubt of its authenticity, which meant that the Noe family held the land legally rather than with "extralegal interest" as the title insurance company ruled. Despite this cloud and the inaccuracies, the title was quieted, someone got paid for the Hall land, and construction of the dam got under way. Completed in 1952, Bull Shoals Dam backed a hundred feet of lake water over the riverbank farmland that had been at the core of the Hall-Caulder-Turner families.

43. Promise Land Cemetery is on a ridge of the same name above the ravine cut by Sister Creek. A mile below the church and cemetery, accessible by a winding one-way dirt road, is the Promise Land Resort, which fronts the lake.

Epilogue

1. The Pape store in the heart of Zalma burned to the ground in March 2002. Historians and researchers of southern Bollinger County lost not only a landmark building but also a wealth of photographs, newspaper clippings, hand written commentaries, and scrapbooks collected by local historians and genealo-

gists that were kept there. Zalma residents lost their only grocery, hardware store, and information center.

2. Interview with Dolores Abernathy Jackson, July 18, 2001, and letter from Dolores A. Jackson in author's possession dated July 27, 2001. Ms. Jackson mentioned that the Caulder and Hall farmsteads adjoined the cemetery which is located in the NE ¼ of SE ¼ section 36, Township 29N, Range 8E, of Bollinger County, Missouri. David Hall Jr./Sr. patented his land in section 25 of the same township and range. Also in the Hall Church Cemetery, which has been preserved by the efforts of Ms. Jackson and other relatives, are graves of several Cato, Deckard, and Randolph family members, relatives by marriage with the Caulder and Hall families. Ms. Jackson mentioned that David Hall Jr./Sr.'s wife, Margaret, who had come with him from Arkansas, died in 1868 (actually 1862). Margaret was buried in Condor Cemetery located upriver two and half miles from the Hall homestead. According to a local legend, David Hall Jr./Sr., who had been gunshot wounded while in service with the Missouri State Cavalry in 1862, was shot again while plowing by a bushwhacker, Sam Hildebrand, after the war. The attacker left him for dead, but he stumbled and crawled to Margaret's grave where he was found the next day lying across it. David Hall Jr./Sr. survived. In 1863, Hall married Mary A. Nelson of St. Louis, who bore him a son, David Hall Jr., and a daughter named Dora. Dora Hall married Benton Randolph. Dora and Benton and children were the last of the family to live in the Hall homestead in Wayne Township, Bollinger County, Missouri. Mary L. Hahn, ed., *Bollinger County, 1851–1976: A Bicentennial Commemorative* (Marceline, Mo.: Walsworth Publishing Co., 1977), 793.

3. David Caulder's place of burial is not recorded, but it seems logical for it to be the Hall Cemetery, which contains some unmarked and unrecorded graves. A widow's pension claim by Matilda Hall dated June 29, 1880, specified 1876 as the year of death for David Caulder. Another document in the pension file had it two years earlier on December 10, 1874. Pension file of Eldridge Hill, Certificate No. 197821, Box No. 34480, RG 94, National Archives, Washington, D.C.

4. The third generation of Halls and Caulders appeared to be illiterate, odd since Dave Hall Jr./Sr. donated valuable property on which to build a school.

5. Jim Abernathy, "Old Time Zalma Services Came from the Heart," newspaper article in author's possession and from Dolores Jackson interview of March 2001. Hall arranged to arrive late on selected Sunday mornings. With the church already full of expectant parishioners, Hall would pull his wagon alongside the front door of the church and his wife, Dora, a jolly woman, would climb down. She would ascend rickety steps into the church while Dave continued on to a hitching rack by the back door. Rushing from the wagon, Brother Dave would begin to sing a hymn, "Send the Light," in his powerful bass voice cueing Dora to commence in harmony. As preacher and wife entered the church from opposite ends, the congregation, excited by the dramatic and stereophonic start to the service would join in, "Send the Light . . . We have heard the Macedonian call today, Send the Light, Send the Light!!!" These enthusiastic Baptists of Hall Church attended services sitting on benches built from sawmill slabs with log stumps for legs.

6. Quit-Claim Deed from Peter Thomas Caulder and Sarah R. Caulder dated November 13, 1894, Bollinger County Circuit Court Record of Deeds, Marble

Hill, Missouri.

7. Silas C. Turnbo, "A Long Time Ago."

8. *Index of Abstracts and Deeds*, Ozark County Circuit Clerk, Gainesville, Missouri, Lien and Mortgage to William Hammonds, November 12, 1878, I, A, 160–61. Joseph Hall and Brown Hall mortgaged crops in favor of John W. Lewis. Moses Caulder consorted after his return from the Civil War with a Marion County woman named Jemima. She eventually deserted Caulder in favor of a man named "Brown." This interloper may well have been Brown Hall, a relative and probably a close acquaintance of the couple. Testimony of T. J. Hall, dated June 14, 1902, in Pension File of Mary A. Caulder, widow of Moses Caulder, Certificate No. 553339, Can No. 48132, Bundle No. 20, RG 49, National Archives, Washington, D.C.

9. Willard B. Gatewood Jr., "The Perils of Passing: The McCarys of Omaha," *Nebraska History* (Summer 1990): 64–70. Professor Gatewood writes that because of "the secretive nature of permanent passing, it is impossible to ascertain how many black Americans actually passed. Estimates ranged from a few hundred to many thousands annually."

10. West Plains *Howell County Gazette*, January 28, 1904. A news article announced the death of Henderson Hall at the supposed age of 105. The editor described Hall's Portuguese heritage as being often mistaken for "Negro blood." So convinced were the school authorities that Hall's children were "colored" that they barred them from admission to the district school.

11. *Muskogee Times-Democrat*, February 15, 1908. Under the heading, "Supposed Negro is White Man says Courts," this newspaper article described the trial. "In the most peculiar trial of its kind ever heard of in this part of the world, Henderson Hall, a well-educated Missourian who came to these parts some years ago, has been acquitted of a charge of neggro (*sic*) blood and, it is believed, will in the future be allowed by his neighbors to take his place among them as a white man."

12. Howell County Circuit Clerk, Circuit Court Records, Book Z, 134–35, May 5, 1890. "Thomas Hall Proof of Race Affidavit." Someone filed the affadivit in Howell County a year and a half after Thomas Hall's death. Most likely, it was used in both of the James Henderson Hall trials of racial verification.

13. Luther P. Jackson, *Free Negro Labor and Property Holding in Virginia, 1830–1860* (New York and London: D. Appleton-Century Company, 1942), 3, 5.

14. John Hope Franklin, *From Slavery to Freedom: A History of Negro Americans*, 3d ed. (New York: Alfred A. Knopf, 1976); Vernon Burton, "The Antebellum Free Black Community: Edgefield's Rehearsal for Reconstruction," *Furman Review* 5 (Spring 1974): 18–26. However, South Carolina legal restrictions on free black rights astutely sewed distrust between races into the body politic.

BIBLIOGRAPHICAL ESSAY

Primary Sources

Military Records

Peter Caulder wrote no letters and kept no diaries and therefore falls into a biographical category termed inarticulate. To compound the problem of a lack of personal papers, Caulder resided most of his life in sparsely settled frontier regions where overall literacy rates were low. Nevertheless, as the investigation proceeded, material documenting his actions if not his actual words surfaced from several sources. Because he was a veteran of the War of 1812 and served in two regiments over twelve years in the United States Army, his name appeared on a number of army muster rolls and monthly inspection returns, available in textual form at the National Archives in Washington, D.C. A pamphlet compiled by Lucille H. Pendell and Elizabeth Bethel, "Preliminary Inventory of the Records of the Adjutant General's Office" (Washington, D.C.: National Archives, 1949), is a starting point for research of these materials. Most accessible of textual records (meaning those that do not appear on the microfilm indexes of the National Archives) are the "Flattened Muster Rolls and Returns," Record Group 94, in which handwritten returns have been preserved, boxed, and organized according to company commander's name. Examples of such textual records and their citation that would allow a pull from the archives would be Box 139A: *Riflemen, July 1815–December 1818, Field and Staff to Company: Bradford*, or Volume 205, *Captain T. J. Robison and W. Coles Company Muster and Receipt Rolls, Third Rifles, 1814–15*.

Inspection returns for the Seventh Infantry between 1823 and 1828 exist but have not been processed and are still housed in their original folders and file boxes, making them more difficult to access and to use. Although military records from the early nineteenth century continue to be processed by the National Archives staff, the progress has been slow and without high priority. Some monthly returns for army posts, including Fort Smith and Fort Gibson, and for the Seventh Infantry Regiment, have been microfilmed. Muster Rolls and Inspection Returns are a part of Record Group 94.

For biographical information about soldiers and their stationing within the army, one may refer to the *Registers of Enlistments in the United States Army, 1798–1914*, Microfilm 233, Record Group 94, National Archives, Washington, D.C., in 81 rolls, organized by last name of individuals, further alphabetized by first names. *Registers of Enlistments* includes age, place of birth, place of enlistment, height, eye, hair, and complexion coloring, and a brief summary of service for officers and enlisted men. See the pamphlet *Military Service Records: A Select Catalog of National Archives Microfilm Publications* (Washington, D.C.: National Archives, 1985). The *Registers of Enlistments* for regular soldiers is far more resourceful than is the *Index to Compiled Service Records of Volunteer Soldiers Who Served During the War of 1812*, Microfilm 602, 234 rolls, Record Group 94, which offers only the name of the unit and the dates of service for the volunteer soldiers. Letter files to and from officers and the War Department are available also in Record Group 94, but seldom if ever do officers mention enlisted men by name in their written reports. Caulder, for example, was not referred to by name in any letter from Bradford or Arbuckle.

Sutler Account Books

Names of enlisted men and civilians appear in handwritten account books of the post store at Fort Smith. Three such account books are known to exist and cover the period from 1820 to 1823. The *Fort Smith Trader's Account Book* for May 1820 to June 1821 is located in the Gilcrease Museum Archives in Tulsa, Oklahoma. The *Fort Smith Sutler's Account Book, 1821–1822*, held by the Arkansas History Commission in Little Rock, Arkansas, has been placed on microfilm as has the *Account Book of the Post Trader at Fort Smith, 1822–23*, in the Beineke Rare Book and Manuscript Collection at Yale University. Store clerks recorded credit sales and purchases. These ledgers reveal a good deal about the habits of soldiers and civilians in and about the fort. Laxness by the army in providing regular pay days for soldiers proved beneficial to modern researchers because day-to-day activities at the store are therefore documented on the account books.

County Tax Records

Existing county tax records in antebellum Arkansas have been microfilmed by the Arkansas History Commission. Useful to this manuscript were personal property tax rolls for Crawford, Izard, and Marion counties. These tax rolls show the value and number of slave and livestock holdings of individual taxpayers and sometimes the description of their real estate holdings. See *Crawford County Records, Tax Records 1821–1851*, Roll #22, Arkansas History Commission (Fort Smith was a part of Crawford County until the creation of Sebastian County in 1852); *Izard County Tax Records, 1829–1866*, Roll #16, Arkansas History Commission (the upper White River and the Little North Fork were part of Izard County until the creation of Marion County in 1836); *Marion County Tax Record, 1841–1866*, Roll #13, Arkansas History Commission.

Censuses

James Logan Morgan, *1820 Census of the Territory of Arkansas—Reconstructed* (Newport, Ark.: Morgan Books, 1984). *The Fifth Census of the United States: 1830* and the *Sixth Census of the United States: 1840* provide the names of heads of household, their race, and the number of occupants in each dwelling assorted by age groups. For the *Seventh Census of the United States: 1850*, marshals and their assistants recorded name and age of each member of a household and their race, literacy, occupation, and place of birth. In addition to the Enumerated Census for 1850, the Agricultural Manuscript Census for 1850 provides an inventory of farm holdings by a number of, but not all rural residents in selected counties and townships within those counties. Census records and the Soundex locator system are on microfilm in dozens of libraries, genealogical research rooms, and archives throughout the state. The Arkansas History Commission will furnish a researcher with a list of their "United States Census Records on Microfilm." County libraries are a source for print copies of enumerated censuses for their county. Special Collections of the Mullins Library, University of Arkansas, holds the original handwritten Agricultural Manuscript Census for 1850 and 1860. Sheriff Censuses taken in a few counties were reprinted in the *Arkansas Gazette* in 1823, 1827, and 1829.

Journals

Journals and letters of contemporary travelers offered details and insight into life patterns, events, and the environment of Peter Caulder while he sojourned at Fort Smith and on the White River. Most of these early journals have been edited by scholars or reprinted by various publishing companies, and as with Nuttall and Schoolcraft, several versions are available. Thomas Nuttall, an English naturalist stayed in Fort Smith for several weeks in 1819 and recorded his observations about the fort, the surroundings, and his adventures with Bradford and his soldiers in *A Journal of Travels into the Arkansa Territory, During the Year 1819* (Ann Arbor, Mich.: University Microfilms, Inc., 1966; originally published 1823). See also the edited version of Nuttalls's journal by Savoie Lattinville (Norman: University of Oklahoma Press, 1980). Several original letters of Nuttall to his Philadelphia-based sponsors are reprinted in Richard Beidleman, "The 1818–20 Arkansas Journal of Thomas Nuttall," *Arkansas Historical Quarterly* 15 (Autumn 1956): 249–59. Young Henry Schoolcraft traveled down the White River over the winter of 1818 and 1819 and touched the same location as David Hall settled a year later. Milton D. Rafferty edited his journal published as *Rude Pursuits and Rugged Peaks: Schoolcraft's Ozark Journal, 1818–1819* (Fayetteville: University of Arkansas Press, 1996). Frederick Gerstaecker, *Wild Sports in the Far West* (Durham, N.C.: Duke University Press, 1968; originally published in 1844), somehow managed to miss Fort Smith and the upper White River, but he did wander about the Ozarks staying with settlers and engaging with them in bear hunts and icy baths. Where bear hunting is concerned, Charles F. M. Noland, an Independence County writer and adventurer of considerable fame, seized upon the vocabulary and attitudes of an antebellum White River bear hunter for his fictional tales, and a number of them have been edited and reprinted by Ted R. Worley and Eugene A. Nolte in *Pete Whetstone of Devil's Fork: Letters to the "Spirit of the Times"* (Van Buren, Ark.: Press-Argus, 1957).

Harlan M. Fuller and LeRoy R. Hafen edited *The Journal of Captain John R. Bell, Official Journalist for the Stephen H. Long Expedition to the Rocky Mountains, 1820* (Glendale, Calif.: Arthur H. Clark Company, 1957). Bell refers to Caulder by name in his journal only because he suspected him. Regrettably, a second man from Fort Smith who accompanied Caulder to Glenn's Trading Post went unnamed by Bell. Long had split his expedition into two trains for the return trek and naturalist Edwin James wrote a journal separate from Bell's entitled *Account of an Expedition from Pittsburgh to the Rocky Mountains, Performed in the Years 1819 and 1820*. (Ann Arbor, Mich.: University Microfilms, 1966; originally published 1823). James referred to the warm reception afforded the group at the house of the soldier and his wife across the river from the fort. For a stirring account of Long's earlier exploration along the western rivers, see Maj. Stephen H. Long, "Voyage in a Six-Oared Skiff to the Falls of Saint Anthony in 1817," in *Collections of the Minnesota Historical Society, Volume II 1860–67* (St. Paul, Minn.: Minnesota Historical Society; originally published in 1889 with introduction by E. D. Neill). Long's river voyage up the Mississippi was in the same skiff that he, Caulder, and six other soldiers would take up the Arkansas later in the winter of 1817. In a letter to Gen. Thomas A. Smith, dated May 12, 1818 a photocopy of which is found in I-105 file, Fort Smith (Arkansas) National Historic Site, Arkansas Major Long described his exploratory route taken from Belle Point to the Red River to Hot Springs and to Belle Fontaine in the company of four soldiers who are unnamed in the letter.

Journals of Santa Fe trail traders who set out from Fort Smith shed light on military and civilian residents here and at Fort Gibson: Elliot Coues, ed., *The Journal of Jacob Fowler* (Lincoln: University of Nebraska Press, 1970; preface and notes by Raymond W. and Mary Lund Settle and Harry R. Stevens); and Milo Milton Quaife, ed., *Gen. Thomas James, Three Years Among the Indians and Mexicans* (New York: Citadel Press, 1966);

Local Histories

Several local writers described people and events of the White River hills in the years of Peter Caulder. William Monks, a Unionist cavalryman and a postwar lawyer in Howell County, described the conflicts between pro-Union and secessionist families that he had personally witnessed in *A History of Southern Missouri and Northern Arkansas: Being an Account of the Early Settlements, the Civil War, the Ku-Klux, and Times of Peace* (Fayetteville, Ark.: University of Arkansas Press, 2003); John F. Bradbury Jr. and Lou Wehmer, eds., *Historical and Biographical Sketches of the Early Settlement of the Valley of White River Together with a History of Izard County by A. C. Jeffery* (Richmond, Va.: Jeffery Historical Society, 1973); W. B. Flippin, "Marion County as She Was When Settled In 1836," *Yellville Mountain Echo*, May 9, 1899. See also John Joseph Mathews, *The Osages: Children of the Middle Waters* (Norman: University of Oklahoma Press, 1961), which is a collection of oral histories of the Missouri-Arkansas-Oklahoma tribe with a warring reputation of which Mathews is a member.

Newspapers

The *Arkansas Gazette* is indexed from its first edition in November 1819. Other Arkansas newspapers from the antebellum era are not indexed and accordingly are less helpful to the researcher than the *Gazette*. They include the *Fort Smith Herald*, available on microfilm beginning in 1848, the *Arkansas Banner*, the *Batesville Eagle 1848–1850*, the *Batesville News 1838–1842*, and the *Arkansas Advocate*.

The *Niles Weekly Register* printed in Baltimore, especially the issues from 1815–1826, tracked the configuration of the United States Army and printed the occasional dispatch from newspapers west of the Mississippi River. For the War of 1812 period, the *Daily National Intelligencer* published in Washington, D.C., kept its readers posted on the ebb and flow of the war and the accompanying politics. Both of these eastern newspapers are on microfilm and are self-indexed. The *Howell County* (Missouri) *Gazette* of January 1900, available on microfilm in the West Plains Public Library, un-indexed, and the *Muskogee* (Oklahoma) *Times-Democrat* of February 1908 available on microfilm in the Muskogee Public Library, indexed, carried articles about descendants of Peter Caulder and David Hall.

Land Records

Circuit clerk records in county courthouses include deeds, mortgages, legal actions, and records of marriages and deaths. Deed books are organized by years and indexed according to grantee and grantor. The search for land patent records in the state is helped by Desmond Walls Allen and Bobbie Jones McLane's *Arkansas Land Patents* (Conway, Ark.: Arkansas Research, 1991) for each county. This index yields a document number to be used on search requests for original purchase records and cash entries by an individual at a United States Government Land Office. Those records are digitized and are accessible online. The address is http://www.glorecords.blm.gov, which allows you to download a facsimile of the original warrant. Cash payments by the patentee were made a year or two in advance of the issue of the deed. Those cash entry records, which provide a little more detail about the purchase, are available from the Bureau of Land Management. The steps to acquiring cash (entry) files are outlined in the pamphlet, *Research in the Land Entry Files of the General Land Office* (Washington, D.C., 1997). Copies of the bounty land warrants issued to veterans of the War of 1812, such as Peter Caulder and Martin Turner, are also available at the glorecords.blm.gov site. These soldiers' applications included their enlistment and discharge papers. For names of Arkansas warrantees, warrant numbers, and dates, see the pamphlet by Katheren Christensen, *Arkansas Military Bounty Grants, War of 1812* (Hot Springs, Ark.: Arkansas Ancestors, 1971). With a warrant number, a researcher may proceed to a request for the Military Service Records and Pension Application Files of a bounty land claimant. National Archives and Records Administration (NARA) forms on which to file requests are available from county and municipal libraries. The NARA accepts no other format for record requests and charges a small fee for successful searches. Virgil D. White has helped speed the process with his *Index to War of 1812 Pension Files* (Waynesboro, Tenn.: National Historical Publishing Company, 1989).

A source for surveyor's reports for the antebellum era is the Arkansas State Land Commission in Little Rock. At the commission, historical surveys are filed according to county and township. Notes and map symbols reveal cultivation patterns and other conditions at the time of survey. A limited number of historical materials including surveys, deeds, title proceedings, and cemetery relocations in Arkansas are available from the Corps of Engineers, Real Estate Division, Little Rock District, Little Rock, Arkansas, if like the White River, a dam impounded farmland and homesteads and private property was condemned for purchase.

Papers

The Thomas Adams Smith papers at the Western Historical Manuscript Collection on the campus of the University of Missouri at Columbia include seven volumes and four folders of letters sent by and to General Smith during the years 1813–1818. The collection of Andrew Jackson papers archived at the Library of Congress is being systematically digitized for online reference. The Stephen H. Long Papers at the Minnesota Historical Society in St. Paul include Herman Ralph Friis, ed., "Stephen H. Long's Unpublished Manuscript Map of the United States, Compiled in 1820–22."

Oral Histories and Interviews

Biographical material on the Hall family of Marion County and on the lives of many other White River hills settlers can be found in the Turnbo Manuscripts. The manuscripts were written by Silas Claiborne Turnbo, an itinerant and self-taught oral historian who lived on the Arkansas-Missouri borderlands in the early twentieth century. Two collections of his works exist, fittingly one in Arkansas and one in Missouri. The complete set of handwritten stories by Turnbo is held by the Library Center of Springfield-Greene County in Springfield, Missouri. The originals have been transcribed and bound in volumes with indexes and are on the shelves of the research room. In addition, the manuscripts have been digitized and made available on the internet by the Library Center. Typewritten Turnbo stories are part of the J. N. Heiskell Collection of the University of Arkansas at Little Rock Library Archives. In addition, two published versions of selected Turnbo stories are available at most libraries and they are: James F. Keefe and Lynn Morrow, *The White River Chronicles of S. C. Turnbo: Man and Wildlife on the Ozarks Frontier* (Fayetteville: University of Arkansas Press, 1996); and Desmond Walls Allen, ed., *Turnbo's Tales of the Ozarks*, 8 volumes (Conway, Ark.: Arkansas Research, 1987, 1989).

Secondary Sources

Race

A few articles and several book-length accounts of free black lives contribute immensely to understanding the variety of responses to rising anti-black conditions in the antebellum South. Willard B. Gatewood Jr.'s thorough research and his organizational talents in editing the diary of a black Virginian in *Free Man of Color: The Autobiography of Willis Augustus Hodges* (Knoxville: University of Tennessee Press, 1982) provides readers with an unaccustomed look into the daily life of and the issues faced by a dynamic Southern free black man. Edwin Adams Davis and William Ransom Hogan coauthored *The Barber of Natchez* (Baton Rouge: Louisiana State University Press, 1954; reprinted in 1973), which relates the unusual story of William Johnson, a prosperous and assertive free black businessman in Natchez, Mississippi. Remarkable parallels can be found in the life and actions of a Kentuckian known simply as Free Frank with that of David Hall, Peter Caulder's father-in-law. See Juliet E. K. Walker's *Free Frank: A Black Pioneer on the Antebellum Frontier* (Lexington: University of Kentucky Press, 1983). William L. Cheek and Aimee Lee Cheek, teachers, humanists, and scholars, reconstructed the life of a prominent free black man born on a Virginia plantation in *John Mercer Langston and the Fight for Black Freedom, 1829–1865* (Urbana: University of Illinois Press, 1989). Ruth Polk Patterson collected oral histories and artifacts of her extended family roots in rural Arkansas. Her book, *The Seed of Sally Good'n: A Black Family of Arkansas, 1833–1953* (Lexington: University of Kentucky Press, 1985), is a wondrous addition to the historiography of the state. The story of a remarkable mulatto South Carolinian, William Ellison appears in Michael P. Johnson and James L. Roark's *Black Masters: A Free Family of Color in the Old South, 1984* (New York: Norton, 1984). Set in the same state, Vernon Burton's study of an 1850s community in western South Carolina demonstrated that rural free black families existed side by side and in harmony with their white southern counterparts in "The Antebellum Free Black Community: Edgefield's Rehearsal for Reconstruction," *Furman Review* 5 (Spring 1974): 18–26. Marie Tedesco supplies substantial evidence that Adam Waterford, "A Free Black Slave Owner in East Tennessee," in *Appalachians and Race: The Mountain South from Slavery to Segregation*, ed. John C. Inscoe (Lexington: University of Kentucky Press, 2001), interacted with his white neighbors and adversaries as equals in business and in court actions. See also Elizabeth Fortson Arroyo, "Poor Whites, Slaves, and Free Blacks in Tennessee, 1796–1861," *Tennessee Historical Quarterly* 55 (Spring 1996): 57–65; and Margaret Ross Smith, "Nathan Warren, A Free Negro for the Old South," *Arkansas Historical Quarterly* 15 (Spring 1956): 53–61.

Hardly any of these studies directed toward free blacks who carved out a degree of independence and respect for themselves and their family members in the South had been published at the time that Ira Berlin researched and wrote *Slaves without Masters: The Free Negro in the Antebellum South* (New York: New Press, 1974). Instead, the prominent scholarship pointed to the subservience of southern free blacks. Wilbur Zelinsky's "The Population Geography of the Free Negro in Ante-Bellum America," *Population Studies* 3 (1949–50): 386–401; John Hope Franklin's *From Slavery to Freedom: A History of Negro Americans*, 3d ed. (New York: Alfred A. Knopf, 1976); Franklin's original scholarship and his commendable insight made his a foundation work for studying the African American experience. Nevertheless, his chapter on "Quasi-Free Negroes" omits discussion of rural and yeoman blacks in the South. Zelinsky wrote that status of the free Negro had been treated "exhaustively in essays" and concluded that they "as a group had not greatly advanced above the slave population." A revealing look at the stilted attitudes held by influential politicians toward free blacks can be found in Bruce Rosen's "Abolition and Colonization: The Years of Conflict, 1829–1834," in the anthology *Freedom's Odyssey: African American History Essays from Phylon*, ed. Alexa Benson Henderson and Janice Sumler-Edmond (Atlanta, Ga.: Clark Atlanta University Press, 1999). Older state studies include James Blackwell Browning, "The Free Negro in Ante-Bellum North Carolina," *North Carolina Historical Review* 15 (January 1938): 23–33; J. Merton England, "The Free Negro in Ante-Bellum Tennessee," *Journal of Southern History* 9 (February 1943): 37–58; Marina Wikramanayake, *A World in Shadow: The Free Black in Antebellum South Carolina* (Columbia: University of South Carolina Press, 1973); and Donnie E. Bellamy, "Free Blacks in Antebellum Missouri, 1820–1860," *Missouri Historical Review* 67:2 (1973): 198–226. These studies reveal three aspects of the free black experience: white antipathy toward free blacks after the Vesey, Gabriel, and especially Nat Turner rebellions; the plethora of legal restrictions aimed at free blacks as a result; and the plight of urban free blacks, who were often older, single, and repressed (but who left more documentation of their actions and thoughts). These studies say little about the rural agricultural communities established by free blacks both in the old northwest territory and in the slave South and their relationships with white neighbors. The older scholarship, crucial as it was, also narrowed the field and the conclusions about the state of mind of free blacks, as well as the state of mind of white Americans that existed in the decades before the Civil War. While Berlin built his compelling interpretation on sturdy scholarship and his work remains a landmark in the field, the recent historiographical trend might modify his thesis, if not undermine his title. While many whites in the South insisted on hard and fast lines of race and the acceptance of that line by both whites and blacks, their view was not universal. Ambivalence, not rigidity, marked attitudes toward free blacks by a considerable number of Southern white yeomen, at least until the mid-1850s. White and black neighbors could and did hammer out mutually beneficial communities. Abject submission, and the requirement for it, did not apply to all southern free blacks any more than it did to all northern free blacks. On the building of a statewide community and an examination of the important question of what groups would or would not be included, see David Sloan, "The Louisiana Purchase, Expansion, and the Limits of Community: The Example of Arkansas," *Arkansas Historical Quarterly* 62 (Winter 2003): 404–22. Colonial, that is to say American, ambivalence in general is presented in a classic study by Michael Kammen in *People of Paradox: An Inquiry concerning the Origins of American Civilization* (New York: Alfred Knopf, 1972; reprinted in paperback by Cornell University Press in 1990).

In the mid-1850s, however, ambivalence became a social luxury that few whites could or would afford as momentum built toward making color the sole delineation for citizenship. Blacks were, of course, the "other people" in the Constitution. The Dred Scott case might have been as Eric Foner wrote, "morally reprehensible, but it was good constitutional law." Foner in his reflective article, "Blacks in the U.S. Constitution," that appeared in *Who Owns History: Rethinking the Past in a Changing World* (New York: Hill and Wang, 2002), reminded us of Roger B. Taney's argument that blacks "had no rights which the white man was bound to respect." Racism thus became the point and accordingly, the legal classification of "black or white" became arguably the most serious test a person of mixed ancestry faced in antebellum America. Certainly the free black communities of Arkansas, made up of mixed-ancestry people who were classified as mulattoes, would be destroyed by state law. With regard to the historiography and bibliography of the Taney court's most-famous, most-hailed, and most-derided decision, see Don E. Fehrenbacher, *The Dred Scott Case: Its Significance in Law and Politics* (New York: Oxford University Press, 1978), or his abridged edition, *Slavery, Laws, and Politics: The Dred Scott Case in Historical Perspective* (New York: Oxford University Press, 1981). It is important to remember that not only was there dissent on the Supreme Court bench, but that many white Americans reviled the Taney majority decision, not just because it expanded slavery into territories but also because it denied free black citizenship.

Defining black as a legal term is the task undertaken by Paul Finkleman, who collects a series of scholarly examinations on the subject in *Slavery and the Law* (Madison, Wisc.: Madison House Publishers, 1997). See also Ariela J. Gross, "Litigating Whiteness: Trials of Racial Determination in the Nineteenth-Century South," *Yale Law Journal* 108 (1998): 107–88. Joel Williamson focuses on the unique status held by mulattoes in colonial and early America in *New People: Miscegenation and Mulattoes in the United States* (New York: Free Press, 1980). Changes in the hectic decades before the Civil War are traced by Robert Brent Toplin, "Between Black and White: Attitudes toward Southern Mulattoes, 1830–1861," *Journal of Southern History* 45 (May 1979): 185–200.

Crossing the color line was, if not common, possible for blacks with enough white genes and sometimes even encouraged by their white neighbors. These intersections of cultural history have been documented in two recent studies: James M. O'Toole, *Passing for White: Race, Religion, and the Healy Family, 1820–1920* (Amherst: University of Massachusetts Press, 2001); Willard B.

Gatewood Jr., "The Perils of Passing: The McCarys of Omaha," *Nebraska History* (Summer 1990): 64–70. See also a worthy web article by Wendy Ann Gaudin entitled "Passing for White in Jim Crow America," located by following links at http://www.jimcrowhistory.org

Other useful studies of free blacks and slavery in antebellum America include Brenda E. Stevenson, *Life in Black and White: Family and Community in the Slave South* (New York: Oxford University Press, 1996); Andrew Jackson O'Shaughnessy, *An Empire Divided: The American Revolution and the British Caribbean* (Philadelphia: University of Pennsylvania Press, 2000); Letitia Woods Brown, *Free Negroes in the District of Columbia, 1790–1846* (New York: Pantheon Books, 1975); and Loren Schweninger, *Black Property Owners in the South, 1790–1915* (Urbana and Chicago: University of Illinois Press, 1990). John Hope Franklin's *The Militant South: 1800–1861* (Cambridge: Harvard University Press, 1956) describes the militancy of whites, as led by the slave owners, toward blacks and mentions that patrols apprehended "all Negroes" who were not in their proper places. Winthrop Jordan's *White over Black: American Attitudes to the Negro, 1150–1812* (Chapel Hill: University of North Carolina Press, 1968) remains an essential study to the understanding of the effects of slavery and skin color, and his earlier article "American Chiaroscuro: The Status and Definitions of Mulattoes in the British Colonies," *William and Mary Quarterly* 19 (1962): 183–200, helps explain how New World colonists developed racial categories.

To examine the stratification of the period under exciting new light, two recent studies reconstructed the antebellum worldview imagined and created by slaveholders *and* slaves. Walter Johnson offers an innovative and original look at the operation of slave markets and their pervasive effect on the societies in which the market existed in *Soul by Soul: Life inside the Antebellum Slave Market* (Cambridge: Harvard University Press, 2000); and Robert Blair St. George edits *Possible Pasts: Becoming Colonial in Early America* (Ithaca, N.Y.: Cornell University Press, 2000), in which a series of articles explore how the concepts of colonialism evolved in the imaginations of colonial people.

Military Histories

An appropriate starting point for study of the War of 1812 is John R. Elting's *Amateurs to Arms: A Military History of the War of 1812* (Chapel Hill, N.C.: Algonquin Books of Chapel Hill, 1991); and see Donald R. Hickey, *The War of 1812: A Forgotten Conflict* (Urbana: University of Illinois Press, 1989). In *The Dawn's Early Light* (New York: W. W. Norton and Company, 1972), the historian Walter Lord presented a scholarly yet highly readable account of War of 1812 events that include a detailed account of the Greenleaf Point Arsenal and its explosion. David S. and Jeanne T. Heidler in their *Encyclopedia of the War of 1812* (Santa Barbara, Calif.: ABC-Clio, 1997) include an entry on Thomas Adams Smith, but omit Bvt. Maj. William Bradford. John C.

Frederickson has published a brief volume on the Rifle Regiment, *Green Coats and Glory: The United States Regiment of Riflemen, 1808–1821* (Youngstown, N.Y.: Old Fort Niagara Association, 2000); J. C. A. Staggs, "Enlisted Men in the United States Army, 1812–1815: A Preliminary Study," *William and Mary Quarterly* 43 (October 1986): 615–45, should not be missed and gives the most complete statistics on men of color who enlisted. Henry Putnam Beers published his University of Pennsylvania dissertation as *The Western Military Frontier, 1815–1846* (Gettysburg, Pa.: Times and News Publishing Company, 1935). Francis Paul Prucha in *Broadax and Bayonets: The Role of the United States Army in the Development of the Northwest, 1815–1860* (Lincoln and London: University of Nebraska Press, 1953, reprinted in 1995) whets the cutting edge that the army became on the frontier with an excellent bibliography of oft-ignored military records. The Cherokee scholar Grant Foreman studied the contributions made by the army in taming and claiming the trans-Mississippi, and of equal importance, in providing later historians with documents to verify that role, and wrote a brace of books: *Indians and Pioneers: The Story of the American Southwest before 1830* (New Haven, Conn.: Yale University Press, 1930) and *Advancing the Frontier, 1830–1860* (Norman: University of Oklahoma Press, 1933). David Michael Delo in *Peddlers and Post Traders: The Army Sutler on the Frontier* (Salt Lake City: University of Utah Press, 1992) omitted any mention of Hugh Glenn and little about Fort Smith sutlers in his otherwise illuminating study on a neglected facet of western expansion.

For enlistment and participation by black soldiers in the U.S. Army, see Gerald T. Altoff, *Amongst My Best Men: African-Americans and the War of 1812* (Put-in-Bay, Ohio: Perry Group, 1996). Jack D. Foner, *Blacks and the Military in American History* (New York: Praeger Publishers, 1974), contains a bibliographic essay that specifies most, perhaps all, of the scholarship that existed then about black soldiers in the War of 1812. Foner mentions, without citation, that the U.S. Army issued an order on February 18, 1820, specifying that "No Negro or mulatto will be received as a recruit of the Army" (27). The General Regulations of 1821, according to Foner, limited enlistment to "all free white male persons." By that date, all of the Marion "colored" soldiers had been discharged at Fort Smith except for Peter Caulder and Joseph Clark. Those two men had either undergone a change in their racial classification by the army or grandfathered under the exclusion. Gail Buckley's *American Patriots: The Story of Blacks in the Military from the Revolution to Desert Storm* (New York: Random House, 2001) adds no new information regarding military service of blacks during the early nineteenth century. Christopher T. George, "Mirage of Freedom: African Americans in the War of 1812," *Maryland Historical Magazine* 91 (Winter 1996): 427–50, sums up attitudes in his title and Scott S. Sheads briefly explains his subject's noble death in "A Black Soldier Defends Fort McHenry, 1814," *Military Collector & Historian* 41 (Spring 1989): 20–21.

For a thorough investigation of commanders and troops of the era interacting daily with their surroundings to obtain food, shelter, and clothing, see the recent study by Wayne K. Bodle on the Continental Army's famous winter spent west of Philadelphia, *Valley Forge Winter: Civilians and Soldiers in War* (University Park: Pennsylvania State University Press, 2002). Albeit on a much-smaller and less-dramatic scale, Bradford and his men faced the same sort of winter survival situation in their less-than-famous winter spent in the west. Similarly, the travails of Revolutionary War riflemen were studied by Don Higginbotham in *Daniel Morgan: Revolutionary Rifleman* (Chapel Hill: University of North Carolina Press, 1961).

Fort Smith, Arkansas Territory

The military history of antebellum Fort Smith has been treated by Edwin C. Bearss and A. M. Gibson in *Fort Smith: Little Gibraltar on the Arkansas* (Norman: University of Oklahoma Press, 1969). Bearss, the start-up historian at the Fort Smith National Historic Site, has a minutely detailed unpublished manuscript entitled "Fort Smith 1817–1824" bound and available at the Fort Smith National Historic Site Library. The parallel study by Brad Agnew, *Fort Gibson: Terminal on the Trail of Tears* (Norman: University of Oklahoma Press, 1980), is a necessary companion to complete the story of military presence on the territorial frontier of Arkansas. While William Bradford and Mathew Arbuckle await biographical studies (as does Gen. Thomas Adams Smith), brief articles deal with their commands at Fort Smith: Harold W. Ryan, "Matthew [sic] Arbuckle Comes to Fort Smith," *Arkansas Historical Quarterly* 19 (Winter 1960): 287–92; Carolyn Thomas Foreman, "William Bradford," *Arkansas Historical Quarterly* 13 (Winter 1954): 341–51. Benjamin L. E. Bonneville has received attention from Washington Irving, who edited Bonneville's journal of his adventures in the Rocky Mountains, and from biographer Edith Haroldsen Lovett, *Benjamin Bonneville: Soldier of the American Frontier* (Bountiful, Utah: Horizon Publishers, 1992). A folksy look at famous Americans who intersected with the region is provided in Joseph Quayle Bristow's *Tales of Old Fort Gibson* (New York: Exposition Press, 1961). The life of one of those famous Americans who passed through is amplified by Harold McCracken, *George Catlin and the Old Frontier* (New York: Dial Press, 1959). On the 175th anniversary of his attempt to find the source of the Arkansas River, Stephen H. Long received welcomed study. George J. Goodman and Cheryl A. Lawson began their investigation at the source of the Arkansas River to write *Retracing Major Stephen H. Long's 1820 Expedition: The Itinerary and Botany* (Norman: University of Oklahoma, 1995), while Roger L. Nichols and Patrick L. Halley concentrated on rehabilitating the "neglected" explorer in *Stephen Long and American Frontier Exploration* (Norman: University of Oklahoma Press, 1995) and along the way contributed a fine bibliography of primary sources.

Aspects of the social and cultural history of territorial Arkansas that bore on Peter Caulder and his free black community have been explored and documented in dozens of articles that have appeared in the *Arkansas Historical*

Quarterly, with recent examples of the scholarship being Mary L. Kwas, "The Spectacular 1833 Leonid Meteor Storm: The View from Arkansas," 58 (Autumn 1999): 314–24; and Joseph Patrick Key, "Indians and Ecological Conflict in Territorial Arkansas," 59 (Summer 2000): 127–46. Two excellent monographs that form bedrock scholarship for the study of the development of Arkansas and the treatment accorded free blacks and slaves in Arkansas are S. Charles Bolton, *Territorial Ambition: Land and Society in Arkansas, 1800–1840* (Fayetteville: University of Arkansas Press, 1993); and Donald P. McNeilly, *The Old South Frontier: Cotton Plantations and the Formation of Arkansas Society, 1819–1861* (Fayetteville: University of Arkansas Press, 2000). For a worthy critique of Henry Rowe Schoolcraft's 1819 observations of the people whom he encountered along Arkansas's White River, see George E. Lankford, "'Beyond the Pale': Frontier Folk in the Southern Ozarks," *University of Kansas Publications in Anthropology*, Robert Smith and Jerry Stannard, eds., 17 (1989): 53–70.

General Works of Influence

Bernard Augustine DeVoto, *Across the Wide Missouri* (Boston: Houghton Mifflin, 1947), and Henry Nash Smith, *The Virgin Land: The American West as Symbol and Myth* (Cambridge, Mass.: Harvard University Press, 1950), gave this author along with legions of other students the lay of the immense Louisiana Purchase lands and the equally immense influence that so much arable soil would have on generations of Americans. No doubt, Peter Caulder, his comrades, and his community agreed with Nash's theory that Americans of the nineteenth century valued living on the farm and simply asked for the opportunity to do just that. David Brion Davis has written widely and profoundly on the ramifications of slavery, but particularly useful to this study was his *Problem of Slavery in the Age of Revolution, 1770–1823* (Ithaca, N.Y.: Cornell University Press, 1975). In understanding the cultural foundations of South Carolina, the rise of black consciousness, and Scotch-Irish sand hill people, see the excellent state history by Walter Edgar, *South Carolina: A History* (Columbia: University of South Carolina Press, 1998); the useful Peter H. Wood, *Black Majority: Negroes in Colonial South Carolina: From 1670 through the Stono Rebellion* (New York: Alfred A. Knopf, 1974); and the prescient and exciting book by Hendrik Booraem, *Young Hickory: The Making of Andrew Jackson* (Dallas, Tex.: Taylor Trade Publishing, 2001). To understand the mentality of the settlement frontier where Indian confrontations were concerned, no better description can be had than Ellen Eslinger's *Citizens of Zion: The Social Origins of Camp Meeting Revivalism* (Knoxville: University of Tennessee Press, 1999). Nancy Britton's *Two Centuries of Methodism in Arkansas, 1800–2000* (Little Rock, Ark.: August House, 2000) comments on racial designations within the church. Pricilla McArthur, *Arkansas in the Gold Rush* (Little Rock, Ark.: August House, 1986), supplies muster lists and day-by-day journals for wagon train communities bound from Arkansas to the west. Salt Lake City journalist Will Bagley in *Blood of the*

Prophet: Brigham Young and the Massacre at Mountain Meadows (Norman: University of Oklahoma Press, 2002) extracts history from legend about a special Arkansas wagon train made up of migrants from Carroll, Boone, and Marion counties. A historian's historian, Merrill D. Peterson, spins fine detail on the interaction of three magnificent politicians with the ebb and flow of American life in *The Great Triumvirate: Webster, Clay, and Calhoun* (New York and Oxford: Oxford University Press, 1967). River and overland travel are described by Walter Moffat, "Transportation in Arkansas, 1819–1840," *Arkansas Historical Quarterly* 15 (Autumn 1956): 187–201; Robert B. Walz, "Migration into Arkansas, 1820–1880: Incentives and Means of Travel," *Arkansas Historical Quarterly* 17 (Winter 1958): 309–24; Dallas T. Herndon, "A Little of What Arkansas Was Like a Hundred Years Ago," *Arkansas Historical Quarterly* 3 (Summer 1944): 117–24; Dwight Pitcaithley, "Settlement of the Arkansas Ozarks: The Buffalo River Valley," *Arkansas Historical Quarterly* 37 (Autumn 1978): 203–24; Duane Huddleston, Sammie Rose, and Pat Wood, *Steamboats and Ferries on the Arkansas River: A Heritage Revisited* (Conway: University of Central Arkansas Press, 1995; reprinted in 1998 by the University of Arkansas Press, Fayetteville); and C. Fred Williams, S. Charles Bolton, Carl H. Moneyhon, and LeRoy T. Williams, *A Documentary History of Arkansas* (Fayetteville: University of Arkansas Press, 1984).

Contextual

Though not contemporary with Peter Caulder's life, certain studies on nineteenth-century white, black, mixed-race, and working-class people contributed to understanding the context of his times, including Ted Ownby's *Subduing Satan: Religion, Recreation, and Manhood in the Rural South, 1865–1920* (Chapel Hill: University of North Carolina Press, 1990), which speaks of universal and timeless traits of being a Southerner, whether white or black; Willard B. Gatewood Jr., *Aristocrats of Color: The Black Elite, 1880–1920* (Bloomington and Indianapolis: Indiana University Press, 1990) describes with his customary perception the stratification that existed within black society in the East.

INDEX

Page numbers in italics refer to illustrations in the text. A t following a page number indicates the subject is mentioned in a table on that page.

Bollinger County, Missouri, 202,
205–6, 207, 209, 211, 218
Bonneville, Benjamin L. E., 111–13,
136, 149, 172; mission to
Batesville, 115–16; remains
in Fort Smith, 119; trip with
Lafayette, 127–28
Bottoms Bridge, Virginia, 21
bounty Irish, 2
bounty lands, 17, 31, 117, 120–22,
138, 307n12
boy planters, 65, 145
Bradford, William, 16, 36, 38, 68,
90, 130, 165, 172; takes command of rifle company, 30, 32;
quarrel with Selden, 34,
291n32; ordered to Arkansas,
40–48; voyage up the
Arkansas, 50–54; at Belle
Point, 57–58; outlook on
Indians, 61; command in first
year, 65; express boat, 69; mission to Red River, 73–75,
77–80; in civil court, 83; and
Hugh Glenn, 86; returns with
paymaster, 98; advertises for
deserters, 100; strategies of,
103–4; as biggest taxpayer,
125; at Fort Meigs,
292–93n14; gift given,
295–96n42; letter, 299n39
Brannum, John, 177
Brower, Emila, 109, 116, 119
Brower, John, 108–9, 113, 116, 119
Buck Swamp Creek, 10, 15
buffalo, 39, 67, 74–75, 136, 143,
292n10
Bull Shoals, 139, 151, 157–59, 175,
180, 322n42
Burch, Milton, 203
Burns, Clarissa, 167t, 185
Burton, Vernon, 192
Byers, John H., 187
Byers, William, 186, 187, 190,
316–17n49

Caddo Indians of Louisiana, 33
Cain, Bill, 204
Calder, Archibald, 13
Calder, Dr. William, 12–13
Calder, Mamie D., 211
Calder, Nancy, 1
Calder, Peter (white), 1
Calder, Peter, Jr., 1
Calder Road, 12
Calhoun, Andrew, 57–58, 98, 100,
102, 109
Calhoun, John C., 14, 71, 73,
172; directive to Andrew
Jackson, 40
Calico Rock, 161
Cape Girardeau, Missouri, 41, 70,
201–2, 207, 212
Carlisle Barracks, Pennsylvania, 22,
25, 27, 31, 36, 40, 289–90n19;
Cole's Company at, 28
Carter, Randolph, 168t
Catfish Creek, 1, 3, 8, 9, 17, 42,
90, 175
Cato family, 202
Caulder, Amanda, 183, 201
Caulder, Caroline Berry, 212
Caulder, Charles, 208, 218–19
Caulder, Eliza Hall, 123, 136,
141–42, 146, 155, 157–58,
174, 182–83, 197, 201
Caulder, David, 142, 144,
157–58, 183, 205–8; at Cape
Girardeau, 202; death, 212
Caulder, Ida, 215
Caulder, James Henry, 202, 212
Caulder, Jim, 215
Caulder, Margaret, 142, 182
Caulder, Mary Anne Nelson, 208
Caulder, Mary Josephine Young, 211
Caulder, Matilda Cato, 202, 206–8
Caulder, Moses (elder): in South
Carolina, 1, 5, 7, 8, 17; con-
tinued in service, 24; descrip-
tion of, 28; discharge from
regiment, 31